FLOWERS IN THE
DUSTBIN

FLOWERS IN THE DUSTBIN

Culture, Anarchy, and Postwar England

Neil Nehring

Ann Arbor

THE UNIVERSITY OF MICHIGAN PRESS

#27187042

Copyright © by the University of Michigan 1993
All rights reserved
Published in the United States of America by
The University of Michigan Press
Manufactured in the United States of America

1996   1995   1994   1993   4 3 2 1

Library of Congress Cataloging-in-Publication Data

Nehring, Neil, 1957–
    Flowers in the dustbin : culture, anarchy, and postwar England /
Neil Nehring.
        p.   cm.
    Includes bibliographical references and index.
    ISBN 0-472-09526-9 (alk. paper). — ISBN 0-472-06526-2 (pbk. :
alk. paper)
    1. England—Popular culture—History—20th century. 2. Anarchism—
England—History—20th century. 3. Avant-garde (Aesthetics)—
England. 4. England—Civilization—1945—   I. Title.
DA589.4.N44   1993
941.085—dc20   92-42085
                                                                        CIP

A CIP catalogue record for this book is available from the British Library.

Photos on preceding pages, reading counterclockwise: Teds at the Wembley
Rock n Roll Festival, 1972; Mods at Clacton, 1964; Punk outside the Rain-
bow Theatre, London, 1977. Photos © The Hulton-Deutsch Collection,
London.

Creating a new culture does not only mean one's own "original" discoveries. It also, and most particularly, means the diffusion in a critical form of truths already discovered, their "socialisation" as it were, and even making of them the basis of vital action, an element of co-ordination.
—Antonio Gramsci, *Selections from the Prison Notebooks*

Acknowledgments

This book is dedicated to Maria Nehring, for her love and steadfast faith and support. My parents and parents-in-law, Earl and Harriet Nehring and Peter and Frances Petkoff, have also provided inestimable support, and, along with Maria, treated every step in the book's emergence as an excuse for a celebration. For specific ideas and references of considerable value, I am indebted to Lance Bertelsen, Greg Carey, Susan Comfort, Simon Cordery, Arthur Efron, Elisabeth Piedmont-Marton, Tom Staley, and Urszula Tempska. Looking back, I'm grateful to Peter Casagrande, James Gindin, June Howard, and Alan Wald for supporting my work when it was pretty raw, and I follow their example in encouraging students who want to make a difference. I also want to thank LeAnn Fields at the University of Michigan Press, for her responsive handling of this book, and the University Research Institute, at the University of Texas at Austin, for providing significant financial assistance towards its completion.

The author gratefully acknowledges permission to reprint the following copyrighted material:

Excerpts from *Saved* by Edward Bond, from *Plays: One* by Edward Bond. Reprinted by permission of Methuen Drama.

Excerpts from *Oi for England* by Trevor Griffiths. Reprinted by permission of Faber & Faber Ltd.

Excerpt from "The Beach Head," from *Fighting Terms* by Thom Gunn. Copyright © 1954 by Thom Gunn. Reprinted by permission of Farrar, Straus and Giroux, Inc.

Excerpts from "Elvis Presley," "On the Move," and "Lines for a Book" from *The Sense of Movement* by Thom Gunn. Reprinted by permission of Farrar, Straus and Giroux, Inc.

Excerpts from *V.* by Tony Harrison. Copyright © 1985 by Tony Harrison. Reprinted by permission of Bloodaxe Books.

Excerpts from *Look Back in Anger* by John Osborne. Reprinted by permission of S. G. Phillips, Inc. from *Look Back in Anger* by John Osborne. Copyright © 1957 by S. G. Phillips, Inc.

Parts of this book have been published in other versions:

"Cultural Studies [sic(k)] in the United States," *Australian Journal of Communication* 18 (1991).

"Revolt into Style: Graham Greene Meets the Sex Pistols." Reprinted by permission of the Modern Language Association of America from *PMLA* 106 (1991):222–37.

"The Shifting Relations of Literature and Popular Music in Postwar England," *Discourse* 12 (1989–90).

"What Should the Politics of Cultural Studies Be?" *LIT (Literature/Interpretation/Theory)* 1, no. 3 (1990): 229–37. Copyright © Gordon and Breach Science Publishers S.A.

The following songs are quoted in this book:

"Anarchy in the U.K.," "God Save the Queen," and "Pretty Vacant" (Paul Cook / Steve Jones / Glen Matlock / Johnny Rotten) © Glitterbest Ltd. (adm. by Careers-BMG Music Publishing Inc.) / WB Music Corp.

"Bad Boy" (Marty Wilde) © Duchess Music Corporation and Youngstar Music Ltd.

"Complete Control" and "White Riot" (Mick Jones / Joe Strummer) © CBS Records

"Emotions" (Mariah Carey) © M. Carey Songs / Virgin Music Inc. / Cole / Cliville's Music Enterprises

"19th Nervous Breakdown" and "Play with Fire" (Mick Jagger / Keith Richards) © Abkco Music Inc.

"The Price of Paradise" (D. Boon) © New Alliance Music

"Rise" (Bill Laswell / John Lydon) © More Cut Music

"Uniform" (Becky Escamilla / Bruce Marton) © Trance Music

Every effort has been made to trace the ownership of all copyrighted material in this book and to obtain permission for its use.

Contents

Introduction

Flowers in the Dustbin was written to help shape cultural dissidence among artists, audiences, critics, teachers, and students—whose functions, it will be argued, should overlap considerably. In the interest of enlarging this avant-garde (in life as well as art), the book presents crucial ideas in its first part, and, in the second, concrete illustrations of them from postwar English literature, rock music, and youth subcultures. Besides a general sense of the stakes involved and concerns in both theory and practice, hopefully more than a little inspiration will be found as well.

The book begins by looking at recent critiques of the whole history of "aesthetics," which emerged as a specialized discipline in the eighteenth century. These demystifying accounts repudiate the way art has long been conceptualized as some exalted form of human activity, necessarily removed from the depredations of everyday life.[1] Of particular concern is the early twentieth century, when some artists confronted assumptions about art's autonomy and the artist's uniqueness, and sought instead to draw together aesthetic and social experience. This impulse defines the avant-garde, which scholars have subsequently conflated into a single modernism, thereby suppressing to some extent the avant-garde's relation to radical politics, and even moreso its most progressive movements' interest in *mass culture* (a term that will simply denote mass reproduction, rather than mass manipulation). The avant-garde will thus be thoroughly distinguished from elitist tendencies in modernism—but also detached from confinement to any particular historical period, considered instead as an ongoing effort to integrate art and life. After rearticulation of the original avant-garde's interests, the contemporary field of cultural studies, in particular, is presented as an important avatar, likewise engaged with the uses of cultural forms both "high" and "low" in everyday life. As a break with aestheticism provoked by modernist extremes, the avant-garde represents the first genuinely *post*-modernism; if, as the first chapter further argues, modernist elitism remains ascendant in much "postmodernist" scholarship, cultural studies offers the most progressive postmodernism available, in continuing the struggle with aestheticism. Both the avant-garde and cultural studies insist that overthrowing the fragmentation of cultural experience, among institutions like academia and the mass media, is essential to a more widespread, lucid rejection of the authoritarian plutocracy that dominates the globe. Invigorating communication in this way might ultimately allow a community in which cooperation presides over humane forms of competition, and the existence of the planet and the life on it matters more than the latest quarterly earnings statement.

The next two chapters synthesize a wide range of more and less academic accounts of mass culture, focused on descriptions of authoritarianism and antiauthoritarianism.[2] These chapters are intended to provide younger readers, in particular, with a fairly comprehensive introduction to recent cultural criticism, and especially with the means to grasp their culture and society as a whole. The broadest tasks of cultural studies underlie part 1: analysis of the institutions of communication "to reveal the complex ways both distorted and undistorted meanings are generated and intertwined within them," to describe how those institutions "have taken their present shapes," and finally "to suggest alternative paths [for their] use and development" (Brantlinger 1990:196). Chapter 2 focuses this analysis on the career of authoritarian ideology in the 1980s, and on the role of the mass media in convincing many young people that the status quo was indisputable. Among adults, too, this authoritarian culture bred a near-hysterical determination to be "positive."

Chapter 3, in contrast, covers a variety of older and more recent theories of the virtue and possibilities of *negation,* understood to be the genuinely constructive force in a positivist climate. This dialectical irony derives from the philosopher Hegel, who understood negation as a critique of conformist common sense and its suppression of contradictions. Given a more material grounding than one finds in Hegel's *Science of Logic,* negation might be understood to attack authoritarian attempts (1) to deny the basic contradictions caused by social injustice, and (2) to suppress political contradictions by defaming and delegitimizing protest against that injustice. Herbert Marcuse describes negation as speaking "a language which is *not* the language of those who establish, enforce, and benefit from the facts" (qtd. in Solomon 1979:533–34, 536), terms that might easily be extended beyond the aestheticism he has in mind. In an authoritarian climate stressing the enormously positive, or at least inevitable, nature of existing social relations, and promoting a compulsive positivity about them, such negation is the genuinely positive force. If, furthermore, it understands its targets and links concrete practices with some larger realizations, some sort of discourse about self and society, it could have profound results.

Working from this antiauthoritarian basis, the third chapter links progressive accounts of individual and collective agency to the potential and form of *cultural anarchism.* As in Marcuse's definition of negation, this cultural anarchism is a matter of language, in particular, in the linkage of cultural and social experience to form accounts of society, and attitudes toward it, starkly refusing those urged by cultural and political authorities. (Reference to Hegel clarifies that negation includes the power of critical thought as much as action on that thought; thus it does not entail wanton physical mayhem, which many associate with all forms of anarchism.) Helping generate new voices—attitudes as well as ideas—not found in the dominant media has essentially been the project of the avant-garde and cultural studies alike. The problem attacked by cultural anarchism is that Western societies preserve their inequitable relations not so much through outright oppression of dissidents (which does go on all the time), as through persuading people that the status quo, if not just, is at least inevitable, and thinking or feeling otherwise is lunatic.

Anarchism, which disappeared from mass politics a half century ago with the Spanish Civil War, hardly has a good name on either the left or right; conservative libertarians, in fact, have shown as much interest as the left in anarchism. Marxism has long dismissed anarchism for its ostensible failure to attempt a larger understanding of how cultural, economic, and political institutions operate. Theorists of postmodernism like Jean Baudrillard and Jean-François Lyotard, emphasizing that no sphere of challenge exists entirely outside those institutions, have added that to celebrate a central contradiction between power and dissent can itself, paradoxically, be the bearer of social control. Given the supposed continuity of the relations between power and its opponents, within a seamless institutional system, radical politics can only enact futile vignettes in which "the means and ends of resistance are always already defined by these relations." Thus anarchism (or Marxism, for that matter) affirms authority rather than transgressing it—not only by identifying and thereby confirming authority as such, as well as providing an excuse for its exercise, but also by supplying it with new forms and ideas to exploit commercially and politically (Plant 1992:75, 134, 184). But anarchists, in response to Marxists and other leftists, have pointed out that more conventional politics may fail to challenge authority in any fundamental way precisely because they address it through established channels and patterns of resistance, hence as supplicants (Marcus 1989:13). Anarchists past and present, moreover, such as Peter Kropotkin and Noam Chomsky, have hardly been less attentive than either Marxism or postmodernism to the machinery of power in the mass media, state, workplace, and so on. And it remains highly debatable, finally, whether the difficulties in achieving social change mean that opposing authority always enacts a drama merely reinforcing it, as postmodernists convinced of an abstract power's omnipresence claim. "The recognition that weapons can be turned against those who wield them is no reason to dispense with them altogether" and lapse into petrification and silence, even if "it is indeed more difficult than ever before to reintroduce any sense of negativity to the systems of power in which we live" (Plant 1992:180, 182–83, 185).

Though anarchism may not be a viable political label at present, outside small movements of disenchanted youth, there is nonetheless no more apt a term for the necessary response to the authoritarian culture and politics that developed in the eighties, particularly under the regimes of Ronald Reagan and Margaret Thatcher. More recently, both conservative and liberal politicians in the United States, bereft of the single monolithic threat of communism, have taken aim at a large array of cultural targets instead, from Murphy Brown to Sister Souljah. With the threat of "permissiveness" replacing the Soviet bogeyman of the cold war, many are now bent on suppressing "difference" in every form (political as well as racial and sexual), particularly through censorship of the arts, rap and rock music, and so on. Hence antiauthoritarian dissent, in creative expression as much as politics, needs to be addressed and valorized in the strongest, most direct terms possible.

Though this book concerns recent forms of authoritarianism, a constant tendency should be noted, summed up in Erich Fromm's argument that people "may voice skepticism toward authority in general, yet still be gullible in each new manipulation by authorities" (Lazere 1987:85). Young Americans sent to the Persian Gulf in late 1990, for example, though questioning their circumstances, were "amazingly willing to trust authority" (Hitchens 1990:794); many in the United States expressed doubt and fear when the Persian Gulf War began, but also their support for whatever the state sets in motion. Authoritarianism of this sort is a constant threat from within nominally democratic societies, persistently constructing acquiescence as positive and opposition as negative. When cast in terms of the "nonpolitical" and "political," respectively, during the war, the positive-negative dualism clearly implied that passivity (except for conformist celebration) is the preeminent virtue of the citizen.[3]

In so drastically reducing the only possible positions on the war to the positive and the negative, however, the explicitness, simplemindedness, and apparent success of recent authoritarianism seem unusual. Immediately after the Persian Gulf War ended, the Republican national chairman denounced those who had resisted the precipitous use of military force as holding "negative and depressed viewpoints," at a time when right-thinking Americans were experiencing a "tremendous uplift" over the onset of war and the resulting slaughter (qtd. in Ridgeway 1991b:22). (The invocation of depression goes so far as to suggest that dissent results from psychological disturbance, a suggestion that should be familiar to women.) The appeal is less to express ideology than to appropriate, positive *emotions*—themselves an important component of ideology—a logical outgrowth of the Reagan-Bush era, in which substance seemingly disappeared from politics. Contrary to a fashionable postmodern academic pessimism about the difficulty of political action (see Grossberg 1989b), recent authoritarian politics have not disconnected affective and ideological experience, but confused and hence fused them through explicit reference to emotions (a politician's optimism, and so on) where one would expect to find ideas. Banal film critics have most conspicuously tapped into the positivist sensibility, repeatedly celebrating popular successes like *Pretty Woman* and *Ghost* as "the feel-good movie of the year!" (The paradox of mean-spirited intolerance passing for uplifted spirits, though, as in the loathing of antimilitarists, is characteristic of authoritarianism in general. And not long after the recent outpouring of euphoria, it became apparent that the coupling of dismay at the status quo with conviction of its inevitability, as described by Fromm, remained more typical of the authoritarian personality.

Perhaps the most notable instance of the association between dissent and negativity was General Norman Schwartzkopf's triumphal address before Congress, which contrasted "the great American people" with the "prophets of doom, the naysayers, the protestors and the flag burners." His self-assurance, in saying "we knew you would never let us down," seems warranted: spectators at the endless war celebrations typically pronounced them a way for the American people to "feel good" about themselves and their country. In the midst of this feel-good euphoria, it was negative and political to dwell on the realities of the war, such as the blowing apart, incineration, and disease of tens of thousands of human beings—facts deliberately expunged by the mass media and military, which were "not terribly interested," as General Colin Powell put it, just as the properly enraptured citizen should not be concerned.[4] Dissent, finally, was entirely removed from the conception of democracy.

In fighting the reduction of political discourse into terms of the positive and negative, cultural anarchism actually works from the same simple yet sweeping dualism, but completely reverses the value of each term. What this book seeks to revive from the anarchist tradition is simply its fundamental emphasis on the *virtue* of negation, summed up in Mikhail Bakunin's famous maxim—found in his early work based in Hegel—that the destructive passion is in fact a creative passion (1971:123; 1980:57). Bakunin's terms pose no irony at all, but a vital dialectic highlighting the way institutional authority reinforces consensus on the status quo by deeming inappropriate, or destructive, what are actually the healthiest activities, emotions, and ideas available. Whether in cultural or political movements, negation is in fact the genuinely creative passion, a democratic urge feared and condemned by those in power, who correctly see in it the seeds of the destruction of privilege. This relation between creative deviance and authoritarian responses has been a striking characteristic of youth subcultures, the topic with which the first part of the book concludes.

A similar description of negation—as a matter of emotion as well as intellect, as the basis of subcultures, and as a political force in its own right—can be found in recent work revaluing the significance of affective experience. The mass media and political institutions, Alison Jaggar points out, preserve the status quo not just by transmitting beliefs and values, but by "forming our emotional constitution." When the resulting positivity comes to seem perfectly natural (as it did during the Persian Gulf War), people lose "the capacity for outrage." That loss, in general, lends "plausibility to the belief that greed and domination are inevitable human motivations" and buries "the possibility of alternative ways of living." But the power to constitute people's emotions is hardly total, and thus "outlaw" emotions frequently emerge as the basis for subcultures that oppose prevailing perceptions. Since emotion is an important component in constructing ideology, such subcultures are even politically subversive, though operating on largely epistemological grounds (by testing the validity of knowledge, in other words). To emphasize outlaw emotions in lived cultural forms, therefore, is not a weak substitute for political analysis and action. Any critical perspective on society necessarily has its beginnings in a dialectical relation with outlaw emotions, which for many people "may provide the first indications that something is wrong" with conventional descriptions of the world (1989:159–61, 164). Critiquing the traditional disparagement of emotion in aesthetics, Peter Middleton argues that emotion is "both cognitive and socially structured," not a capacity to be set below intellectual activity (especially as feminine weakness): "Feeling always has elements of belief, judgement, and intention inscribed within it" (1990:133).

The second part of this book, to illustrate responses to authoritarianism more concretely, works through exemplary moments in postwar English culture. The general suggestion is that avant-garde practices—in everyday life, though seldom expressed as such, as well as art—have never disappeared from the world. In seeking out, in postwar England, the "neglected works" lionized by Raymond Williams (one of the progenitors of cultural studies), this book shares his concern with "break[ing] out of the non-historical fixity of postmodernism." Academic studies too often stop history dead, in his view, by treating modernism, or the early twentieth century, as the terminus of meaningful possibilities for development not only in art, but seemingly in life; the late twentieth century is thus futilely "after" or "post." The avant-garde lineage constructed throughout parts 1 and 2 will "counterpose an alternative tradition taken from the neglected works left in the wide margin of the century, a tradition which may address itself not to this . . . quite inhuman rewriting of the past, but, for all our sakes, to a modern future in which community may be imagined again" (1989:35).

This hopeful sort of reconstruction, in part 2, is indebted to British cultural studies, specifically its sociological description of the various artifacts, commodities, and texts making up subcultural styles. To find literature drawn into various frays, in postwar England, confirms the original avant-garde's insistence that *all* cultural forms "high" and "low" share in material social experience. Looking across art and everyday life in England between the 1950s and 1980s, furthermore, one finds a striking exchange of power between conservative literati hostile to mass culture, which was genuine pabulum in the fifties, and the habitués of that culture. By the 1960s, in Swinging London, rock musicians and their followers were appropriating literature itself into a parody of dominant ideological propositions concerning "affluence" and "consumerism." In the late 1970s, working with both avant-garde theory and embittered working-class musicians, a group of bohemians fought a pitched battle, couched in terms of *anarchy,* against the incipient forms of the authoritarianism of the eighties, which generally traded on a presumed crisis of *authority.* That tomes like *Flowers in the Dustbin* continue to appear, on the Sex Pistols in particular (see Marcus 1989; Savage 1991), indicates the significance of punk's historical position, at the onset of the authoritarianism that subsequently ravaged both England and the United States. The persisting interest in punk reflects the persistence of its nemesis; punk's moment, in this light, bears lessons not failed or lost, but still being worked out. British punk's introduction of a longer avant-garde tradition into *popular culture* (a term that will refer to the actual social use of mass-reproduced texts) is thus the core event from which every other concern in this book has emerged.

As the product of work originating in literary studies, though, *Flowers in the Dustbin* must be acknowledged to work more with texts than with firsthand ethnographic data, even in discussing everyday lived culture. The description of different cultural forms, however, also articulates the author's own experience and that of people around him, which represents an important, legitimate resource in cultural studies (given moderation of the resulting claims). The account of the significance and potential of voices of contumacy, resisting authoritarian ideology, is thus deeply felt, if the materials are sometimes second- or thirdhand. Outside of reading, the immediate experience informing the book is largely that of rock and roll, especially punk rock, in public and private since the early seventies. This experience has confirmed Simon Frith's belief that the voice of antiauthoritarianism—"essentially youthful—is still heard publicly only in rock music" (1988b:75). The argument is not that music and related styles can produce significant social change by themselves, but that they may provide a crucial opening onto it. Czechoslovakia's recent "velvet revolution," for example, took its name from a band of the sixties, the Velvet Underground, that had a considerable influence on the music and attitudes of punk a decade later. When Lou Reed, the best-known member of VU, suggested to Czech president Vaclav Havel in 1990 that he "obviously [felt] and [proved] that music can change the world," Havel both qualified and endorsed the relationship of popular music and social progress: "Not in itself, it's not sufficient in itself. But it can contribute to that significantly in being a part of the awakening of the human spirit" (Reed 1991:106).

A contribution to that awakening is as much as this book will attempt, in keeping with the anarchist theory of art, which encourages "the *presentiment* of an art still to be born" (Reszler 1973:43). The projection of creative possibilities in everyday life, in other words, is more helpful than concentration on immediate political results, which are seldom profound in popular culture. This sense of futurity, like Havel's, does not presume that significant social change will occur directly through current cultural forms, but that it might result from their cumulative pedagogical function. It is not at all limiting, from this view, to celebrate the fact that the attitude of negation continues to reappear in a variety of forms, and to leave the possibilities they hold to future discovery.

Such celebration, however, frequently raises objections to its lack of political rigor, along the lines that it is "uninterested in party organisation, revolutionary strategies, or consciousness raising"—the last accusation entirely false—and only in "mocking the established order, not working for a new one" (Street 1986:176). To measure cultural and/or political strategies by a single absolute standard of revolutionary consciousness, first of all, is elitist and unproductive; second, cultural analysts posing such qualms about anarchist avant-gardes virtually never offer any vision of an alternative social order in their own work, merely chiding those presumably less high-minded or serious. But it is true enough that Bakunin indulged in a virtual "cult of the unknown," in his belief that "man cannot and should not stipulate to the men [and women] of ages to come what they should do" (Reszler 1973:46).

To balance this reticence, briefly, an issue that arises at a number of points in this book should be emphasized: the authoritarianism of contemporary culture has its basis in the concentrated economic control of mass communications, or the "media monopoly" (discussed in chapter 2). An essential, practical project to which a cultural anarchism can contribute quite forcefully, it will be seen, is the exposure of the mass media's role in maintaining the constricted range of political discourse (one ideology presented as two parties, the left rendered invisible, and so forth). As a matter of public policy, which cultural studies is also sometimes criticized for neglecting, the corporate conglomerates controlling information and entertainment should be broken up, in the interest of democracy.

But if the prospect of antitrust laws being applied to the mass media is virtually nil, given the seemingly ineluctable partnership between big business and government, a genuinely open public discourse is likely to remain unrealized for some time. It is hardly irresponsible, then, to countenance the anarchist reluctance to define the shape of future social change, arguably a more realistic approach when such change has not even begun to be widely discussed; the critical task at present is simply to initiate such discussion. This reluctance is inarguably less restrictive, as well, especially if "any emerging mass movement is as likely as usual to take the intellectuals along with everyone else...by surprise" (Buhle 1990:174). A grave error of much anticapitalist doctrine and its prognostications, in this respect, has been a failure in humaneness and openness: a limitation, "so often, to the terms of its opponents, [in proposing] a political and economic order, rather than a human order" (Williams, qtd. in Brantlinger 1990:55). André Reszler, writing on anarchism and art, leaves the form of future social organization to be developed through action upon "the senses of the insurgent by [an] inexhaustible motley of new events, new objects, and '*unexpected* news' [that] abolishes the barriers between the known and the unknown, the new and the old, the impossible and the possible" (1973:46–47).[5] Such change is not necessarily abrupt and cataclysmic, predicated as it is upon the knotty task of achieving more genuinely democratic communication.

In keeping with anarchism's presentiment of expressive forms yet to be born, this book concentrates on the prepolitical dissent of youth subcultures, out of concern more with the process by which young people escape the confines of consensus, than with persons already radicalized. That process can hardly be expected to yield immediate, radical results, and thus many left intellectuals dismiss it, leaving the field to the authorities they ostensibly want to fight. The concept of the *political* thus needs to be "broadened so that the struggle for control [of meaning] in which subcultures are engaged is not dismissed as peripheral and temporary." If the making and transmitting of meaning is fundamental to the social order, such struggle may be quite significant, even when political ideology is not explicitly at issue (Muncie 1982:57–58).

In the author's own experience, a long-term process of education has occurred through often unexpected encounters with dissenting ideas and voices, found in "high" and "low" culture alike. These experiences have had an impact as much affective (or emotive) as directly ideological (or intellectual)—again a source of scorn by some on the left. If, for this reason, the culture of the young often appears trivial and unpromising, it must be acknowledged that young people are making do with what they can control. It is precisely "because they *lack* power that the young account for their lives in terms of play, focus their politics on leisure" and its pleasures (Frith 1981:201). Young people at present may believe "deeply in their own powerlessness," disdaining discussion of economic and political realities, but the subject of popular culture produces "a different response from them," George Lipsitz has found. Popular texts "unleashed the memories and experiences suppressed by the dominant rhetoric of their private and public lives. Here hope was still an issue, and happiness was still possible" (1990:xiii).

The prospect of cultural experience leading on to political transformation, however, inescapably raises troublesome questions, developed most thoroughly by Jürgen Habermas. One can certainly identify in the present as well as the past "which crisis tendencies are transformed into deviant behavior and in which social groups." But the sore point is always whether "the expected [disruptive] potential permits directed political action, or [leads] rather to undirected dysfunctionalization" (1975:40). Past and present youth subcultures, for example, have been neither purely dysfunctional, as cultural and political authorities typically insist, nor as politically oriented as many radicals, both intellectuals and politicos, would like. In the latter case, for example, punk's introduction of avant-garde and anarchist ideas into popular culture created "an expansive, libertarian culture of often 'politically incorrect' desires, [which] continues to command a deep social power that meshes uneasily with the more purist . . . definitions of culture advanced by activists hewing to the . . . dictates of political theory alone" (A. Ross 1989b:109).

Some take problems of the sort raised by Habermas as reason for pessimism, while others employ them with the anarchist's eye to the future, to help prompt contemporary efforts to discover the political unknown. He poses three crucial questions for the latter:

> (1) Can the new potentials for conflict and apathy, characterized by withdrawal of motivation and inclination toward protest, and supported by subcultures, lead to a refusal to perform assigned functions in such a scale as to *endanger the system as a whole*? (2) Are the groups that place in question, possibly passively, the fulfillment of important system functions identical with the *groups capable of conscious political action in a crisis* situation? (3) Is the process of erosion that can lead to the crumbling of functionally necessary legitimations of domination and motivations to achieve at the same time a process of politicization that creates potentials for action? (qtd. in McCarthy 1978:385; italics added)

The last question is critical in an authoritarian climate, when the "crumbling" falls more easily in a regressive direction. The erosion of capitalism's claims to legitimacy spawns both anarchist punks and racist skinheads, but the latter are a shorter step from recent neoconservative ideology, with its heavy charge of racism (as in rhetoric about hiring "quotas").

Another problem raised by Habermas has been discerned by

many, the seemingly limitless ability of capitalist culture to incorporate dissident expression. "Blows directed against stone walls bounce off rubber screens," when the response to imaginative provocations is not necessarily open repression, which does occur, but in many cases an increased tolerance reflecting strategies of commercial defusion and dispersal (1975:129). One has a choice, again, of despairing at this phenomenon, or trying to assist efforts to counteract it. In the latter case, one recognizes first of all that recuperation is never completed: "By highlighting elements of resistance (the formation of subcultures, nonconformity, anti-authoritarianism, and so on) we can see that while incorporation of commodity forms"—like popular music, for instance—"may be [nearly] complete, the struggle for ... control of meaning is alive and ongoing" (Muncie 1982:58). Incorporation is not necessarily "without risk for the system.... The endless caricaturing of the most deeply felt revolutionary desires can produce a backlash in the shape of a resurgence of feelings, purified in reaction to their universal prostitution" (Vaneigem, qtd. in Plant 1992:85).

On a similar, more hopeful basis (for which he is often ridiculed), Habermas advocates attempts simply to foster the identification of antagonistic class interests, of the contradictions between the dominant ideology and the actual fundamental interests of most people. With the resulting renewal of competence in communicative action, he believes, "conflict becomes manifest, [breaking] out in a questioning, rich in practical consequences" (1975:27, 69). Like theorists ranging from anarchists to subcultural sociologists, he does not attempt to specify those consequences, and stipulates that they may result from cultural conflict seemingly peripheral to conventional political organization, in particular, notably, from conflicts initiated by youth. Frith (to return to the beginning of this discussion) has grown more pessimistic about the possibilities of youth cultures, after the apparent failure of punk's promise. But he did believe, in the not-so-distant past, "that even if youth culture is not political in the sense of being part of a class-conscious struggle for state power, it nevertheless does provide a necessary pre-condition of such a struggle" (Hall and Jefferson 1976:238). Dick Hebdige, perhaps the best-known theorist of youth subcultures, similarly recognizes the ambiguity of a form of resistance constructed underneath authorized discourses, but based in signs provided by commercial culture: "The 'subcultural response' is neither simply . . . resistance against some external order nor straightforward conformity with the parent culture. It is a declaration of independence, of otherness, of alien intent, a refusal of anonymity, of subordinate status.... And at the same time it is also a confirmation of the fact of powerlessness, a celebration of impotence" (1988:35). The question, then, concerns the direction—insubordination or acquiescence—in which a subculture's activities lead its members, and the answer, at present, is almost invariably a mixed one.

Given the uncertainty of attempting a significant cultural and political intervention in any form, but especially in an academic text, the study that follows will only claim a very specific virtue: the injection of volatility into the study of literature, by examining a few provocative moments at which literary texts have been mixed up with popular cultural forms in everyday life. Even in this respect, though, the implications are political, not just in counteracting institutionalized value judgments on literature and popular culture, but in illustrating one important source of dissent identified by the avant-garde—different cultural forms learning from one another, the most vital sense of montage. Chapters 3 and 6 develop the avant-garde's theory of the long-term instructive significance of such "moments" of irruption, a theory the material on postwar English culture bears out in building from relatively small kernels: an imitation of Anthony Burgess's *A Clockwork Orange* on a Rolling Stones record sleeve; quotations from Graham Greene's *Brighton Rock* in a biography of the Sex Pistols. In seeking out the social uses of texts, an approach to literature based in cultural studies necessarily starts, perhaps, from minor incidents beneath the notice of cultural authority. Such an approach expands upon the implications of those incidents for future practice, in large part by building outwards into a larger network of cultural forms and the ideological and institutional constraints with which all the texts and audiences in question grappled. Richard Johnson suggests that the aim of cultural studies should be to "decentre 'the text' as an object of study" by considering its social life, by placing it in "a larger discursive field or *combination* of forms" (1986/87:62)—in essence an act of montage. The "exclusivity of literature as a category," to put it bluntly, should be discarded: "All kinds of texts ... must be taken as the occasions for further textuality. And textual studies must be pushed beyond the discrete boundaries of the page and book into institutional practices and social practices" (Scholes 1985:16).

This book works across different media, accordingly, recasting the relations between the forms and texts in question—literature, rock and roll music, and youth subcultures—through attention to their actual social life. With regard to the intersections between literature and mass culture, says Colin MacCabe,

> we must recognize the extent that one of the major functions of literary criticism as an institution is to preserve a cultural form, with a very specific class history, by ignoring those cultural forms based on *mechanical and electronic reproduction* which threaten to enlarge the audience in unacceptable ways.... [L]iterary criticism can only develop within a genuine humanities by recognising that its object of study is the whole range of cultural productions. It is only then that we will be able to seriously investigate the cultural movements of the twentieth century and the place of writing within them in ways which seriously engage with the gains and losses of these hugely enlarged audiences.... [T]he chauvinist connotations of English and the class connotations of literature must be abandoned in favor of a commitment to cultural studies. Such cultural studies would find an inevitable place in the analysis of a "linguistics of conflict." (1987:301–2; italics added)

Flowers in the Dustbin has its basis in just such a "linguistics of conflict," in a material attention to the power of dissident voices expressing outlaw emotions and ideas, cutting across a range of forms including the literary and the electronic. The point is not to privilege any one form over another, but to suggest how each might learn from others.

It should be stressed immediately that the voices contained herein do not always emerge from groups with entirely progressive memberships, notably with regard to gender and race. Thus the importance at the beginning of understanding the book's main purpose: to volatilize the relations between literature and mass culture, while to a lesser degree valorizing some of the specific subjects. But the lessons all the subjects offer, hopefully, will prove broadly relevant and useful despite the glaring faults of some. One reason for the extensive theoretical sections that follow, in the first half of the book, is the desire that negation be understood in as large a context as possible, as a response to alienation not dissimilar among men and women, nor among ethnic and racial majorities and minorities. Cultural anarchism is not intended to supplant the politics of difference, whether oriented to gender, race, sexual preference, or some other category of identity, but to suggest the usefulness of negation as a reminder of what all dissident politics have in common—contumacy, the angered resistance of authority. The important thing, with respect to difference, is to recognize the differing barriers to expressing that resistance faced by various groups (especially those faced by women,[6] as the first chapter indicates).

With regard to the specific subcultural actors in the second part of the book, however, it must be said frankly that they are not subjected to standards by which any group with some politically incorrect members is dismissed out of hand.[7] Paul Willis has leftists in mind when he observes, in the case of English youth subcultures, that "it is mean spirited, uncharitable and pedantic to list all the things these cultures were not, when they so clearly were something—something . . . which teaches us about a whole unexpected range of cultural struggle and transformation." Those subcultures remain significant precisely because they show how the "political programmes and theoretical perspectives" of left intellectuals and politicos often "utterly fail to supply or even sense the importance of the cultural level of transformation, [in the specific sense] of change in routine and daily consciousness" (1978:58).[8]

In the postmodern climate—and just what that implies will be contested throughout the book—cultural criticism in academia is almost required to be pessimistic by the prevailing, overlapping "posts": post-Marxism, postmodernism, and poststructuralism. As opposed to some balance between intellectual pessimism and optimism of the will (a formulation variously attributed to Antonio Gramsci and Romain Rolland, and now derided by some scholars on the left), the epoch of postmodernism is characteristically theorized as one in which all expressions of resistance are of negligible moment, presumably received with the utmost complacency. The resulting pessimism "masquerades as critique," but is "so one-dimensional that it ultimately serves as a form of collaboration with the oppressors" (Lipsitz 1990:xvi). Thus the conventional, distanced abstraction of academic work in relation to everyday life ought to be "undermined and supplemented by critical involvement," if analysts genuinely wish to understand, for example, the play between popular music, sartorial style, and the bodily experience of desire (Chambers 1987:242–43).[9]

Instead, postmodernist pessimism, sometimes nihilism, has proved infectious (in the negative sense), even outside academia. Retrospectives on punk rock, for instance, have adopted the fashionable despair of postmodernist theory. This development is evident in a music journalist's argument that

> punk is responsible for our future-less impotence, the pernicious inadequacy of things. Its have-a-go dynamic, its invitations and incitements, somehow only seem to have rendered pop small and common, in an age when what people secretly want is a large rarity. Ten years or more—this final throb of the rock narrative has shattered and de-mystified the monolith, long since outlived its usefulness. Its notion of 'threat' is in tatters. . . .
>
> Today, what must be rekindled are mystery and fascination—in essence, the un-punked 'ghost' of rock [to a] music that occupies larger premises. . . . Sexless, beerless, function-less, far-out noise—a new 'purity,' perhaps. (Stubbs 1989:275)

There are any number of problems here, especially the explicit invocation of "mystery" and "purity," which pits an elitism similar to that in modernism and much of postmodernism against punk's avant-gardism. As for the nostalgic desire to return to prepunk rock music, no one in their right mind would look to the dinosaur rock of that era—the primary cause of the punk upheaval in the first place—considering the oppressive persistence of moneygrubbing geriatrics such as Phil Collins, the Rolling Stones, and so forth.

Personal experience (as well as extensive documentation by critics, journalists, and sociologists) confirms that *something* profound happened a little over a decade ago, with punk, and this book tries to work from its nostalgia for that moment to create a climate in which more such moments will occur, however different in form. Walter Benjamin describes this attention to the struggles of the past, in order to inform those in the present and future, as something considerably more than wistfulness—a "revolutionary nostalgia." To examine moments in the past when, "even if in brief flashes, people showed their ability to resist, to join together, . . . is to hold out, even in times of deep pessimism, the possibility of surprise" (Zinn

1980:10–11, 573) of the sort sought by cultural anarchism. One should not simply prefer the failed rebels of the past to a history focused on the victors, but learn from the former's aspirations and defeats, putting their lessons to further use. This interest in radical historical recovery is common among avant-gardists: Raoul Vaneigem of the Situationist International, shortly before the student revolutions of 1968, hoped that "awareness of just how nightmarish life has become is on the point of fusing with a rediscovery of the real revolutionary movement in the past. We must reappropriate the most radical aspects of all past revolts and insurrections at the point where they were prematurely arrested, and bring to this task all the violence bottled up inside us" (1983:138).

More recent analysts (some soured directly by the failure in 1968) discern instead a precipitous loss of historical reality in the postmodern world. If that loss reduces "culture to a flattened juxtaposition of disparate images," nostalgia, in particular, working through "allegory and *bricolage*—a piecing together of encompassing stories" out of postmodern fragments—might be the source of historical and social redemption (Stewart 1988:239). For artists and audiences alike, the electronic mass media, the "very forms most responsible for the erosion of historical and local knowledge," sometimes serve in actuality as the sources of reconnection with the pasts of others, and the moral and political lessons therein (Lipsitz 1990:261). These last two views, far more productive than most theories of irremediable postmodern fragmentation, continue to discern possibilities for individual and collective agency. Their conviction, based as much on material experience as theory, is that human beings right now engage in all sorts of very effective practices, even critical discourses, or are perfectly capable of doing so given some direction and motivation by a committed, humane pedagogy. Such a pedagogy issues not just from teachers or an artistic vanguard, but from social interaction with one's peers.

With regard to education of this sort, the excesses of academic postmodernism pose a more specific concern, regarding the fate of cultural studies since it emerged from the University of Birmingham's Centre for Contemporary Cultural Studies. In its origins, cultural studies concerned the recovery, description, and propagation of moments in everyday life when "ordinary" people find strong voices of dissent, using cultural materials conventionally deemed degraded or banal, themselves ordinary. This concreteness was amalgamated with a concern with the more abstract "structural" context against which such initiatives were played out—the constraints as well as the liberating potential of ideologies, language, signs. The sense was always that these structural forces, in their impact on subjectivity, had to be considered in terms of specific social practices. Now, however, particularly in the United States, where cultural studies has been a trendy rubric, " 'cultural studies' has become an umbrella for just about anything" (Hall 1990:22).

The greatest harm to the field of cultural studies has occurred in filtering it through virtually nihilistic versions of post-Marxism. Such theories are usually derived from Ernesto Laclau and Chantal Mouffe's *Hegemony and Socialist Strategy* (1985), a treatise replacing the older, arguably static Marxist conception of social class with a theory of the necessarily shifting alliances between various individuals and subordinate groups, as mediated by the complex field of "discursive practices."[10] Structuralism first identified such structures, beginning with the sign system of language itself, which provide the conditions for expression, behavior, and so forth; poststructuralism, on which Laclau and Mouffe rely in part, often considers those conditions the causes, so to speak, of expression by their "subjects." Some exponents of post-Marxism, on this basis, view the array of discursive practices and their intersections in "articulations" as the real social agency. Human subjects appear to be just fragmented meeting points for the multiplicity of articulations, to use post-Marxist jargon (as if the actual social use of structural rules does not to some extent modify them as much as the user). The unquestionable realities of social fragmentation, in essence, are highly questionably extended into descriptions of a fragmented subject (or individual, that is), with issues of postmodernity replacing older, supposedly antiquated concepts of ideological struggle that assume the existence of functional human agents (see McRobbie 1991b).

The upshot for cultural studies has been a rejection, based in pessimism over contemporary politics, of the very possibility of considering culture as a coherent field of human practice, in favor of notions of a virtually infinite if not incoherent diversity in experience. Lawrence Grossberg, for example, an admitted pessimist, goes so far as to declare the necessity of cultural studies becoming "anti-humanistic"—literally, not just in terms of academic disciplines. In his reading of Laclau and Mouffe, "We are always constrained by a history we did not make, . . . by the effective force of the multiple histories of articulation. . . . Thus, the process of making history is always anonymous since we are never in control of the effects of our struggles" (1989a:414, 417). (The literal post-Marxism lies in the extrapolation from Marx's statement that people make history in *conditions* not of their own making; presumably they controlled to some extent the *effects* of their acts, which Grossberg now denies.) When Grossberg does portray "a struggle to find progressive meanings and pleasures," as a result, it "seemingly must be waged *within* the dominant social signifying institutions." In U.S. cultural studies in general, optimism and affirmation similarly seem "to mask a kind of desperation" (Budd et al. 1990:171). Stuart Hall, who helped guide Birmingham cultural studies to prominence, has chided poststructuralist inflections of cultural studies, for formalizing politics and history as matters of language and textuality in the abstract. Such theories have done so specifically by constituting *power* (à la Michel Foucault) as an unassailable floating signifier, and treating the discourses it generates as virtually the sole constituent of experience (1992:286; see also R. Johnson 1991).

The post-Marxist abandonment of conventional notions of social class, in favor of a more mobile sense of the various collective identifications made by a subject, does contain a corrective to unexamined homogenization of diverse groups into the categories of class.[11] The static teleological understanding of history in conventional Marxism, based in the dialectics of class struggle, is also certainly open to revision. Taken to an extreme, however, overemphasizing social fragmentation, post-Marxist criticism of the old conception of social class for its "totalization" only reflects a morbid, even more overarching sense of the complexity of multinational capital—or the now "impossible totality of the contemporary world system" (Jameson 1984:80). The network of corporate capitalism has not, presumably, "for a long time shown itself quite as total," given the intricacy and seeming invisibility of its operations (from the view of the detached intellectual specialist at least). But authoritarian ideologies, economic crises, and so forth certainly remain "palpable," argues Terry Eagleton. Thus the irony that "at just this historical moment, when it is clear that what we confront is indeed in some sense a 'total system,'... elements of the political left begin to speak of plurality, multiplicity, schizoid circuits, microstrategies and the rest" (1990:381).[12] If an older faith in the teleology of history, in the stable subject (individual and collective), and in something better than the present has its pitfalls, a refusal to develop a critical engagement with these entities is more dangerous still: "It is little wonder that the world appears chaotic and boundless when we have so thoroughly denied ourselves the critical tools with which to understand it" (Plant 1992:186). The result merely reinforces the perceived postmodern condition, the "end of history" line promulgated by left and neoconservative academics alike. Contradictions and even open dissent on a fairly large scale remain discernible, however, as do the most complex, far-flung operations of multinational capital. The will to *act* "is neither foolish nor malign," as one might conclude from academic pessimism concerning subjectivity, but continues as always to require "imagination and a readiness to risk," qualities still perfectly alive in the postmodern world (Hebdige 1988:222). The only necessarily fragmentary politics, in postmodern life, is the vulgar self-interest encouraged by the mainstream.

Andrew Ross sensibly focuses post-Marxism on the totalizing categories of the older Marxist analysis of class, which "are no longer enough to help us make sense of the fragmented and various ways in which people live and negotiate the everyday life of consumer capitalism" (1988:xv). The invocation of fragmentation is not entirely innocent of the post-Marxist affinity for micropolitics, however: in *No Respect* his cause célèbre is the small field of feminist "anti-antiporn" pornography, far less visible in its circulation than most other popular forms (pornography in general remaining a furtive if immensely profitable pastime). Dick Hebdige, in contrast, defines the insubordinate subculture as forming in the highly public "space between surveillance and the evasion of surveillance," where scrutiny is turned "into the pleasure of being watched" by authorities of all sorts, and publicly conveying some direct or indirect form of disrespect for them (1988:35). Ross, however, does underpin his more general accounts of everyday culture with a strong materialist sensibility, likewise emphasizing the expression of disrespect for cultural authorities. Since both the domination and subordination enacted through ideology are active, shifting phenomena, one should not always be "in the position of unveiling a truth beyond the ideological facade of popular 'sense,' [but] engage with the concrete effects of that sense in the everyday culture at large" (1988:15).

For the effects of popular cultural forms are not just intellectual, of course, but affective or emotional. Recent critics such as Henry Giroux and Roger Simon have pointed out that both semantic meaning *and* pleasure have to be accounted for in the analysis of texts. Like Ross, they refute the conventional Marxist tendency to reduce all mass culture to a simple matter of ideological manipulation: the effects of mass culture should not be defined "around a set of ideological meanings [presumably] permanently inscribed in particular cultural forms." In such a "search and destroy mission based on uncovering the particular meanings and messages that mediate between any given film, popular song, or text and its audience," far too great a premium is placed on "ideology and rationality as the interests which structure behavior and move us." Lost is the plain fact that the effectiveness of popular texts depends even more on their engagement of pleasure, of corporeal desires, emotions, passions, and so forth, the ways "in which the *body* learns, moves, desires, and longs for affirmation." A critical pedagogy must realize that cultural forms involved in struggles over producing and reproducing corporeal desire do involve power and ideology, but cannot be analyzed simply in terms of meaning, "rather than through the primacy of pleasure and affect" (Giroux and Simon 1989:9, 15–17).

This materialist emphasis has been characteristic of British cultural studies, which has always posited a dialectical relationship between material experience and consciousness or ideology. The dialectic of affective and ideological experience binds together the study of both text and context, artist and audience, and the whole array of human agents and creative forms in everyday culture. Williams, who helped significantly to implant this materialism in cultural studies, was an avid follower of the avant-garde in his youth, in the 1930s, contemporaneously with theorists of the avant-garde such as Mikhail Bakhtin and Walter Benjamin, featured prominently throughout this book. The playwright Bertolt Brecht, a strong influence on Benjamin, held that "realist" or materialist art and cultural analysis should be dialectical in the sense that it is *"concrete* and so as to encourage *abstraction"*—linking physical experience and intellectual realization—a point recently cited in work on cultural studies (Brantlinger 1990:170).

Cultural studies might thus be conceived as an avatar of the avant-garde: in the theory of the avant-garde, expressed best by Benjamin, the discovery of formal innovation appropriate to radical content, in a particular production, is essential to sparking a simultaneously affective and intellectual response in its recipient, a "bodily presence of mind." For Bakhtin, form and content were one, in the everyday use of language as well as avant-garde works, and he complained six decades ago about linguists and literary scholars who persisted in abstracting human expression from its social context. Brecht sought in general to convey an *attitude*—a disposition to question conformist common sense—a term that suggests both affect and intellect. Much like Jaggar's recent reminder of the role of emotion in ideology, and thus in any outlaw or dissident culture, Brecht argued that "emotions, instincts, impulses are generally presented as being deeper, more eternal, less easily influenced by society than ideas, but this is in no way true" (1964:101).

A cultural materialism of this sort, attuned simultaneously to the sensuous and the rational, the felt and the articulated, is essential to the "linguistics of conflict" called for by MacCabe. Eagleton, writing on the place of materialism in the history of the aesthetic, finds that aesthetic theory has persistently divorced the sensuous into a "baroque aestheticism"—as in postmodern celebrations of the body as pure corporeality (see Fiske 1989)—and the rational into the "brutal asceticism" characteristic of more quietist aesthetics in the tradition of Kant (discussed in chapter 1). Capitalist society already comprises the dual forces of a chaotic possessive appetite (or bodily gratification) and "a supremely bodiless reason," in the rationalization of human relations along economic lines. The perversity of aesthetics, therefore, has long been to mirror the very world it usually execrates, merely taking one or the other tendency to an extreme. If this "rift between raw appetite and disembodied reason is to be healed, it can only be through a revolutionary anthropology"—like cultural studies—"which tracks the roots of human rationality to their hidden source in the needs and capacities of the productive body" (Eagleton 1990:207–8).

In proposing the avant-garde as a benchmark for studies of contemporary culture, it should be noted that many people have made connections between avant-garde insurgencies like "the Sex Pistols, dada, the so grandly named Situationist International, and even forgotten heresies." The problem, though, is that "no one had made anything of them," as Greil Marcus says in his own history of the avant-garde, *Lipstick Traces.* The story of the avant-garde, he finds, if one does try to make something of it, emerges as "a story seemingly endemic to the century, a story that repeatedly speaks and repeatedly loses its voice." Cultural revolt has a distinct tradition, then, but he finds its appeal in large part in "its *gaps,* and those moments when the story that has lost its voice somehow recovers it, and what happens then." The history of the avant-garde seems to contain gaps, however, in part because of his distinction between propagandist vanguards of a fairly immediate, visceral rebellion (Dada, the Lettrist and Situationist Internationals, and punk) and more scholarly theorists. Benjamin, as a result, is unfortunately and curiously dismissed as a "careful absolutist" (1989:19, 22–23), and inaccurately tied to the Frankfurt School's ascetic aloofness from mass culture, while Bakhtin receives one passing mention.

If one considers instead Benjamin's role in articulating Dada and surrealism with the work of Brecht; the Situationist International's citation of Brecht as the only artist with similar methods and aims; the Situationist influence on English punk rock in the seventies; and, finally, critical readings of punk through Benjamin, the avant-garde appears to have a quite encouraging continuity, to have been a *constant* presence. Its actors have indeed spoken *directly* to each other. Admirable, exciting, and important as Marcus's book is, it does its subjects a disservice in describing their relationship in mystified terms of "familiars," communicating "blindly" across time. As opposed to Marcus's "weak perception that this continuity is 'transcendentally odd'" (A. Ross 1989b:116), his own privileged subject, the SI, declared that *any* dissatisfied persons who had attempted to enact new responses to the emptiness of their culture were "pre-situationist" (Gray 1974:14). With the recovery of their history, previously misrepresented or actually rendered invisible, it becomes possible, in criticism and teaching, to connect radical aesthetics to social practice. It is simply not true, one discovers, that "no new aesthetic movements of collective importance, operative across more than one art form, emerged after Surrealism," nor even that the Situationist International, in 1968, "marked the last time when art and politics mingled powerfully" (Anderson 1988:328; Ball 1987:106).

To construct a coherent alternative tradition out of the neglected (or misrepresented) works of modernity, one might begin with Paris, "the Capital of the Nineteenth Century," as Benjamin put it. According to the Situationists, the precursor of genuine avant-gardism is the poet Lautréamont, who asserted that "poetry must be made by all." Art, in other words, should at least engage members of an active, critical audience, the distinction between artist and audience eradicated. He worked and died immediately before one of the high points of cooperation in human history, the short-lived, ruthlessly suppressed Paris Commune of 1871, not only "a pivotal event in modern history . . . whose echoes have not died away," but "a positive experiment whose whole truth has not been rediscovered or fulfilled to this day" (Avrich 1988:229; Debord et al. 1981:315; see Marcus 1989:123–27, 140–42).

The collective human endeavor in Lautréamont's revolutionary Paris, reflected in his maxim on poetry, presents an absolute contrast with the Paris of Baudelaire, and the spurious revolution of 1848 (as viewed by Marx in *The Eighteenth Brumaire of Louis Bonaparte*). Frequently described as the first modernist, Baudelaire recoiled from the perceived ravages of urban life, particularly its crowds. As a result, his "theory of the transitory beautiful" held that "the shock-like experience of the new can only have an effect upon itself," or within the realm of art. With the arrival of modern industry, then, the engine of urbanization, "the first consciousness of the degeneration of experience" led to "the withdrawal of poesy into itself" (Jauss 1988/89:48–49).[13] Working at this key moment, Baudelaire set the tone for nearly a century of derision of new aesthetic technologies, particularly in his execration of photography as a popular art, in "The Salon of 1859": "If photography is permitted to supplement some of art's functions, they will forthwith be usurped and corrupted by it, thanks to photography's natural alliance with *the mob*." As an accessible, readily employable means of both representation and reproduction, photography in essence threatened the autonomy of art, and the uniqueness of the artist.

In the bitter attack on injustice in *Les Chants de Maldoror* (1869), Lautréamont, on the other hand, created an unprecedented language, or style, of negation. He continued his assault on mindless positivity in *Poésies* (1870), but did so through ironic mockery based in a profane form of montage, a collection of plagiarized, altered maxims. Lautréamont's social indignation in the first book, leading him to prune "false idea[s] of the beauties of literature" and to refuse to create a poetry "outside the ordinary," and his subversive collage-like collection of maxims, in the second, have a considerable affinity with the Paris Commune, which broke down "hierarchical divisions [in] the realm of cultural production" between aesthetic and political discourse (as in *Maldoror*), and between genres (as in *Poésies*), as well as those drawn between high and popular art. Kristin Ross's description of this sort of *bricolage,* in the Commune—"the wrenching of everyday objects from their habitual context to be used in a radically different way" (1988:5, 36)—seems to take its terms directly from the Birmingham work on subcultural style, and thus invokes, as does Marcus, a lineage between Paris in 1871 and the present.

Lautréamont was only fully recovered to aesthetic theory by the surrealist movement between the world wars in this century, when the limits of modernism's quest for artistic autonomy were being reached, and radical artists pursued instead the possibility of the opposite aim, to render art and life inseparable. Dada's historic role just prior to surrealism, says Situationist Guy Debord, "is to have delivered a mortal blow to the traditional conception of culture," one so purely negative, however, that Dada dissolved almost immediately. But "the dadaist spirit has influenced all the movements that have come after it, and a dadaist-type negation must be present in any later constructive position" (1981d:18; see also Marcus 1989:187—244).[14] As Benjamin similarly puts it, Dada enabled the conception of the work of art as "an instrument of ballistics," but kept that tactile shock effect wrapped "inside the moral shock effect," at the expense of politics (1969:238).

A little over a decade later, in the 1930s, response to the Depression and to the rise of fascism compelled the high point of the avant-garde. This epoch is exemplifed by Brecht's epic theater, which sought to create a theater full of experts with a critical attitude towards themselves and their society, and by Benjamin, whose criticism integrated Dada and surrealism with Brecht's distinctive interest in new artistic technologies. Contemporaneous (or nearly so) with the development of the Benjamin-Brecht position, but in the face of Stalinism rather than fascism, Bakhtin likewise defined an aesthetics of contumacy (under the guise of studying Rabelais). Bakhtin's cohort V. N. Volosinov found electric sparks in language, considering all spoken and written forms the products of social dialogue, and hence laden with simultaneously affective and ideological struggle. This tactile understanding of communication led Bakhtin to champion carnival, the avant-garde borderline at which art and life meet, especially the curses and oaths (or billingsgate) it directs against authority.

In the postwar period, the most crucial avant-garde movement has been the Situationist International, which formed in the midfifties, at the end of Brecht's life, and disbanded shortly after the May Revolution of 1968 in Paris. In 1968 (a formative moment for a Czech fan of the Velvet Underground named Havel, too), the SI dramatically revivified the anarchist belief that liberated speech initiated concerted political resistance, in attempting the great project of all the figures here, the generation of negation in everyday life. The SI insisted on the full realization of the implications of Lautréamont's plagiarisms, which it renamed *detournement,* in specifying that such a montage should level cultural hierarchies in the interest of radical ends. The detournement of Greene's *Brighton Rock* in a biography of the Sex Pistols, written by English Situationists in 1978, fully realizes a "revolutionary literary criticism" as Eagleton defines it. The authors not only reinserted the novel into the whole field of cultural practices and social activities, but corrected, in Greene's case, received judgments about his literary status as well. Thus punk, "in many respects, was the moment when it became inescapably clear that the traditional concerns of the avant-garde would henceforth be addressed and worked through in relation to popular culture" (A. Ross 1989b:116).

Prior to the economic depression and authoritarian ideology of the midseventies that spawned punk, the confluence of literature, popular music, and youth subcultures in postwar England generally revolved around the highly successful ideology of the "Age of Affluence," propagated in the fifties. The general argument was that class distinctions had diminished or even disappeared due to postwar prosperity, and that a consensus on the social-welfare state had been reached that likewise minimized or even foreclosed past political differences. Subsequent economic decline and Thatcher's reign of terror certainly make these notions seem a bad joke. But the brief period when the ideology of affluence reigned supreme remains significant, having generated responses in popular culture instructive in attacking contemporary myths—very similar to that of affluence—which bear a disturbing degree more authoritarianism. Thus the chapters on authoritarian and antiauthoritarian culture do not concern England much at all, but set a larger context for the signficance of cultural events in that nation's recent history, so that their examples might be put to further use.

Over the period covering the work of Colin MacInnes, Anthony Burgess, the Rolling Stones, and the Sex Pistols, 1958–78, subcultural groups arrived at a conscious understanding of the antiauthoritarian possibilities in appropriating and recasting "high" art. The suggestive if peripheral role of literature in this milieu, though alluded to very generally, has not been developed in subcultural sociology. The literary connection, though, serves all the more to confirm Hebdige's linkage, over a decade ago, of subcultural style and the avant-garde tradition. The astute use of literature in youth subcultures undermined cultural authorities along distinctively avant-garde lines, violating the boundaries drawn around high culture, and contradicting elitist value judgments on popular cultural activity. The increasingly sophisticated use of literature, in postwar youth subcultures, provided Williams with more than sufficient reason to assert that "no dominant culture ever in reality includes or exhausts all human practice, human energy, or human intention" (1977:125), all of which continue to emerge. If there is anyone who still questions whether supposedly distinct levels of high and popular culture might be legitimately melted down—and it is certainly still possible to have execration heaped on one's head for suggesting it—the relations of literature and rock music in postwar England must surely lay objection to rest. The reversal in those relations between 1958 and 1978 indicates a thoroughgoing embroilment of the different forms. Initially the literary condescended to evaluate the music and its social significance; ultimately, in remarkably short order, the musicians and their fans—"flowers in the dustbin," in the Sex Pistols' "God Save the Queen"—taught the literary about their enterprise, both its past and its possibilities.

Part 1

CHAPTER 1

The Avant-Garde Tradition and Cultural Studies

In a brief essay entitled "The Destructive Character" (1931), Walter Benjamin celebrates the "destructive" action of making art practicable, or useful. His aphoristic style, as in all his work, veils a powder keg: the conflict of authority and contumacy, played out in culture, that provides an important source of hope for the course of human history. At stake, more specifically, is the issue of whether the habit of critical thought—actively drawing one's entire range of cultural and political experience into coherence—will become widespread enough to enable new visions of human society.

The destructive character creates art, or passes on the art of others, with a consciousness of history, an awareness of the efforts of human agents to change the circumstances and conditions of their lives. To the destructor's opposite, the "conservator," who attempts to sanctify art outside these social processes, its embroilment with history can only appear a destructive practice. The conservator's quietism serves the purposes of dominant social groups by denigrating any significant social function for the artist, implicitly or explicitly denying human historical efficacy in general. Thus the conservator's perspective on what constitutes creativity and destructiveness is granted the privilege of institutional status and its weight.

Because of this institutional power, says Andrew Ross, the "education of taste has become an important area of contestation within the academy." A history concerning or including popular culture, in other words, cannot confine itself to producers (or artists) and consumers (or audiences): "It must also be a history of intellectuals—in particular, those experts in culture whose traditional business is to define what is popular and what is legitimate, who patrol the ever shifting borders of popular and legitimate taste," exercising their prestige and privilege (1989a:5, 210). What follows here at the outset, accordingly, in a brief history focused on literary modernism, describes the origin and growth of a cultural hermeticism of two centuries' standing, which pervades the practice and study of the humanities and arts generally. It must be supplanted by a dialectical attention not only to texts, but to their uses in everyday life as well; not only to privileged cultural forms, but to those "grotesque" popular forms that contain, Benjamin believes, the most crucial energy of their time.

Interdisciplinary efforts in the field of cultural studies, in its British origins, had a specific interest in conducting "an ideological critique of the way the humanities and the arts present themselves as parts of disinterested knowledge." Searching the past for "the genealogy of the present situation," and from that starting point constructing "a possible alternative scenario," proved to require an "alternative conception of *modernity*" (Hall 1990:15; 1988:14). A number of recent critiques of canonical modernism and postmodernism are available to such an enterprise. These reevaluations have laid bare the arbitrary notions generated by elite institutions of art, particularly the dichotomy drawn between "high culture" and everyday life—the latter the presumably ephemeral, merely utilitarian realm of mass culture and politics. Two historical periods are particularly important in this regard: the overlap of the Enlightenment and Romanticism, when the aesthetic in its present construction was first defined, and the cold war, when modernism was canonized by quietist scholars. The collision at present between this asocial establishment and cultural studies, as a conflict over the construction of modernity, in essence continues the battle between modernism and the avant-garde—a schism often suppressed by their conflation in conventional scholarship.

Even intellectuals who wish to encourage resistance of elitism, however, face the contradiction of inveighing against "cultural capital," or institutionally sanctioned cultural authority. They, too, gain preferment through the skilled manipulation of language and symbols within their respective fields, and challenge to cultural institutions often remains confined and specialist, as a result. The recent confrontation of this dilemma, though, has at least brought "the historical confinement to the political margins of the fraught relationship between intellectuals and popular culture... onto center stage" (A. Ross 1989a:213).

Placing that relationship in the foreground, furthermore, might redeem not just popular culture, but high culture as well. If one does not stop belonging to high-culture institutions simply because he or she disavows the old distinctions between high and low, one way of redeeming work in that sphere would be to draw out the potential of the various aesthetic languages it sequesters, "in order to turn [scholars'] inescapable social distance from other... people into a critical one" (Gripsrud 1989:204). The latent potential even of high culture to inform dissent must be kept in mind in the following sections on the aesthetic, modernism, and the avant-garde, as an important reason for moving through them to arrive at cultural studies. The point is not to forsake entirely "high" art and literature, but to open them finally to material use, considering that traditional notions of creative genius soaring "above material conditions, society, politics" have only brought the arts "an honoured place... at the cost of limited influence, marginality, even irrelevance" (Sinfield 1989:28).

Cultural Capital

The dominant fractions of the dominant class, says Pierre Bourdieu in *Distinction: A Social Critique of the Judgment of Taste,* understandably demand of art and its keepers a high degree of denial of the social world and its injustices. Thus the dominated fractions of that class, intellectuals and artists, purvey notions of the purity of art, compensating for their status as "poor relations" and its abnegation by promoting the ascetic aspect of aesthetics. In essence they accept control of cultural capital, in lieu of economic capital, thereby reinforcing (wittingly or unwittingly) the dominant taste for quietism. Beyond simple confirmation of the status quo, the particular stock-in-trade is pessimism concerning the social world and the possibilities for its change. Though Bourdieu describes cultural conservators as poor relations, he stresses in general the more logical basis for their behavior, the actual privilege of the intelligentsia: "The detachment of the pure [ostensibly disinterested] gaze cannot be dissociated from [conditioning by] a life of ease [that] tends to induce an active distance from necessity" (1984:176). The intellectual specialist's distance from social life fuels alienation, at the very least, if not pessimism. At a deep level, in either case, has traditionally been "a conviction that there is nothing but the [aesthetic] past to be won," a restriction of attention that amounts to "a determined refusal [to consider] any genuinely alternative social and cultural order" (Williams 1989:124–25).

By abstracting works of art from the historical and social conditions of their production and reception, the conservator preserves art against any usefulness besides a mystified, purified "appreciation." But if one considers the oppressive conditions, throughout history, that have enabled a few to enjoy the leisure to produce and consume art, cultural treasures appear instead a record of barbarism, in Benjamin's view. The authoritative keepers of art, for example, have traditionally enforced cultural hierarchies—based in highly abstract, hence mystified assumptions about Beauty, Form, Taste, and Truth—that justify *other* forms of authority. Hierarchy in art, by claiming a natural, immutable status based on disinterested judgment, helps legitimate clearly interested claims in society, for the natural superiority of elites and the immutability of the social structure. Cultural hierarchies of "high" and "low," to put it bluntly, are directly analogous to social class (Berger 1972:11, 29; Stallybrass and White 1986:2–3). Such a social context, not surprisingly, including the actual relations between different "levels" of cultural production, has traditionally been suppressed in the study of art and literature. Students have learned for decades that "personal response" alone is sufficient, in encountering art, that one should be sensitive about nothing in particular, just about abstractions like beauty and genius (Bennison and Spicer 1991:19).

A good example of blithe assumptions about the purity of literature is a digression in Paul Fussell's *The Great War and Modern Memory*, in which he stops to instruct the reader in the "illiteracy" of writers with political convictions: "As it grows politically conscious, literary discourse naturally takes on the rhetorical characteristics of postwar political adversary proceedings. And that is fatal for it" (1975:109). As these terms indicate, notions about the necessary autonomy of high culture from politics have been closely linked with the intellectual quietism of the cold war. By identifying with "'value-free' investments" in art—a pretense of disinterestedness, devoted to some general human condition rather than any specific one—the intellectual purist empties out the political contents of art (whether explicit or implicit), in a craven effort to win and preserve the tolerance of public officials (Lasch, qtd. in Sinfield 1989:105). Cultural institutions tied directly to political power, like the National Endowments for the Arts and the Humanities in the United States, can thus exploit quite explicitly the notion that there is some aesthetic realm pure of any political taint.

Even with the recent declaration of an end to the cold war, prominent critics continue to police the institution of art for dissent, now on the part of women and minorities as much as Marxists. In 1990, for example, Richard Bernstein insisted in the *New York Times* that art is not "obliged to be socially responsible," or, in the prevalent conservative stereotype of leftist thought, "politically correct." All such claims that art and its study should be "nonideological," however, merely represent the actual, more stringent enforcement of political correctness, which has long "meant to *ignore* issues of social and human concern" (Pindell 1990:5). This *apolitical* correctness concerning art and literature wishes to forestall the evaluation of works without concern for "refinement, etiquette, and 'taste,'" and, thereby, to prevent efforts to tell the truth about social injustice both past and present (Brantlinger 1990:155). Not *all* politics are wrong, either, in the conservative argument; the intent is obviously to make dissident politics wrong, a priori. The modernist poet and critic T. S. Eliot was at least more honest than his postmodern epigones, in *After Strange Gods,* when he declared that Tradition in the arts buttresses orthodoxy, or a culturally, racially homogeneous community resisting excessive tolerance of difference.

Control of cultural capital (specifically the power to define hierarchies of high and low culture) also allows the conservator to deem aesthetically illegitimate large portions of everyday popular culture, as well as art by subordinate groups. One continues to find in art, criticism, and scholarship tirelessly repeated "apocalyptic denunciations of all forms of 'levelling,' 'trivialization' or 'massification'" (Bourdieu 1984:469). The left and the right have been equally guilty in this regard; the legacy of aesthetics born in the eighteenth century informs the dismissal by many Marxists, as much as conservative elitists, of both mass culture and popular life. At best, all too often, popular texts and everyday practices are subject to conventionally detached intellectual contemplation. A genuine challenge to institutionalized tastes, instead, would draw upon forms of popular culture "in ways that *explode* the 'objective' canons of aesthetic taste rather than simply... expanding them by appropriating, as a new colony of legitimate attention, cultural terrain that was hitherto off-limits." It does no good to submit marginalized cultural forms "to yet another round of clever formalist 'readings'" (A. Ross 1989a:211).

In contrast with the constriction of institutional art's parameters, the "destructive" effort to draw art and popular life together is clearly the genuinely creative force. Benjamin, in "The Destructive Character," surely has in mind Mikhail Bakunin's formulation that the destructive urge is also a creative one, if based in the power of critical thought. Breaking the boundaries of the institutions of art, to engage with everyday life, clearly suggests Bakunin's dialectic.[1] When modernism was just becoming a spent force, Benjamin, accordingly, linked the conservators of art of his own day with the secular cult of beauty encouraged by earlier movements advocating *l'art pour l'art* (art for art's sake). The concept of the autonomous, self-contained work of art, in his view, attempts "to seal art off from the development of technology" and mass culture, in particular (qtd. in Jauss 1988/89:48). Thus both art and critics are associated with fascism, in "The Work of Art in the Age of Mechanical Reproduction," and he referred to scholars, in his personal correspondence, as trained apes.

Another anarchist, Pierre-Joseph Proudhon, had already attacked notions of art's autonomy in the mid–nineteenth century, declaring art for art's sake to be "*debauchery* of the heart and *dissolution* of the mind." When construed as the highest thought of the soul, aloof from material social experience, art is "reduced to nothing more than an excitement of fantasy and the senses" (qtd. in Bourdieu 1984:49).[2] In citing anarchism here, Bourdieu draws upon a significant antecedent of his critique of cultural capital; from their origin, theories of aesthetic autonomy have been shadowed persistently by such criticism, as the chronological range of Proudhon, Benjamin, and Bourdieu's work indicates. One of the first complaints about the absolutist, authoritarian function of art appeared in an early anarchist treatise, William Godwin's *An Enquiry Concerning Political Justice* (1793). Bakunin, in *God and the State* (1871), condemned the "immutable, impersonal, abstract and insensitive science" of a new class, the *savants,* who exercised their knowledge so as to "paralyze the movement of social forces." In launching "the first fullscale attack of modern times" on the institution of art, these anarchists saw a connection between esteeming the "artist of genius" and justifying social inequity. To acclaim the artist's uniqueness suppresses the creative potential of popular life in favor of the isolated, superior individual, and validates, in essence, the general economic process by which people are dispossessed for the benefit of a minority (Reszler 1973:43, 46).

To the cultural anarchist, with regard to creativity,

> what are works of art alongside the creative energy displayed by everyone a thousand times a day: seething unfulfilled desires, daydreams in search of a foothold in reality, feelings at once confused and luminously clear, ideas and gestures presaging nameless upheavals, ... the hurricane of hatred, and the wild impetus of the *urge* for *destruction*.... The search for new forms of communication is now part of a collective effort. In this way the old specialization of art has finally come to an end. There are no more artists because everyone is an artist. The work of art of the future will be the construction of a *passionate life.* (Vaneigem 1983:147, 154–55)

The arts possess a fairly long tradition of such anarchism in both theory and practice, more familiarly referred to as the avant-garde. The impact of anarchism on art, in fact, "reached its peak precisely when the historical avantgarde was in a crucial stage of its own formation," in the modern period (Huyssen 1986:5). But the avant-garde, by the end of this chapter, will be understood to thread through the supposed disjunction between modernism and postmodernism, and to include forms from both mass-reproduced culture and popular life.

The Avant-Garde, Modernism, and Postmodernism

In 1960, Harry Levin declared the modernist period to have ended with World War II, in one of the first descriptions of a postmodern period. But essentially modernist attitudes towards art and everyday life nonetheless continue to dominate institutions of art (whether academic departments or museums). Useful accounts of the avant-garde have been choked off, as a result, through its conflation into one undifferentiated modern mass (a tactic with subtler variations, like treating avant-garde movements as precursors to individual masterpieces). It has recently been said, for example, that the only feature of modernism that lends the concept coherence is a "self-conscious break with tradition" (Eysteinsson 1990:52), terms generalized enough to include every individual and movement in the modern period. As the Surrealist André Breton pointed out at the time, though, "every intellectual creator who appears to break with tradition... because of certain formal innovations in his poetry" is spuriously lumped together, as a "revolutionary," with the efforts of the avant-garde "to define a systematic action aiming at the transformation of the world" outside art (1969:213–14). Some modern artists and critics clearly stand apart for having sought, beyond aesthetic innovation, to make art useful, to integrate it with everyday life in the interest of democratizing communication. Among the avant-garde movements themselves, an even more distinctive minority thought modernism's despised Other (as explained below), mass culture, might actually be essential to making life an art in its own right.

The formal experiments of modernist art—such as James Joyce's *Ulysses* or Eliot's *The Waste Land*—have generally been synonymous with the avant-garde, whether in popular parlance or scholarship. But modernism, in ensconcing internal individual experience away from the perceived ravages of mass civilization and culture, was an attempt to create an art autonomous from the everyday. *Ulysses* concerns its own production above all else; the "unity of material life and self-exiled artistic consciousness which Joyce seeks is achieved not *in* the work but *by* it." In resisting (if also recording) the realm of commodities and mass culture, through the difficulty and self-absorbedness of his work's parade of allusions, Joyce becomes a producer without consumers, except for the elite described by Bourdieu.

Eliot, for one, believed that Joyce's formal tactics in *Ulysses* were necessary to shape the "anarchy and futility" of the modern period, though the order Joyce achieved scarcely engaged the material causes of those conditions. *The Waste Land*'s own esoteric allusions point to an off-stage cultural knowledge or Tradition; hence its intended value likewise resides only in the form of the text itself (Eagleton 1976:149, 156–57).

At the same time Levin and others declared the arrival of the postmodern period, Raymond Williams recognized instead how little had changed. He launched a career-long critique, as a result, of the persisting construction of literature and criticism as necessarily isolated, nonpolitical opponents of industrial society, even of democracy itself (Brantlinger 1990:40–41). A lecture near the end of his life, on modernism, casts his critique in its strongest terms: modernism, he finds, is confined to a highly selective field of aestheticist works and ideas, "and denied to everything else in an act of pure ideology [that] stops history dead. Modernism being the terminus, everything afterwards is counted out of development. It is *after;* stuck in the post"— the post-modern, that is.

Williams distinguishes "two faces of Modernism" that confront the present: first, the original texts that at least had the merit of destabilizing fixed forms; second, the modernist/postmodernist academics who stabilized those texts "as the most reductive versions of human existence in the whole of cultural history," while preserving a reactionary tendency toward popular culture that "should have culminated with Eliot." These two stages both embrace conservative ideologies, but nonetheless differ dramatically. Modernism was genuinely innovative in its "desperate images" of the fragmentation of identity, but later postmodern critics and scholars merely consolidated that achievement as a new establishment. The original modernists were often "literally exiles, having little or no common ground with the societies in which they were stranded." But the later postmodernist establishment, "near the centres of corporate power, takes human inadequacy [and] self-deception...as self-evident routine data," helping propagate a sense of helplessness the corporate world would like people to feel (1989:34–35, 45, 76, 130). The transition between the modern and postmodern periods, therefore, amounts to "a shift from a strong to a weak form of nihilism" (Newman 1989:141), from the genuinely alienated to the perfectly comfortable.

The distinction Williams draws between modernism and its sub-sequent canonization is critical to the comprehensibility of a critique of modernism; part of the confusion about modernism lies in the transmission of its own claims to radicalism (such as those noted by Breton), usually highly ironic in retrospect. The art critic Herbert Read, for example, a contemporary of the moderns and a theorist of anarchism, considers autonomous art "permanently revolutionary"—though abstract, purely formal, irrational, and so on. The artist is "an upsetter of the established order" because he or she does *not,* in particular, give "clear expression to the confused feelings of the masses." A revolutionary art, paradoxically, is an elitist art: "The greatest enemy of art is the collective mind" (1967:24). Borrowing from Bakunin, Read agrees that in order "to create it is necessary to destroy," but, despising "not only the plutocracy ... but also the industrial proletariat," identifies the autonomous artist (or "poet") as the appropriate "agent of destruction, ... necessarily an *anarchist*"— but in an asocial sense. An artist only "acquires significance by being a member of a society," he stipulates, but there is no extant society, in his view, capitalist or nominally Marxist, in which any relations to practical activity but "dereliction" and "resentful independence" are appropriate (1971:58–59, 61, 63, 228).

The problem with such constructions is the association of revolution in art with the freedom of the unique, superior individual. This elitism, in fact, is symptomatic of modernism's ambiguous relation with anarchism in particular, a relationship suppressed until recently in scholarship. Read embodies both problems: as a critic he denies any actual political connection in modernism, describing Picasso as "devoid of ideologies of any kind" (1971:77), though Picasso's best-known early work was actually created in close proximity to anarchism—put to the same elitist uses one finds in Read. In the 1950s, Roger Shattuck observed that anarchism, the "most turbulent force of all" in the social background of avant-garde art (in the general sense of an art of scandal), was "almost forgotten" in histories of art and literature dealing with the first half of the *belle époque* (1885–1900) (1968:20).

More recently, Patricia Leighten, writing on Picasso, contemporaneous artists, and anarchism, has pointedly noted the academic suppression of the political connections and content of modern art, well under way in U.S. universities when Shattuck wrote, in the midst of the cold war. Modernist aesthetics do discount content in favor of formal abstraction and innovation, but their repute in this regard also has a good deal to do with their academic transmission, which jettisoned, for example, the political contents of Picasso's early work (a suppression assisted by Picasso himself, later in life). Even with a renewed picture of the actual political context of Picasso's work, however, Leighten finds that anarchism licensed for modernists a "faith in the pure, direct expression of the artist, [a] cult of extreme individualism." If expressed as radical anti-intellectualism and instinctual primitivism, this individualism is not far different from institutional notions about art. "The appeal of anarchism for many," she finds, "was that it was more an anti-politics than a politics," inseparable from solipsistic, "Nietzschean convictions regarding the importance of the 'natural' spontaneity of the 'true' artist" (1989:6, 9, 11, 17, 43–44, 50; see also Sonn 1989). The artist-as-revolutionary, to the modernists, presumably fulfilled "the duty of genius to tear up norms, to shatter the confines of rule and to permit a whole new world of reality, uniquely perceived, conceived, and expressed" (Graña 1964:52).

Though stunted by inherited conceptions of the artist's uniqueness, the relation between art and radical politics in the modern period, in its sheer volatility, verifies Williams's belief that the modernists are sometimes less execrable than the subsequent employment of them to enforce elitist, quietist values. The inwardness of modernist aestheticism has served more exclusively conservative purposes since it migrated into the institutions of art in the 1950s, when the "emergence of modernism as a literary category coincided with the explosion of the *academic* study of modern literature" (Bergonzi, qtd. in Sinfield 1989:191; see Eysteinsson 1990; Nelson 1989). The dominant school in literary studies at the time, New Criticism, eschewed not only political commitment, but any social interests at all, in favor of close textual reading, in which "no raising of the eyes from the page to the wider world is required." In the midst of the cold war, this intellectual quietism, along with the ascendency of American universities and critics (such as Hugh Kenner and Lionel Trilling), played a particularly decisive role in the canonization of modernism. The myth of free (or autonomous) literary endeavor and the myth of the Free World helped "to generate each other" (Sinfield 1989:102, 105).

In the McCarthy era, with "freedom" in general honored only

in the abstract, the conception of aesthetic freedom, after the brief moment of the original avant-garde between the world wars, was reconfined as the abstracted freedom of isolation from popular culture. In one stroke, the revolutionary avant-garde movements were discarded, or else denuded of their politics and conflated with modernism on the basis of superficial features, like the use of montage. In a well-known essay published in 1957, "The Fate of the Avant-Garde," Richard Chase could thus treat "aesthetic experimentalism" and "social protest" as identical categories (see Bérubé 1991). Working from the same equation, Trilling declared that modernism was an adversary culture because it sought to *escape* from social bonds (1967:82)—a formulation dating to the Enlightenment, and equally popular with academic Marxists of the same period, like Theodor Adorno and Herbert Marcuse of the Frankfurt School.

Such a safe, purely symbolic sort of freedom was held by the art critic Clement Greenberg, most notably, to be epitomized by the significantly titled Abstract Expressionism. In a now-familiar corollary, he set abstraction in modernist art—in terms of both technique and the artist's social disengagement—against the simplistic "kitsch" of mass culture, celebrating the migration of the main premises of modern Western art, abstraction and formalism (and elitism) to the United States. In his view, the achievements of American modernist painting did not just befit, but essentially justified the experience of alienation under capitalism; the freedom to dribble paint somehow compensated for the suppression of other freedoms in the McCarthy era. In the catalog for an Abstract Expressionist exhibit—sponsored in fact by the Central Intelligence Agency[3]—the director of New York's Museum of Modern Art extolled the paintings as "symbolic demonstrations of freedom in a world in which freedom connotes a political attitude," or connotes only an abstraction, in other words, rather than practical experience (Sinfield 1989:102–3, 190). There was no contradiction in the fact that if Jackson Pollock had decided to produce agitprop, rather than harmlessly dripping paint to the glory of the Free World, he would immediately have been blacklisted, shunned, and so forth.

The greatest loss in the postwar depoliticization of art, however, resulted from the conflation of the original avant-garde with this harmless version of modernism, as still more essentially trivial formal innovation. Artists and critics who attended not just to the production of art but also to its social purpose and reception, in order to discover a role for it in everyday life, were absorbed into the general arcana of aesthetic history and theory. George Steiner, for example, absurdly and crudely enlists Benjamin in the ranks of elitism, as one "committed to abstruse thought and scholarship," who knew that critical intelligence "resides in the always-threatened keeping of the very few" (qtd. in Eagleton 1981:xiii). In actual fact, Benjamin held that intellectual production must "become politically useful," by surmounting "the separate spheres of competence" into which it is divided (1973:95), especially the division between an elite minority culture and mass culture. Intellectuals in general, he believed, should follow the lead of the avant-garde in this respect.

Only recently have repudiations of the Anglo-American conflation of modernism and the avant-garde begun to appear, nearly all sparked by Peter Bürger's *Theory of the Avant-Garde* (1974; trans. 1984). Unlike an earlier book with the same title by Renato Poggioli, Bürger sharply distinguishes modernism from the avant-garde "critique of the aesthetic as an autonomous realm," a subversion typified by Dada and surrealism.[4] Looking back to Benjamin, as well as Bertolt Brecht, Bürger describes the truly avant-garde purpose as the eradication of "art as an institution." The oft-criticized, near-absolute dichotomy he draws on this basis, between hermetic modernism and the avant-garde attack on the institution of art, must be taken as a *polemic,* directed beyond the refutation of their equation in scholarship, to the task of generating a contemporary avant-garde (however pessimistic he may be on that score). If the dichotomy he draws between modernism and the avant-garde works better in theory than in application to actual aesthetic events in the past, in other words, his work might be understood to help sharpen the conceptualization of present-day and future art and their reception.

Williams likewise distinguishes even the more truly radical innovations of modernism—such as the development of independent means of production and distribution (like Leonard and Virginia Woolf's Hogarth Press)—from the avant-garde's fully oppositional initiatives. The avant-garde was determined not simply to promote its own work, but to "attack its enemies in the cultural establishments and, beyond these, the whole social order, in which these enemies had gained and now exercised and reproduced their power" (1989:50–51). One critic summarizes Williams's position thusly: idealist artists and critics have perpetrated a hoax, in disseminating "the prevailing image of modernism as a relatively coherent syndrome" including the avant-garde (Nixon 1989:16). Though Williams's *Politics of Modernism* never mentions Bürger by name, it seems fairly clearly informed by his polemic.

Another recent critic endorsing Bürger, Michael Newman, adds an important further distinction, within the avant-garde itself. Only some avant-gardists espoused and practiced the absorption of cultural forms "extrinsic to the Western high-art tradition," namely mass culture and popular or "subcultural forms" (1989:100), without preserving some privilege for traditional genres,[5] as surrealism did, for example. In the "Manifesto of Surrealism," Breton made explicit his "complete indifference" to mass culture, especially film: "The cinema? Three cheers for darkened rooms." He had no use for new cultural technologies in general, which "properly speaking belong to the realm of the laboratory" (1969:46). In the cityscape *Nadja,* his indifferent filmgoing habits—"never looking to see what's playing, [which] would scarcely do me any good, since I cannot remember the names of more than five or six actors"—lead him to prefer "the most absolutely absurd French films," ones he understands "quite poorly, [that] I follow too vaguely," as opposed to polished commercial cinema. But his real fondness, a nostalgia in fact, is reserved for a disappearing popular theater, and other "old-fashioned, broken, useless, almost incomprehensible" objects. Given the similarities in cultural attitudes, therefore, including an insistence on artistic autonomy as well as active hostility towards mass culture, surrealism and other movements like Dada differ from modernism almost solely in their revolutionary claims. Since some artistic practices are also largely indistinguishable (like simple forms of montage using newspaper cut-ups), the avant-garde and modernism certainly do lend themselves to conflation—unless one recognizes as the genuinely significant break the turn to mass-reproduced culture and popular lived culture.

The portion of the avant-garde interested in mass and popular culture, represented most prominently by Benjamin, Brecht, and later the Situationist International, has expanded the parameters of "art" to include the neglected works championed by Williams. These include 1) mass-reproduced culture and its new technologies; 2) works, though in traditionally esteemed genres, deemed marginal by cultural authority; and 3) the uses audiences make of either or both of these two areas in everyday life—a shift in priority from the individual creator to collective reception—with antiauthoritarian uses the ones that matter most. The avant-garde's dialectic with both mass culture and anarchism represent vital dialectics, Andreas Huyssen argues, that have been lost, methodologically severed by quietist academic interpretation (1986:4–5), as Leighten confirms concerning anarchism. Those conservators include left academics who combine infatuation with detached, dense theory with pessimism about the culture of everyday life.

The first concern here, however, is the origin of the institutional status of art. That institutionalization resulted from specialization, in the actual production and distribution of art (through private galleries and salons, for example), and in the purveyance by artists and critics of ideas about art in the abstract, particularly concerning its autonomy from social life. Bürger dates the first expression of art's autonomy in the eighteenth century, with the rise of urban industrial capitalism; the decline of aristocratic patronage; and the artist's consequent economic free agency in relation to practical life—or the illusion thereof, since any production requires some sort of distribution. With the Enlightenment, according to Max Weber's analysis of specialization (or social rationalization), which informs Bürger's study (and virtually all Frankfurt School work), art and aesthetics first became detached as an institutionalized culture of experts.

In the experience of artists themselves, the decline of patronage opened greater possibilities for original artistic discoveries. Given the uncertainties of value in the marketplace, however, originality itself (a value in the abstract) became "the sole point and foundation of literary creation" (Graña 1964:41). The old relationship between patron and artist, by the modern period, had been "so reversed that the contemporary artist must form the taste and recruit the public (through the intermediary of the art critic, in himself a modern phenomenon) on whose patronage he will then depend. The modern artist is miserably dependent on the media of publicity. That is his deepest humiliation," and thus a significant source of hostility to the bourgeoisie, commerce, and mass culture. The effect of the industrial revolution on art was the artist's sense of exclusion (and alienation, as a result) from the economic processes of production (Read 1953:18, 26).

As a separate dimension from the making of commodities, in fantasy at least, art pits creation against production, culture against mass culture. This "narrowing abstraction" requires neglect of the continual transformation, in actuality, of works of art into commodities. Hence, "Art and thinking about art have to separate themselves, by ever more absolute abstraction, from the social processes within which they are still contained. Aesthetic theory is the main instrument of this evasion." It typically lauds the higher or spiritual nature of art, since the materiality of art has associations with work and production (Williams 1977:153–54, 162).[6]

This notion of art's autonomy from commercialism was and remains disabling, "making a virtue out of grim necessity." If all artifacts necessarily become commodities, with no distinct audience besides those with some taste and money, artists and their work therefore have the compensation, presumably, of "existing entirely and gloriously for themselves." Art at the dawn of modernity in the Enlightenment, just released from its traditional linkage with the church, court, and state into the anonymous freedom of the marketplace, thus perceives itself as altogether autonomous of the political. The aesthetic, posited as a realm in which individuals are free of politics, potentially held radical possibilities, such as fueling anticipation of a liberated social order. But ultimately it left the prevailing order unchallenged, and thus only legitimated existing social relations and their inequity (Eagleton 1990:9, 97, 368, 370).

The Romantic period (dated roughly here from 1790–1848, from Kant to Baudelaire) set the creative imagination against the rise of industrial capitalism and a concomitant rationalism in the eighteenth century. The work of art had become, in both perception and reality, a commodity like all others, and thus the Romantics were "idealist in a more than philosophical sense of the word, [feeling] increasingly driven back into the solitariness of [the] creative mind" (Eagleton 1983:20). Experiencing a "tension between the heroic self-image of the creative person and the impersonal commercialization of the market," Romantic literature "glorified strong passions, unique emotions, and special deeds," despising normalcy and concern with the affairs of everyday life (Graña 1964:57, 68). Subsequent critics of mass culture, ranging from Matthew Arnold to Adorno to Jean Baudrillard, have borne a striking resemblance to the self-exiled Romantic artist "elevated above those below, elevated through the refinement of 'his' sensibilities" and discrimination (Collins 1989:13).

Ever since the eighteenth century, notions of art's autonomy have featured a glaring contradiction resulting from contempt for the market. Aestheticians wished to protest the effects of capitalism, such as vulgar materialism and philistinism, yet their definition of art was quite favorable to the maintenance of capitalism—emphasizing the externality and inconsequence of art in relation to practical affairs, except as harmless consolation for their depradations (Sinfield 1989:109). A more basic contradiction in relation to the marketplace appears in complaints about social negligence and misunderstanding, oddly "decrying the lack of appreciation of the inherent value of literary creation because of the absence of material remuneration for it." Commerce is bad because one is not profiting from it as much as one would like. This conflicted connection with commercialism bred "arrogance and almost utopian self confidence on the one hand; fear, impotence, and martyrdom on the other" (Graña 1964:55–56). The same angry, contemptuous ambivalence has been characteristic of subsequent academic epigones, as well, who disdain utility in their work and then complain that they aren't paid enough.

As the circulation of capital became more complex and rapid, particularly around the pivotal year of 1848, there arose a still stronger alienation, the modernist sense of "the fleeting, the ephemeral, the fragmentary" condition of life, and the lack of any historical continuity. Grappling with that experience is undeniably important, but the ambivalence lies in the question of whether the modernist response was in the final analysis "a pure bowing down to the force of spatial and temporal restructuring of the period" (Harvey 1989:11, 262–64, 271). In the essay "Crisis in Poetry," for example, Stéphane Mallarmé advocated withdrawal into the mysterious musicality of poetry, condemning ordinary speech as a "commercial approach to reality.... Language, in the hands of the mob, leads to the same facility and directness as money."

Bourdieu traces the origin of claims for aesthetic autonomy from commerce and ordinary people, specifically the conception of a "pure gaze" in the contemplation of art, to Kant's *Critique of Judgment* (1790). Kant's definition of art as a purposive activity *without* a purpose—with beauty resulting from disdain of utility—directly reflects the German "reading debate" in the eighteenth century, a controversy over the increase in literacy with the rise of the bourgeoisie. The original definition of aesthetics as a discipline contained "an alarm at the way readers were turning from works that demanded a modicum of mental exertion—a modicum of reflection and meditation—to ever lighter forms of entertainment" (Woodmansee 1988/ 89:207). In England as well, in the eighteenth century, "classical bourgeois" authors like Alexander Pope and Jonathan Swift condemned the vulgar popular appeal of Grub Street hacks, in essence elevating reason over bodily response (see Stallybrass and White 1986).

Kant accordingly formulated an opposition "between the 'taste of sense' and the 'taste of reflection,' and between *facile* pleasure, pleasure reduced to a pleasure of the senses, and *pure* pleasure, pleasure purified of pleasure. [His] principle of pure taste is nothing other than a refusal, a disgust—a disgust for objects which impose enjoyment [and for] the crude, vulgar taste which revels in [it]." Having defined pleasure and enjoyment as responses of the cultured elite and barbarous masses, respectively, he proceeds to distinguish "free" (or autonomous) art from "mercenary" (or commercial and popular) art. The former is "agreeable on its own account," in no way compelling action on the beholder's part, while the latter, servile to the market, "forces itself on the beholder with the enslaving violence of its sensible charms" (Bourdieu 1984:3, 6, 488, 492).[7] Kant's dichotomy was imported into English letters by Samuel Taylor Coleridge, who disdainfully contrasted (in "On Poesy or Art") the "so called music of savage tribes"—the mere expression of passion—with poetry, which takes "all its materials...from the mind [and] for the mind." The body, he held, "is but a striving to become mind." An immediate successor to Kant in Germany, Johann Adam Bergk, likewise condemning the excitement of passion by commercial art, further specified that political subjects were inappropriate to fine art (Woodmansee 1988/89:213).

By the modern period Kant's original dichotomy had become a proposition about language itself, pitting banality against authenticity. "Ordinary" language, presumably, is clichéd and one-dimensional, while poetic language is experimental and difficult, the only qualities capable of revitalizing perception (Pinkney 1989:5). Mallarmé's pupil Paul Valéry set the music of the "poetic universe" against the "practical order" of speech (in "Poetry and Abstract Thought"). The difficulty in creating the former, he lamented, was that one had to "borrow language [from] the voice of the public," to draw "a pure, Ideal Voice [out of] everyday language" by swinging pendulum-like between pure sound and banal meaning. Like Mallarmé, Valéry described that ideal in terms of music—as if everyday expression bears no significant tonalities (a notion destroyed by Mikhail Bakhtin's dialogical linguistics, discussed in chap. 3).

Terry Eagleton's *The Ideology of the Aesthetic,* prompted to some extent by the work of Bourdieu and Bürger, amplifies their description of the eighteenth century, before working out at great length its legacy to the present. The contemporary notion of the aesthetic artifact, says Eagleton, is "inseparable from the construction of the dominant ideological forms of modern class-society, and indeed from a whole new form of human subjectivity appropriate to that social order." The construction of this aesthetic realm, however, was and is contradictory, for it does contain a potential challenge to those dominant ideologies. The contradiction revolves specifically around body and mind, or affect and ideology, in other words. The aesthetic has always represented a contest between "on the one hand a liberatory concern with concrete particularity, and on the other hand a specious form of universalism," in which the sensuous is subjugated to the intellect and reason (1990:3, 9). As a result of this contradiction between liberation and pacification, the aesthetic has been a significant site of struggle between authority and contumacy.

When definitions of the aesthetic first arose to account for both intellectual and physical aspects of human experience, they did so under considerable influence by the necessities of political authority in a unique situation in Germany, at the historical intersection between feudal absolutism and the rise of the bourgeoisie. The old ruling class in that country continued to take a leading social role, particularly in industrialization, with the bourgeoisie necessarily finding a secondary power in cultural leadership, as a professional intellectual caste made up of bureaucratic functionaries, scholars, and so on. The development of the aesthetic, in a period and place hardly free of absolutism, thus bore symptoms of an ideological dilemma inherent in absolutist power. Such power needs for its own purposes to take account of 'sensible' life, for without an understanding of this no dominion can be secure. The world of feelings and sensations can surely not just be surrendered to the 'subjective' [and potentially unruly], to what Kant scornfully termed the 'egoism of taste'; instead, it must be brought within the majestic scope of reason itself.... Aesthetics is born of the recognition that the world of [sensory] perception and experience ... demands its own appropriate discourse [in order to regulate it].

Enlightenment aestheticians, and most of those subsequent to them, extended "rationality into vital regions which are otherwise beyond its reach," exercising with relish their intellectual power (or their cultural capital, what was left to them by real social power). Aesthetics, dating from Alexander Baumgarten's effort in 1750 to reconcile the senses and reason, fairly quickly fell under the sway of an antisensuous idealism. Kant expelled all sensuousness from the aesthetic experience, by privileging pure form and a disembodied appreciation of beauty. A true aesthetic practice, a relation to society "*at once sensuous and rational*," was bifurcated in aesthetic theory into either an idealism repudiating the body or an opposed extreme, a libidinal orgy of anarchic desire (Eagleton 1990:4, 15–16, 196, 207).[8]

The underlying main current of aesthetics subsequent to Kant, in the nineteenth century, extended in particular the original formulation of the individual artist's genius and uniqueness. This view was submerged somewhat after Romanticism, by realism and Naturalism, but reemerged in Symbolism, says Edmund Wilson. A "second swing of the pendulum away ... from a social conception of man" in art, Symbolism made "poetry even more a matter of the sensations and emotions of the individual" (1984:2, 19–20, 25).[9] Realism could not satisfactorily address, in particular, the sense of temporal and spatial displacement caused by the acceleration of the circulation of capital.[10]

However one reads the course of the nineteenth century, by its end Symbolism had indisputably mounted the ultimate, most intense effort to prove the autonomy of art, in the aspiration to achieve a "silent," more accurately *asocial* music, a notion of formal indefiniteness Baudelaire had borrowed from Poe (Wilson 1984:13).[11] The world transmitted by the senses, as represented in the material word, might thereby reveal a spiritual (actually only an intellectual) universe. "Spirit," Mallarmé claimed, "cares for nothing save universal musicality [in] the intellectual and written word in all its glory" (as opposed to speech, the medium of commerce and the mob). The Symbolist poem would provide a revelation through something like Baudelaire's *correspondance,* or synesthesia, in which the poetic word is simultaneously transient and eternal, both "material in its embodiment and metaphysical in its revelation of a spiritual but still sensual reality." Modernism's preoccupation with the creation of new languages results from this sense of the poetic word's ephemeral significance, of the necessarily transitory representation of the eternal. The ostensibly spiritual "inner forms" of languages would presumably enable at least brief expression of the inner lives of their authors (Williams 1989:71). "But the words of our speech are not musical notation," Wilson points out, "and what the symbols of Symbolism really were, were metaphors detached from their subjects," fleeting and vague (1984:21). In construing obscurity of meaning as a condition of poetic music, Symbolist theory disdained content in favor of formal innovation, "entirely separate from what Mallarmé described as the 'journalistic'" or everyday (Newman 1989:98–99).

In English letters, Walter Pater would declare in 1888 that "all art constantly aspires to the condition of music," or pure form, and his aestheticism exercised a considerable influence on Joyce (as well as Virginia Woolf).[12] Joyce also relies on German idealism (inflected with his scholastic background), especially Kant, for the description of aesthetic stasis and kinesis in *A Portrait of the Artist as a Young Man* (McGrath 1986:237, 250–51; Buttigieg 1987:141–42). Stephen Dedalus associates the static with formal beauty, the kinetic not just with pornography, but even with any didactic, instructional function, because it moves one to action of some sort. The artist, not surprisingly, is in Dedalus's view uniquely able to apprehend and represent the "luminous silent stasis" of the epiphany, a theological phenomenon imported into the new secular religion of art. The physical manifestation of "spiritual" meaning, in the epiphany, resembles the aesthetic goal sought by Symbolism. But Joyce's novel is hardly static, moving from infant stream-of-consciousness to Symbolist prose-poetry; the discussion of aesthetic stasis and kinesis must thus be understood to concern the appropriate *outcome* of art, rather than the work itself. The disdain for "didacticism," simply for moving someone to *do* something, eschews a social role for art.[13]

The opposition of stasis and kinesis is very much like aesthetic distinctions ranging from Kant's, between free and mercenary art, to Valéry's, between poetry and prose. Kant's follower Coleridge held that beauty is aloof from any interest; Baudelaire, disdaining the heresy of any didactic function in art—appeals to conscience, concern for truth, the demonstration of something useful—declared poetry to have "no object but itself" (in "Theophile Gautier"). Like walking, in Valéry's formulation, ordinary language involves practical activity aimed at attaining some goal, while poetry is like dance, with no end outside itself: "It goes nowhere" and "answers no need." In "Mr. Bennett and Mrs. Brown," Woolf maintains that the best literature is "self-contained," leaving one, as Joyce would have it, "with no desire to do anything."[14] Eliot similarly held, in "The Function of Criticism," that the perfect literary work does not "serve ends beyond itself."

The Symbolist "revolution" reconstructed by Julia Kristeva (in *Revolution in Poetic Language*), a subversion of ossified meaning and ideology (or "symbolic" content) by the fluidity of poetic language (or "semiotic" form), might thus be construed as just the opposite of revolution. It amounts only to construction of a purely negative space beyond everyday processes of communication.[15] From Kristeva's restricted position, confined to Symbolist poetry, "the infraction of *formal* literary codes of language is identical to challenging official law, [which is] very rarely the case." It would be wrong to associate the freedom such transgression affords, however exhilirating, with any automatic political progressiveness. Only a challenge to institutional hierarchies (like "high" and "low" culture), one which emerges from areas of the culture " 'situated' by the dominant in *low* or *marginal* positions, carries the promise of politically transformative power" (Stallybrass and White 1986:18–21). By "investing the alleged modern condition with a romanticism of extremity," Kristeva's and other such theories actually discourage political analysis (Sinfield 1989: 201).

Modernist aesthetics deriving from Symbolism, Bürger believes, represent a reaction specifically against the means-end rationality of capitalist production (or its effect on culture, at least). But if the instrumental rationality of means (labor) and ends (commodities) entails the alienation of men and women from the products of their labor (and hence from the labor itself and from others involved in it), modernism characteristically excoriates capitalism's victims, the "masses"[16]—somehow responsible for their own subjection—not its institutions. Well before the advent of scientific management and its assembly lines, Gustave Flaubert, for example, saw the way "stupid professions" like that of Manchester pin makers turned workers into "a quantity of human machines," language not unlike that of Marxism. But such revolutionary perceptions are typically accompanied by reactionary sentiments (a phenomenon dating to the Romantics). Immediately after his observation on factories (in a letter to Louise Colet), Flaubert concludes that "humanity hates us [artists]; we do not minister to it and we hate it because it wounds us. . . . The distance between myself and my fellow men widens every day" because of their participation in the debased culture of bourgeois society, as if bourgeoisie and proletariat were identical.

Accounts of modernism as a counterpart to Marxism, a "displaced" anticapitalist politics (see N. Larsen 1990), commonly begin with the aftermath of the revolutions of 1848, when the bourgeoisie consolidated its power. Some artists, such as Baudelaire, did find in the effects of the marketplace on art "at least a negative identification between the exploited worker and the exploited artist" (Williams 1989:54). Pragmatic events like revolutions, however, were always perceived as merely utilitarian—extraordinary objects of amusement at best. Baudelaire appears to have seized the moment in part for personal reasons, to call for the shooting of his stepfather, and his interest in the working class seems "at times more taken with the aesthetic consequences of revolution than with its political benefits. . . . Eventually he dismissed 1848 in the Flaubert style as 'amusing' and 'charming by reason of the very excesses of its absurdity.'" Expressing the belief that the political revolutionary was "nothing more than another mass man, another cultural equalitarian, 'an enemy of art, of perfume, a fanatic of utensils,'" or utility, Baudelaire admonished the police to attack anarchists (Graña 1964:113, 119–21).[17]

Complaints about the bourgeois treatment of art as a commodity, moreover, clearly took on the "moralistic and spiritually narrow figure of the *aristocratic* complaint." The idealistic artist, berating commerce and philistinism, at first registered dissent and division in the middle class. The strongest element in Romanticism and early modernism derived from the notion of the artist as the authentic aristocrat in a debased civilization. That assertion of superiority did not have to be made very often, though, before it was extended "to a wholesale condemnation of the 'mass' that was beyond all authentic artists: now not only the bourgeoisie but [the] ignorant populace" (Williams 1989:55). Baudelaire and Flaubert associated democracy itself with the hated bourgeoisie, and because "bourgeois ambitions had now [supposedly] penetrated to every class, this hatred must be extended to 'all humanity, including the people,'" who were complicit in their own alienation. The "new aristocracy" of artists, then, was "individualistic without being democratic" (Graña 1964:69, 113).

The modernist abhorrence of the crowd, the common thread linking Baudelaire and *The Waste Land,* reflected metropolitan experience in particular, the prospect of teeming masses and their amusements. The preference for intellectually demanding art has a close relation to fear of the crowd, to perception of its political impulses arising from the body more than the mind (P. Middleton 1990:138). Due to their pessimism about the masses and "further social and political change," in fact, modernists ultimately "prefer *order*—both aesthetic and political." Thus the formal fluidity achieved by modernism frequently washes away into right-wing irrationalism, as is the case in English literature with Eliot, D. H. Lawrence, Wyndham Lewis, Ezra Pound, W. B. Yeats, and so on, or simply "nothing much at all" (Eagleton 1983:190).[18] Alienation, as a result, is typically construed as a miasma in modern life, rather than a concrete function of capitalist social and economic organization; aesthetic hermeticism reflects a misanthropic revulsion against everyday life. Georg Lukács appropriately defines the "ideology" of modernism as an ontology of solitariness, growing out of Romanticism but advanced well beyond it, in modernism's ahistorical sense of solitude as a universal human condition.

Thus in its preoccupation with form (or artistic "means" alone), set against social utility (or any "end"), modernism not only fails to overcome alienation (the split between means and ends), but actually reinforces it, often deliberately. Modernism, in this respect, marks an extreme form of Kant's dictum on purposelessness; to avoid social engagement, modernist social criticism is confined to the weapons of style. Flaubert, to whom the phrase "taking up a position" was "meaningless language," aspired to write "a book about nothing" (he wrote Louise Colet), "held together by the strength of its style,... which would have almost no subject, or in which the subject would be almost invisible." In the formal impenetrability and inwardness of modernist texts, the "apartness" from social life "that always constituted the institutional status of art in bourgeois society now becomes the content of the works," says Bürger (1984:27)—the technique itself a statement of alienation, that is.[19]

One of the persisting, crippling legacies of modernism, in this regard, is that of the Frankfurt School. Adorno, Marcuse, and Max Horkheimer did believe that Kant's notion of ascetic disinterestedness was wrong, leading only to an "affirmative culture," or an ideal realm requiring no transformation of actual existence (hence affirming it). But they nonetheless considered autonomous art the only way to critique capitalism, provided that a work's effort to harmonize its form and content retains contradictions (like the modernist priority on formal abstraction) that reflect an alienated reality. The autonomous work, presumably, thereby embodies a desire for a different society (Jay 1973:179–80; cf. Eysteinsson 1990; Hunter 1992[20])—a notion as abstracted and mystified as any other modernist aesthetic. In light of the ease with which Greenberg and others used autonomous art to legitimate the free market, instead, during the cold war, the Frankfurt School's linkage of Marxism and modernism seems utterly specious. In the hands of intellectuals on the left like Dwight Macdonald, furthermore, who condemned mass culture's violations of high art's autonomy, the Frankfurt line appears downright culpable in the McCarthy era's assault on excess democracy (see A. Ross 1989a:42–64).

Only in the loathing of mass–reproduced culture, finally, did modernism oppose in any way the effects of capitalism. The modernist attempt to render art impossible to appropriate sought specifically to trump the perceived reduction of every creative form to the end of commodity exchange. Since commercial or mass culture is characterized by the ready accessibility of its forms, modernism meant to be relatively inaccessible. Its difficulty and esoterica offered a "passive resistance to the all-pervasive commodification of experience" (Felski 1989:163). Mallarmé is the most brazen critic, in this regard, explicitly extolling a difficulty and mystery only the aristocrat of taste can master (in "Art for All"). A poet keeps away the stupid mob "by inventing an immaculate language, a series of sacred formulae which would blind the common eye with dull study," but reward those with sufficient erudition and patience; such a poetry would thereby resist commerciality, in particular, or being "bought cheap." In light of such views, mass culture and modernism can thus be said to represent "dialectically interdependent phenomena," though antithetical in their forms (Jameson 1979:133, 135; see also Huyssen 1986). In "The Salon of 1859," Baudelaire describes painting and photography, fine art and mechanized culture, as "two ambitious men who hate one another with an instinctive hatred." When the two "meet upon the same road, one of them has to give place."

The premium placed on difficulty marked a reaction specifically against new technologies in mass communications, which allowed a more rapid, hence (presumably) more facile circulation of ideas and images. Echoing Benjamin's account in "The Work of Art in the Age of Mechanical Reproduction" and his work on Baudelaire, Williams insists that any explanation of modernism must start with the the mid- to late nineteenth century, when "the greatest changes ever seen in the media of cultural reproduction" occurred. "Photography, cinema, radio, television, . . . and recording all make their decisive advances during the period identified as Modernist, and it is in response to these that there arise . . . defensive cultural groupings" (1989:33). Cesar Graña connects the mid–nineteenth-century belief in a "new intellectual aristocracy," doctrines of "pure intellectual symbolism," loathing of mass culture, and the formation of cultural capital:

> the intellectual must retain his identity and his position by making ideas inaccessible to the masses. Since goods and even luxuries are now available to them, thought and art should be made rare, precious and, in their own way, expensive. . . . Anything which is public, available to numbers, must be readily used by them. . . . *Useful*, therefore, emerges out of this reasoning as the antithesis of the personal. . . . Artistic creation became something formidable, awesome. (1964:52, 109–10)

In "The Symbolism of Poetry," for example, Yeats declares that "only those things which seem useless . . . have any power."

The problem here is modernism's indiscriminate rejection of both exchange value (market salability) *and* use value (actual utilization).[21] Adorno and Horkheimer found a double sin in commercial art: after use value malignantly destroyed the "liberation from the priniciple of utility" that a properly "useless" art provided, use value itself had been eradicated by exchange value and thus held no interest (1987:158). Put another way, the general conflation of bourgeoisie and proletariat by modernists led to a failure to distinguish the activities of cultural producers and consumers; the latter's responses could thus be treated as a given in commodities and entertainments. The modernists continually fail to distinguish people's leisure pastimes from the commercial transactions involved, a tendency persistent in epigones like the Frankfurt School. Modernist art deliberately and perversely cripples itself, as a result, its inaccessibility giving body to that misanthropy. This loathing of utility, as the last part of this chapter indicates, has been perhaps the most persistent legacy of modern aesthetics.

Outside of high culture, however, that legacy has been highly ironic: commercial culture easily appropriated art forms that were only formally subversive, assigning them precisely the utility in the marketplace that the modernists sought to resist. The purely formal revolution of alienated visionaries not only reinforced the bourgeois ideology of the sovereign individual (including the consumer), but actually served to nourish the culture of advertising, given the "lack of social direction in such self-absorbed inventiveness" (Nixon 1989:16). Williams finds that modernist forms eventually "lent themselves to . . . the commercial interplay of obsolescence, with its shifts of schools, styles, and fashion so essential to the market. . . . The isolated, estranged images of alienation and loss, the narrative discontinuities, have become the easy iconography of the commercials" (Williams 1989:35). This incorporation includes movements identified with the avant-garde, as well, such as surrealism, that failed to establish a connection between the formal disturbances they created and the political ends to which they pretended. Montage, in the simple sense of juxtaposition or pastiche, has often been cited as a staple of MTV and so forth. Despite its often adversarial relationship to capitalist ideologies of modernization and progress, modernism is thus "deeply implicated in the processes and pressures of the same mundane modernization it so ostensibly repudiates" (Huyssen 1986: 56). Pound's formalist dictum "make it new" could just as easily be a pitch for the purchase of modern commodities, with their built-in obsolescence, as a program for poetic language. As long as art "does not connect its formal subversion to an analysis of social situations, it becomes little more than a further example of the disturbances that go on as we live through a day" (Polan 1987:351).

At present, however, in reading modernist and many other texts, cultivated pleasure continues to feed on complex, "intertwined references, which reinforce and legitimate each other, producing, inseparably, belief in the value of works of art, the 'idolatry' which is the very basis of cultivated pleasure, and the inimitable charm they [supposedly] objectively exert on all who are qualified to enter the game" (Bourdieu 1984:499). Standards of allusiveness, erudition, and "difficulty" (venerated by Steiner in a well-known essay) are scholarly, not at all universal aesthetic standards, elevating intellectual power over material affective power (which the modernists certainly possess), complexity over simplicity, the unique over the common, and so on. To argue from this basis "that only certain stylistic features constitute real difference (thereby rendering all else identical) reveals a profound elitism" (Collins 1989:12). The result is the disdain for "ordinariness" attacked by Williams throughout his career, and the preference for abstraction and obliquity in aesthetic form and academic discourse alike.

Many academic accounts of postmodernism, operating from similar biases, have only represented an attenuation of modernist alienation from the culture of everyday life, scarcely a movement beyond modernism. The postmodernists, including practitioners in the arts as well, take from the avant-garde "the dissolution of art into social life, the rejection of tradition, an opposition to 'high' culture as such, but [cross them] with the unpolitical impulses of modernism" (Eagleton 1986:146–47). Thus even in "the very act of turning away from high culture and spurning the pieties lavished on the canon, academics demonstrate how incomplete the postmodernist break with traditional forms of artistic analysis has been," in remaking figures like Madonna "into Theory incarnate." In wild overanalysis and excessive theoretical claims, even popular culture, like literature before it, is valued for its (supposed) complexity, as proof "that there is no stable and empirically verifiable 'reality' [beyond] the vagaries and impermanences of language" (Harris 1992:792–93). "It is as if the creative powers of modernism had migrated into theory," Huyssen says quite bluntly (1986:209).

The actual postmodern break lies in an increasing pessimism over that presumed impermanence or evanescence of language. If modernism detaches itself from reality by treating language as a personal refuge, retreating from the nightmare of history into highly subjective forms of consciousness, postmodernism simply goes its predecessor one better by disavowing the individual as well, or the efficacy of language at any level, perceiving absolute fragmentation where the moderns did alienation. The common thread running through every field identified with postmodernism, whether in the arts or academia, is a perceived crisis of individual identity. In repudiating the basis of modernism's already troubled claims to truth, the internal processes of the individual, postmodernity has thus been "modernity without the hopes and dreams which made modernity bearable" (Hebdige 1988:195). But if postmodern art and criticism push modernism's inward turn to the breaking point, they also rely considerably on appropriations of modernist motifs such as self-reflexiveness, montage, and uncertainty, in the very attempt "to create the impression of some recent and radical break in cultural experience" (Callinicos 1989:6, 12). This persisting reliance on techniques already established by modernism does not necessarily stop history dead, though, leaving it stuck in the "post"; the issue, it will be seen, is what forces from the modern period—the apolitical sensibility of modernism, or the radical engagement of the avant-garde—influence the way practices like montage are construed.

Most of the various postmodernisms (whether accounts of mass culture or theories of subjectivity) suggest a morbid academic fascination with the approaching millenium, little different from the millenarianism intellectuals deride when expressed by televangelists and their ilk. The roots of postmodernist analyses, Alex Callinicos argues (like many others), can be found in a "combination of the disillusioned aftermath of 1968 throughout the Western world," and intellectual dismay at the subsequent success of the hyperconsumer life-style "offered upper white-collar strata by capitalism in the Reagan-Thatcher era" (1989:7; see 164–71; Plant 1992:111–12). Whatever its basis, the discovery of postmodernism, in Graeme Turner's view, has yet to justify the explosion of academic work on the subject, or, more specifically, "the considerable support it has lent to an evacuation of politics from cultural studies analysis" (1990:228). While he has in mind celebrations of postmodern consumerism and pleasure such as those offered by the "New Times" group in England (see McRobbie 1991b)—more like a surrender based in the same dismay identified by Callinicos—the same abandonment of politics occurs at the opposite pole of disillusioned bleakness. The postmodernist academic establishment typically takes modernism's "originally precarious and often desperate images...of fragmentation, loss of identity, loss of the very grounds of human communication," and converts them from dynamic compositions into static truisms. That establishment, as a result, whatever its express politics, buttresses capitalist culture's "versions of cognate theories—psychological alienation;...natural competitive violence; the insignificance of history; the fictionality of all actions; the arbitrariness of language"—thereby confirming the inevitability of the multinationals' operations and effects (Williams 1989:130).

If postmodernist art is generally rooted in daily life and popular culture—or "roots" in them, at any rate—it makes sense that the will to autonomy would gravitate into the cloistered world of academe. The invocation of postmodernism easily becomes "a kind of lament for one's own departure from the center of the world" (Hall 1990:23), for the ineffectuality and irrelevance (largely self-elected) of academic work. In general, at present, postmodernism marks a total acceptance of ephemerality, wallowing "in the fragmentary and the chaotic currents of change as if that is all there is," reinforcing those conditions to the extent they do exist (Harvey 1989:44). Much of poststructuralism, for example, steps outside the world, removing into "the sphere of the far-away and the archaic the spontaneous powers of imagination, self-experience and emotion"—the same abstraction and mystification of the nature of art found in modernism. Thus, just like the modernists, "to instrumental reason they juxtapose in Manichean fashion a principle only accessible through evocation, be it will to power or sovereignty, Being or the Dionysiac force of the poetical" (Habermas 1983:14). Literary and cultural studies must choose, therefore, between two contradictory attitudes toward language, in particular: one which treats language as part of material social processes, and the assertion of much poststructuralism that language inhibits authentic consciousness. This last orientation reaches its antimaterial apogee in characterizations of the sublime (or unrepresentable), of the impossible totality of the universal systems or structures that presumably rule human experience by virtually ineffable means, whether discursive practices, ideologies, or language itself (Williams 1989:77–78).

If the categories of modern and postmodern seem less than distinct in aesthetics, they might better be dissolved into a continuous complex tracing the cultural contradictions of capitalism as they have evolved through the century. Such a continuity would be a far more sensible way to deal with problems like the fragmentation of experience—hardly unique to the postmodern period—rather than making eschatological announcements of a new historical epoch, an apocalyptic rupture in human experience. In *The Condition of Postmodernity,* David Harvey argues that recent cultural changes constitute more a shift "in surface appearance rather than [a sign] of the emergence of some entirely new postcapitalist or even postindustrial society." Much postmodernist art and criticism, in their emphasis on ephemerality, mimic the "emergence of more flexible [and rapid] modes of capital accumulation" that have evolved since the economic crisis of the early 1970s. Such shifts in perception, identifiable in 1848 and the period just before World War I, "are by no means new," and are "certainly within the grasp" of historical, material interpretation (1989:vii, 54, 59, 302, 306–7, 328, 339; see also Callinicos 1989).[22]

In many accounts of postmodernism, for instance, the sublime consists to a considerable extent of man-made cultural and scientific technologies, which required human representation and understanding to be produced in the first place. Thus when the postmodern sublime is assigned a downright eschatological character, it paradoxically includes perfectly secular components like the workings of the computer, controlled by human beings. Fascination with the outer limits on expression and activity persists nonetheless, leaving the implication "that we are left stranded in a world of meaningless surfaces: 'lured' this way and that by the 'fatal' fascination exercised upon us by mirrors, icons, images." It is impossible, in such theory, "to countenance the prospect of any historically constituted collective changing anything for the better" (Hebdige 1987:64, 66, 69).

In the postmodern academy, this insistence on the difficulty of effective expression is clearly the legacy of modernism. Like the modernists, the postmodernists extol "the extraordinary, the eccentric, and the estranged," ignoring or suppressing, with politically crippling consequences, voices more representative of everyday life. The effect in academia, in particular, is to discourage regard for the radical possibilities of ordinary culture (Nixon 1989:16). To the poststructuralist Jacques Derrida, for example, the value of a text lies in its neutralization or denial of the social, a value "proportionate to its unreality, its gratuitousness, its sovereign indifference" (Bourdieu 1984:495). Thus he privileges an innocuous avant-garde for its refusal to transmit any content, in such forms as Artaud's theater of cruelty.

In perpetuating modernist alienation from everyday life, poststructuralist theory has been especially egregious in misrepresenting the avant-garde practice of montage, speciously amalgamating Benjamin's description of montage with Derrida. Derrida's theory of montage, or collage, assumes that his linkage of different literary fragments "alludes to *nothing*, ... can *do nothing* more than cite"—the height of abstracted, antimaterial quietism, if not nihilism. The "castration" of texts presumably befits a culture of mechanically reproduced simulacra and its fragmented incoherence, its "loss of reference, the undecidability of allusion." Fittingly enough, the deconstructionist's literary model is the aimless esoterica of John Cage, quotations of literary texts that render them "*empty* words" (Ulmer 1983:86, 89, 92, 96–97, 102–3; see Harvey 1989:51). Newman sharply criticizes such readings of Benjamin through poststructuralist theory, for reversing "the trajectory towards Marxism" in his conception of the allegorical capacity of montage (1989:128), which held that the reassembly of cultural fragments could invoke "the real," or social life (see chap. 6). The Situationist practice of detournement (montage-as-highjacking), moreover, to which postmodernist practices are considerably indebted, actually affirms like Benjamin "the possibility of some strategic sense of purpose and analysis of the social relations it contests," contrary to the postmodern use of montage to mirror the fragmentation of life "in isolation from some wider purpose." Postmodernists like Baudrillard, Gilles Deleuze, Felix Guattari, and Jean-François Lyotard mine the entire avant-garde tradition like a "Dada without the war or surrealism without the revolution; postmodern philosophers are sold-out situationists who wander without purpose" (Plant 1992:112, 131, 148, 150).

This postmodern pessimism concerning the absorptive power of mass culture has led to a theory of contemporary culture as *pastiche,* in essence the bankrupted practice of montage discerned by Derrida. Because every aesthetic form is susceptible to appropriation by the mass media, presumably "the intermingling and confusion of forms means the final collapse of traditional (or, rather, in this context, *modernist*) cultural values, the reduction of art to the vacuous routines of mechanical reproduction" (Frith and Horne 1987:4). And even if judgments on such heterogeneity are not cast in explicitly negative terms, much postmodernist theory nonetheless serves to maintain academic insistence on complexity and difficulty, the standard of taste descended from modernism. "By recognizing the intrusion of popular culture into the ostensible spirituality of high culture, heterogeneity allows the writer to claim an everyday relevance for critical work, while the very fact of heterogeneity as a complexity . . . reserves a privilege for the critic as someone who has superiority over mass taste," in being able to grasp that complexity (Polan 1988:50–51).

Work on postmodern heterogeneity is typically based in a belief that the needs of multinational corporations predominate absolutely, particularly the need to produce ever more novel commodities. Given this frantic emphasis on novelty, says Fredric Jameson, "Overt expressions of social and political defiance no longer scandalize anyone, and are not only received with the greatest complacency but have themselves become institutionalized." He offers confident assurance, citing the Clash (a rock group that helped shake many people, as a number of accounts attest), that no form of oppositional expression is now possible in popular forms. Jameson has continually derided any expression of negation in contemporary culture as inevitably inauthentic and trivial, "secretly disarmed and reabsorbed." All cultural dissidence lacks "a certain minimal aesthetic distance" (1984:56, 87)—an assertion that smacks of nostalgia for theories of art as an autonomous institution.

Jameson's antipathy to mass culture is little more than a rehash of the antitechnologist elitism of the Frankfurt School, especially Marcuse, and the academic currency of Jameson's work on postmodernism thus seems rather suspect.[23] The notion that a cataclysmic break in history has become discernible in the last decade is highly disputable, when the same observations have been around far longer. Sadie Plant even argues that "all theorisations of postmodernity are underwritten by situationist theory," with the postmodernists turning that theory against itself by discarding the Situationists' passionate criticism and belief in the possibility of change. Jameson does indeed cite Guy Debord's work on the spectacle (or mass culture), which, Plant finds, prefigures "the world of uncertainty and superficiality described and [sometimes] celebrated by the postmodernists" (1992:5–7; see Jameson 1979:132; 1984:66). Marcuse's *One-Dimensional Man,* however, published in 1964, seems the more heavily utilized source in Jameson's case, particularly in his description of the postmodern waning of affect. This loss of affective capacity in art and its audience presumably results from a culture of pastiche, wreaking havoc on aesthetic hierarchies and history through a blank mimicry of past styles, especially the modernist styles both critics eulogize. "The absorbent power of society depletes the artistic dimension," says Marcuse, "by assimilating its antagonistic contents. In the realm of culture, the new totalitarianism manifests itself precisely in a harmonizing pluralism, where the most contradictory works and truths peacefully coexist in *indifference*" (1964:61). He concludes, as Jameson would under the new rubric of postmodernism, that even the negation and rebellion of "anti-art"[24] are drawn into the complacent "daily universe, as an enjoyable and understandable element of this universe." Any effort to represent the world as a whole is inevitably the work of a "pseudo- and crackpot opposition," since all speech is false, part of a mutilated whole—something like the linguistic fragmentation of social life into specialized discourses, described by Jameson. Marcuse bases his pessimism in the presumed omnipotence of technology over the subject, now that "reality has become technological reality" (qtd. in Solomon 1979:522–23, 536–37, 539). Jameson merely updates this perspective by invoking Ernest Mandel's *Late Capitalism*—somewhat erroneously (see Callinicos 1989:133)— to describe the sublime evolutionary stage of the machine in the computer era.

His conclusions on cultural levels, accordingly, have been persistently nihilistic: modernist literature and a manipulative mass culture were the *only* possibilities for art under capitalism. The dialectic between modernism and mass culture is presented as acknowledgment of a legitimate need for mass-culture studies, but what he gives with one hand, he clearly takes away with the other. He dismisses a number of subcultural forms—"black literature and blues, British working-class rock, women's literature" and so on—by consigning them to "marginal pockets" of social life, not yet "fully penetrated by the market and by the commodity system" (1979:140). This is a patent absurdity; these forms have long been distributed via the same commercial processes as any other musical and literary forms. The Sex Pistols have in fact been prized as *rebellious commodities,* as "the first rock act to turn their aggression against the industry itself" (Carr 1988:40; Harron 1988:195). Ultimately Jameson rules out any possibility of a political art: "No useful purpose is served by speculation on the forms such a third and authentic type of cultural language might take" (1979:140). Summarily dismissing any activity remotely resembling that of the original avant-garde, he severs the dialectic between the avant-garde and mass culture.

Severance of the avant-garde from mass culture (and anarchism), along with the frequent conflation of the avant-garde with modernism, has the effect of diverting what "taste for innovation [exists] toward certain degraded, innocuous, and confused forms of novelty." When avant-garde artists do become well known, argued the Situationist International, critics generally suppress radical elements with a society-wide focus, treating avant-garde works in isolation, as the stuff merely of diverse aesthetic interpretations. The closely controlled and manipulated term *avant-garde* has thus acquired "a ridiculous and dubious aspect" (Debord 1981d:18). This reductive, conformist process depoliticizes the avant-garde as "an elite enterprise beyond politics and beyond everyday life, though their transformation was [its] central project" (Huyssen 1986:4).

An attack on the institution of art that instead actively sought a social function, the original avant-garde was a self-criticism possible only when art had arrived at the limit of specialization—in essence forcing a confrontation with long-standing presumptions about the separateness of art. Debord, the leader of the Situationists, recognized well before Bürger the source of avant-gardism: because art had "a perpetual privileged concession" under capitalism for "pure creative activity, an alibi for the alienation of all other activities," inevitably

this sphere reserved for 'free creative activity' [turned into] the only one in which the questions of what we do with life and of communication are posed practically and completely. Here, in art, lies the first locus point of the antagonism between partisans and adversaries of the officially dictated reasons for living. The *established* meaninglessness and separation [of art] give rise to the general crisis of artistic means, a crisis linked to alternative ways of living, to the demand for a new way of life. (Qtd. in Marcus 1989:211)

The avant-garde thus *succeeded* aestheticism historically, and is scarcely identical with modernism; if there is a truly *post*-modernism, it lies in the original avant-garde and its successors. Modernism was a necessary precondition for the avant-garde, as Bürger puts it.

The avant-garde would overcome means-end rationalization not through sheer formalism, but through a dialectic of formal innovation and some social content. ("Social content" does *not* imply propaganda, socialist realism, and so forth, it should be stated at the outset.) To break down, in this way, distinction between art and everyday life would resonate through a "liberating life praxis," in Bürger's terms; the roles of artistic producers and recipients, ultimately, should be rendered less distinct. The avant-garde sought, by reintegrating art and social experience, to overthrow aesthetic specialization generally, whether in art or criticism. It correctly perceived that aesthetic autonomy, both real and imagined, was merely the obverse of the alienation in bourgeois society that art purported to resist (Russell 1985:18–19). Thus the term *avant-garde* should not refer simply to aesthetic innovation, especially not to the modernist effort to establish an absolute autonomy for art. The avant-gardist seeks just the opposite: the volatile interpenetration of art and everyday life through a mutual activity on the part of artistic producers and recipients, with the latter putting aesthetic forms to uses creative in their own right. Popular life should emerge as the ultimate avant-garde, even if not expressed as such.

The Benjamin-Brecht Position

The avant-garde itself contains negative and positive moments that require distinction; many movements identified as avant-garde, it must be admitted, are not easily disentangled from modernism. In terms of engagement with everyday life, Benjamin and Brecht—not Dada, given its nihilism, or surrealism—provide the most consistent avant-garde theory available. Eagleton distinguishes Dada and Brecht in terms of their relationship to institutional art: Dada resisted it through self-consuming gestures, while Brecht sought a real political significance for his art, through its integration with everyday life (1990:372). Many avant-gardists, in other words, if they attacked aesthetic traditions, essentially continued to conceive of art as an autonomous source of imaginative transformation, even when they professed to seek revolutionary results. In Brecht's materialist view, purely formal innovation could never challenge injustice, and thus the shock of the new alone was a poor substitute "for discovering an innovative response 'appropriate' to the given conditions" (Russell 1985:208).[25]

As opposed to the surrealists and others, furthermore, who believed they could directly attack and destroy the institution of art, Brecht's work seeks more sensibly to change the function of the specific media with which it works, "stick[ing] to what is concretely achievable" (Bürger 1984:89). In contrast with the frequent failure of other avant-garde movements to shed entirely the elitism of modernism—or its constriction of concern to traditional genres, at least— he does not take the term avant-garde to refer literally to being in "advance" of one's time. The Russian Futurists (including Vladimir Mayakovsky) illustrate both these liabilities: first, for all their similar concern with provoking the expressive capabilities of the audience, literature remains a privileged medium; second, as Leon Trotsky pointed out, they "anticipate history and contrast their scheme or their prescription with that which is. They thus have no bridge to the future" that their name invokes. Brecht's work and theory, therefore (and its articulation by Benjamin, one might add), are virtually unique, and not just in most fully bearing out Bürger's thesis distinguishing the avant-garde from modernist aestheticism. (Brecht and Mallarmé are certainly polar opposites, in their views of popular life.) The Benjamin-Brecht position, more importantly, is the one remnant of the original avant-garde movements that suggests "the potential of a continuing avant-garde tradition" (Russell 1985:178–80, 235).

Brecht's concept of the alienation effect, an interruption or fragmentation of his dramas by a variety of formal devices, did have the same aim as other avant-garde tactics, to break down the traditional "organic" work of art. The organic work, following the original definition by Kant, intends the impression of wholeness; its individual elements are significant only in the larger harmonious unity—that is, the whole is greater than the sum of the parts. That wholeness constitutes the work's autonomy, an intended imperviousness to everyday life. Brecht, in contrast, did not consider the nonorganic avant-garde work to be a political statement in its fragmentary form alone. It simply served to allow, in his words, its discontinuous, independent parts to be "confronted with the corresponding partial events *in reality*" (Bürger 1984:72, 91)—formal innovation provoking alert reception of some social content. The political significance of the work, that is, results only from further critical activity on the recipient's part. Brecht believed that his "work was only a particular part of and contribution to larger, shaping historical forces," and in this sense that formal innovation must be productive (Russell 1985:208). The dialectic of form and content[26] in the aesthetic experience should lead onto the dialectic of art and everyday life, of individual creation and collective experience.

Through the estrangement of his audience by a variety of formal devices, including popular music, placards, self-reflexive acting, and stage-settings—summed up as the *gest,* or the alienation effect— Brecht meant to make it consider what was being done to it not only inside the theater, but especially in everyday life outside. (He despised the Aristotelian concept of catharsis, in particular, because it implied wholesale absorption in drama, a loss of critical awareness.) The social content of his works, characteristically, is scarcely propagandistic; plays like *The Caucasian Chalk Circle, Galileo, Mother Courage,* and *The Threepenny Opera* "do not present a doctrinaire picture of political action." The characters, instead, are caught in ambivalent, decidedly nonprogressive situations, much as everyone is in everyday life; the audience was supposed to reach a perspective not actually contained in the play (Russell 1985:219, 228, 232). In prompting the question of why life is as it appears in the play, and whether it need be, Brecht's work "embodies a difference between the way things are and the way they can be" (Polan 1987:352).

The surrealists, on the other hand, were less lucid about integrating the realms of art and everyday life. They never really shed a residual formalism, in a sense, in finding politically conscious works of art intrinsically revolutionary (Eagleton 1986:147). The innovations in their works, furthermore, can be as self-absorbed and idealistic as anything produced by the modernists. Surrealists tend to call for the transformation of conscious social life, and then "drop back unexpectedly to self-conscious play within the apparently hermetic domain of pure art, . . . protest[ing] the valorization of the benefits of rationality in opposition to the irrational or the suggestive states of dream experience" (Russell 1985:24, 33). The central figure in the surrealist movement, Breton, "insisted always on retaining the . . . autonomy of artistic revolution, intellectually and organizationally" (Wollen 1989:79–80). Despite his Marxism—which as both a poet and a psychiatrist he related more to the mind than to society—and professed concern with the transformation of everyday life, he perceived a dilemma for the artist caught between expression of "the secret . . . within himself and himself alone" (quite mystified terms) and support for any "practical plan of action for changing this world." He resolved the dilemma by holding that art "resides in imagination alone, independently of the exterior object [or material reality] that brought it to birth." The imagination properly portrays *"only itself"* (Breton 1969:214, 220), a description of autonomy indistinguishable from modernist aesthetics, like Tristan Tzara's assertion that "what interests a Dadaist is his own mode of life" (1989:251). Breton's "Manifesto for an Independent Revolutionary Art," written with Trotsky, stresses artistic independence far more than revolution; after extensive insistence that "the imagination must escape from all constraint" and achieve "complete freedom for art," Breton feels compelled to deny that he wishes "to revive a so-called pure art" (1978:185–86), a denial necessary because he gives every indication of doing so. One can date the failure of the surrealist movement, says Maurice Nadeau, from the moment Breton classified himself in the detached category of the artist (1965:201–3).

The Situationist International, while acknowledging the important emphasis on desire and surprise in surrealism, criticized its failure to enact, in any material way, its proposal for a new use of everyday life. The surrealists' continuing devotion to painting and literature came nowhere near the Situationists' own eventual abandonment of original works of art. They entirely inverted surrealism, then, most fundamentally through "a semantic shift in the meaning of the word 'desire' (from unconscious to *conscious*) which enabled the SI to endorse the surrealist slogan, 'Take your desires for reality'" (Wollen 1989:82).[27]

When Benjamin argued for the "melting down" of hoary antinomies like art and the everyday, or high and mass culture, he had most in mind not surrealism, but Brecht's objective, the elimination of the distinction between artist and audience. The ambition of the Benjamin-Brecht position is to make every man and woman not necessarily an artist, but a critical thinker or "expert," at least, a person equipped to act on his or her world. Passing the tactics of Dada and surrealism through the medium of Brecht, Benjamin sharpens the theory of montage,[28] the technique that melts down cultural levels like "high" and "low." Montage, in the commonly understood sense, involves the juxtaposition of dissimilar cultural artifacts, a disruption of their conventional social (or antisocial) contexts.[29] The fragments in montage, in Benjamin's description, are torn altogether out of their original cultural contexts, either the autonomous realm of "high" art or its degenerate Other, mass culture, upsetting their distinction. The purpose is hardly mere pastiche: only freeing the fragment of conventional cultural assumptions can open it to use in everyday life. As an "interruption" of familiar experience, montage generates a shock— Benjamin's "shock effect," or Brecht's alienation effect—that provokes potentially critical response from an audience. Ideally, as in Brecht's theater, an audience forced to reevaluate its habits in receiving aesthetic texts might also begin to question its reception of ideas and images beyond the particular cultural event.[30]

"The Author as Producer" (1934), the high point of Benjamin's essays derived from Brecht's work, provides a thorough yet compact definition of avant-garde aims. The essay develops, most importantly, a dual understanding of montage central to the Benjamin-Brecht position. In somewhat the traditional sense of montage, literary forms, Benjamin argues, must be "melted down" with the technical innovations made possible by new technologies in mass culture, such as film and phonograph records. But he pushes the understanding of montage beyond the provocative amalgamation of diverse forms, in insisting that an individual text—whether filmic, literary, musical, or theatrical—must strive in its *own* form to generate interruption. Shock, in other words, can result not just from linkage with other forms, but in learning from and *emulating* their formal possibilities. The author-as-producer understands his or her work in the context of living social relations, specifically the constraints of economic and social relations in literary production, and will look to various means of cultural production and reproduction, both "high" and "low," for sources of technical innovation. The audience's *own* reception and use of a variety of cultural artifacts and texts, ultimately, would be tantamount to the avant-garde work's employment or emulation of the techniques it finds at hand.[31] If an avant-garde text invites such production from the spectators, that production entails the specific pleasure of knowing the world can be remade (Polan 1987:353), a dialectic between pleasure and knowledge, the affective and the ideological.

In the case of either the producer or the audience, the result must be, to some degree, what Benjamin and Brecht call the "functional transformation" of existing institutions.[32] That transformative activity, says Benjamin, must be cognizant first of "the decisive difference between merely supplying a production apparatus," the field in which one works and/or plays, and actually *changing* it. The capability of commercial culture to assimilate, even propagate, a seemingly unlimited number of revolutionary themes (1973:93–94), or content, must also be kept in mind. Hence the necessity of disruptive technical innovation, if the content itself is to have any significant impact. Brecht, in "The Modern Theatre is the Epic Theatre," makes the same dialectical point with the emphasis on content instead: the "fun" of formal innovation should be accompanied by a requisite attention to the conveyance of the subject matter.

More concretely still, the emotive, bodily impact generated by an avant-garde text is understood to convey in itself a social content—the *attitude* of contumacy. In Brecht's jargon, attitude is synonymous with gest, alienation effect, and so on. For him, "the attitudinal position" of the audience "springs from an attitudinal position in the work. [The] 'audience must be entertained with...the anger that is a practical expression of sympathy with the underdog'" (Polan 1987:352–53). Thus the term *attitude,* in its dual connotation of the intellectual and the emotional, suggests in general the simultaneous, dialectical relationship between affect and ideology sought by the positive moment of the avant-garde (and now by cultural studies). Still more specifically, to disrupt conventional reception in an authoritarian system, in a material, sensuous fashion, is to strike an immanently as well as eminently anarchistic blow. A contumacious *tone* (in whatever form), furthermore, by injecting refusal into the affirmative complaisance of the dominant culture, thereby breaks open a door for much more historical "content," or action, than that borne in the individual text.

This materialist sensibility is essential to enacting a genuinely avant-garde social engagement, rather than simple alienation. Negation of the status quo requires appropriate material form, an appeal to intuitive feeling as well as intellection. Brecht advocated removing the conflict between feeling and reason not just in art, but in capitalism generally (by giving life more depth than the instant gratifications of consumerism, for instance). Brecht's aim was a productive conflict between emotion and reason that would lead onto the pleasure of changing reality: "Our feelings impel us towards the maximum effort of reasoning, and our reason purifies our feelings" (qtd. in Fischer 1986:10). Williams likewise argues that cultural experience consists of "thought as felt and feeling as thought," and that "the true social *content* [in art and literature] is in a significant number of cases of this present and affective kind" (1977:133). The artist or creative individual, it should be noted, does not somehow have to disappear; the point is to understand his or her activity in a material, rather than mystified fashion.[33]

Eagleton, in *Walter Benjamin,* finds a "revolutionary literary criticism" based in the concept of montage. His terms reflect Benjamin's work, naturally, but what might be noted in the following is the presence of the language of Williams, in the general terms of cultural practices and social activity. A revolutionary literary criticism

> would dismantle the ruling concepts of 'literature,' reinserting 'literary' texts into the whole field of cultural practices. It would strive to relate such 'cultural' practices to other forms of social activity, and to transform the cultural apparatuses themselves.... It would deconstruct the received hierarchies of 'literature' and transvaluate received judgments and assumptions; engage with the language ... of literary texts ... and mobilize such texts ... in a struggle to transform ... a wider political context. (1981:98)

The distance between this program and actual practice, in literary studies, indicates the desperate need to recover the materialist tradition.

In the unstated influence of Williams, Eagleton's tenets suggest a readily available basis for such an effort, the fairly recent field of cultural studies. Recognizing the strong traces of the avant-garde in the original, defining work in cultural studies helps clarify the purposes of the field, now that it has become an academic growth industry (see McRobbie 1992). A fairly direct link exists between the avant-garde and early British cultural studies, in fact, in the person of Williams. His late essays on the quest of Brecht and others to unite art and everyday life, posthumously collected in *The Politics of Modernism,* serve as a reminder of his youthful enthusiasm for the avant-garde, in the late 1930s.

If it seems dubious to compare even a highly progressive academic field with the avant-garde, given the distance of academia from popular life, this is precisely the problem cultural studies should attack. Benjamin and Brecht's theory of functional transformation—the work done to change one's field, in hopes of altering society as well—includes the transformation of the artist into a *teacher;* in cultural studies, the teacher and/or scholar should become an *artist.* The ultimate aim must be to inform and encourage avant-garde practices outside as well as within the sphere of education.

Cultural Studies

Cultural studies should not only recover moments of dissent in lived or "ordinary" culture, as Williams ironically puts it, but seek to propagate them, as the avant-garde did. The common ground of the avant-garde and cultural studies lies in an understanding of popular culture as a productive process, in which texts and their uses are inseparable. The avant-garde's interest in transforming reception as well as production is revived in the most distinctive feature of cultural studies, "the connections made between lived cultural ensembles and public [mass] forms. Typically [such] studies have concerned the appropriation of elements of mass culture and their transformation acccording to the needs of social groups," highlighting those moments when an outburst of desire, or negation, has fractured common sense concerning existing social relations (R. Johnson 1986/87:72). Claims for distinctive creativity remain viable in cultural studies, but have to cut across artists and audiences, with a material grounding in the question of a text's social utility (or use value), rather than an abstract judgment on its aesthetic quality. For the avant-garde and cultural studies alike, there can be no clear-cut distinction between artist and audience, no political preference for either individual or collective creativity.

The renewal of the avant-garde's concern with the practices of cultural consumption began in the Centre for Contemporary Cultural Studies, at the University of Birmingham, under Stuart Hall's guidance in the midseventies (see Brantlinger 1990; Turner 1990). As opposed to traditional text-bound scholarship, cultural studies recognizes the simple fact that audiences make their own, sometimes quite subversive meanings (though more often just the opposite) out of music, television, and commodities in general.[34] This humane realization reflects very specifically Williams's "culturalism," along with the work of E. P. Thompson and Richard Hoggart. Hall and his cohorts subsequently extended into contemporary popular culture the central emphasis of Williams's work, on the volatile coexistence of both dominant and emergent (or oppositional) cultural practices. In this domain of meaning formation and affective investment, literature and art cannot be separated from other social activities, or whole ways of life. The material, "experiential pull" of culturalism, as Hall puts it, helps uncover the potential for creative agency in "sensuous human praxis, the activity through which men and women make history" (Hall 1981:24–26; see Hall 1980; Williams 1977:121–35).

Iain Chambers has linked cultural studies and the avant-garde on the basis of their similar material interest in the body (or, better put, affective experience).[35] The avant-garde project, overthrowing conformist common sense, might now be found in the subject of cultural studies, the languages of daily urban culture (a view influenced very much by punk): "Here [the] shock of the historical avant-garde, the transitory immediacy of perpetual sonorial and visual reproduction, and the 'dense and concrete life' of subordinated cultures are . . . mixed together" (1988:610–11). Cultural studies shares the belief of the original avant-garde that *culture* refers neither to autonomous art nor commercially manipulated popular forms, but to a field of social differences and struggles.

This overarching materialist perspective, in cultural studies, is complemented by structuralist theory, concerned with the more abstract mental structures referred to as ideology. Richard Johnson describes structuralism as the study of public, mass communication, and its control by the social groups who determine in part language, signs, ideologies, and discourses. Culturalism, in contrast, concerns comparatively private, though sometimes quite notorious uses of those materials by various individuals and social groups, especially subordinate ones. Linked together in cultural studies, ideological conceptions of the world and the shared, lived principles of everyday life are understood as common sources in a single process producing individual and collective consciousness, emotions, desires, and so on. In both approaches, therefore, regardless of their differences over the appropriate extent of theorizing, "cultural studies is necessarily and deeply implicated in relations of power" (1986/87:45, 53).[36] The impetus of cultural studies should always lead outside merely academic ends, especially by breaching what is all too frequently a barrier between academic theory and practical experience; hence comparison with the avant-garde is not inappropriate. As an interpretive practice entering into ongoing struggles over the uses of texts—or *articulations* of them, in Antonio Gramsci's terms—cultural studies should attempt "to change our lives for the better." The democratizing recovery of cultural contradictions, "disregarded evidence, . . . and denigrated social practices" serves to fracture fictions of cultural and social homogeneity (Turner 1990:215, 227).

In the interest of subverting the manufacture of consensus, Hall, Williams, and others have been ardent proponents of Gramsci's theory of hegemony, the process through which "common sense" is formed and delimited. Gramsci acknowledges the power of dominant social groups to win consent and set limits on common sense, in ideological discourse; his virtue is to emphasize as well the continual struggles of subordinate groups over interpretation of the world. The hegemonic process, grasped in its real fullness, belies gross abstractions about totalitarian cultural and political discourse, long typical of elite Marxisms. The turn to Gramsci, in the 1970s, was particularly important in reconciling structuralist and culturalist approaches, which tended to isolate dominance and opposition, respectively, phenomena integrated in his view of popular culture. His example, furthermore, helped correct the tendency of both paradigms to posit ideology as a monolith "imposed from without, as an alien force, on the subordinate classes." The theory of hegemony provided a more nuanced reading of popular culture, as a field of relations shaped by contradictory pressures, both subordination and insubordination, deformation and self-affirmation. This position was neither opposed to the popular nor uncritically for it (Bennett 1986:xiii, xvi; see Turner 1990:70–72, 210–15).

As Williams puts it, "the reduction of the social to fixed forms remains the basic error" in ideological analysis that takes "terms of analysis as terms of substance," operating at too great a level of abstraction. One may rightly speak of a prevailing ideology, but should remember that it is "lived specifically and definitively, in singular and developing forms" (1977:129). Gramsci himself wrote that analyses of hegemony had no significance unless they informed practical oppositional activity. Cultural studies, accordingly, should describe and reconstitute "in concrete studies the social forms through [which] human beings 'live,' become conscious, sustain themselves subjectively," with that materialism *reinforced* by broader structuralist insights (R. Johnson 1986/87:45). Work on the framing of consciousness should always remain grounded in material activities and conditions. The "strongly coupled," essentially synonymous concepts of culture and ideology pose together "the problems consequent on trying to think both the specificity of different practices and the forms of the articulated unity [or ideology] they constitute" (Hall 1981:36).

From this integrated view, the use of artifacts and texts of all sorts, in popular culture, constitutes "a production process, in which the [original] product becomes a material for fresh labour" by its audience. Critical approaches concerned primarily with texts and their original, usually elite producers only highlight "the separation between specialist critics and ordinary readers," listeners, or viewers. Johnson singles out the tendency of literary criticism and theory to remain obstinately technical or formal, an abstraction of literature out of everyday social practices (1986/87:58–59). Cultural studies, which emerged from literary criticism (via Hoggart and Williams), has long fought that discipline's confinement, combining with literary theory the approaches of disciplines including anthropology, history, and sociology.

The field of literary study has in fact only recently begun to refute the presumption that the question of use value is a vulgar one; the crippling and pervasive influence of modernism can be seen most clearly in the continuing antipathy to any question of social utility in art. Barbara Herrnstein Smith, most notably, has demolished the hermeticism of literary scholarship, the long-standing, disabling opposition between texts and contexts in aesthetic evaluation:

> To those for whom terms such as "utility," "effectiveness," and "function" suggest gross pragmatic instrumentality, crass mate-

rial desires, and the satisfaction of animal needs, a concept such as use-value will be seen as irrelevant to or clearly to be distinguished from aesthetic value. There is, however, no good reason to confine the domain of the utilitarian to objects that serve only immediate, specific, and unexalted ends or, for that matter, to assume that the value of artworks has altogether nothing to do with pragmatic instrumentality or animal needs. (1988: 33)

In work more closely identified with cultural studies, John Fiske likewise supplants older, arbitrary aesthetic critieria with those of utility, or relevance, which "can only be located in the social situation of the reader; they can reside in the text only as a *potential,* not as a quality." The critic might rightly hypothesize that potential, but evaluation of any text should also consider (as much as possible) specific moments, time- and place-bound, when that potential is activated. In examining the uses of a text, the criteria of judgment become the relevances made out of it, and their political effectiveness. Fiske's assertion of utilitarian questions, however, reaches the point of relativism, when he finds that any one use cannot be evaluated as better than another (1989:130–31). Celebrating the sheer prolificity of textual possibilities, in this way, suppresses the lack of possibilities in the social system as a whole: "making over the meaning of a television program may be much easier than climbing out of a ghetto" (Turner 1990:122).

The defense of utility leads seemingly inevitably to terms of relativism, a continuing failure, in the final analysis, to breach the realm of intellectual specialization. Cultural studies, as a result, "needs to consider what it should do with notions of value, with qualitative discrimination among the texts and practices of popular culture" (Turner 1990:228). An understandable reluctance to add to elite judgments of the past, to be sure, may contribute to the hesitance to make such evaluations. It is ultimately self-contradictory if not quietist, however, to assert the criteria of social utility in examining texts and then pull up short, refusing to judge the uses of those texts by utilitarian criteria as well. The relativist refusal to make positive and negative discriminations in evaluating popular culture, ironically, makes the *utilitarian* critic *useless* to the world outside academia. If cultural studies exists to suggest particular political directions to the culture at large, it needs to offer forthright illustrations of practices it considers exemplary.

Such judgments will always be subjective to some extent, since no critical evaluation, even cumulative or consensus judgments, ever represents perfect objectivity. It would be a mistake, then, to equate a utilitarian standard with greater objectivity; the point is to replace arbitrary, hopelessly abstracted traditional standards such as beauty, genius, and truth with more material standards based in actual social experience. On this basis, one can certainly identify with some confidence the superiority of active disrespect and irreverence, for instance, as opposed to complacent authoritarianism. Despite her extensive interest in relativism, Herrnstein Smith does also suggest that the utility of cultural goods, "in the sense of their satisfaction of some obvious . . . bodily . . . need or desire," must be evaluated in light of their contribution to social *scrappiness*. The scrap she describes very closely resembles the hegemonic process, the continuously conflictual interactions in which people construct themselves, explaining and justifying their actions and beliefs. Those human interactions, in her view, do "operate reliably enough under recurrent conditions to permit their more or less coherent description," and thus can inform provisional conclusions, at least, good enough to keep humanity going (1988:132, 148).

The question for value judgments on texts and lived culture, in Johnson's terms, concerns the "outcomes" of the use of various cultural forms. If the preferable outcome for those with power is apathy, stasis, and torpor, for cultural studies it should be desire running beyond cultural and political stasis. The three general concentrations in cultural studies he describes, separable but *not* discrete, all look to serve this last end, whether in cultural production,[37] the resulting texts, or their use in lived cultures:

> Production-related studies imply a struggle to control or transform the most powerful means of cultural production, or to throw up *alternative means* by which a counter-hegemonic strategy may be pursued. Such studies are usually addressed to . . . radical political parties. Text-based studies, focusing on the forms of cultural products, have usually concerned the possibilities of a *transformative* cultural practice. They have been addressed most often to *avant-garde* practitioners, critics, and

teachers.... Finally, research into lived cultures has been closely associated with a politics...*upholding* the ways of life of subordinated social groups and [their] *hidden wisdoms*. (1986/87:72–73; italics added)

Johnson's schema is reflected in the plan of this book: the next chapter, on authoritarian ideology, concerns the dominant cultural institutions, drawing together the classic negative theories of mass culture (in order ultimately to move beyond them). Subsequent chapters recover, develop, and theorize exemplary moments of subversive response, in literature, popular musical texts, and the audience subcultures formed around them. These elements, to reiterate, are inseparable: "the familiar dichotomy of 'text' and 'lived' is meaningless" (Mercer 1991:63). And the discovery of dissent should not be separated from the persistence of domination—by exaggerating the extent of either one—or else one loses the "complexity of cultural relations, [which] both enable and disable people" (Giroux and Simon 1989:7).

It is also important to qualify Johnson's question concerning use value, or whether desire in everyday practices breaks hegemonic constraints. Some desires, of course, can be expressed in deviant, unconventional, but ultimately authoritarian fashion, as in fascism. Paul Willis, in *Learning to Labour,* describes a less extreme paradox along these lines, in the "self-damnation" of young working-class males whose resistance of authority in school, and the mental work emphasized there, serves to confine their opportunities to manual labor. A moment of freedom leads onto a lifelong entrapment. Willis, however, presents his study as reason for optimism as well as pessimism, stressing the continuing possibility of producing different outcomes. If his subjects only reproduced the "prior authority relations [of] 'them and us,'" diminishing the possibility of direct political challenge through their refusal of education, they did exercise at the same time a real creative, interpretive ability, "a partial penetration" of the determining conditions of working-class existence "superior to [the] official versions of reality. [T]he possibility of strengthening and working from this base always remains" (1981:3, 103, 109, 119–20, 172, 174–75). Related sociology, concerning youth subcultures, is often dismissed for seeming to suggest that the revolution will occur through fashion. But the whole point of cultural studies is to identify and bring to wider attention the potential in "partial" realizations of resistance.

If such possibilities for desire in lived culture are often too easily dismissed, they can also underwrite uncritically populist polemics. The work of Chambers and Fiske, in particular, Meaghan Morris has argued, tends to refuse any evaluative discriminations whatsoever. Chambers, for example, places the tactile experience of popular culture in opposition to the "cerebral world," associated with official culture, suggesting that a sheerly pleasurable *lack* of attention to aesthetic objects somehow opens up democratic prospects (1986:12–13). Morris, in contrast, describes the appropriate concern of cultural studies as a positive discrimination, an emphasis on moments when the "unambivalently discontented, aggressive *theorizing* subject" appears in popular culture (1988:20). Used to elaborate Johnson's question concerning desire in lived culture, this is an essential formulation for work in cultural studies. In supplementing his terms of desire overrunning stasis, Morris's reference to "theorizing" is critical, for it emphasizes persons engaged in critical thought as well as in practice—in *praxis,* in other words—who link and make sense out of a wide range of cultural and social experience and act, in some form, on that basis. Such exemplars have healed, in a sense, the damaging schism between mental labor and immediate material practice found in Willis's subjects, who feel "that practice is more important than theory" (1981:57).

The central concern of Dick Hebdige's *Subculture: The Meaning of Style,* for example, is precisely the intentional, avant-gardist elimination of the distance between audience and performance, in youth subcultures formed around rock and roll music. At the zenith of punk rock, Hebdige and others have pointed out, the audience's creative involvement in forming the general punk style frequently led its members into making the music itself. The impetus to eradicate barriers to performance in punk was *style:* as Benjamin would have it, an embodiment of refusal as shock effect or "noise," common to both the music and the audience's own creative visual ensembles, which expressed "a fundamental tension between those in power and those condemned to subordinate positions" (1979:130, 132).

Angela McRobbie, more recently, has pitted Hebdige's *Subculture* against the recent spate of scholarship on postmodernism, which diagnoses the breakdown of cultural levels as the demise of aesthetic autonomy, and the loss of distinctions of taste and value in a culture of indiscriminate pastiche. Questions of postmodernity, she finds, seem since the mid-1980s to "have replaced the more familiar concepts of ideology and hegemony" (1991b:1). *Subculture,* as McRobbie reads it, suggests that the ransacking and recycling of culture in "a cross referencing between forms, and notably between pop music and 'art,' between aesthetics and commerce, between commitment and the need to make a living, . . . can create a *vibrant critique* rather than an inward-looking second-hand aesthetic" of pastiche. So far, then, only Hebdige "has broken out of [the] reproduction of the old divide between high culture and the pop arts," by illustrating a productive relation between them—where many postmodernists actually leave the divide untouched by merely announcing its demise, however playful and subversive their descriptions of chaotic pastiche. Thus his work still seems unique, even among positive versions of postmodernism (McRobbie 1986:109, 114).[38]

Hebdige himself, more recently, has sought to rescue pastiche and collage "from the aura of despair which surrounds them" in postmodernist work. Rather than some sign of entropy, they may represent the "means through which ordinary consumers can not only appropriate new technologies, new media skills to themselves, but can learn a new principle of assemblage, can open up new meanings and affects." If postmodernism refers to such a process—opening up critical discourse to prohibited subjects and new voices, eroding the cultural capital of experts, and enhancing the collective sense of cultural and political possibilities—then "I for one am a postmodernist."[39] He continues to believe in the living textures of popular culture as a means to effectively contest authority, and eschews purely theoretical analysis of them (1988:204, 222, 226).

McRobbie points out, however, that Hebdige has also disavowed "the more playful elements of *Subculture,*" in reaction against commercial celebration of stylistic excess (1986:109). By Hebdige's own account, he had a "change of heart in relation to the putative importance of 'style' in life, politics, and art," and thus dissociated himself from the fetishization of style in popular magazines (in England) like *The Face.* For him the "idea of subculture-as-negation grew up alongside punk, remained inextricably linked to it and died when it died." His work does remain optimistic about the possibility of negating dominant forms of expression, but prefers the sort of shifting, decentralized alliances, comprised of individuals occupying fluid, plural positions, theorized in post-Marxist readings of Gramsci. A subculture, in contrast, represents a relatively discrete collective, its members more fixed in their identification with a stylistic ensemble. The actual plurality of stylistic possibilities available in popular culture, says Hebdige, suggests that "it no longer appears adequate to confine the appeal of these forms—the multiple lines of effect/affect emanating from them—to the ghetto of discrete, numerically small subcultures" (1988:8, 10, 211–12). The assumption throughout this book, therefore, is that the term *subculture,* in its most useful sense, refers not to full-time participation in a visual style, but to a relatively diffuse phenomenon formed around a widely shared attitude, with bases possible in any combination of contumacy, class, gender, race, and sexual preference. More at issue is the assemblage of different texts and commodites one discovers in a subcultural style, the perfectly verifiable evidence of people putting all manner of cultural resources to work.

A qualified account of the nature of subcultural activity is certainly essential, Simon Frith points out, considering that Hebdige's *"Subculture* has, after all, long been essential reading for ad agencies," and that the head of MTV once waved a copy of the book while claiming to be a "subcultural force" (1988a:79). As for cultural studies in academia, "just as rock lost its privileged place as any sort of counter-culture"—in Frith's view—with the reconsolidation of the record business after the disruptiveness of punk, "cultural studies emerged to restate its radical significance—on the syllabus. By 1983–4 the music industry may have been organised 'like punk never happened,' but the cultural studies industry was still wallowing in its consequences—semiotic readings of style, postmodernist accounts of video, psychoanalytic interpretations of the voice." Lacking was a concern with the material organization of the music industry, with the power of the dominant means of cultural production. Instead, according to Frith, cultural studies has too frequently addressed consumption alone, asserting some authenticity in commodities (like rock records) through overly idealistic recourse to the consumer, who ostensibly rescues "the real meaning of a record from its market form" (1988c:2, 6). Different forms of popular music can thus seem to have just as many different ideological effects, emerging from a seemingly benign production process.

Cultural studies has indeed, at times, celebrated audience uses of mass culture simply for their pluralism, finding a radical potential (à la Fiske) in the simple fact that "mass cultural texts are complex and contradictory, therefore people using them produce complex and contradictory culture" (M. Morris 1988:19). Perhaps, says Hebdige, "the myth of the inert masses is in danger of being replaced by a counter-myth of the robustly iconoclastic, healthily corporeal and debunking culture of the popular classes" (1987:61). The endorsement of pluralism, in cultural studies, thus poses a danger to "the need for a sharply focused politics of culture." Both textual and ethnographic studies rely excessively "on a limited number of concepts such as empowerment and resistance, with nobody asking 'Resistant to what?' 'With what degree of success?' 'In what social and historical context?'" other than the broad rubric of postmodernism (McRobbie 1991a:20).[40]

From a more discriminating approach, one's primary concern should be the "grittier experiences" of unambivalent discontent and aggression, conscious or "theorized" in some fashion. That grittier sensibility gets obscured when everyday life is assumed to be inherently positive, with "a way to redemption" always optimistically discerned (M. Morris 1988:21). As opposed to Fiske's stark dichotomy between commercial culture and the seemingly universal guerilla warfare in everyday life, consumption and production are not so easily dissociable, but complex, variable phases of a single process. Johnson (1986/87), for example, describes very thoroughly a circulation between mass and popular culture, between public and private cultural forms, in a mutual process of appropriation and exploitation.

It is important to note that a feminist critic, Morris, would have cultural studies seek out aggression and grittiness, just as it is McRobbie who cites the importance of a similar attitude in subcultural style. "For as long as I can remember," she says, "collective expressions of disaffiliation from Authority and the hegemony of the dominant classes (by either sex) have sent shivers of excitement down my spine" (1980:48). Others believe, however, that the "hardness" celebrated in resistance of authoritarianism has historically had its material basis in the relative autonomy possessed by men (Worpole 1983:47). Oppositional sub- and countercultures constructed largely by black males, for instance, like hiphop and Rastafarianism, can address oppression and be harrowingly sexist at the same time.[41] Among all oppressed groups, women face the greatest obstacles to the aggressive expression of discontent, even simply in style.[42]

This phenomenon is understandable in light of conventional mores of femininity: since public displays of deviance and insubordination on the part of men are considered the relatively tolerable product of masculine physical energy and high spirits, one must look to more private forms of consumption to find something like subcultural resistance on the part of women, as the work of McRobbie and Janice Radway (1984) indicates. Thus Julia LeSage finds it essential to question first and foremost why "in the sphere of cultural production there are few dominant ideological forms that allow us even to think 'women's rage.' . . . It is a task open to all our creativity and skill—to tap our anger as a source of energy and to focus it aesthetically and politically" (1988:421–22). For women (and also men) to arrive at progressive "uses of anger," in Audre Lorde's terms, it may first be necessary to confront how difficult the construction of femininity makes the very conception of anger. At the same time, feminine and masculine experience should not be considered entirely disjunct: Kim Gordon of Sonic Youth points out that "a lot of people" in rock bands like hers "get motivated to write from a point of anger," with unconventional men and women alike facing the fact that "if you're too opinionated, or too vocal, or too loud, that's always sort of frowned upon." Rage or "screaming," for both sexes, "is a kind of vehicle for expressing yourself in ways society doesn't let you" (qtd. in France 1992:24). The concern of cultural studies with the expression of discontent—with the "outlaw emotions" described by Alison Jaggar (1989)—should be universally suggestive, therefore, despite the striking failure of British subcultural sociology to consider feminine experience.[43]

But if its content is predominantly masculine, even that original British work on youth subcultures is "clearly also attuned to feminism, as a political theory that insists on breaking down false conceptual divisions between . . . private and public" (Brantlinger 1990: 131). Johnson, for example, besides describing at some length the continual circulation between private and public cultural forms, also specifically suggests a greater scholarly reliance on personal experience: if popular life is often overestimated in the abstract, students of culture should resort to the perfectly valid access they have to lived culture "through their own experiences and social worlds. This is a continuous resource, the more so if it is consciously specified and if its relativity is recognized.... [I]n general, students of culture should have the courage to use their personal experience more, more explicitly and more systematically. In this sense cultural studies is a heightened, differentiated form of everyday activities and living" (1986/87:69, 79). One's personal experience and awareness of that of others certainly hold some utility; they even furnish a good deal of information about the production process itself, about its constraints on texts and their audiences—inferential knowledge, perhaps, but significant nonetheless.

The inclusion of personal materials would overcome a significant reason for the neglect of feminine cultural pastimes, which McRobbie finds inherent in subcultural sociology: the "tendency to conceive of youth almost entirely in terms of action or direct experience," most apparent to the observer, while neglecting more private, less immediately visible activities and internal processes common to males and females alike (qtd. in Turner 1990:118).[44] But she also finds the concept of subcultural style perfectly relevant to feminine experience. Feminists, for example, "wage a similar semiotic warfare" in their daily lives: "all the signs and meanings embodied in the way we handle our public visibility play a part in the culture which, like the various youth cultures, bears . . . living evidence that although inscribed within structures, [women] are not wholly prescribed by them." McRobbie suggests that the classic subculture, providing its members "with a sense of oppositional sociality, an unambiguous pleasure in style, [and] a disruptive public identity . . . could have a positive meaning for girls" in general, as well (1980:49; cf. Lewis 1990).

One response to masculine bias in cultural studies (and other fields), though, has been a search for purely feminine expressive forms. But this approach, by itself, may miss the possibility that if "patriarchy has defined and placed women as the other," then women who "speak and act from the same ground . . . men have traditionally enjoyed" automatically effect a useful form of resistance (P. Smith 1988:137). The appropriation of a masculine edge in rock music, for example, breaks with the conventional expectation that a woman must be a "singer/songwriter/folkie lady" characterized by "sensitivity, passivity, and sweetness" (Frith and McRobbie 1990:377). Critiquing claims for gendered aesthetics, Rita Felski questions whether men and women actually express themselves in distinctively different ways at all. Like

Benjamin and Brecht, she finds that revolutionary style alone—in this case the "development of uniquely 'feminine' or 'subversive' styles"—fails to surmount the separation of art from everyday life, if reception is not politicized as well. Lived culture should also be a feminist concern for a reason important to cultural studies in general, the need to "reevaluate a long-standing and dismissive association of the popular with the feminine," of commercial culture with a somehow feminizing pacification (1989:156, 159–60, 174).

While "difference" must be recognized in the barriers to public discourse various groups encounter, that commonality should always, in the final analysis, be brought out. The experience of alienation and rage is common to men and women, white people and people of color alike. The so-called punk novelist Kathy Acker, for example, in *Don Quixote,* makes the familiar feminist point about gender, that "you can only be who you're taught and shown to be." In the very next sentence, she expresses a more visceral sentiment shared by a wide range of people, one which was certainly at the core of punk: "Those who have [shown] and are showing you [who you are], most of the controllers, are shits." Cultural anarchism, it should be stressed again, does not necessarily involve aggression and rage in physical action at all; the urge to destruction entails both an emotive, intuitive response and intellectual, critical activity—the power to *think,* as Bakunin held. Anarchism, in this sense, is hardly the exclusive province of men, nor inaccessible at all to women.[45]

The experts sought by Benjamin and Brecht would be the aggressively discontented, theorizing subjects sought by Morris. Fay Weldon, in *The Life and Loves of a She-Devil,* a testament in part to the force of "hate," or resentment, also suggests the radical importance of theory (the power to think), or the abstract that emerges from the concrete, as Brecht put it. She depicts repressed suburban housewives who "discuss things, rather than ideas; . . . exchange information, not theories; . . . keep ourselves steady by thinking about the particular. The general is frightening." The refusal or reluctance to confront systemic social contradictions is hardly the exclusive province of housewives, however, as the next chapter on authoritarianism indicates. The effort to prompt people to confront those contradictions, conversely, has been limited to a small number of provinces—among them the avant-garde, in the arts, and cultural studies, in scholarship and teaching—from which it may yet emerge.

CHAPTER 2

Theorizing Authoritarian Culture

The concentrated nexus of economic and state power, in advanced Western nations facing incurable economic crises, has in recent years strategically drawn culture further than ever into politics. Corporate control of mass communications has become more concentrated, narrowing the range of public expression; efforts increase to institute official and "voluntary" censorship at every level of state and culture, affecting everything from government information to rock music; political leaders frequently trade in appropriated mass-culture imagery and rhetoric, confining political discourse almost entirely to either feel-good inanity or its dark obverse, simplistic appeals to hatred (usually on a racial basis). A new authoritarianism pervades everyday life, as a result, transmitted through the verbal and visual media of entertainment and information.[1]

Dire conclusions on those media have historically been the one area in which commentators from both ends of the political spectrum agree (see Brantlinger 1983). The right bemoans the leveling of high culture; the left despairs at the utter pacification of consumers by capitalist culture, in an "unholy combination of technological determinism and cultural pessimism" (Williams 1989:120). Though rightly criticizing, for example, the specious individualism of consumer society—as an illusory, materialistic satisfaction of people's needs—the left has managed to be self-defeating nonetheless, blithely invalidating "the needs themselves instead of looking for more progressive ways of meeting them" (Fiske 1989:165). Most regrettable are those puritanical forms of leftism that throw out "the baby of pleasure with the bathwater of ideology, [creating] an immense gap between left cultural criticism and the people it purports to serve" (Stam 1988:142). The Situationist International execrated left academicism, observing that

> people in the streets, in the offices and factories know damn well what's going on, even if they can't write essays about all its theoretical ramifications. The point is that they can't do anything about it. What needs understanding is the state of paralysis everyone is in. Certainly all conditioning comes from society but it is anchored in the body and mind of each individual, and this is where it must be dissolved. Ultimately the problem is an emotional, not an intellectual one. All the analyses of reification in the world won't cause a neurosis to budge an inch. (Gray 1974:167)

If theories of reification (defined below) are insufficient, the SI did recognize the necessity of other more immediate tasks of analysis, such as debunking the mass media's pretense of neutrality and independence.

Another problem with judgments on mass culture, more recently, has been the postmodernist abandonment not just of dire accounts of ideological manipulation, but of any evaluative discrimination whatsoever. In theories of postmodernism, "the necessarily moral and teleological dimensions of cultural critique [are] lost in the current championing of multiplicity and difference" (P. Smith 1989:43).[2] Some sort of "fixed" cultural models are needed, however, if cultural criticism is not to be worried into atomization and relativism. For all the past excesses, radical approaches to mass culture should refuse to give up their moral and political dimensions, and continue to recognize the volatile tensions underlying apparent resignation (as in the theory of hegemony).

The quality that differentiates the best work on mass communications is a dialectical perspective. One-dimensional critics find political passivity practically irrevocable, the postmodernists as much as traditionalists like Frankfurt School epigones.[3] Metaphors of *bread and circuses, spectacle,* and so forth hold some truth, but only if left as terms of description, not assertions of actual fixed, monolithic conditions. This chapter includes some of these classic negative views, but must be understood as a partial description, and not the sort of totalizing critique characteristic of academic approaches on both the left and the right. What follows below attempts for the most part to describe the specific ideological components of contemporary authoritarianism. Ultimately, like William Morris speaking on popular culture a century ago, this study "could not go through the dreary task of speaking to you of a thing with no life in it; I must speak of a living thing with hope in it, or hold my peace" (1984:106). The next chapter, on cultural anarchism, will qualify, even refute much of this chapter's analysis of authoritarianism (though recent positive assessments of popular culture, especially the treatment of consumerism as a generally oppositional activity, can be just as absolutist as traditional negative criticism).

Oppositional cultural forms must first understand who and what they are fighting, though, in order to mount productive challenges to authority. Creative forms of dissent, for one thing, when they manage to attract much attention, face an ever-intensifying process of commercial appropriation and reconstitution. Invigorating a common political sentiment with punk fury, for example, the Clash sang on their first record that "all power's in the hands / of people rich enough to buy it"; shortly thereafter, with more experience of the music business, the group had to confront the fact that the economic power it railed against entails "Complete Control / even over this song."[4] With regard to the political economy of mass culture, therefore, the problem "is not just to organise subcultural resistance, ... but to do [so] with reference to the contradictions that are necessarily built into cultural consumption" (Frith 1980:61).

Descriptions of those dilemmas include both *realist* and *formalist* theories, a crucial distinction to make in forming a perspective on mass communications. Realist analyses treat the mass media as a relatively transparent conveyor of ideology, which can be tested against alternative sources of experience for its truthfulness. The concern is control over content, in the belief that a change in ownership, or seizure of the means of message production, would allow dramatic change in the ideology conveyed. Formalist analyses, however, consider the mass media to work primarily through their form, their techniques or structures, prior to any content. The media, from this view, have the same, usually pacifying ideological effect regardless of who owns them. The formal means of making meaning so thoroughly construct reality for their consumers, presumably, that even the notion of some independent reality, in realist approaches, is questionable (Frith 1980:51–52). The technology of mass cultural production, for example, in the Frankfurt School's view (see Adorno 1941; Horkheimer and Adorno 1987), institutes a standardization of entertainment—the pleasure of "a passive, endlessly repeated confirmation of the world-as-it-is." As in the rationalized (measured and quantified) discipline of industrial labor, in "a rational leisure discipline [the] traditional forms of release and riot became bound by the timed routines" of technology (Frith 1980:59).[5]

From a realist perspective, however, insubordination and domination coexist, and the mass media's effort "to win popular respect and consent for authority is *endlessly* waged," never a closed issue. One should not "attribute any purity of political expression to popular culture," certainly, in its use of mass-produced commodities and texts. But, at the same time, one must acknowledge its not infrequent power to generate "ideas and desires that are relatively opposed, *alongside* those that are clearly complicit, to the official culture" (A. Ross 1989a:3, 10). Commercial culture may package spurious beliefs and needs, but never merely dictates them; they are also repackaged, after they circulate through popular life and receive sometimes unpredictable utilization and alteration.

This chapter is more concerned with the first, direct stage of "packaging"; the next chapter will discuss the demolition of its effects. The objective for now is a widely applicable historical and theoretical context for understanding contemporary authoritarianism. Analysis of specific texts has largely been omitted, since it goes on constantly in many other places, often on an ad hoc basis lacking much connection with the larger cultural and political system from which those texts emerge. The following synthesis of ideas and theories, hopefully, will supply a useful systemic overview for more closely focused studies. Since close textual description is a lesser concern, affective experience is scanted somewhat in favor of ideology, though some attempt is made to consider the general affective climate. Subsequent chapters will correct this imbalance, demonstrating that what matters most, finally, is not the "historically fixed objects of culture, but the state of play in cultural relations" (Hall, qtd. in Giroux and Simon 1989:9).

Authoritarian Populism

The absence of analysis of the cultural industries, their political economy, and how they work to make meaning has been described as "a missing link at the heart of the cultural studies project." Mass communications comprise an economic formation as well as a cultural system, and their study requires investigation not just of ideologies, but of how economic dynamics—particularly conglomeration—contribute to shaping ideology (Murdock 1989:436, 439; see Budd et al. 1990).[6] In reviewing the variety of analytical approaches to mass culture, the first essential point must therefore be an incontestable realist one: access to the dominant means of communication, as is the case with other sophisticated, expensive technologies, is restricted by the extreme concentration of their ownership. In plain statistical terms, as few as five to ten corporations will soon control most of the world's important newspapers, magazines, book publishers, radio and television stations and networks, movie studios, and record companies. Of the 25,000 communications outlets in the United States, ninety percent will be held by fifteen to twenty-six corporations, by 1995 (Bagdikian 1987:xii; 1989a:805). Public expression is largely the property of the likes of General Electric, Gulf and Western, and Time Warner Inc., and a few allied independents like the Reverend Moon, Rupert Murdoch, and the Newhouse family.[7] For all the progressive cultural initiatives one can certainly cite, the "marginalization and impoverishment of oppositional media" effected by these conglomerates ensure that "most members of the mass audience rarely contact messages overtly designed to challenge [the] dominant culture" (Budd et al. 1990:172).

The close corporate control of new communications technologies, in particular, increasingly enfeebles public access to information, however great the torrent of discourse in the "information age." No one committed to freedom could be pleased with the consequence, "a national discourse that is increasingly one-sided," drowning out less affluent opposing voices (Schiller 1987:6; see Schiller 1989a). The predominance of the voice of corporate America does not just quash hope for individual liberty, but also counsels the inevitability of a variety of disasters, including widespread poverty, the destruction of the environment, and international military intervention. This postmodern world has even been characterized as an outright schizophrenic one, in which the individual personality (or an awareness of one's own and society's past, present, and future development) has ostensibly been eradicated in a delusional, perpetual present, a fixation on the commercial and political image-mongering of the moment (see Jameson 1984:71–73).

Certainly the schizophrenia George Orwell described in "Politics and the English Language," more a matter of simple disjunction between rhetoric and reality, has reached its zenith. *Freedom* is equated with "free enterprise," dominated by a relatively small number of large corporate interests; economic *reform* means redistributing income to the wealthy, while *prosperity* is equated with that minority's conspicuous consumption; *defense* refers to militarism; the selective application of the term *terrorism* (e.g., to Palestinians, but not to Nicaraguan contras and other "freedom fighters") defies reason. Thus for

> a realistic picture of society there is no such thing as a central authority.... The result of the overwhelming power of relatively narrow corporate ideologies has been the creation of widely established political and economic illusions in the United States, with little visible contradiction in the media to which a majority of the population is exclusively exposed. [P]olitical and social ideas, in news, books, broadcasting, and movies, [foster] distorted reality and impoverished ideas. (Bagdikian 1983:xiv, 46–47)

Mainstream discourse has been dominated in particular by "authoritarian populism," in Stuart Hall's terms, an ideological formation that emerged in the late 1970s, as a period of economic stagnation and crisis reached its climax. (The discussion of authoritarianism here will be limited to this objective social phenomenon, at the exclusion of more general psychological studies like those of the Frankfurt School, such as *The Authoritarian Personality* and Erich Fromm's *Escape from Freedom*.)

Authoritarian populism can hardly be read according to the base-superstructure model, which treats ideologies as the epiphenomena of economic change. This new authoritarianism actually bridged two very different economic situations, at the beginning and end of a

massive economic restructuring. At first a stern, mean-spirited response to "stagflation," scapegoating and repressing those who ostensibly caused it, authoritarian populism changed its spots entirely
once the new order was well under way, serving as the "feel-good"
bellwether for an era of greed, intolerance, and bellicose militarism
that has yet to abate. But if ideology should not be read off an economic "base," some account of the economic restructuring that occurred is helpful in understanding the arrogant, plutocratic tenor of
contemporary authoritarianism. That basic meanness is typically
tricked up with pseudo-folksy appeals to common sense like that of
H. Ross Perot, whose plutocratic authoritarianism represented a logical outgrowth of the eighties (though his meteoric rise, ironically,
depended on disgust with that decade's results).

   With the saturation of world markets by developed and developing nations, the response of nations with older productive facilities,
like England and the United States, was to reorganize as global financial centers, and upwardly redistribute contracting economic resources. Corporations in the United States

> cut costs, directly, crudely, and unimaginatively: by demanding
> wage concessions, speeding up production processes, substituting
> part-time workers (generally without benefits) for full-time ones,
> resisting or rolling back unionization, and farming out work to
> low-wage subcontractors here [in the anti-union Sunbelt] and
> abroad [in Third World nations on the Pacific Rim and in Central
> America, but most brazenly in Mexican *maquiladoras*]. Equally
> important was finding politicians who would repeal, weaken, or
> refrain from enforcing the environmental, occupational-safety,
> consumer-protection, antitrust, securities, banking and fair-
> labor-practice laws; cut social-welfare spending, which forced
> people into the labor market, further driving down wages; and
> above all, lower taxes on the business class, collectively and indi-
> vidually. (Scialabba 1988:26)

By the end of the eighties, not surprisingly, the wealthiest ten percent
of American households controlled about three-quarters of the nation's wealth, with the wealthiest one percent holding about half of
that amount. The boom in the only economic sectors to receive
influxes of capital—financial services, health care, and the military-

industrial complex—hardly revived production facilities and skilled labor.[8]

What occurred, David Harvey finds, was a crisis of the old "Fordist" model of capital accumulation, and a transition to a new, more intense process of "flexible accumulation." This was not a rupture creating some unprecedented postmodernist epoch, but a continuous, necessary development of capitalism. Fordism had evolved from the beginning of the century (as the term implies), employing the techniques of scientific management to regulate the whole cycle of production and consumption. But the full development of Fordism only came in the long postwar boom from 1945–1973, with a "tense but nevertheless firm balance of power between organized labour, large corporate capital, and the nation state." The state took on new Keynesian roles in managing the economy, priming it with deficit spending (chiefly devoted to the military), while maintaining a modest social safety net to help keep the peace (quickly undermined when the economy faltered).

With the shock of the oil embargo in 1973, the torpor of stagflation became untenable, and a greater flexibility proved necessary, in greatly intensified rates of innovation "with respect to labour processes, labour markets, products, and patterns of consumption." The results include the proliferation of financial services and the service sector in general, particularly the management of communications and information, and uneven development between geographical regions (national and international), with industry rapidly relocating wherever labor is cheapest. In general, an increasing "time-space compression" has occurred, with the shrinking of "the time horizons of private and public decision-making" and the global financial network's porous complexity. This compression took material form, for example, in the "discounting [of] time future into time present" by the brokerage of fictitious capital, from commodities futures to junk bonds. As a result of all these developments, capitalism is paradoxically "becoming ever more tightly organized *through* dispersal, geographical mobility, and flexible responses" to labor and consumer markets. The continuity with Fordism lies in a number of areas, one the increasing role of the state in controlling economic cycles. Federal Reserve Chairman Paul Volcker's brutal control of inflation, in the early 1980s, precipitated the primary scandal of the decade by raising the cost of money for savings-and-loan institutions, leading them to lobby Congress to abandon controls on their operations. Another continuity is apparent in the power that the well-organized corporation continues to derive from control of information. This monopoly was further enhanced by deregulation (essential in general to flexible accumulation), which stripped restrictions on media ownership (Harvey 1989:132–33, 145, 147, 158–59; see also Callinicos 1989:132–44; Lang 1990; Melman 1991).

For anyone who cares to notice, the contradictions of this economic system would be surreal, were they not so commonplace. Whether auto companies make or lose billions of dollars, their executives take bonuses in the millions, while still more tens of thousands of employees are released. Coal companies provoke strikes, employ right-wing mercenaries to instigate violence, and cut all medical benefits for the widowed, retired, and disabled. Such reports, in the abstract, evoke a sense of déjà vu that indicates the reversal of historical gains by labor, recalling the abuses prevalent until the postwar settlement on cooperation between management and labor, abrogated in the mid-1970s by business (see Giardina 1989; Schwartz 1989; Davis 1986).[9]

What has taken place, however, is only in its general features—monopolism, union busting, and so forth—a rollback of history to an earlier epoch in the economic sector. Appropriately enough, authoritarian populism likewise only appears to hearken to the past and traditional beliefs. Hall, in his extensive work on authoritarian populism, describes it as "the attempt to 'educate' and discipline the society into a particularly regressive version of modernity by, paradoxically, dragging it backwards through an equally regressive version of the past" (Hall 1988:2). This effort has been required by the seemingly baffling ephemerality of the most basic material processes, under the regime of flexible accumulation. Profound questions of interpretation have arisen, a "legitimation crisis" recognized by Jürgen Habermas in the pivotal year of 1973. With the torpor of capitalism at that point in time, the state's intervention increasingly included the cultural realm, with "meaning" becoming an ever more scarce resource. The formation of meaning became critical, an essential part of managing the crisis caused by the inability to proffer the expected rewards for "conforming to the system" (1975:73).

Since Habermas wrote, the dislocations and inequities caused by flexible accumulation have wrought even greater problems of legitimation. The multinational cultural conglomerates and the state, dominating public communications, have responded by channeling the resulting anxieties into a "search for authenticity and authority in politics" (Harvey 1989:292). The result, predictably, has been the most inauthentic and authoritarian of politics, appealing to a mythical past of free-market bounty and relying on both external and internal enemies for confirmation of national identity. Isolationist at home (with respect to economic misery), interventionist abroad, the new authoritarianism has embraced the ethos of flexible accumulation, rapidity making a virtue of rapaciousness, whether on Wall Street or in the Persian Gulf: "If quick, profitable victories can be achieved, they become right" (Tesich 1991:334).[10]

In the rhetorical recourse to the earlier epoch of laissez-faire capitalism ("Morning in America," the "Victorian" in England), the characteristic appeals of authoritarian populism to the past and traditional beliefs seem to coincide with the rollback of economic and social relations developed under Fordism. But that rollback is a response to a new world economy; thus appeals to traditional values are not, in fact, nostalgic at all. One might recognize instead in the "seemingly endless flow of colourful retrospect, simple idealizations of a happy and privileged past," an avoidance of the present in "merely temporary alternatives to the pain of any kind of connection" between anxiety and the policies of corporation and state. Nostalgia, in contrast, is predicated on some engagement with the present, however unhappy (Williams 1989:96). Reagan, for example, "appealed to a kind of nostalgic utopianism, couched in the language of community," yet his policies in the present were ones "that ultimately shatter community," a contradiction not widely faced (Stam 1988:139). Hence the further, unstated paradox in authoritarian populism: "Such [false ideological] propaganda preserves within people *outdated* structures of feeling and thinking whilst forcing *new* experiences upon them." The strain brought about by the transformation of the economy, when felt by many "as inevitably incoherent frustration," thus receives no widespread resistance (Berger 1985: 169–70).

The unusual achievement of authoritarian populism has been the linkage of appeals to traditional values with new economic arrangements (tied rhetorically to the old free market) like "merger mania" and supply-side or trickle-down economics (in reality an upward, torrential redistribution of wealth). The result may seem similar to what were known as trusts in the Gilded Age a century ago, to which Reaganism and Thatcherism often hearkened, but the eighties were "far more mercenary, far more narrowly defined by bucks" than even Thorstein Veblen's epoch of conspicuous consumption. At a time when most people were becoming functionally poorer and the middle class increasingly anxious, the mainstream media continually hailed the engineers of corporate takeover and other arrivistes as the most vital, patriotic personalities in American life. Their profits, though, "tended to come at the expense of other people's jobs, . . . homes, neighborhoods, or small businesses, [and] opportunity was becoming something of a spectator sport" (Shames 1989:71). The most insidious, inhumane revival from almost exactly 100 years before, however, was the language of social Darwinism, recast in theories of "welfare dependency." The "welfare scrounger," often a person from an "alien culture" or race, was the demonic Other of the the possessive individual, the presumably ordinary person (Hall 1988:145). Herbert Spencer's century-old argument that nothing should stand between a man and his suffering was the stuff of State of the Union addresses in the eighties—omitting only Spencer's premise, his bald assertion that social misery afflicts those unfit by nature, who deserve their fate.[11] Advancing the notion that destitution was somehow determined by dysfunctions innate to the individual (not the society), theories of the "pathology of poverty" abounded by the early nineties, most prominently among neoliberal Democrats backing Bill Clinton.

Thatcherism and Reaganism thereby "robbed the word *public* of any positive resonances (as in public welfare or public good), made *private* (private enterprise, private property) a ripping great hurrah-word, and bound *free* hand and foot to the concept of enterprise" (Nixon 1989:17). Legitimizing self-interest, the two leaders damned long-established efforts at social remediation as inherently repressive. Thatcher went so far as to declare that Jesus Christ's self-sacrifice for others was a matter of idiosyncratic personal preference. When "the people" of the United States and England allowed common sense about the state to be defined in this way early on, by Reaganism and Thatcherism, those demagogic, populist appeals could then be accompanied by the imposition of authority and order—the actual *expansion* of state power—against the supposed drags on the economy, from well-paid workers in troublesome unions to social-welfare recipients (Hall and Jacques 1983:10–11). The ruling economic interests broke more expensive labor and curtailed spending on social relief, while fueling the immensely profitable military industry.

It is difficult to understand public tolerance of this plutocratic revolution, unless one bears in mind Hall's emphasis on the populist side of the new authoritarianism. Simply put, the dominant bloc succeeds most when it takes seriously the real concerns of subordinate groups. In the eighties, the state executive branch and big business successfully tapped the "resentment of the 'little non-political person in the street' " by directing it against the *other* large corporate entities, "big government" and "big unions," characteristic of Fordist social democracy as it evolved over the last half century (Hall and Jacques 1983:10–11; see Hebdige 1988:218). The result was "an ideology of selfishness and scapegoats" (Hall 1988:251), and one of the most common Orwellian coinages at present, the description of all groups not representing big business and its politics as "special interests." Corporations, "development," and "growth" presumably serve the general public interest, if through unrestrained individual acquisitiveness: the association of social democracy with the bureaucratic state, as a negative power bloc, allowed "possessive individualism [and] personal initiative" to be counterposed as the positive pole of "freedom." Against social democracy, cast in this light, Reagan and Thatcher, the representatives of the real power bloc, could seem aligned with the people (Hall 1988:142),[12] though the attack on big government was hardly populist, in relieving big business and the wealthy of governmental regulation and progressive taxation.[13]

The appeal to traditional moralism did exploit a space in popular ideologies that is not necessarily regressive, including as it does concern for community and so on. But traditional common sense is also "a massively conservative force, penetrated thoroughly [by] fixed conceptions of the unchanging and unchangeable character of human nature" (discussed in the conclusion to this chapter), and by "ideas of retributive justice." In the absence of genuine educational preparation for democratic citizenship and of any exposure in the mass media of alternative insights into society, the exploitation of conventional popular morality has the greatest "power to map out the world of problematic social reality in clear and unambiguous moral polarities." The theme of crime, for example, allied with "wider scenarios of 'moral degeneration' and the crisis of authority and social values," allowed political issues to be displaced into conventional moral absolutes (Hall 1988:142–43). Extraordinary witch-hunts resulted, like the furor in the United States over "ritual" (satanic) conspiracies and prurient art (see Nathan 1990; Carr 1990b). In the cultural arena, renewed efforts at censorship—not just of pornography, but of phonograph records, radio stations, and schoolbooks as well—aim to stamp out not immorality, as the censors pretend, but dissent. The moral panic over rap music, for example, has fastened on that key word in the avant-garde, summing up dissent in both form and content: *attitude* (see Adler 1990). An accompanying effort at suppressing troublesome information goes on, meanwhile, in government agencies (see Scialabba 1988; Ridgeway 1991a).

Authoritarianism also justified itself in a time-honored manner, through manipulation of paranoia over a bogeyman, an Other responsible for all that ails the society and individual. With dissent and demands for change tied to a vague conspiracy, in a society "mesmerized by *consensus,* whatever the state does is *legitimate* [if done in the service of free enterprise], and whoever threatens the consensus threatens the state." The crisis of advanced capitalism, like any crisis, has necessitated an explanation of its causes, and, of course, the "causes cannot be structural, public, or rational, since they arise in the best, the most civilized, most peaceful and tolerant society on earth." So an enemy is required, a generalized "moral panic" extending even to simple dissent and difference, finally, implicated in the vague sense of a general threat "out there" (Hall 1988:23–24, 33). Thus flag burning, an extremely rare occurrence, could mesmerize the United States, not only as the desecration of the national idol, but also as the threat represented by freedom of speech.

As Hall documents, a significant bogeyman in authoritarian populism was a long-standing one, Communism; "Red Scares" in England had long been linked to the Labour Party in particular (1988:24; see Hall et al. 1978:307, 312–13). In the United States, the election of Reagan revived the cold war and the national religion of anticommunism formed immediately after World War II (see Zinn 1980:416–34). Stressing eternal, absolute essences—the Evil

Empire and American innocence—anticommunism has traditionally dumped the possibility of progressive change in either society down a "black hole" (Kovel 1988:85–86; see also Parenti 1986:113–72), just as neoconservatives assured Americans in the eighties that governments in the Eastern bloc could never be changed. The resuscitation of the national security state served to confirm the preeminent elite interests: massive expenditures on the defense industry, and harrassment of dissidents at home (in presumably Communist-tinged environmental, nuclear-disarmament, and peace movements) and abroad (in Third World nations, like Nicaragua, daring to experiment with independence and social reform).

When Communists refused to play their role and the cold war became unsustainable, the international threat was shifted first to the "drug war," then to the Arab nationalist threat to Western control of oil. Given the reality of the drug problem, it need only be focused narrowly enough, on the Third World and the inner cities, to continue a number of plutocratic policy goals from the old Cold War, including the erosion of civil liberties, and the containment of the domestic underclass and Third World dissidents (see Chomsky 1989). The sudden shift in 1990 from drug lords to Saddam Hussein seemed distinctly Orwellian—as in *1984,* however frequently the enemy changed, the hatred induced by the state and mass media was equally intense.

The neoconservatives, furthermore, tied simple exercise of freedom of speech to the spectre of Communism (though dissent in the East was applauded), linking even the mildest opposition of authority to undermining democracy. During the Persian Gulf War, as a result, protest became synonymous with treason. By this schizophrenic logic, freedom is protected only by surrendering it, while defense of civil liberties is equated with extremism and immorality. One succumbs to totalitarianism in order to escape it; freedom of speech, in many people's minds, applies only to expression favorable to power, not to dissent. The prevailing tone towards difference—in culture, economic status, politics, race, sex—became one of sheer meanness. Deprived of the monolithic specter of communism, conservatives and liberals alike were forced to conjure up an extraordinary range of cultural and social enemies such as the cultural elite, environmentalists, "feminazis," gay activists, the pathological poor, and rap singers.

Authoritarianism and Youth Culture

With the advent of flexible accumulation, wealth is increasingly derived directly from mass communications, from the superstructural
processes with which cultural studies is sometimes accused of being
preoccupied, at the expense of economic matters. Advertising and
media images have increasingly served an important function in the
growth dynamics of capitalism, by accelerating the pace of consumption and instantaneous obsolescence. The resulting "throw away values" suit authoritarianism very well: the "cultivation of the blasé
attitude, myopic specialization [in leisure pastimes], reversion to images of a lost past, . . . and excessive simplification (either in the presentation of self or in the interpretation of events)" (Harvey 1989:285–
87). The culture of flexible accumulation represents a "circulation of
detached and imponderable representations of value, with an occasional freeze-dried hamburger thrown in as a stabilizer." This ficti-
tiousness in communications is now inseparable from the circulation
of fictitious capital. With production (either automated or relocated
in the Third World) of secondary importance in relation to consumption, "Advertising, public relations, and other industries of image and
hype are consolidating into global megacorporations; their prime role
is to envelop a jerry-built material world with provocative tenuous
meanings, suggesting fathomable value" (Ewen 1988:158–59).

The culture of youth, the terrain of the most intensive efforts at
acculturation into authoritarianism, is a useful starting point in as-
sessing the difficulty of resistance against this system. In writing on
the legitimation crisis of advanced capitalism, Habermas finds that
youth is especially relevant to the question of how widespread dissent
might emerge, "as a critical phase in the socialization process in
which it is decided whether the adolescent crisis has a conventional
outcome" (McCarthy 1978:385). A rigid sociocultural system, in his
view, one not moving with the requirements of economic and political
change, can cause "a *motivation crisis*—that is, a discrepancy between the need for motives declared by the state, the educational
system and the occupational system on the one hand, and the motivation supplied by the socio-cultural system on the other" (1975:74–
75). The experience of youth supplies perhaps the most immediate
indication of the correlation, or lack thereof, between the required
motivation and its actual cultural supply.

In this respect, two conclusions might be drawn about the eighties. One is the extreme postmodernist suggestion, derived from the likes of Jean Baudrillard, that motivation is simply no longer required for the horde of passive automatons working in deskilled service economies. Less farfetched and elitist is the second possible conclusion, that the apparent quiescence and authoritarianism of the young might be attributed to a fairly close, successful correlation between the state, education, and mass culture. Both education and entertainment, since the end of the Vietnam era, have clearly worked to reinstill deference to authority figures in young people (see Shor 1986; Giroux 1988), complementing Reagan and Thatcher's denunciation of the 1960s and the "hedonistic anarchy of the decade as a moral wasteland" (Marcus 1989:135). The neoconservative obsession with revenge on the sixties and its youth culture was particularly pronounced during and after the Persian Gulf War, with widely repeated, wildly exaggerated myths about young protestors spitting on troops returning from Vietnam, and so on.

In the field of education, authoritarian populism "has made itself the guardian of the 'return to standards' and of authority in the classroom," as part of its appeal to moralism (Hall 1988:144). Demagogic pundits featured in mainstream media, such as William Bennett, advance what would seem bizarrely contradictory prescriptions for the educational system, calling for students better intellectually equipped for the high-tech world, who have at the same time uncritically absorbed the most hackneyed authoritarian versions of national history—the glories of past wars and so forth. After Allan Bloom wrote his best-selling, if unread book on educational decline, heavily promoted by establishment media, conservative nonscholars like Roger Kimball and Dinesh D'Souza assaulted a largely mythical "political correctness." Such fabrications exploited the general authoritarian construction of good "nonpolitical" conformism and bad "political" dissent, recasting the old academic pretense of disinterestedness as a "nonideological" position.

Authoritarianism among the young, however, is a function not simply of cultural manipulation, but of economic decline as well. Quiescent attitudes reflect the quite real dearth of meaningful employment opportunities for most, and, as Barbara Ehrenreich puts it, the resulting "fear of falling." In Habermas's terms, a crisis in motivation (and hence legitimation) lurks near the surface of the apparent acquiescence of the eighties: it can be quite cathartic for students to confront why, if they live in essentially the best possible social organization, they are so apprehensive about entering it. The young are well aware of the contradiction between the promises of society and its actuality.

Anyone who teaches older adolescents and young adults can recount far gloomier evidence, on the other hand, of a widespread return to traditional shibboleths of conformity, accompanied by a new edge of despair, a tribute to the success of authoritarian culture: the common refrain that "you can't change anything." Young iconoclasts disenchanted with injustice certainly still exist, including both a small minority of activists and a nebulous larger group that responds with anger at the rationalization of social inequity (if confronted with it by their teachers), and empathy for its victims. But many of the latter seem morose, convinced of the cynicism of their doubts by a culture that incessantly affirms the inevitability of the status quo—the *real* cynicism.

Many of their peers simply have no wider perspective than the prevailing politics of self-interest. In the United States, the conformists have actually claimed the following in the classroom: that economic inequity results from some inescapable process, akin to the social Darwinists' survival of the fittest, since everyone has plenty of opportunity, even the same (!) opportunity (though the recent backlash against affirmative action, or "quotas," if logically consistent with this view, may mark an abandonment of any pretense of fairness); that political protest of social injustice is thus unreasonable, unpatriotic, and even unprotected by the right to freedom of speech; that demonstrators representing labor and the left are, consequently, potential bomb-throwing terrorists. To contemporary students, the "simple act of public engagement" in any form is "half-crazy," especially when it involves dissent (Loeb 1990:59). These political views, presented without their context, would likely be agreed to define fascism (in part), yet they simply reflect the typical experience of acculturation at present, particularly the mean-spirited intolerance licensed by Reagan and Bush.

One theorist of postmodernism, Lawrence Grossberg, argues that young people have not really been prey to conservative ideology in the mass media, but suffer from a larger historical diminution in the possibilities for affective investment, or commitment. Many young people, both the best educated and those less privileged, "find it impossible to represent their mood, their own affective relationship to the world" in the postmodern period, in which a valueless world of frantic consumerism, environmental disaster, and nuclear proliferation have rendered terror and boredom indistinct for the young. Nihilism, not conservatism, is the problem, presumably; thus a critic or teacher would be mistaken, says Grossberg, to read the politics of young people "from their tastes, their emotions, their moods, their 'mattering maps.'" One should not conclude that "if some youths like Rambo, Reagan, Madonna, and *Top Gun,* if they felt good when temporary military victories were won, if they want comfort and security for themselves, they have been duped into conservatism."

Grossberg attributes youthful nihilism to the impact of two apocalyptic transformations in social life since World War II, represented by nuclear terror and a new "cultural logic of simulation," in which reality and the image have not simply collapsed but actually imploded into each other, their difference disappearing. Ronald Reagan's ideology scarcely mattered to young voters, presumably; he was more real to them precisely because his handlers were the most successful at constructing him as a media object. The "media logic of indifference or simulation" that produces "authentic inauthenticity" (a mere pose of commitment understood as such) ignores the concrete, encouraging instead the assumption "that all images, all realities are equal—equally serious, equally deserving and undeserving of being taken seriously." For the young, as a result, "the relationship between *affect* and *ideology* . . . has become increasingly problematic. . . . It has become increasingly difficult, if not impossible, in other words, to make sense of our affective experiences and to put any faith in our ideological constructions, even though they still operate as common sense" (1989b:94, 97, 100, 107, 109; italics added).

But one might conclude instead that nihilism *complements* conservatism and the maintenance of the status quo, that conservative ideology, particularly in promoting self-interest, encourages and thrives on a general affective malaise—that emotion, therefore, is a crucial component of ideology. Grossberg's primary example of the purely affective appeal of authentic inauthenticity, Bruce Springsteen, inarguably has an ideological impact as well: recent studies have found that a majority of students ranging from grade school through college erroneously believe that "Born in the U.S.A" is a patriotic song.[14] The simultaneity of conservatism and nihilism, furthermore, is hardly historically unique, considering Fromm's description (in 1941) of the crippling effect of simultaneous credulity and cynicism, of willing authoritarianism and pessimism.

Any realistic portrayal of affect and ideology among the young must be a mixed one. Leading young people through articulation of their experience of both positive and negative ideological meanings and affective responses, moreover, can have results that need not compromise with the perceived "nihilism" and inauthenticity of postmodern culture. Grossberg, however, conveniently dismisses the "self-interpretations" (or "mattering maps") of the young, who presumably can't articulate their experience anyway, and thus believes that employing traditional political categories only reinforces the ideology of the right in youth, unwittingly legitimating its discourses. But in moving beyond critique of the dominant ideology, as well as exposition of oppositional views, he offers only a sparse postmodernist conclusion, outright mummery concerning "empowered nihilism." The oxymoron is belied by his own description of the inability to make any genuine commitment, hardly an empowerment.

This postmodernist embrace of irony, of the prevailing absence of seriousness and commitment, plays into the dominant culture's hands far more than discussion couched in traditional politics does. At a time when a resurgent authoritarianism has attempted to delegitimize altogether oppositional ideas, the postmodernist acquiesces to the argument for their insignificance. The abhorrence of commitment among the young is not a product of epochal historical decline, however, but a specific function of media like television, for example, and its smug irony towards all excessive emotion, especially rebelliousness. Christopher Lasch's *The Culture of Narcissism* ascribes the general flight from commitment not to nihilism, but to the pervasive cultural instruction in the cool management of impressions and images, and the tendencies to cede self-definition to experts and to live through celebrities. At the same time, the fact that the alleged postmodern sensibility is so eminently articulable and representable indicates that its opposite, a critical contumacy, is equally possible. The Trance Farmers, in their recent anthem "Uniform," refuse to embrace the resignation they sum up with clear irony: "Don't be outrageous / Just play it cool / The ruling class is always gonna rule."[15]

If one retains an insistence on moral and political judgment, it is simply impossible to ignore the success of the ideology of the multinationals, generally embodied in some paladin of authority, and in general actively encouraging a distaste for critical reflection on competing ideas concerning the social organization. The infamous film *Top Gun,* for example, actually made with Pentagon script approval, predictably celebrated military technology, as have numerous spin-offs. It subsequently generated a persisting fascination with high-tech weaponry that pervaded soft-drink advertisements and music videos (the sources of the film's techniques, in a stultifying circularity or "synergism," defined later here). Thus, in phenomena like the contemporary cold-war cinema and MTV, a dramatic reversal of meanings in youth culture has occurred: rock and roll "is widely accepted cultural shorthand for anti-authoritarianism; but in these films, the wielders of the absolute freedom of action that is celebrated *are* the authorities" (Levy 1986:443). Acquiescence to the status quo in rock music, furthermore, has been accompanied by renewed efforts at censorship: "the 1980s marked the rise of yuppie rock, in which the ideology of teen is translated into an affluent adult life-style; on the other hand, there has been a moral panic about the rock 'threat' to the family that seems like a throwback to the fifties" (Frith 1988c:127). The coincidence of these developments would seem to be logical enough—after yuppification, what deviance remains is eradicated by state legislators, concerned politicians' wives, and the religious right.

Such phenomena, many have pointed out, indicate that distinction between entertainment and some more real world of politics no longer seems possible. The crisis of legitimation posed by the slowdown of capitalism in the 1970s, and the greater administrative power required to manage the processes of flexible accumulation, make "necessary mass loyalty for new functions of state activity, [and] the boundaries of the political system vis-à-vis the cultural system shift as a result" (Habermas 1975:71; see McCarthy 1978:369). With culture no longer taken for granted, one finds such phenomena as the carefully orchestrated integration of politics with entertainment and public relations in the Reagan era, and the intensifying push for censorship of dissenting voices, the latter reflecting the increasing policing of the private sphere in general.

As a result of the confusion of culture and politics in the new celebrations of authority, the youth-culture audience actually expects the presentation of social conflict—but only if it reflects authority's point-of-view. When confronted with, say, a contumacious political song by the Clash, many young people profess to seek only innocent escape in their entertainment, and to disdain any music or film that reminds them of the world's problems by expressing an uncomfortable social anger, or otherwise demanding their engagement. Yet, paradoxically, their favorite escapist entertainment is full of politics; thus, "By 'politics,' they mean the sticky reality out there, while the fantasy politics of a Stallone or a Reagan offer [a] complete . . . escape from that reality" (Levy 1986:443). The mass media in general rely on "weak or truncated forms of carnival that capitalize on the frustrated desire for a truly egalitarian society by serving up distorted versions of carnival's utopian promise: Fourth of July commercial pageantry, jingoistic singalongs, authoritarian rock concerts, festive soft-drink commercials" (Stam 1988:137). On the other hand, when a star-studded 1990 rock concert honoring Nelson Mandela was broadcast around the world, along with a speech by him, no American television network would broadcast the event, out of concern over its "political nature."[16]

The benumbed contradiction in "fantasy politics"—the professed evasion of ideology coupled with actual immersion in it—reflects the repetitious resolution of social conflict in popular films, music, and television, especially spectacular police actions against any opponents of the prevailing social order, both domestic and international. Such narratives legitimate the power of those "in control of 'The Law' to impose that law upon others" (Fiske, qtd. in Turner 1990:38). When cynicism towards authority does appear, it is often expressed by right-wing vigilantes. Through incessant confirmation of the exercise of power, the defense of economic and political authority comes to appear not political, but *natural*—even "nonpolitical"—with sufficient repetition. The benchmark in characterizing the eighties, of course, is frequently Sylvester Stallone films: when Rambo refought and won the Vietnam War a decade after it ended, slaughtering scores of Asians, audiences chanted "U-S-A," just as they did for Rocky's total victory over the Soviets in *Rocky IV*. In disseminating neoconservative exultation in tests of "will" or "resolve," which required Americans to stomach "charred babies" without guilt (Kupperman, qtd. in Cockburn 1987:398), Stallone and his ilk did a great deal to advance the assault on the "Vietnam Syndrome," or reservation about U.S. violence in the Third World.

Not surprisingly, given the intertwining of authoritarian politics with education and entertainment, the critic of public education (or "indoctrination") and the analyst of mass culture frequently echo each other.[17] The critic of education finds that "school is the ether of our lives . . . that qualifies the young to be effective citizens, . . . cognizant of horror but well-inoculated against vigorous response" (Kozol 1975:11); the critic of mass culture that "enough practice in passivity will make [the audience] cease to value the capacity to judge individually; at the same time it will discourage [it] from forming the alliances . . . that could give [its] responses social force" (Levy 1986:442). College students certainly seem to confirm this pessimism, whatever the combination of sources for such views, in their insistence "that they have the power to achieve six-figure private dreams," at the same time "they believe they neither can nor should do anything to affect the arms race, poverty, race relations, or the other critical public issues of their time" (Loeb 1990:57). The passivity of the young, finally, from the less formal view of the late Abbie Hoffman, has consequences even more immediately tragic than the abdication of democracy:

> people say, Don't waste your time, nothing changes, you can't fight the powers that be—no one can. You hear it a lot today from young people, [who] live with awful nightmares: AIDS will wipe us out; the polar ice cap will melt; the nuclear bomb will go off at any minute. Young people are detached from history, the planet and, most important, the future. I maintain to you that this detachment from the future, the lack of hope and the high suicide rate among youth are connected. (1987:563)

Such frustration and despair are hardly the sole province of youth, of course.

No one is young when a jaded failure of faith in the ability to understand an irrational society, and to change it, is so widespread. If images of youth dominate the media, their audience only "reads them as signs of domestic economic regeneration and a new freedom to impose our will in foreign policy" (Levy 1986:444). There is no essence of youth here, only culturally constructed positions to occupy that connote youthfulness. It is, in fact, "precisely our inability to define 'youth' that signals its status as an increasingly central site of ideological struggle" (Grossberg 1989b:95). On the one hand, youth, the preeminent tool of marketing and entertainment, "is in no way the property of those who are now young, but of the economic system," employed as an expression of its dynamism (Debord 1983:#62). On the other hand, in a more positive light, it is also possible to "call young any individual, no matter what his age, who does not yet [accept] his function, who acts and struggles to attain the realm of activity he truly desires, who fights to achieve a career in terms of a situation and a form of work other than that which has been planned for him" or her (Isou, qtd. in Marcus 1989:271). But the result of the fusion of culture, politics, and the rhetoric of youthful vitality has been a crippling ideological effect, universal arrested adolescence. This arrested development typifies cultural and political authorities—self-interested, narrow in outlook and sympathy, and enamored of the apparent ease of using force to resolve conflict.

The Culture of Images

In order to contain this continual frustration and barely submerged rage, the culture of consumerism preserves a stunted illusion of liberty. Consumption does remain relatively free, certainly; the experience of freedom must have some reality, and thus there exists a "balance between freedom and order. . . . Leisure must give pleasure, but not too much." In the resulting tension between choice and constraint, many cultural commodities "are not necessarily conducive to good order" (Frith 1980:59, 61).

Much more dire views of leisure tend to predominate, however. The flow of commodities and related publicity images in the consumer society, according to many critics, has succeeded in turning their consumption "into a substitute for democracy. The choice of what one eats (or wears or drives) takes the place of significant political choice. . . . All hopes are gathered together, *made homogeneous, simplified.* . . . Capitalism survives by forcing the majority, whom it exploits, to define their own interests as *narrowly* as possible" (Berger 1972:149, 152–53). Consumerism only allows one to be " 'exceptional' within the constraints of conformity," or the specious self-realization of buying things, a distinctly impersonal activity engaged in by everyone else (Ewen 1988:108). People flounder, as a result, in "an anxiety-ridden quest for lost difference" in individual *qualities,* following a logic of mass consumption, or the *quantitative,* "from which difference is banished" (Attali 1985:5). By the logic of consumerism, one becomes more fully oneself the more one is like everyone else. Hence, in part, the increasing antagonism towards difference— whether political, racial, or sexual—that marks recent authoritarian ideology.

Hall, discussing the heavy reliance on images in the construction of authoritarian populism, finds that "people aren't wrong to imagine that what is required of them as citizens is simply to express a broad, undefined 'preference' for one scenario or another, this image or that." But he refuses to conclude simply that politics has been trivialized by the likes of Roger Ailes, Lee Atwater, and their ilk, for images are not trivial things, when "fundamental political questions are being posed and argued through [them]. We need to take them more seriously than we do" (1988:260–61). Nearly every critic who does so arrives at the same conclusion about a culture based on images: the minimal, purely materialistic freedom to consume a plethora of images and goods is uncritically equated with political freedom. In the film *Moscow on the Hudson,* a Soviet defects in the midst of Macy's plenty, and later is reduced to grateful tears by the numerous brands of toilet paper in the United States; in Wendy's ads, a Russian fashion show pathetically features the same outfit for every occasion. The contest between nations and economic systems is thus "reduced to a war of appearances. American capitalism is validated by the suggestive surfaces with which it wraps its products." An extensive choice of images and goods "is regularly equated with a choice and variety in ideas and perspectives" (Ewen 1988:111–12).

Imagistic cues, or fashion, serve in general as a "reference point by which we have come to understand life *in progress.*" Consumption, in other words, habituated to the world of fashion and its built-in obsolescence, becomes the measurement of both personal development *and* social change. Corporations, political institutions, and the wealthy and powerful "employ and project images of stability for themselves," while daily life for most others "carries a visual message of unpredictability and impermanence," reflecting their real social situation, but also acclimatizing them to it. Although this account of the power of images tends towards postmodernist pessimism, anyone involved in teaching, in particular, would find the following a familiar concern: "The danger is this: as the world encourages us to accept the autonomy of images, 'the given facts that appear' imply that substance is unimportant, not worth pursuing." With appearance eclipsing substance in every area of life, especially discourse, and the resulting discouragment of critical thought, the "evanescent becomes increasingly 'real,' [while] reality becomes increasingly evanescent" (Ewen 1988:23, 52, 262, 271).

Contrary to some theories of postmodernism, this debilitating devotion to the ephemeral is not a recent phenomenon: "it is a mistake to exaggerate the novelty of the cultural tendencies detected by contemporary commentators" like Baudrillard or Fredric Jameson (Callinicos 1989:148; see 148–53). The corporate creation of an ideology of leisure, designated "consumerism," actually took place after World War I, as an aggressive "development of an ideal of consumption [that] responded *both* to the issue of social control and the need for goods distribution." From the earliest stages of Fordism, corporate America, through the advertising industry, explicitly set out to imbue the masses with "the character of machinery—predictable and without any aspirations toward self-determination," instead "solving their life's [sic] problems through the benefit of commodities" (Ewen 1976:19, 73, 84). In the postwar stage of Fordism, as automation permitted increasing leisure time,[18] it was further necessary "to ensure that leisure was as boring as the new forms of work," the Situationist International found: "More boring, if leisure was to replace work as the locus of everyday life, a thousand times more. What could be more productive of an atomized, hopeless fatalism than the feeling that one is deadened precisely where one ought to be having fun?" (Marcus 1989:50). The Situationist view is characteristic of anarchism in particular. Other anarchists agree that the "banalities of everyday life, the meaninglessness of most work, our profound isolation from others, and our being treated (and treating others) as objects . . . are *not* byproducts of capitalism: they are *key* mechanisms of social control" (H. Ehrlich et al. 1979:3). The images and goods in capitalist society may present themselves as an abundance of variety, but self-definition on their superficial basis eradicates individuality and difference; quantity supplants quality as the basis of desire.

The illusion of consumer choice, that one has a cornucopia of commodities to choose from—when automobiles, colas, hamburgers, and motels are essentially identical—helps win mass acquiescence to a political system likewise without any really significant variety. Incessantly replenishing a "fantasy of choice,...ad campaigns and brand names drill in us the lesson that sameness *is* difference.... Commercials, which secretly aspire to mesmerism while publicly espousing active choice, provide a model for a politics that aims to maintain diversity in theory while diminishing it in practice" (Levy 1986:443). As politics degenerates entirely into image marketing, the difference between a Dukakis or Clinton, and a Bush, or any Democrat and Republican—though never great—is truly no more significant than that between Pepsi and Coke. In the tendency toward cinematic cliché characteristic of Reaganism, all problems, even real social ones, are reduced to matters of perception; in politics generally at present, as a result, "instead of social change, there is image change" (Ewen 1988:269).

Descriptions of a constricted culture of images represent a classic formalist position (more sweeping than realist concern with content), often informed by the concept of *reification*, which describes an abstraction from material social relations. Reification literally means "thingification: turning into an abstract thing or matter,...the process by which the concrete products of history (social forms, commodities) are abstracted and frozen in an ideational state, where they acquire the aura of 'nature' or permanence" (Ball 1987:26).[19] Authoritarian ideology exploits reification by giving it articulated form, in the "*eternalization* of relations which are in fact historically specific, [a] *naturalization* effect—treating...specific historical development as if universally valid, and arising...from Nature itself" (Hall 1986b:34).[20]

The phenomenon with which reification is often conflated, "commodity fetishism," refers to one effect of alienation in economic production, the perception of commodities as things with a life of their own. (This occurs most conspicuously in the advertising of some products as things coming to life in human form—the Michelin tireman, the Pillsbury doughboy, and so on.) The result is a loss of awareness of the social relations—namely those of exploitation—involved in the manufacture of commodities. In leisure, reification refers generally to any abstraction from real human social relations.[21] This occurs, for example, when a product, a mere *thing*, claims the ability to create a more satisfying life, seeking to efface and supplant the consumer's impulse to test his or her *human* capacities to do so. The "once evanescent phenomena [of] individual emotions and experiences," brought out of oneself by oneself, become associated with commodities presented with "irresistibly alluring images of what [one] could be." Thus the commodity becomes more human while the human being becomes increasingly like a commodity (Marcus 1989:101, 131). Marx wrote in the 1844 Manuscripts that the sense of *having*, the desire for possession of things and their supposed social power, makes human beings stupid, persuading them to yield their "inner wealth to the outside world" (1964:139). Since then, life under capitalism has frequently been perceived to be "caught between the polarities of *doing* and *having*" (Ewen 1988:108). But with new forms of mass communications, emphasizing visual images, the commodity has become an ever greater abstraction. One no longer really buys an article of clothing (like blue jeans), for example, but the designer name (or image) associated with it, no longer desiring "having," but now "appearing" (Debord 1983:#17).

In *Society of the Spectacle* (1967), Guy Debord refocuses the young Marx's and Georg Lukács's descriptions of alienation and reification, respectively, on leisure consumption. The spectacle consists of stultifying repetition, a stream of exchangable images that keeps the spectator-consumer pacified. It is "not a collection of images, but a social relation among people, mediated by images," primarily producing "separation," or alienation. Debord says that one may see what is *possible* (e.g., to be wealthy, to stage a protest), but also learn, by dint of his or her separation from these activities— mediated by mass communications—that they are *not permitted*. And separation from other people, in the isolation of driving a car or watching television, undermines any collective sensibility; the spectacle's monopoly control of appearances forestalls dialogue.

Simply in its form, then, as much as its content, the spectacle generates the "total justification of the existing system's conditions and goals," presenting "itself as something enormously *positive, indisputable* and *inaccessible*. It says nothing more than 'that which appears is good, that which is good appears.'" One no longer understands oneself or one's social existence, having accepted an alien version of them: "the more he [or she] contemplates, the less he lives," says Debord (echoing his own citation of Lukács); "the more he accepts recognizing himself in the dominant images of need, the less he understands his own existence and his own desires" (1983:#4, 6, 12, 30). The decline of having—the already attenuated desire for

possession—into appearing reflects the completed domination of social life by spectacle, the image taking on an even greater "life" than
the commodity. With regard to the consequent alienation, though,
Debord concludes that it would be ludicrous to suppose that an objection to electronic media is that one cannot answer back directly, a
fact omitted by many commentaries on his work. As Raymond Williams says, "the situation is that of almost any reader" of print media,
and thus represents in itself no extraordinary decline in cultural literacy. The techniques of the mass media, if "relatively impersonal, . . . are at worst neutral," and should not be confused with the
uses to which they are put (1983:301).

Authoritarianism, Entertainment, and Information

The reductive appeal of authoritarian images in politics, casting a
contest of moral absolutes in the world, has been simultaneously
played out and affirmed in entertainment. Reagan peddled nostalgia
for an imagined past of national and theological inerrancy, predating
the perplexing, intensifying contradictions of contemporary horrors;
his reference points often included mass culture both past and present, from the Western and frontier myth to new myths of success and
a revived cold-war cinema (see Traube 1992). The entertainment industry clearly served up a concomitant wish fulfillment, in films like
Peggy Sue Got Married and the aptly named *Back to the Future,* both
about time travel to the 1950s. This appeal to the past, the essence
of authoritarian populism, serves the quest for images of stability
necessary to legitimize the hyperaccelerated economy of flexible accumulation. The irony of addressing new economic circumstances
through a rhetoric of outdated beliefs and values is abundantly apparent: working people's *traditional* patriotism, for example, celebrated
in contemporary advertising for automobiles, beer, and so forth,
hardly jibes with their employers' *new* preference for labor in other
nations; these and other *newly* obsolescent economic victims are offered the recourse to *tradition,* or flag, family, and law and order (or
gravitate to right-wing televangelists who trade in traditional theologies of apocalypse).

It must be reemphasized, though, that if mass-reproduced culture
has deleterious ideological effects, much of that ideological work is

done through forms and ideas transformed, even generated by popular life itself. There is no unidirectional, entirely top-down manipulation of the sort taken for granted by the most pessimistic theories. Mass culture does not impose "arbitrary materials on a stunned and passive populace," but instead transforms "elements at large in the culture,... appropriating meaningful elements already extant" (Kipnis 1986:31). There is a circulation, in other words, between the public realm of production and the private one of reception, as cultural studies argues. Commercial culture (the field of production) and popular culture (the uses of those commodities in everyday life) each inform the other. Mass communications, since they "remain dependent on achieving understanding in language," remain open to challenge (Habermas, qtd. in Brantlinger 1990:196).[22]

Most purveyors of mass culture certainly have a benign enough view of themselves, often averring that their motivation in handling topical issues is more financial than ideological. The egregious Stallone simply believes (or so he claims) that film is not "show art" but "show business," and professes merely to pander to prevailing prejudices accordingly. But if the simple drive to maximize profit—the essence of the existing social system—underlies films, music, and television programs, their materials will inevitably contain any conflict within the dominant order, in the quest for popular success. The greatest profit lies in confirming conventional expectations of familiarity and repetition, in both form and content, and certainly not in disrupting them. Interruption, in Walter Benjamin's terms, the effort at functional transformation of the field in which one works, is not a smart commercial tactic.

Perhaps "the crucial distinction for communication in our time, then, becomes that between mass communication in which consumers pay little and are asked only to be counted as witnesses to the ads, and specialized communication that may be noncommercial,... in which there is a shared subculture between makers and consumers that either does not interest most people or offends them" (Budd et al. 1990:173). This distinction is hardly universally applicable, however; the corporate music industry, for example, maintains a close if exploitative relation to independent record companies, which often produces unexpected breakthroughs like Nirvana. The anticommerciality in the commercial/noncommercial distinction, in fact, serves to police such violations of its spheres by feeding an essentially Romantic idealism, verging on elitism, that writes off the possibility of genuinely radical art being produced by anyone with a following larger than a cult. But if the distinction often serves reflexive condemnations of cultural commerce, from a less rigid standpoint it usefully clarifies a significant difference in commercial attitudes, between lusting with an unquenchable thirst for profit and making a living from one's art while preserving idealistic motives. There is no necessary schism between political commitment and making (some) money; many of the individuals and groups valorized in subsequent chapters did take a profit on their productions. As Benjamin puts it, an artist chooses either to supply the field in which he or she works, or to attempt to change it. If the latter course by some fluke pays off, actually attracting some attention to a dissenting perspective, this should be cause for celebration. All too often, "commercial oblivion spoils the aesthetic effect," as in the case of the great Mekons, a distressingly unsuccessful anarchist rock band: "Oblivion is no fun for artists, especially artists working popular forms with putatively political intent, and it's hell on their protein intake. Materially, the Mekons have fuckall to show for their critically acclaimed studio output" (Christgau 1991a:75).

In Stallone's province, Hollywood, the all-consuming drive for profits (typifying the epoch of authoritarian populism) compels media monopolists "to resell again and again whatever sold before, just as the advertisers do." Endless sequels are "franchises"; in a classic example of commodity fetishism, human stars have long been "assets" (Miller 1990:64). The more marked the individualism of such a star, in popular music, "the more convincingly the capitalist order appears as the true basis of individual self-realisation and the more convincing . . . purchasing his record as an expression of the consumer's same individualism" (Wicke 1990:115). The view most commonly expressed by members of Elvis Presley's widespread working-class following, for example, is that he proved "anyone can make it" in America, can rise from poverty to riches and fame.

In the age of "synergism," communications corporations exert their total control of expression not simply by excluding idiosyncratic ideas (with the exception of those of oft-reviled, actually harmlessly muddled mavericks like Spike Lee and Oliver Stone), but especially by converting corporate-generated material in one medium "to as many forms of media as they control" (Bagdikian 1989a:812), as in the cases of *Top Gun, Ghostbusters, Batman, Dick Tracy,* and so forth. The profitability of this repetition would be undermined by innovation at any point in the process—hence innovation refers to superficial devices such as special effects, always much ballyhooed in mainstream coverage of film. The form of repetition represented by synergism eclipses old critical complaints about derivativeness within an individual medium or text, now that "exchangeable homogeneous units" and " 'completely equipped' blocks [of] pseudo-cyclical time," as Debord describes them, occur across different media. The point, he says, "is to wait for [their] cyclical return"—even "if none of them is exactly the same as another, the immense majority of them are so undifferentiated and so dull that they give a perfect impression of similitude" (1983:#149, 152–53; 1981d:24). The new repetition "increases what is already a drug on the market: commercially safe, generic, all-purpose books, films and TV programs," created with an eye to order and routine (Bagdikian 1989a:815).

Regardless of occasionally express "liberal" politics, profit-driven productions must necessarily reinforce at least some of the social institutions that either legitimate or forcibly preserve the status quo, as well as the profit motive itself. When marketing research drives cultural production, "images and ideas not already acceptable to broad segments of the population" are inevitably suppressed, along with cultural and historical conflicts likewise inimical to uniting the audience as a "homogeneous buying public." Petty divisions based on brand loyalty, for example, constitute the extent of difference (Lipsitz 1990:259). Texts aiming only to reproduce the dominant ideology, ironically, may be more likely than liberal ones to have the effect of "challenging the dominant libidinal economy" and its mores (Grossberg 1989b:93), though the libidinal excesses are often merely sexist and/or violent, as in recent horror films.

No matter how critically authority is viewed in the narrative content of profit-driven productions, the resolution of conflict inevitably occurs within the prevailing social order. In 1979, Jameson argued that mass culture effects ideological control by, ironically, actually universally raising utopian desires, or legitimate, "fundamental social anxieties and concerns." But that utopian element is always repressed, in the final analysis, through "the narrative construction of imaginary resolutions," and "the projection of an optical illusion of social harmony" (1979:141). Mark Crispin Miller has suggested more recently that narrative resolution in Hollywood film became entirely insane during the 1980s, in the form of perfectly identical, illogical, unmotivated happy endings. This phenomenon might be inferred to reflect the general authoritarian emphasis on positivity: "each cheery climax functions not to end the story but to liquefy it. [T]he 'problems' that had kept the story going, however minimally, need no longer be resolved" because they are *dis*solved, "in the bliss of being in the spectacle, of being, like the stars, lovingly looked up to and watched over." In stark contrast with Brecht's alienation effect, intended to create a critical distance in an audience, Hollywood narratives offer "the infantalizing promise of *no distance:* no separation, never any feeling of exclusion—not even from the spectacle itself" (Miller 1990:64, 67).

Jameson's account has also been revised in a positive way, to emphasize more the audience's response in the process of arriving at narrative resolution. Andrew Ross points out that the "sexism, racism, and militarism that pervade [popular] genres is never expressed in a pure form; it is articulated through and alongside social resentments born of subordination and exclusion" (even if that sense of exclusion is laid to rest by the end of a story). Stallone's *Rambo* sequels, for example, may resolve fundamental concerns over the cold war and the Third World in the most mindless, militant way imaginable, the violent total victory of the United States, but they do so while appealing to utopian longing for individual self-assertion against state power (in the form of military bureaucracy). A theoretical description of popular culture of this sort, "in its appeal to authority and self-respect alike," improves upon the "conspiratorial view of 'mass culture' as imposed upon a passive populace," Ross finds. Where Jameson (endorsing the Frankfurt School) ultimately emphasizes pacifying resolutions, Ross is less inclined to conclude that the desires, or affective responses, raised in the process are very thoroughly repressed. Jameson would likely agree that preaching only "about the sexism, racism, and militarism while neglecting to rearticulate the popular, resistant appeal of the disrespect will not be a popular politics, and will lose ground in any contest with the authoritarian populist languages" (A. Ross 1989a:4, 231). But in light of his belief (in subsequent work on postmodernism) that all expressions of resistance are received with equal complacency (or passivity, in his earlier terms), he would hardly allow that there is much difference between Stallone and Nirvana, though the latter is not at all authoritarian or exploitative in addressing youthful disillusionment.

Just as Jameson moved on to descriptions of postmodern schizophrenia (a collapse of identity), recent formalist analyses have gone well beyond any claim for coherent ideological effects in popular narratives. Where Ross reminds one of the affective impact of individual texts, the postmodernists find instead that the eroded distinction between image and reality has created a complete dysfunction in the mass audience's affective relationship to the world. Thus, in the worst cases, they rather abstractly assert both the schizoid fragmentation of the subject amidst a plethora of discourses, and hence the supposed irrelevance of the ideological machinations aimed at it, as in Baudrillard's claim in *Simulations* that power no longer exists.

Postmodernist critiques do have a material basis, though, in flexible accumulation and the rapidity of its information-based economy, as well as its dissolution of distinctions between present and future (as in brokerage) (Harvey 1989:291). In their acceleration, ephemerality, and imagistic disembodiment, cultural production and consumption become "progressively dehumanised and 'etherealized'— focused [as they are] round information-and-image-as-product" (Hebdige 1988:165). Because the postmodern information society no longer needs effective social subjects, an ostensibly new mass culture allows one "to luxuriate in one's own loss of will." Where mass culture in the past offered simplistic social identities and models, postmodern mass culture, in its chaotic intertextual flow, "calls into question each and every role that one might care to adopt. There is no position except that of an alienated cynicism" (Polan 1986:178–83). In the "global shopping center," which places a premium on reproducibility in order to maximize regularity in consumption (as in Hollywood's narratives and synergistic spin-offs), consumers "become 'decentered,' and a well-formed interior life becomes an obsolete encumbrance" (Gitlin 1989:55).

In their basic form as much as their content, the argument goes, commercial productions confirm the status quo, particularly in the paradoxical simultaneity of their repetitive sameness and rapid turnover:

they match the intertwined processes of commodity production, predictability and obsolescence, in a high-consumption society. [T]hey help instruct audiences in the rightness and naturalness of a world that, in only apparent paradox, regularly requires an irregularity, an unreliability which it calls progress. In this way, the regular changes in TV programs [and other forms], like the regular elections of public officials, seem to affirm the sovereignty of the audience while keeping deep alternatives off the agenda. Elite authority and consumer choice are affirmed at once.

Choice merely in consumption—here in entertainment—no matter how varied, supplants genuine political choices. Viewers or listeners properly habituated to this intersection of leisure time with the prevailing economic and political interests "experience themselves as anti-political, privately accumulating individuals" (Gitlin 1982:430, 433). In the seemingly unrelated flow of television, therefore, "form responds to function: those heterogeneous fragments start to look and sound more alike once you consider their economic purpose" (Budd et al. 1990:172). The larger "supertext" of television, for example—the program and its interstitial advertisements, and their serial recurrence in the overall schedule—"helps produce and render 'natural' the logic and rhythm of the social order," of the workday, workweek, and leisure. Beyond the role of the advertisement, which implicitly offers a symbolic restitution, a commodity, for the sense of lack in the narrative of the program, the overall repetition of serial forms serves "to continue the subject along the itinerary of habituated consumption, . . . as an answer to the problems of everyday life" (Browne 1987:588–89, 592, 596–97). The "presence of volatile and unstable elements" in culture and society is stifled by "the simultaneous rapid change and deadly repetition [of] simply producing more and more objects for more and more people" (McRobbie 1992:162).

There is something more at work than sheer inundation, though; one should not stop with the observation that television as a whole "purports to offer us a world of 'choices,' but refers us only to itself," just as its advertising offers "no respite from the marketplace but the marketplace itself." That hermetic world also attempts to convince viewers "that our spectatorial inaction is the only sort of action possible" by flattering viewers for the automatic skepticism, the "very boredom and distrust which [TV] inspires" in them. In the process of pandering to those jaded devotees, furthermore, every program from the news to sitcoms actually refocuses that antagonism on the subjects portrayed, through a "seductive irony" lying specifically in more and less subtle derision of any strong feeling alien to passivity—exuberance, negativity, resistance, tension, waywardness. Fed by "the cold thrill of feeling ourselves exalted above all concern, all earnestness," the smug jeering gaze encouraged by television shields the spectator from his or her own actual boredom, rage, and cynicism; the reflexive consumption encouraged by advertisers, not surprisingly, is the only activity safe from mockery (Miller 1986:188, 193–94, 218, 223, 225).

In contrast with television, popular music has been far less narrowly concentrated in access to performance, production, distribution, and audience, and thus the source of the most significant oppositional initiatives in mass culture. But here, too, the corporate recording industry, in its drive to render consumption more predictable, persistently constrains access to innovative and/or dissident records, and to new recording technologies.[23] The abrupt abandonment of vinyl records occurred in part because the temporarily more expensive technology of compact discs could be more exclusively controlled (and a higher price charged). With the technology's dispersal, that control has already slipped (though prices have been artificially maintained), as is the case for many developments in musical recording, such as digital-audio tape (DAT) and equipment. The drive for control of eighties technology, however, did significant damage: the music industry compromised considerably with censors operating in and through the Congress (like the Parents' Music Resource Center) because of pending legislation affecting the industry's ability to police the use of its music, particularly home taping, and its technologies, such as DAT.

The music itself, furthermore, has dwindled in significance with the corporate emphasis on organizing around single heavily promoted, interchangeable figures, thus fueling "a sort of consumer-fan panic . . . that suspends one's very identity in the fear of missing out on what's happening, or what is said to be happening" (Marcus 1990:476). This reliance on pure hype represents another species of synergism, the bulk of the profits from popular music now coming from its use in other forms of mainstream entertainment, including advertising and film. These developments have a great deal to do with the ascendency of the music video, a promotional medium more exclusively controlled by major multinational media organizations, and hence closer to the "world of lifestyle sales." If success in popular music long depended on marketing and promotion as well as music, the two fields coexisted in a potentially volatile equilibrium; try as they might, record companies have never been able to manipulate either the creative process or the audience in such a way as to guarantee musical hits. Video, however, has liberated advertising techniques from the musical product and much of its uncertainty, at the very least bringing promotion more into the foreground. As a result, the forms of music most successfully linked to video have exhibited the "sterile technical perfectionism" of advertising, relying on "quickly threadbare fashionable effects inhabit[ing] a social vacuum"—think of Mariah Carey, Phil Collins, Whitney Houston, and so on (Wicke 1990:127, 162, 166, 169, 172).

The inclination to be either as innocuous or as calculatedly titillating as possible, fueled by the linkage of music and video promotion, has also fed the music industry's willing acquiescence to censorship: "it is commercially important . . . to appear to be on the right side. This is another aspect of the record industry's charity work: rock musicians are now *responsible*" (Frith 1988c:128). The simultaneity of the corporate concern with appearances and the pressure of state censorship also reflect, in general, the prevailing authoritarianism (see Marsh and Pollack 1989; Steinhorn 1990). If popular music has been and continues to be the most significant cultural outlet for the expression of youthful deviance, at long last, it seems, authority finds minimal opposition to a repression beyond the wildest dreams of the racist Citizens' Councils of the 1950s and Spiro Agnew in the 1960s. With many rock musicians celebrating the Persian Gulf War in 1991, and the presumably progressive ones silent, "there can be no other conclusion than that anti-war dissent, . . . in the face of an apparently overwhelmingly popular war, disappeared from sight in a self-serving move to protect access to a mass audience. Music careers, record sales, and stardom prevailed over moral courage and human feeling" (Carter 1991:92).

Political authorities can also count on the the news media to confirm economic and political power, and the state's perception of domestic and foreign adversaries. The selective distortion and suppression of information, like the ideological repression in entertainment, is a function of the concentrated economic control of communication, and likewise keeps significant social alternatives off the agenda, giving the status quo the appearance of inevitability. Myths about a free press remain viable only because the less visible "structures of control within the U.S. media are different from the institutionalized formal censorship we might expect of a government-controlled press." The news media's narrow perspective, "tied to the rich and powerful but not totally immune to the pressures of an agitated public, [can be] propagandistic yet sometimes provid[e] hard information that is intentionally or unintentionally revealing" (Parenti 1986:6). In general, on the basis of self-preservation as well as that of ideology, the editors and producers who decide what is news, appointed by the owners of the mass media, are unlikely "to be interested in emphasizing those events and interpretations that undermine the owners' political and economic interests" (Bagdikian 1989b:32).[24] Hence everyone outside the orbit of corporation and state—consumers, environmentalists, feminists, left-wing activists, the poor, racial minorities—is judged outside the mainstream, if not "extremist." The news media bear considerable responsibility for the widespread perception that "partisanship toward the status quo is . . . nonpartisan. In America, the very notion of criticism is so alien to the national creed of positive thinking that 'bias' is widely believed to *mean* criticism of the status quo" (Lazere 1987:92).

Edward S. Herman and Noam Chomsky, in *Manufacturing Consent,* describe the actual bias of the news media, toward power, not as a function of conspiracy, but of a market system directed by government, business leaders, media owners, and their employees with some power of initiative. Because media organizations, like other institutions, essentially preselect right-thinking people for their "internalized preconceptions [about] market and governmental centers of power," self-censorship prevails at every level. Those persons may believe they reflect as much as shape consensus, but that belief only helps conceal (from themselves as well as the audience) the fact that an orientation to consensus inevitably helps *produce* consent to it. Chomsky and Herman's "propaganda model" of American news media is comprised of a set of filters, including the concentrated ownership of the mass media, the influence of the economic power of advertising over most of those media, and the almost exclusive reliance of the news media on government and corporate information. Right-wing flak, from media-watchdog groups heavily funded by corporations, serves to discipline the media still further (1988:xii, 2).

The first and foremost result is that the news media simply provide constant access to political leaders while excluding strongly opposed views, "delegitimiz[ing] all but a narrow wave band of commentators—either friendly or innocuously dissident" (Cockburn 1986:447). Groups like FAIR (Fairness and Accuracy in Reporting) have convincingly documented the news media's consistent presentation of conservative politicians and corporate spokesmen, and virtually absolute exclusion of any significantly differing views. With the news media oriented to the centers of power, political discourse becomes homogenized, "sterile in ideas for necessary change, deficient in its confrontation with the realities of social injustice, and therefore narrow in plausible alternatives held out to the public" (Bagdikian 1989b:34).

The problem is not only ideological distortion, but also outright omission. When a U.S. Senator (John Kerry), ordinarily a venerated official, investigated drug smuggling by Nicaraguan contras and CIA operatives, NBC (owned by the major defense contractor General Electric) refused to air his findings, labeling him and his information "not in the mainstream." The dominant news sources more typically suppress readily available evidence, usually found in easily ignorable smaller journals, that contradicts the statements of political leaders.[25] There is simply no objective reason, however, that such "rebuttals cannot be given equal exposure and treated with the same urgency and importance as the original charges" by the state—apart from being more factual, rebuttals are certainly no less sensational and hence newsworthy (Parenti 1986:169). Omission also works through the absence of economic, historical, political, or social *context,* from which the spectacle "isolates all it shows," barring any extensive probing of authority's intentions and the consequences of its actions (Debord 1991:28). Anytime the context of events is provided, one begins to interpret them, to be political; thus presenting simple facts, "with interpretation by high officials, is much safer." If independent analysis of the causes and consequences of events is missing, though, the result is not neutral, obeying some stricture of objectivity, but instead "a picture of an uncontested and inevitable status quo" (Bagdikian 1989b:33; see Lee and Solomon 1990). Objectivity, then, entails a strategic confinement of attention to trivial issues (which political players won and which ones lost, for example) that raise no substantive questions about the legitimacy of governmental and corporate policies and activities. Much of the work of the news media is containment, emphasizing unity and normality, and reassuring the audience either that nothing is fundamentally wrong with the political system generally, or that the government is responding adequately whenever crisis is at hand (Hallin 1986:33). Even in presenting the ills of society, when the general imperative to "feel good" may be inappropriate, the function of the mass media is still essentially positivist.

One unique, more specific result of narrow economic control of the news media, contributing mightily to the era of authoritarian populism, has been what Alexander Cockburn calls "news spasms," concerning events like the Soviet destruction of a Korean airliner, the bombing of Libya, and the invasions of Grenada (inspired by the media success in England of the Falkland Islands War), Panama, and the Persian Gulf. The news spasm presents a sensational, usually abbreviated event by allowing the state to dictate not only information, but emotional response as well. Any troubling complicity of political authority in tragic incidents passes without comment.[26] Characteristically "totalitarian in structure and intent, obsessively monopolistic of newsprint and the airwaves," news spasms force "a 'national mood' or consensus in which rituals of grief and vengeance can be carried forward" (Cockburn 1987:406).[27] One critic was finally moved to ask, concerning a renewed spate of hysteria over Arabs holding American hostages (in Lebanon in 1989), "When exactly did TV newspeople become bloodthirstier than the National Security Council?" (Ireland 1989:8).

During the Persian Gulf War, the Pentagon's censorship, disinformation, and orchestration of hostility toward the news media, combined with the latter's obsequiousness and outright cheerleading, painted a reductive picture of a sanitary, just war between good and evil. Both parties were expressly indifferent to determining the actual extent of death and suffering.[28] The euphoric celebration after the war was no doubt facilitated by the destruction of all pictures of dead Iraqis by American newsphoto agencies,[29] not unlike Winston Smith sending inconvenient photos and stories down the "memory hole" in *1984*. Cockburn's conclusion that the American press exhibits a virtually totalitarian unanimity and deference to power fittingly echoes Orwell's suggestion that "when one looks at the all-prevailing schizophrenia of democratic societies, ... the silence about major issues"— that is, the failure to report beyond the line of authority—and "the distortions of the press, it is tempting to believe that in totalitarian countries there is less humbug, more facing of the facts" (qtd. in Sinfield 1989:100). This would certainly seem to be the case given the recent popular revolts in Eastern Europe. In nations nominally committed to free expression, the Situationist International observed some time ago, "What the tolerant people who are in a position to express themselves tolerate, fundamentally, is the *established power* everywhere" (Knabb 1981:178).

Conclusion

According to presidents, teachers, Hollywood producers, and news editors alike, then, only established power deters evil Others, whether Arab dictators or simply all those who are "different," though casting about in the post-Communist world often yields Others as innocuous as performance artists, politically correct academics, public television, or rap singers. Television evangelists, closely allied quasi entertainers who profit from organizing socially powerless, more desperate fringe groups, invent additional Others—in the United States, for example, "secular humanism" and ritual/satanic conspiracies. When such fringe groups and the dominant ideology have verged on one another, in different places and at different times, the result has been some form of fascism. Some worry over this fate in Western democracies; in the United States

> We have watched [the reallocation of] the economic resources of this country, in an exponential leap, to military goods; we have watched ... the dismantling of legislation worked out historically ... to make a more equitable society—the antitrust laws, the labor protection laws, the civil rights laws. We have watched [arise] from dormancy a new generation of know-nothings to [affirm racism], to raise hell with the books in school libraries and texts in grade schools and to support the ideological simplism of [current] foreign policy; we have seen ... contempt for poor people on welfare and for environmental law, as if ... only

poor people on welfare breathe air or drink water. (Doctorow 1986:327)

Treatises otherwise concerned purely with politics and economics now have to allude to mass culture, as well, to explain their perception of a new fascism. A history of the American working class concludes thusly on the present: "Girding themselves for the defense of their accumulated affluence, the new and old middle strata are taking on the armor of merciless resolution—...iconized in popular consciousness by films like *Rambo* and *Sudden Impact*—to exclude and repress the dangerous classes that prowl the circumference of their pleasure dome" (Davis 1986:305).

To create and participate in a politicized art instead, encouraging antiauthoritarianism, it is first necessary to overcome the frustrated sense that society's mainspring is too complex to understand, grasp, and remake. The problem is to step outside and contest what seems natural, but only arises from a particular form of social organization, and its maintenance by dominant groups. An abstract notion like that of "human nature," often invoked by authoritarian populism, poses an interesting example of the difficulty involved, since concrete experience would certainly seem to confirm conventional assertions about it.[30] A variety of cultural sources instruct that no change of social institutions, however radical, would affect human nature, the perpetual darkness of the human heart, manifested in competitiveness, that forever prevents any social organization based on cooperation and trust.[31]

Competition that no one denies to be chaotic is in fact the essence of one particular form of social organization, the one that happens to be in place now—capitalism. The coincidence ought to raise questions about the possible usefulness of human nature in mystifying the current social system. If a competitive society merely reflects common sense about the utterly untrustworthy motivations of human beings, that society's own irrationality would be justified. Reagan, for example, spoke (in a particularly racist code) of holding back the "jungle and restraining the darker impulses of human nature" (qtd. in Gresham 1989:120). In general, says one skeptic, "As long as we each spend our time trying to knock lumps off one another then, apparently, a great civilisation is assured." Authority figures like Reagan, on the other hand, in their self-presentation, seem "by and large exempt from the dark, awful, obscene, violent, greedy promptings of nature that the rest of us are liable to" (O'Flinn 1975:11, 73).

The argument here is not that human beings do not have competitive instincts, or that competition can be eliminated from society, but that "progress must consist in elevating the level and humanizing the terms on which the vital contests are fought" (Eastman 1955:105). Above all, one must recognize who one's real enemies are: if unbridled, cutthroat competitiveness lies at the core of human nature, why do the most successful capitalists—apparently the most perfectly natural members of society—always aim to eliminate competition, through monopolies, cartels, price-fixing, union busting and other often eminently cooperative, hence, one would assume, unnatural activities?

On the historical rather than the individual plane, another form of very general common sense prevails: if capitalism is inevitable, dissent and resistance against it must be chalked up to misguided idealism, if not outright lunacy (both individual and collective). The result of radical change, from this view, is essentially that it produces "big mistakes," apparently regrettable events like the Russian Revolution. Given the number of rebellions against capitalist modernization in every part of the world, however, since at least the French Revolution of 1789, "the number of events that have gone right in the last 200 years can seem oddly small. [A]s long as you assume history and [the development and progress of] modern capitalism are the same thing, you are going to be stuck explaining too many large events with mummery about madness and violence" (Malcomson 1989:59). In a telling self-contradiction at the heart of these sorts of neoconservative arguments, the supposed darkness of human nature that logically compels capitalist economic organization appears insanity when it opposes it. Young people in the United States, whose nation and personal liberties were created by an event entitled, at least, a revolution, will now almost unanimously aver that revolution is both a condemnable event in real life and a negative word in the abstract. But the contemporary neoconservative argument here goes even further: social revolution is a thing of the past; the age of multinational corporate capital will prove eternal (see Hitchens 1989). Competition is supposedly an immutable fact of human nature, on the one hand, yet conflict between ideologies supporting and opposing capitalism has ostensibly ended.[32]

Despite the widespread encouragement of cynicism about both individual and historical action, however, the exploitation of many human beings by a relative few remains a simple but profound fact, known not always theoretically, but certainly intuitively to everyone. That intuition alone, fortunately, continues to supply a basis of antiauthoritarian action. Because the contradictions of capitalism, like the increasing extremes of wealth and poverty, are easily discernible by many people, reification should not be construed as a total, absolute phenomenon: "Not a moment passes without each one of us experiencing...the contradiction between oppression and freedom; without each one of us being caught up and weirdly twisted by two antagonistic perspectives simultaneously: the perspective of power and the perspective of transcendence" of that power (Vaneigem 1983:8).

CHAPTER 3

Theorizing Antiauthoritarian Culture

In converse response to authority's aestheticized politics, subordinate individuals and groups politicize art, publicizing dissenting attitudes. These efforts usually remain limited, at present, to a brief half-life prior to commercial appropriation. But celebrations of anger and resentment, along with expropriations of dominant cultural forms, continue to appear nonetheless. In light of their persisting potential, the study of everyday life matters as much as analysis of power. In examining popular life, furthermore, critics and teachers must heed Antonio Gramsci's warning against a well-intentioned elitism: describing what language will best serve dissent requires one to "demonstrate that 'everyone' is a philosopher and that it is not a question of introducing from scratch a scientific form of thought into everyone's individual life, but of renovating and making 'critical' an already existing activity" (1971:185, 330–31).

To argue generally that popular culture does have resistant elements, on a basis like Gramsci's, ought to be unnecessary by this time, since one posits an academic Other whose "concept of culture [is] so rudimentary that it excludes" that possibility (M. Morris 1988:19). Those Others are still all around, though, particularly in academic institutions, and on the political left as much as the right. On the left, "postmodern disdain for the old Frankfurt School approach to media—the view that mass art is hopelessly degenerate and the tool of the ruling classes—[sometimes reveals], at heart, trendy revisions of

Frankfurtian elitism and pessimism about the ability of average people to be anything but passive cultural dopes" (Rapping 1990:17). The Frankfurt School's presupposition of "the fundamental centrality and cohesiveness of all cultural activity," controlled by a "cabal of executive authorities," has hardly lost its appeal to academics. Where, however, does one "locate such a 'master control room' or institution responsible for monitoring *all* cultural production" (Collins 1989:10)? Contemporary "intellectualocentrism," to use Pierre Bourdieu's unwieldy term, continues to mistake the scholar's subjective relation to culture and society—especially its ineffectuality—as the measure of some objective social condition. Thus the cultivation of avant-garde dissent may still need to argue with the canonized observation that the mass media and political discourse expropriate and incorporate popular languages without contest.

Rather than despairing at the contemporary situation, the anti-authoritarian artist, critic, or teacher seeks out the ways "dominated social groups [can] reappropriate language, allowing it once again to become a medium for expressing the needs and material, concrete experiences of individuals and groups" (Schulte-Sasse 1984:xvi). Untroubled celebrations of popular culture that too steadfastly oppose the curmudgeonly academic Other, however, lose a sense of dilemma in considering the successes and failures of artists and audiences. To discredit the pessimism of the Frankfurt School does not entirely displace it, nor render it an outdated analysis. The "voxpop style of cultural studies," for example, tends to admit the existence of oppression and then, through a simple "yes, *but* . . . ," to find a happy saving grace in the sheer profusion of popular culture, taken as evidence of active resistance—when it ought "at least to do both simultaneously, even 'dialectically'" (M. Morris 1988:20–21). It makes no more sense to valorize popular culture "as a realm of rebellion" than it does to construct mass culture as an abyss "against which all resistance is impossible" (Brantlinger 1990:180).

In their affirmation of the potential of mass-culture technologies and popular responses to them, earlier avant-gardists like Walter Benjamin and Bertolt Brecht never pretended to refute entirely the pessimism of other artists and scholars. But it does seem about time to seize optimistically on the disintegration of the myth of aesthetic autonomy, the collapse of traditional cultural authority in the postmodern era, that allows greater credence for "the displaced, fractured experience of the dispossessed" (Frith and Horne 1987:175). Many younger postmodern critics and scholars, however, dwell on the phenomena of disintegration and fracture alone (hence preserving the Frankfurt gloom), rather than the possibilities they open up. With social fragmentation interpolated into individual fragmentation, questions of ideological struggle are replaced by those of postmodernity. Treatises on how to challenge coherently the dominant culture, and on those actual concrete moments when such cultural rebellion occurs, remain fairly rare.

Analyses and practices that place culture in the foreground, with some hope for its possibilities, have also been condemned for their attention to ideological struggle, at the expense of the "structural underpinnings" of domination, the comparatively "dull compulsion of economic relations [and] different state forms," including the making of public policy (Jessop et al. 1985:122). Stuart Hall, however, chides those on the left who have not kept pace with the enormous cultural changes of the last few decades, even resisting them, out of a profound sectarianism. A damaging tendency has been to minimize the relevance of cultural politics, while valuing only direct political action. The left in general has failed "to see and make contact with the popular and democratic elements in daily life because of the forms in which they are presently packaged or observed." It isn't the commodities and technologies spewed out by mass culture that matter most, but "*attitudes* and practices ... established through the social use of [those] things and techniques" (terms common to cultural studies and the avant-garde alike). Why should any form of radicalism "be a popular political force when it is not a force in the popular cultures and aspirations of the masses?" (1988:211, 215–18, 257).

Cultural activity matters just as much as battles for workplace and state, first of all, at a time when preserving any positive conception of such dissent has become an issue, in developed Western nations; cultural questions, furthermore, pertain to the largest part of life in the consumer society. Fredric Jameson's pessimistic conclusion on the relation of culture and politics, in the epoch of the spectacle, might easily be given a positive inflection: "until the omnipresence of culture in this society is even dimly sensed, realistic conceptions of the nature and function of political [struggle] today *can scarcely be framed*" (1979:139; italics added). They have been framed, belying Jameson, by theorists of cultural and communicative action ranging from the Situationist International (SI) to academics such as Jürgen Habermas and Raymond Williams. The SI's "search for the loci of social power in relations of language, knowledge, and everyday experience," in fact, "provided postmodernism with much of the ammunition for its attacks on established genres of thought and social organisation" (Plant 1992:6).

Scholarship on the left more commonly tends to conceive of cultural politics in the agonized and agonizing abstractions characteristic of postmodernist and/or poststructuralist theory. The problems with much of that theory reflect a mesmerization by the culture of images, in particular, probably greater than that actually experienced by the popular audience. Jameson recently declared video the "cultural dominant" of postmodernism and the schizophrenic loss of social memory (1987:201–2). The abstraction of such cultural theories, at times, seems to surrender to the abstraction of communicative forms, rather than critiquing it. In a dark moment, Stuart Ewen ascribes the greatest power in postmodern life to those "who can mobilize abstractions to the third power, to the formlessness of electronic blips, the record of which is kept in the evanescence of a magnetic charge" (1988:160).

The study of mass culture has long been predicated on the predominance of the image, conveyed by electronic visual media like film and television. To critics emphasizing vision—the least tactile, most abstract sense—the apparent effect of the mass media is a retardation of any very material sensibility. Conventional wisdom does quite rightly hold that "the electronic media have provided a new kind of cultural experience and symbolic environment that *increases* the importance of *images* and *decreases* the importance of *words*" (Kellner 1982:389; italics added). From this view, a subject "external to its world, as the *observer*-subject is,...becomes increasingly impoverished and isolated, and estranged from itself, from others and from the reality of the world it aspires [futilely] to know and control merely by *looking*" (Finn, qtd. in Shepherd 1987:155).

But far from confirming some insidious capacity in the technology of electronic media, "aversion to a relation of ease between the spectator and the art work" also perpetuates a historical mistrust of visual representations, which can be traced to the Talmudic prohibition on graven images and Plato's cave in *The Republic* (Hebdige

1987:50, 53). The conception of the aesthetic developed by Kant led immediately to Johann Adam Bergk's observation that the audience for popular fiction "watches events appear and disappear as in a magic mirror,...stifled by the mass of impressions" (qtd. in Woodmansee 1988/89:215). This criticism of eighteenth-century readers sounds exactly like contemporary criticism of television viewers, which should come as no surprise: in his once-famous history of communications technologies, Marshall McLuhan argued that the printing press, by enabling widespread literacy, first elevated vision and individualism over sound and sociality.[1]

The contemporary culture of the image, therefore, hardly has effects observed only since the advent of recent electronic technologies. Its effects reflect less the form of communication than deliberate commercial attempts to produce easily consumed fodder, which entails rendering "silent and inert a social world that is bubbling [and] evanescent" (Shepherd 1987:155, 157). Williams repeatedly made the same realist argument, that technologies are not identical with the institutions that control them. But many intellectuals, even those genuinely interested in mass culture, continue to reproduce, in essence, the schism between two ways of looking—elite and popular—first formulated by Kant: the first a critical theoretical gaze, properly contemplative; the second a gaze conducive only to simple pleasure.[2] Minimal expectations of the popular audience infect much of the voluminous academic work on Madonna, for example, which has been chided for its "unremittingly visual focus," however celebratory. By reducing all postmodern cultural experience to enthrallment with television, such work misses the fact that "the specifics of Madonna's *music* contribute in no small part to her total triumph" (Christgau 1991b:31).[3] The result of such abstraction from material experience, in recent scholarly analysis, has been particularly disastrous in theories of the subject, in which individuals and the possibility of their self-determined collective organization have very nearly been dismissed altogether. Williams's major legacy to cultural studies, in this regard, is his insistence that "*no* dominant social order and therefore *no* dominant culture ever in reality includes or exhausts all human practice, human energy, and human *intention*," however difficult the emergence of new practices and relationships opposing the dominant culture may become (1977:123–26).

Agency

According to most poststructuralist theories, the sense of oneself as an individual exists because of language, which wholly constitutes and incorporates the subject—as in the process of "interpellation" or "hailing" of the subject, theorized in different ways by Jacques Lacan and Louis Althusser. The power of varioius institutions, as described by Michel Foucault, lies in their domination of language through their discursive practices. In postmodernist theory in general, a similar bleakness over subjectivity has led to a cult of schizophrenia, exemplified by Jean Baudrillard, whose decentered, somnambulant subject floats through "the 'hyperreal' space of an image-bloated simulacrum" (Hebdige 1988:194). The only subversion possible for the "silent majorities" lies in passive hyperconsumption, a "black hole" absorbing all cultural directives. Far from some new insight, this portrayal of hyperreality derives from Baudrillard's early contact with Guy Debord, whose theory of the spectacle is simply taken to a fatalistic extreme: "content to describe and celebrate the ahistorical world of image, sign, and appearance," Baudrillard precludes all critical appraisal of the spectacle. The Situationists, however, considered the fragmentation and "free-floating aimlessness of modern society as qualities specific to the spectacle, arguing that capitalism is largely maintained by its ability to present itself as a chaotic society which has broken free from all sense of historical progress." In Baudrillard's description of the mass of reproduced images and information, in contrast, the fact that there is human agency involved in generating pseudo-events (and so forth)—and in exposing and opposing them—is suppressed. Construing the simulations of reality as reality itself, he merely reproduces the myopia encouraged by the owners of the mass media, and thus happily accepts the spectacle's own account of itself as the only possible world (Plant 1992:112, 150, 168–69).

Two other postmodern theorists indebted to the SI, Gilles Deleuze and Felix Guattari, at least want to base an actual revolution on schizophrenia (see Plant 1992:122–25). Postmodernist and/or poststructuralist theory of this sort even invokes anarchism itself, though it does so in the heavily abstracted terms of "multiple regimes" of power, in which a chaos of desires circulates. As Lawrence Grossberg unhelpfully describes postmodern anarchism, in working with Deleuze and Guattari's *The Anti-Oedipus,* desiring or "analytic machines" engaged in practices of resistance can traverse a complex "multidimensional surface . . . only by mapping [its] various planes." Anarchism is reduced to still another form of postmodern nihilism, distinguished merely by a heightened affective sensibility, a cultivation of molecular (or fragmented), micropolitical desire for the sake of sheer excess, set against a power defined only by its sublimity, or untouchability (1983:68).

This withdrawal from sociality, says Dick Hebdige, "by problematising language as tool and language as communicative medium," tends "to limit the scope and definition of the political (where politics is defined as the 'art of the possible')" (1988:201–2). The real cultural and political crisis, for intellectuals, has resulted from having to face challenges to the prestige of elite judgment, and the increasing impotence of negative academic critiques. Intellectuals, out of pique more than anything, posit their own alienation as a universal condition, an absolute value: "Rather than surrender mastery of the field, the critics who promulgate the line that we are living at the end of everything . . . make one last leap and resolve to take it all—judgment, history, politics, aesthetics, value—out of the window with them." Feminist critics have pointedly noted that when the culture of women and minorities is becoming increasingly prominent, white male critics declare an end to the subject, in a last-ditch effort to forestall the erosion of their privilege. Recourse to concrete cultural practices, in contrast, reveals fairly readily that "lived culture—the experience of actual women and men—can intervene against the bleak perspectivism of certain currently fashionable kinds of crystal-ball gazing" (Hebdige 1987:67, 70, 73; 1988:164–65, 194, 224–25).

The form such pessimism takes is scarcely oppositional, since the frequent accounts of the schizophrenic postmodern subject only succeed in describing the ideal consumer from the perspective of the multinationals—a person who lives entirely through fragmentary libidinal contacts with the cultural technology of an unprecedented sensorium. The emphasis on evanescence, along with merely theoretical invocations of the body, merely confirms the abstraction of a culture ruled by the nonsensuous experience of visual images. The cultural theorist, as readily as the dominant culture he or she wants to fight, eclipses material experience.

The pacifying effect of the spectacle, though, is never the result simply of its collection of images, but the social relation among people—the powerful and their subjects—mediated by images. The dire accounts of ideology, knowledge, and power associated with many poststructuralisms, however, remove this social element, denying the viability of the subject. To Foucault, for example, "the play of signs defines the anchorages of power," without reference to any resistance in the process: "the individual is carefully fabricated" by power (1979:217).[4] As in so much theory in the postmodern period, a residue of modernism remains, in Foucault's aestheticization of power and its "triumphant Nietzschean growth, unfolding and proliferation." Foucault's version of power "has much in common with the classical aesthetic artefact, self-grounding, self-generative and self-delighting, ... a kind of subject all in itself, however subjectless it may be" (Eagleton 1990:388, 390).

According to Ferdinand de Saussure's linguistic structuralism (developed at the beginning of the century), in any use of language the signifier and signified, or form (acoustic image) and meaning (concept) of a word, are disjunct; their connection exists only by dint of arbitrary convention. The larger structure or laws of language (*langue*) and actual individual speech acts (*parole*), on the other hand, are presumably inextricable; in the absence of historical and social context, in Saussure's work, the former appears to determine the latter. Whether in micro- or macrocosm, then, language is treated in essentially absolutist fashion, without regard for the actual dialectical relation that exists in each case. In the poststructuralist adaptation of Saussure, the Symbolic Order of a linguistic system, to use Lacan's terms, represses the expression of desire and imagination by subsuming altogether the individual, who becomes a "subject" in the most fully abject sense of the term. If *langue* virtually dictates *parole,* the subject's use of language manifests only an utter absence of authenticity; any sense of a speaker or writer's "presence" is therefore illusory. Jean-François Lyotard, writing on the "postmodern condition," finds that "the social bond is linguistic," but consists of an indeterminate number of language games that do not add up to "stable language combinations" and "are not necessarily communicable," the subject dissolving in those myriad games (qtd. in Harvey 1989:46). This sort of poststructuralist theory, as chapter 1 argues, only updates modernism's preoccupation with the evanescence of meaning, based in its pessimism about history, by writing off the individual as well.

In fact, "the *laws* (of language) can never explain the *act.* ... Language as a system furnishes the formal *conditions* of *possibility* of speech but has no purchase on its actual *causes*" or results (Anderson 1983:48). Mikhail Bakhtin's dialogical theory, in contrast with the various structuralisms, considers discourse as a material social phenomenon, in which a dialectical relation exists between between linguistic structure and the individual (and between form—sound or visual sign—and content in language, a relation elaborated in chapter 6). The considerable career of postmodernist/poststructuralist theory is particularly disheartening in light of Bakhtin's long-standing, unheeded call for a more concrete approach to discourse. Bakhtin counters the Saussurean tradition by refusing to regard "speech as individual and the language system as social, and therefore as antinomies." The original Saussurean *langue/parole* dichotomy actually "implicitly reproduces the venerable bourgeois individual-versus-society trope" running through Romantic and modern aesthetics of autonomy (before postmodernism evacuated even that modest faith in the individual), aesthetics Bakhtin takes pains to reject. (The divide Paul Valéry draws between pure poetic sound and banal practical sense, or signifier and signified, actually uses Saussure to update Symbolist ideas.) Language, in Bakhtin's view, may to some extent be a medium of oppression, just as the modernists believed. But in contrast with their desperate experimental escapes from commonplace language, he understands everyday discourse to be perfectly capable of enabling the individual's process of self-definition. Language from every source, including the mass media, is "processed dialogically so that the words in a sense become half 'one's own words.' With maturity, these words transform themselves [into] internally persuasive discourse," separated in the individual's consciousness from authoritarian discourse (Stam 1988:119–20; see also Bourdieu 1991).

Bakhtin's epistemology, developed at the same time the avant-garde was challenging modernism, absolutely reverses the relation perceived by many poststructuralist theories between the individual agent and language (or power or ideology). He begins with the acquisition of language and the individual's development through it, in which language and ideology are not the same thing; ideology is always articulated through language. Identifying the operations of ideology with those of language (as when Althusser borrows from Lacan the concept of interpellation) typically construes ideology as irresistible, deeply embedded in language acquisition, and the subject as passive, formed entirely from without by discourse. In cultural studies, in contrast, "the articulation of ideology within language and within institutions" is always understood to involve a "dialectic between *autonomy* and *determination*," between the subject's active production of meaning and passive absorption of it. This theoretical approach to ideology underlies all the key debates in cultural studies, concerning "the study of texts, of audiences, of subjectivities, of institutions, and of the construction of everyday life." If the split between culturalism and structuralism (discussed in chapter 1) has dissolved, says Graeme Turner, "the three-way split of economic versus cultural determination versus individual agency still dominates" arguments about ideology. He finds that the turn to Gramsci and the idea of hegemony, with its sense of a contested process between and within each area, "appears to accomodate all sides of this theoretical triangle" (Turner 1990:205, 209–11). But Bakhtin describes even more fundamentally, in language itself, the underlying basis of the continual dialectic between independence and incorporation, in a subject's ideological life.

A section of his essay "Discourse in the Novel" (entitled "The Speaking Person in the Novel") only briefly develops issues relevant to large bodies of work in linguistics and psychology,[5] but does so with an unusually pointed emphasis on the subject's relationship to *authority*. The subject, he says, does not develop into the iron grip of the various discursive practices already arrayed to ensnare it, but instead grows more independent of them (to a varying extent, certainly). This is not to equate agency with voluntarism or free will, but to its production out of contradictoriness (Fiske 1989:181). This epistemology has the virtue of according with what would certainly be a consensus concerning individual experience: even if circumspection or training inhibits overt antagonism, maturity brings a greater, not lesser ability to resist authority.

Bakhtin begins his epistemology with the recognition that "our speech is filled to overflowing with other people's words," not unlike the structuralist point that the codes of language precede and incorporate the individual subject. But he does so to assert the ways in which the individual makes those words partially his or her own. If one pays attention "to the speech sounding everwhere around us," the materially present, speaking person might be recognized as a genuine "*subject* for the engaged, practical transmission of information, and not as a [mere] *means* of representation"—not, in other words, as a mechancial conduit for language. From this perspective on the speaking person, Bakhtin goes on to "the deeper semantic and emotionally expressive levels of discourse," and the way they seem to work "to determine the very bases of our ideological interrelations with the world." But, he argues, authoritative discourse only *attempts* to perform as one's own internally persuasive discourse. The authoritative and the internally persuasive are in fact characterized by a sharp gap. A continual struggle goes on between these two categories, and it is this struggle that determines consciousness.

The authoritative word is distanced from the subject, "organically connected with a past that is felt to be hierarchically higher" (as in poststructuralism)—connected with a prior discourse, that is, demanding unconditional allegiance, indissolubly fused with authority. But, crucially, that discourse can be profaned, once the subject "awakens to independent ideological life" and an awareness of the alien discourses surrounding oneself. At some point "rather late in development" begins the process of distinguishing between internally persuasive and authoritative discourses. The internally persuasive word remains "half-ours and half-someone else's," but this recognition is a far cry from ignoring such nuances, which "leads to a reification of the word," an abstraction of the word as an object or thing, removing it from its living use. The internally persuasive word in fact awakens new, independent words, or new *inflections* of old words at least, in response to new material and conditions, struggling all the while with any number of other internally persuasive discourses one has acquired. In the dynamic process of finding one's own voice, through struggle with another's discourse, individuals "will sooner or later begin to liberate themselves from the authority of the other's discourse," Bakhtin believed (1981:337–48, 352). Authoritarian cultures certainly inhibit this development, but the optimism in the phrase "sooner or later" is not untenable, if taken to refer to a historical potential rather than an inevitability at every place and time.

More recently, Paul Smith has described subjectivity in not dissimilar terms, while adding an important consideration of the role of the unconscious. Bakhtin was a severe critic of what he perceived to be the ahistoricism of Freud, and had little patience for theories of the unconscious. Smith begins with the firm assertion that the subject should never become, as in so much poststructuralist work, a purely theoretical entity removed from political realities. He insists on distinction of the human *agent* from both the "subject" and the "individual," as "the place from which resistance to the ideological is produced or played out." For him, as for Bakhtin, the subject exists within ideological experience, such that conformity and resistance operate on the same ground. No theory of agency could sensibly posit that resistance comes from somewhere outside language, ideology, and other structural fields—it is produced in the same processes that can also inhibit it (a point prominent in cultural studies). Accounts of the process of interpellation (through which the subject's very sense of its existence is constructed) must acknowledge the temporal life of the subject, a singular, "whole history of remembered and colligated subject-positions" (P. Smith 1988:xxxiii–xxxv, 37).

Smith's essential thesis about the interaction between particular cultural texts and agents must be kept in mind, in descriptions in later chapters of subcultural activities: "practices of resistance do not necessarily function with any coherent sense of what it is that informs and necessitates them. [R]esistance involves not just conscious self-constituting acts, but also the agent's individual history" or memory. It may be questioned whether the idea of fully conscious, knowledgeable, intentional activity must in fact be abandoned, but to some extent, certainly, "social meanings and practices are negotiated [in the unconscious] *prior to* and *simultaneously with* any activity of the conscious agent." Though this thesis flirts with post-Marxist erasure of the agent's volition, Smith clarifies that the unconscious is not the cause of the subject, but the "active break" or " 'edge' at which the 'subject' is structured" in relation to language and ideology. There is conflict at that edge, the unconscious standing *between* subject and authority. Human action is always mediated in part by the unconscious, and the pressure of structural forces, as well as conscious volition, has something to do with that action (1988:66, 68, 72–73).[6]

The materialist sense of the development of agency through language has more recently been a critical component of cultural studies, which would, as in dialogical theory, reconcile the structural (or abstract systems) with the cultural (or concrete practices in everyday life). Richard Johnson points out that poststructuralism seems to have no theory of subjectivity at all, given its reduction of "productivity" to that of dehumanized signifying systems of language and other codes, abstracted from social processes. In particular, it offers no satisfactory account of the "continuity of self-identities from one discursive moment to the next" (a point made by Smith as well), no sense of the constant *cumulative* rearrangements of a sense of self, where postmodernists perceive only fragmentation. Crucial insights into language have thus been foreclosed: "namely, that languages are produced (or differentiated), reproduced and modified by socially-organized human practice, that there can be no language without speakers, and that language is continually fought over in its words, syntax, and discursive deployments." Attention to the reader or speaker in society reminds one that "the flows of inner speech and narrative... are the most empirically obvious aspect of subjectivity." These internally persuasive discourses provide the basis for recovering, in theories of agency, not just the elements of self-production in language, but the outright struggle in which individual or collective subjects "produce accounts of who they are, as conscious political agents." The concern of cultural studies with this process might be thought of as "post-post-structuralist" (R. Johnson 1986/87:63–69), in the sense that cultural studies is "anti-individualist or anti-subjectivist because it locates the sources of meaning... in social relations, communication, cultural politics" (Brantlinger 1990:16).

Working in part from the Marxist psychoanalytical criticism of Julia Kristeva (while noting the problems posed by her absolute valorization of bodily over ideological experience), Paul Willis further argues that less consciously directed will and action can make *collective* interaction possible, as well. A "pure expressive purpose," or full consciousness, is not absolutely essential. The creative activity of social groups who "expose and cast into doubt the workings of the larger ideologies, [may be] achieved without any necessary direction, intention or purpose. It happens almost by the way, as if a by-product, in the immediate concerns of the day to day culture," and its "unconsciously revelatory probing of the world and its fundamental organisational categories." The results provide a sense of self-determination and a fuller "grounding for cultural activities, style, and attitudes which [are felt to] hold a greater relevance and resonance than can be directly explained" (1981:120–22, 125, 173)—an apt description of youth subcultures in particular.[7]

In the turn from the individual to the collective, the crucial question concerns how individual anarchs band together in the larger collectives necessary to make any inroads against an authoritarian culture and society.[8] The description of a genuine dialectic between individual and collective agency, in aesthetic theory, has been the province of the avant-garde, which in a sense seeks to enact the original promise of the aesthetic. The aesthetic held at its origin "a vision of human energies as radical ends in themselves which is the implacable enemy of all dominative thought" (Eagleton 1990:9). The pedagogical aim of the avant-garde, accordingly, is an empowered community of agents, but the work of Benjamin and Brecht concerns just the initial relation between artists or producers and their audiences. The further question concerns what goes on in lived culture among the critically empowered members of those audiences, once they have appropriated and used a text.

With regard to such activity, Raoul Vaneigem of the Situationist International presents a stark contrast with Deleuze and Guattari, in his argument—derived from a number of anarchists—that individual agency is realized precisely through collective solidarity (rather than a fleeting plurality of molecular desires). He cites Saint-Just, for instance, a revolutionary of 1789, who held that fighting for everyone else only results from fighting for what the individual agent discovers that he or she loves most, namely other human beings. That love, Vaneigem specifies, emerges from the desire for communication (1983:184, 190). He might have cited Bakunin as well, who held that "man completely realizes his individual freedom as well as his personality only through the individuals who surround him" or her. A materialist "conception of freedom is therefore a very positive, very complex thing, and above all, eminently social" (1980:236, 238).

Radical subjectivity, in Vaneigem's terms, hardly entails the fragmentation or outright evacuation of identity, as in poststructuralism, but the rediscovery of it in a dialectical, pedagogical exchange between individual and group. The very "reflex of identity," in his view, consists of "the desire to find the richest and truest part of ourselves in other people." Through such identification with others, "we lose our uniqueness in [a] multiplicity of roles," but at the same time "strengthen the wealth of our *individual* possibilites in the *unity* of federated subjectivities." In terms resembling Bakhtin's work on Rabelais, Vaneigem describes revolutionary moments as "carnivals in which the individual life celebrates its unification with a regenerated society," a solidarity achieved through the playful invention of identities. This conception of a new game that everyone involved helps elaborate, he realizes, gives the appearance of a relatively untroubled faith in the subjective will. He adds, therefore, that if "everything starts from subjectivity, . . . nothing stays there" since collective activity is imperative: subjectivity "is rooted in the desire to realise oneself by transforming the world" (1983:7, 82, 105, 190–91; italics added).[9] As Debord puts it, the "subject can only arise out of society—that is, out of the struggle that society involves" (qtd. in Plant 1992:73). Vaneigem's subject, in other words, "is not waiting in some haven for the day of its release," secure in the sort of universal foundation postmodernism has picked apart. Radical subjectivity only "emerges in the course of its daily resistance to the spectacular relations in which it arises" (Plant 1992:62, 74)—much like Bakhtin's subject struggling with various authoritative and internally persuasive discourses.

Though Vaneigem emphasizes eroticism and play more than organization and reason, he obviously retains a faith in collective interaction that violates postmodernist strictures on any residue of the Enlightenment, in this case the notion that social transactions occur among coherent subjects. But the field of aesthetics, at least, that developed during the Enlightenment could have been and could still be emancipatory (as the first chapter indicates), in its initial concern with both pleasure and intellect, or experience both exterior and internal, social and individual. That long-standing potential is reflected by the continuity between recent versions of interindividual agency, like Habermas's theory of communicative action and Williams's "long revolution" in communication, and earlier progressive aesthetics like those of Bakhtin, Vaneigem, and other anarchist avant-gardists. Sharing their fundamental materialism, Habermas and Williams insist that language is a constitutive element of all social practice. In the work of both critics, language refers to ordinary everyday communication, "a quite different starting point from the abstractions of language that appear . . . from Saussure to Derrida." In Habermas's theory (as in earlier Frankfurt School work, by Theodor Adorno and Max Horkheimer, on the "dialectic of enlightenment"), the enthronement of human reason as the basis of social organization in the eighteenth century was a double-edged sword: instrumental reason (oriented to material goals and success) has distorted discourse, predominating over communicative reason (oriented to reaching communual understanding). If communication became truly social, or dialogical, the "project of modernity" or Enlightenment (the rational organization of society) could be revived and redeemed (Brantlinger 1990:183, 190).[10] In the cultural and democratic revolutions since the Enlightenment, Williams finds a persistent human energy springing from the conviction that men and women can discover new common institutions: "If man is essentially a learning, creating, and communicating being, the only social organization adequate to his [or her] nature is a participating democracy, in which all of us, as unique individuals, learn, communicate and control" (qtd. in Brantlinger 1990:59, 183). Far from rosy idealists, Habermas and Williams realize that such communication necessarily depends upon the mass media, which will only facilitate democracy if the present concentration of their control is broken; both invoke the avant-garde (to a greater extent in Williams's case), particularly Benjamin and Brecht, to indicate the need to engage with new cultural technologies.

Terry Eagleton—like Patrick Brantlinger, above—synthesizes Habermas and Williams, noting that the latter's emphasis on specific social situations, in communication, serves to ground the universalism of Habermas's theory. On the basis of this synthesis, Eagleton argues that a truly radical, dialogical politics would ask what the reciprocal self-fulfillment of *love* "would mean at the level of a whole society," exactly the question addressed by Vaneigem (and other anarchists—see Read 1971:30). And just as Vaneigem stipulates that the collective resolution of this question requires "the most thoroughgoing fusion of reason and passion" (1983:183), Eagleton calls for a materialist ethics, concerned with "pleasure, fulfillment, [and] creativity" as well as "the most rigorous analysis and discussion." This dialectic would, in effect, realize the original promise of the aesthetic, by drawing together affective and intellectual experience. In the subsequent argument over "which and whose desires should be realized and which constrained," finally, the dialectic of individual and collective emerges: in "demanding an equal right with others to discover what one might become," individual difference necessarily passes through collective identity, "if it is to come into its own" (1990:413–14).[11]

These theories of the potential of dialogic interaction have had especially strong confirmation in cultural studies, in work on subcultural styles—ensembles in the sense of persons as well as objects. One's political identity "derives in large part, and this is not sufficiently remarked, from involvement in a milieu. So an individual discovers a certain kind of selfhood in relation to others," precisely the way a "subculture sets the framework of understanding" (Sinfield 1989:266). Embracing the different attitudes and forms of expression presented by others liberates the subject from the alienated atomization, the separation characteristic of the society of the spectacle. Willis grounds this sort of group interaction specifically in a "battle" fought through language, including symbolic systems stretching from language itself "to systematic kinds of physical interaction; from particular kinds of [antagonistic] attitude, response, action and ritualised behavior to expressive artefacts and concrete objects." The group's demystification of social conditions, of course, is not necessarily conscious and deliberate. As "a subject in its own right," the group likewise responds to unconscious pressures in the sense that it is "not limited by the previous knowledge, experience or ideology of its individual members," and the collective creative results are irreducible to "any one person's head [or] individual subjective will." Willis, like Bakhtin, does not mean "to deny individual consciousness and language use in their dialectical connection with class [or group] practice," but to clarify how critical meanings first arise, before being "diverted back into the group . . . to inform, enforce and shape many other kinds of physical and stylistic practices" by individual members (1981:124–25, 172). In a fine dialectical expression of this exchange, Pete Townshend once said that the mod subculture, in the 1960s, "taught us in [the Who] how to lead by following" (qtd. in Wicke 1990:76). The initial formation of a subcultural style may not be entirely intentional, either, as the case of the teddy boys indicates in the next chapter, but once identified, that style may be used quite deliberately.

The last question with regard to agency concerns just what federated agents can accomplish, in confronting authority in cultural and political institutions. That question is best answered by the concrete examples of subcultural activity in the second part of this book, activity that the remainder of this chapter introduces on a theoretical basis. The essential achievement of collective subcultural agency might at this point be expressed in terms of the struggle over hegemony, over the power to define ideological common sense. The ruling bloc of social groups seeks to contain common sense within as tight a frame as possible, to render strongly oppositional voices and their content virtually unspeakable and unthinkable for subordinate individuals in general. The subculture has functioned in one of two ways.

First, some groups consciously break that hegemonic frame around common sense by injecting significantly deviant voices, images, and ideas into cultural and political discourse. Such activity, however, requires some sort of intrusion into the mass media, and those media often serve the leading role in constricting common sense by either omitting or incorporating oppositional expression. Hence one key problem concerns how one becomes unignorable and (briefly at least) unincorporable, short of the outright destructiveness, even self-immolation, that confirms common sense about the virtual criminality of radical alternatives to the status quo. But this last ploy of the mass media, demonization and ostracism of deviance, raises the second function of the antiauthoritarian group, characteristic of the English youth subcultures described later. The subculture has often not contradicted common sense—indeed, even confirmed it—but done so through a sort of parody of it, even if that parody was relatively unconscious on the part of some members (in the progressive sense of the unconscious, as the "edge" at which the subject encounters ideology). That parody, typically in caricatures of mainstream images and ideas, amounts to an exposé of common sense, specifically its formation out of a range of demagogic stereotypes. In winning vituperative response from the mass media, which typically disapprove of youth cultures as "meaningless" or unreasonable, the significance of youth subcultures lies in bringing fully to light the continual "attempt by the dominant culture to reaffirm its own view of society as the only correct one" (Clarke and Jefferson, qtd. in Muncie 1982:58; see Leland 1991). The function of subcultures accords quite well with the Situationists' insistence that "any critical project must endeavour to sidestep and expose the whole process by which criticism is turned against itself" (Plant 1992:76).

The element of parody in some postmodernist art and literature might easily be perceived in everyday life as well, likewise functioning "to foreground the *politics* of representation," even the entire representational process. Subcultural activity, in this respect, is a far cry from the fragmentary, "value-free, decorative, de-historicized quotation" usually associated with postmodernism. If that parody "both legitimizes and subverts" its object, it nonetheless offers "a certain self-consciousness about our culture's means of ideological legitimation," not unlike the mixture of conscious and unconscious responses in the youth subculture. As the avant-garde would have it, artist and audience are as one in parody of this sort, in that it also contests "assumptions about artistic originality and uniqueness" (Hutcheon 1989b:93–95, 101).[12]

In postwar England, the first function of the subculture, the intrusion of deviant voices, has typically occurred as a result less of subcultures than of particular musical groups. Larger collective initiatives, coalescing around music, have performed the second function, the parody of the dominant culture's response to both the music and its audience. The same phenomenon has occurred more recently in American culture, in the outrage courted and encouraged by rap music and the hiphop subculture. Their success has been to throw back hyperbolic versions of deprived and depraved black youth at authoritarian culture, which peddles terror over urban crime rather than outrage over urban blight. Just as writers living in dangerous times may use allegorical indirection to express dissent, a subculture may necessarily be confined to the symbolic tactics of caricature, to find some space for expression.

This sort of imaginary, symbolic activity does not have immediate political results, as subcultural sociology has always acknowledged. Subcultural styles are invariably incorporated to some extent, ideologically (through official tolerance, naturalization by the media, and so on) as well as commercially. Their significance lies not in direct politics, but in the pedagogical exchange described by Willis and Townshend, in the lesson of contumacious, critical response for members of the group and whoever else might comprehend them. There is obviously a great deal of teaching and learning to be done, however (unless increasingly dire straits accelerate the process), before the number of people demanding a different, better world will be sufficient to counteract the current plutocratic ruling bloc. The incipient collective agency of a genuine community of individuals needs first to find requisite forms of expression, to arrive at a mutual identification based in sensibility—in indignation, moral compulsion, and so forth—as well as ideology. The aesthetic has plumbed both areas of experience; if it has rarely done so with any sort of dialectic between affect and ideology, body and intellect, that is precisely the problem that avant-gardes, including popular cultural initiatives with similar if less theorized objectives, propose to remedy.

Cultural Materialism and Everyday Life

If alternative views of society are to emerge from something akin to subcultural interaction, it is the dominance of surface over substance, in particular, that must be overcome, whether in everyday life or scholarly assessments of it. "Only then will people be able to ensure that the imagery of pleasure is joined to the experience of pleasure," and to "the principles and practices of a human community" (Ewen 1988:271). The goal, therefore, is not to substitute one form of abstract consciousness, or ideology, for another. Instead, consciousness and its expression in ideology must be understood to be inextricable from material social processes of making meaning. Williams, the champion of cultural materialism, stresses the "human-sensuous" production of meaning through the variety of discourses, objects, and activities that generate signs of all sorts. The density of his later, more theoretical work in this area represents a determined attempt to express the simultaneity and interrelation of the two paradigms of cultural studies, culturalism and structuralism (discussed in chapter 1).

Culture, in Williams's work, is a material practice, including both consciousness, or definitions of experience, and actually enacted ways of living—both the meanings and values through which individuals and groups respond to the conditions of their existence, *and* the lived practices through which those understandings are expressed and embodied (Hall 1981:26). Ideology by most definitions includes the first category, the conscious and unconscious mental structures acquired through discourse, but Williams's second sense of culture—as active expression, not mere consciousness—leads to a conception of ideology grounded in affective experience. A practical consciousness develops in labor through material processes and social relations (through forms of discipline like work speedups and drug testing, for example); in leisure, through the thinking and imagining produced by the equally material, social experience of sights, signs (both verbal and written), and sounds. In every area of experience, "meanings and values are actively lived and felt" through the physical "elements of impulse, restraint, and *tone*," found in all communication. Ruling out no form of art, Williams pointedly includes printed material, voices, and music. Emergent, oppositional cultural forms, finally, effecting changes in "structures of feeling,"[13] include both "thought as *felt* and feeling as *thought;* practical consciousness of a present kind, in a living and interrelating community" (1977:62, 128, 132).

The practical links between ideas and everyday life, as Bakhtin insists, lie in the processes of signification, which are all fundamentally material, *shared* ways of both feeling and thinking. The dynamic, transforming activities that go on in everyday life, in which signs "are translated into personalized styles [and] inhabited, appropriated," do produce consent as well as rebellion, to be sure. But in determining the difference, one should not, since ideology is all around us, measure "the struggle for change along the yardstick of a non-ideological reality, ... which contests the 'false' world of ideological appearances" (Chambers 1986:185, 212).

In the midst of the predominantly empty moments of everyday life, everyone already experiences virtually poetic moments of desire, according to sociologist Henri Lefebvre, when love of one's fellows and hatred of authority burn for justice. At once all-powerful and powerless, such moments, if recognized, "could form the basis for entirely new demands on the social order," because the thoughts that arise are not satisfied "by the systems of compensation. The rub [is] that no one [knows] how to talk about such moments." A theory of *moments* requires a still "unknown language necessary to talk about the pieces, fragments, moments" that only emergent cultural forms have the power to provoke, and thereby "spark a 'permanent cultural revolution.'" The Situationists derived in part from Lefebvre[14] the basic concept of the *situation,* or "moments of rupture, of acceleration, revolutions in everyday life." Situationist theory held that "the nature of social reality and the means to its transformation were to be found *not* in the study of power, but in a long, clear look at the seemingly trivial gestures and accents of ordinary experience" (Marcus 1986:79–80; 1989:146, 239). Like Bakhtin, Lefebvre describes everyday life, in its material actuality, as a contested ground between the subject and the structures of language and institutions (K. Ross 1988:9).[15]

Recent work in cultural studies on everyday culture, however, has more often featured work like Michel de Certeau's theoretical treatise *The Practice of Everyday Life.* De Certeau pits consumption, the "tactics" employed in everyday life, against production, or the institutional "strategies" of surveillance described by Foucault: "the goal is not to make clearer how the violence of order is transmuted into a disciplinary technology, but rather to bring to light the clandestine forms taken by the dispersed, tactical, and make-shift creativity of groups or individuals already caught in the nets of 'discipline.' " The languages available in everyday life, de Certeau asserts, are appropriated by "an art of using" imposed systems, of "making do" with systems of representation converted into "tools manipulated by users." Cultural consumption is an intelligent form of production in its own right, in the manipulations that "use as their material the vocabularies of established languages," or "imposed symbolisms" (1984:xiv–xv, 21, 34).

This argument is widely admired, but its execution involves contradictions between the seeming populism and its theoretical expression, the latter indebted to poststructuralism despite the refutation of Foucault. The problem lies in the marriage of optimistic descriptions of collective activities with poststructuralist theories of the subject; elsewhere de Certeau explicitly states that his work on everyday practices does not mark a resurrection of the individual. The "multitude" is seen in a positive light, the subject as a relic of the past. The book may be dedicated "to the ordinary man," but that entity is understood to make up "a multitude of quantified heroes who lose names and faces as they become the ciphered river of the streets, a mobile language of computations and rationalities that belong to no one." The collective is heroic, the individual "incoherent." As objectified in written discursive practices, power has presumably inscribed itself on the body (much as Foucault, Deleuze, and Guattari describe it in *The Anti-Oedipus*) to the extent that the *voice* is broken into bits, and thus the everyday practitioner cannot "command a clear view of the use of words." No individual, as a result, has "the options of planning general strategy and viewing the adversary as a whole within a distinct, visible, and objectifiable space." There is no point in pursuing the voice of the body "because it is always determined by a system," and, in its recorded form in particular, " 'cleaned up' by the techniques of diffusion." The tradition of the body in everyday life persists only in the "aphasic enunciation [of] bits of language," or fragments dropped through the forest of signs into "contextless voice-gaps," in the attempt to recover an "impossible presence." Resistance in everyday practices is held to drift in heterogeneity like the currents in the sea, as a result. This tendency in de

Certeau's treatise leads him to compare cultural consumers not only with ghosts (the dead, in other words), but also with ants and other insects, fishes, and plants. With the erosion of the individual, the heroism of the everyday lies in the collective "anthill society," and in "indefinite citation of the other" rather than authorship (1984:v, xi, 1, 10, 37, 132, 163–64), akin to the postmodernist's pastiche.

The same problems appear in subsequent work in cultural studies that invokes de Certeau. John Fiske has made the most prominent use of de Certeau, borrowing the terms of *making do* and *guerilla* tactics, seeming to suggest that everyday life in all its aspects stands a hair's breadth away from open insurrection (1989:32–43). Like Iain Chambers, Fiske has acquired a reputation for "a kind of hip populism that finds subversion of mass culture everywhere, ... com[ing] perilously close to suggesting that critical inquiry isn't really necessary anymore" (Benn 1990:15–16). His distinction between commercial culture (the production of commodities) and popular culture (the use of those commodities in everyday life by "the people") tends to become an absolute dichotomy. One admits the existence of oppression along class, gender, and racial lines, but then proceeds to find the saving grace of "the complexity and creativity by which the subordinate cope with the commodity system and its ideology in their everyday lives" (Fiske 1989:18–19).

This reduction of everyday life into one large field (or *habitus,* after Bourdieu) of "bottom-up differences" (1992) fails to distinguish its more powerful elements. Popular culture seems to be one large refusal of commodification by the people, in asserting their "right to make [their] own culture out of the resources provided by the commodity system" (1989:15).[16] Lost in this celebration is the role played by consumerism in domestic life, for example, as "the work of reproduction, the sustaining of self and others, in preparation for the return to work." Consumption, in other words, includes both potentially subversive pleasures *and* an interaction with less pleasant facts of social experience, which reproduces the existing system. If nothing else, obviously, buying things perpetuates the cycle of commerce in its present form, even if one treats making do as a heroic, "grand gesture," and consumption is often disappointing or less than pleasurable (McRobbie 1991b:8–9).

Fiske, however, argues that evaluative discriminations are alien to "the people." Though acknowledging that many academics use popular forms in much the same way as nonacademics, he insists that positive as well as negative evaluations of popular forms by academics are inevitably elitist, top-down readings.[17] Left with little basis for positive discrimination in evaluating popular culture, he lauds frayed blue jeans, professional wrestling, sensationalist tabloids, shopping mall guerillas (1989:15, 37, 97–98, 114–16)—even extolling the use of television as background noise, and the selection of apples while grocery shopping (1992). The popular pleasures of evasion in everyday life, however, are distinguished from the "production of contrary meanings," which would require conscious critical reflection on social identity and social relations (1989:56, 69, 161). Since making meaning is disjunct from the body's capacity to evade and/or scandalize power through uncontrolled excess, loud rock and roll is described as an experience *only* for the body (apparently without any specific affective results, let alone intellectual ones, the sort of imprecise reference to the body evident in de Certeau as well). To recast as a modest virtue, in critical assessments of popular culture, the dichotomy often drawn between physical pleasure and reason hardly improves upon long-standing problems in aesthetics.

Hebdige, in contrast, constructs a more adequate dialectic between the "polemological" and "utopian" spaces identified by de Certeau in everyday life. The first term acknowledges the control of discourse by the powerful, while the latter preserves a continuing expectation of the miraculous, the historical realization of social justice. Together they fulfill the old axiom requiring both pessimism of the intellect and optimism of the will. Hebdige recognizes at once the multinational corporations' domination of communication technologies, and, in contrast, the continuing possibility of those technologies serving networks of mutual affinity by "working from 'the other side.'" To note that ordinary people react to a reality "out there"—to the presentation of real and terrible things happening somewhere else to which everyone is connected—and bond together accordingly, need not be sentimental. There seems "little evidence of what Jameson calls a general 'waning of affect' [or] an immunity from feeling" in some outstanding moments, such as the Band Aid concerts organized by former punk rocker Bob Geldof in response to African famine—a significant blow against Thatcherism and its ideology of selfishness (Hebdige 1988:216, 221).

An even stronger contrast with de Certeau's work can be found in Lefebvre's theory of moments, a crucial component of avant-garde theory underlying not only earlier, classic avant-gardism, but also subsequent critical claims for everyday cultural activities. Walter Benjamin's work contains the most complexly developed theory of the moment, emphasizing "a moment (a year, a decade) when a self-consistent cultural language comes into being." Benjamin, as always, dialectically reverses an apparently negative phenomenon, the experience of urban, mass existence as a series of discontinuous moments. He perceives in montage the power to reassemble those moments and awaken the vocabulary of everyday life. Such lived moments can be reconstituted "as the text of a single story," that of struggle between authority and subordinate groups, and become "a potential locus of resistance" (Rolleston 1989:18, 23–25). This avant-garde legacy in cultural studies shows up in Hebdige's study of punk, which ends with the assertion that subcultural style does have its moment, despite the inevitability of commercial incorporation.

The language of the avant-garde generally features an emphasis on the moment, and subsequently on *movement,* the quest to generate new moments of insurrection in everyday life. Such terms do not designate some constant, frenetic quest by any one individual or group for moment after moment of new sensation, always one desperate step ahead of incorporation. The Situationist International, at its origin, claimed for its own brand of avant-gardism only one essentially transitory, brief moment in time—but a moment serving as a passageway to future possibilities for others, as it subsequently proved in England (Carr 1990a:18–19). Asger Jorn, at one time a member of the Situationists, describes the rhythms and passions of materialist art in similar terms, as both "spontaneity" and "movement" (Wollen 1989:84).

Theories of such moments have been articulated with increasing frequency by younger scholars on the left, whose personal experience of mass culture obviates older institutionalized elitism. Those persons who grew up in popular culture in something like its present shape "have long been sensitive to its complications—its restrictions of experience but also its effective and potentially expansive plays on pleasure, . . . its reifications of convention but also its discoveries of innovation and alterity" (Polan 1988:52). An emancipatory culture, from their view, would be very much like Benjamin and Brecht's, generating a shock effect that forces "people to see aspects of the society that they had previously overlooked, or . . . focuses attention on the need for change." The audience might thus reject "idealizations and rationalizations that apologize for suffering in the present social system," refusing authoritarian ideology and its conceptions and stereotypes, which prevent insight into the complexities of social life. At its best, an emancipatory cultural practice "suggests that another way of life is possible" (Kellner 1982:409). It does so, in Laura Kipnis's terms (derived from Ernesto Laclau), in a fashion very similar to the avant-gardist montage: "A left popular culture would undertake to articulate the antagonistic moments *already* there in popular culture into moments when 'popular-democratic' elements are presented as an unassimilable option *against* the ideology of the dominant bloc" (1986:33).

As Williams's work indicates, the alliances and projects necessary to a truly popular culture (one laying bare irreconcilable interests) require as much concern with affective relations as with economic and ideological ones. Finding the means to embody unenacted desire, in other words, matters as much as constructing new meanings. Henry Giroux and Roger Simon argue that "the idea and experience of pleasure must be constituted politically," by recognizing the "possibility for extending unrealized and progressive moments in the production of corporeality." But that discourse should also retain the dialectical recognition that uncritical celebrations of the body (such as Fiske's) are "theoretically and politically misplaced," since the popular experience of corporeality certainly has repressive effects as well (1989:13, 18), as in film violence or the use of sexuality in advertising. The emancipatory effects of bodily excess are hardly identical in the degree of their articulation, either, a discrimination lost in such celebrations (but neither are they universally inarticulate, as Fiske's indiscrimination allows him to suggest). Like Giroux and Simon, Hebdige stresses the importance of a discriminating "sensitivity in aesthetic critique and practice to the incandescence of the particular," or material experience, in considering the uses of cultural technologies. Modernism and postmodernism, he finds, have only caused criticism to forget "that the seat of being is the belly not the eyes, . . . that the essential processes are visceral ones." Only by acknowledging and working from the actual grain of dissenting voices can one offer arguments that take popular culture seriously and "engage directly with it on its own terms, and in its own language," encouraging questioning not only of the structures of power, but also of the way it is registered and resisted. The impact of such voices to discomfort dominant groups and promote the will to act might thereby be articulated and "brought to bear in and on concrete situations as a *transforming force*," a process requiring imagination and a willingness to take some risks (1988:204, 222, 230, 242).

Andrew Ross offers a nuanced but largely positive view, too, on the relationship of cultural technology and sensual experience, with reference to Donna Haraway's "cyborg politics," which deny "the assurance of a tidy division between the utopian, unalienated organic body" and technology. Coming to terms once and for all with new technologies and their practical, democratizing possibilities enables "a contest for that new impure space which is neither organic nor mechanical." Intellectuals should recognize that popular uses of the resulting products likewise pose "none too resolvable contradictions, arising out of desires and fantasies that do not always 'obey' politically conscious ideas about correctness." (Ross's own terms of "disrespect" suggest anarchism, generally unacceptable on the left.) In however impure or compromised a form, popular culture indisputably contains "structures of feelings that draw upon hostility, resentment, and insubordination." If approached with less doctrinaire preconceptions, popular forms might then be appreciated as a basis for inventing new collective relations to sensual experience, in a politics of everyday life "informed by the matrix of power, pleasure, and desire experienced by all other consumers." That politics can "not be remote, utopian, compensatory, or authoritatively deferred until all struggles are over," but based in the immediate accessibility of popular culture (1989a:12, 213, 230–31).

The avant-garde similarly valorized affective experience against both verbal and visual abstractions remote from concrete human relations. If highly commercialized visual media predominate in contemporary culture, the renewal of perception, more specifically, might necessarily take its lead from the media of sound. The result of the culture of images, whether in entertainment, politics, or even personal relations, does seem to be that what a person has to *say* scarcely matters a whit nowadays (a point exemplifed by recent television shows employing silent home videos). Those who would oppose the cultural and political monopoly engaged in image mongering still have the force of reason and their voices for weapons, but at a time, apparently, when hardly anyone *hears* anything anymore. The visual sometimes displaces the verbal altogether, as when George Bush, hand over heart in front of a waving flag, deigned only to improvise incorrectly the text of the Pledge of Allegiance. As the previous chapter notes, Bruce Springsteen's ambivalent "Born in the U.S.A.," which prominently displayed the American flag in its visual packaging, is still understood by many young people as a straightforward celebration of patriotism. The impact of one culprit in this case, MTV, has often been described as the attenuation of music and voices—and the wide range of possible responses to them—by linking them with visual images that drastically narrow the free play of associations.[18] Postmodern cultural forms, it would seem, must always "self-consciously embrace the problem of image creation, and necessarily turn inwards upon themselves as a result. It then becomes difficult to escape being what is being imaged" (Harvey 1989:323), as in Springsteen's case.

Media of sound like music and literature, then, may be essential to a positive, materialist form of postmodernism, based in "those social groups who can claim access to true (because hitherto unpackaged) critical experience (often taken to be rooted materially in the body)" (Frith and Horne 1987:176). Bakhtin, for one, would shift the critic's priority from the visual to the vocal, as a way of restoring voice to the silenced (Stam 1989:19). Kenneth Burke, though writing on negation in the literal sense, provides a thesis befitting the material power of the voice, set against the abstracted experience of visual media: "The essential distinction between the verbal and the nonverbal is the fact that language adds the peculiar possibility of the Negative" (1966:453–54).

Language, the Situationist International held, "still remains the necessary mediation for the awakening of consciousness of the world of alienation," and for contesting the ideological justification of power, especially positivist imperatives. Words may work "on behalf of the dominant organisation of life," but they also "embody forces that can upset the most careful calculations." Insubordinate words rescue some semblance of authentic experience from power, which, through its mechanized reduction of language to simple information, has made communication an imposture and a dupery. But even on the terrain of the machine, it should be noted, "resistances are being manifested; *electronic music* could be seen as an attempt (obviously limited and ambiguous) to reverse the domination relation by [subverting] machines to the profit of language." What is generally required, in any medium, is the denunciation of unilateral communication and its feel-good directives. A language thus liberated "simultaneously embraces words, music, cries, gestures, acts," and art and consequently reinvents poetry itself, an activity "indistinguishable from reinventing revolution." Creating events and their language, in other words, represents a poetry no longer expressed in actual poems. Those "who have rejected all hierarchical power can use any word [in any form] as a weapon to beat out the *rhythm* of their action. Lautréamont and the illegal anarchists were well aware of [this]; so were the Dadaists" ("All the King's Men" 1981:114–15; Khayati 1981:174; Vaneigem 1974b:55; italics added).

Sound integrates and relates human beings, as opposed to the isolation of passive viewing. The vibratory essence of timbre, especially in the human voice, "puts the world of sound in motion and reminds us, as individuals, that we are alive, sentient and experiencing.... The texture, the grain, the *tactile* quality of sound brings the world into us and reminds us of the social relatedness of humanity" (Shepherd 1987:157–58). In order to serve the creation of genuine dialogue, a cultural activity must emphasize the sensuous, and the disruption of the passively received monologue of the spectacle. If electronic commercial art, for instance, "has radicalized noise by seeking to eliminate it," or to channel it for profit, *noise* thus "functions to name that which stands opposed to the information system as a whole" (Mowitt 1987:194, 196), especially in negating that system's relentless positivism. This valorizing of noise echoes the Dadaist Richard Huelsenbeck, who held that "Every [avant-garde] movement naturally produces noise; ... noise is a direct call to action" (1989:26).

Cultural Anarchism

The aim of such noise is not so much "cultural revolution," in the terms of Lefebvre's theory of moments, as cultural *anarchism*. Simply put, genuine freedom requires a contumacious attitude; if the ideas of freedom and equality held by millions are to be clarified "by a common name," there is "no better name than anarchism" (Read 1971:36). Besides momentary forms of open resistance to the guises and voices of authority, anarchism here means the persisting habit of critical thought, as well as action on it. The critical mind rejects abstractions and images contradicted by concrete evidence and experience. One chooses to believe either the obscurantist cultural organs owned by the ruling class, or the material social experience of its victims. This choice is crucial to one's humanity: the negation of authority implies, in the terms of Bakunin, the constructive power to think as much as the desire to rebel, and "these faculties [create] all that constitutes humanity in man" and woman (1971:126–27). In the desire of anarchism to expose "the potentialities residing in our actual human situation," negation is the foundation of creation (Wieck 1979a:331; 1979b:154–55).

Rather than the simple license to do anything and its resulting chaos, anarchic freedom should be understood to "mean the chance to discover what it is you truly want do do." Such a grasp for self-affirmation is rooted specifically "in a negation where freedom is glimpsed" (Marcus 1989:53, 56). Whether artist, critic, student, teacher, or man or woman in everyday life, the anarchist must be understood to exercise intellectual as well as emotive impulses, particularly in placing creative forms in practicable, usable situations. What must be destroyed, ultimately, is the limited range of expression concerning the possibilities for self and society, a task requiring the voice of refusal. Only then does it become apparent that negation represents the actual positive cultural force, given the feel-good shrillness of authoritarian insistence on the (specious) positive, on passive acceptance of the status quo. Personal and collective identity might then be defined through critical examination, not unreflective absorption of dominant cultural norms; the critical mind makes active connections between different areas of cultural and social experience.

Anarchism does not mean and has never meant sheer anarchic violence, "malign chaos," "unthinking revolt," or "a philosophy of destruction simply." But "many people still identify anarchism with unmitigated destruction and nihilism and political terror," though "propaganda by the deed" (or assasination and bomb throwing) was only a short-lived offshoot of anarchism, confined to the last two decades of the nineteenth century. In reality anarchism means libertarian spontaneity, in the lucid critique of the concentration of power—an *attitude* of social condemnation, not utter disorder and lawlessness. Like their political antecedents (Godwin, Proudhon,

Bakunin, Kropotkin), anarchists in recent youth culture, for example, represent "a succession of loose and impermanent groups and confederations of propagandists who see their duty not to lead the people so much as to enlighten and give example to them." The best have abjured as much as possible the role of an elite vanguard entirely responsible for collective consciousness. Instead, freedom of interpretation and variety of approach have been the hallmark of "intellectuals and artists in rebellion against mass values" (Woodcock 1986:11, 14, 17–19, 25).[19] They have sought "to convince people in a rational way, not create another...unthinking acceptance [like that] which people now possess" toward power (Woodworth 1979:35).

Anarchism would dissolve the exercise of "*all* power, sovereignty, domination, and hierarchical division" (Wieck 1979b:139), especially by the state, but even, sometimes, in its own activity. Thus it has tended in the past to counsel, quite facilely, immediate revolt, with total decentralization and absolute autonomy for the individual. Marx repudiated Bakunin not only for this reason, but also because the anarchist cells of the time, conceived as a conspiratorial elite, bore their own tinge of authoritarianism. Bakunin, on the other hand, correctly observed that Marx's own brief, subsequently manipulable descriptions of a socialist society based in the state (if only for a time) were an invitation to disaster, especially the terms "*dictatorship* of the proletariat." Subsequent anarchists have similarly condemned authoritarian tendencies in Marxist-Leninist conceptions of the revolutionary society, led by an elite vanguard.[20] It should be pointed out, though, that Marx's own voluminous work on capitalism, "far from bearing any authoritarian imprint," shares with anarchism "a powerful anti-authoritarian and anti-bureaucratic bias" (Miliband 1984:22).

But collision (in 1871) was inevitable, given that Marx created systems, while Bakunin refused any doctrine and any plans for the future. The result, in essence, was a polarization of thought and instinct in revolutionary ideas (Reszler 1973:49), much like the polar dislocations in aesthetic theory between reason and feeling. Debord, after recounting the mutual accusations of Marx and Bakunin, concludes that anarchism in its past forms has had the merit of rejecting existing conditions in favor of the whole of life, fusing disparate, relatively incoherent desires. But anarchism also tends to perceive such a fusion well before its actual realization, thus condemning anarchism to repeat tirelessly the same untenable ideology of an impending pure liberty. Debord makes it clear, though, that the Situationists' program, if more realistic about the cultural and social barriers to realizing genuine freedom, did retain the anarchist objective, containing "no other promise other than that of an autonomy without rules and without restraint" (1983:#92; qtd. in Marcus 1989:118).

The editors of the more recent *Reinventing Anarchy* attempt to move beyond this abstract ideal, arguing that even with radical change, there would still be some form of social organization. "Some conflict between individual autonomy and social control" would continue to occur, but take place at "some ascertainable level of 'creative conflict'" (H. Ehrlich et al. 1979:2, 4).[21] Anarchism should therefore involve "the constant search, within society as it is, for the opportunities to put anarchist principles into action without waiting for a revolution" (Woodcock 1986:386), especially in cultural forms. Debord and the SI share this practical sense of anarchy: with challenges to the spectacle's fantasy of cultural and political choice, people might "begin to develop real desires in place of the present compensations," to refuse behavior dictated by the spectacle, and to "reinvent their own unique fulfillment," individually and collectively (1981c:309).

If the weakness of political anarchism in the past has been to consider proletarian revolution something immediately present in every crisis, Marxism, in contrast, has required a scientific attention to economic and political organization, in anticipation of the inevitable revolutionary outcome of the class struggle—an outcome now indefinitely postponed in the most developed nations. Western Marxism thus reveals a "consistent pessimism," the product of "its formation by defeat" (Anderson 1979:93), including the seeming irrelevance of its grand historical narrative by the end of the twentieth century. One particularly damaging result has been a profoundly antidemocratic conviction of the weight of ideological domination in capitalist culture. This pessimism results in part from a failing worth reiterating in the terms of Lefebvre, who believed that "Marxism had been wrongly restricted to the domain of the economic and the political, and that its analysis should be extended to cover every aspect of life, wherever alienation existed—in private life, in leisure time, as well as at work. Marxism... should be involved in cultural studies; it should not be afraid of the trivial" (Wollen 1989:77).

The postponement of the revolution Marx believed imminent is often attributed to unanticipated adaptations in capitalism, including pacification of the labor force through mass consumption and culture—which thus mark a crucial point of attack. The SI observed that the bourgeoisie, through culture as well as politics, had proved much better at defending itself than past revolutionaries expected, but also that revolutionary criticism might still "recognise the failures of the past and learn from the implications and effects of this failure" (Plant 1992:77). Just before the revolutionary events of 1968, Debord correctly predicted that protests launched by rebellious currents of youth would directly reject older specialized politics, including the conventional separation of art from the needs of everyday life. Art and everyday material experience would become instead "two sides—now united—of a new spontaneous struggle." Debord himself turned out to be the "new 'General Ludd' who, this time, urges [the young] to destroy the machines of *permitted* consumption" (1983:#115)—not the machines themselves, but the monopoly controlling them.

Yet questions of aesthetic pleasure and value in everyday life, crucial to Lefebvre's theory of moments, continue all too often to be deemed politically immature, let alone less crucial than economic and political questions. The excesses of some academic postmodernists, such as Fiske, in extolling pleasure as resistance have only exacerbated its disrepute. Those on the left who consider aesthetic forms of contestation ephemeral—particularly when significant economic and political struggle seem so remote—help leave any prospective "radical cultural intervention in a relatively weak position" (Barrett 1987:78). Eagleton notes that "mainstream leftist politics has often enough breezily edited out . . . issues of desire, everyday life, the importance of microscopic gestures" (though he proceeds to do so himself, in writing on punk anarchism). He has similarly held, elsewhere, that "few oversights have more drastically impoverished Marxism than its deafness to the libertarian tradition [of] anarchic revolt" (while entirely undercutting the point by charcterizing anarchism as a matter of the "fractured, libidinal, disordered subject," and "an infantile disorder known as instant gratification"). The Paris Commune's break with exclusively economic concerns in favor of a cultural politics, in his view, represents an enduring triumph, but also, in the final analysis, its downfall (1989:12; 1988:viii, xiv). In the postmodern period, though, when education, entertainment, information, and politics have become inextricable, concern with the political must necessarily be extended into all domains and practices in the culture, putting aside the rank-and-file state of mind. The left cannot insist on a concept of "politics—*real* actions and events in the political sphere—that is always above and beyond what continues to be disparaged as the (merely) potentially political effects of cultural transformations" (A. Ross 1988:xv–xvi).

Whichever "ism" one chooses to prefer, a well-known stricture of Vaneigem's must be kept in mind: "People who talk about revolution and class struggle without referring explicitly to everyday life, without understanding what is subversive about love and what is positive in the refusal of constraints," in all manner of emergent cultural forms, "such people have a corpse in their mouth" (1983:15). The Situationists thus prohibited the derivation "situation*ism*," which would suggest a political ideology, rather than a "synthesis of aesthetics and politics [in a] life-as-art which must be actively realized" (Ward 1985:148). Debord pointedly remarked that "when we speak of a unified vision of art and politics, this absolutely does not mean that we recommend any sort of subordination of art to politics whatsoever" (qtd. in Sussman 1991:149). The potential relation of everyday life to rebellion must logically be creatively or critically articulated before it can be politically enacted. The question of actually appropriating the means of production themselves (cultural and otherwise) could only emerge, perhaps, subsequent to such activity.

Just how resistance can be articulated in art and in everyday life in ways satisfactory both aesthetically and politically, for both producers and audiences, cannot be prescribed, and "will remain open to trial, error, and debate" (Huyssen 1986:220–21). Anarchism in art entails an eye to futurity, a presentiment that a truly revolutionary art has yet to be born. Given this prospective sense, artistic practice retains some significance in its own right (though never an absolute autonomy), as "a *project* which leaves the door wide open to the future." The anticipation of a fully liberating art "allows the anarchist to resist the iconoclastic temptations" of claims to autonomy from the everyday, common among purely artistic heretics, "and to avoid the dangers of a purely destructive nihilism." One might thereby contribute to the realization of a genuinely popular art "of the people, for the people, *by* the people," by arousing "the creative artist lying dormant in each of us." An anarchist art must establish "the principle of creativity in all realms of human activity, [b]oth artistic and social creations" (Reszler 1973:43, 46).

The truly revolutionary society (as envisioned by Marx), says Eagleton, would in fact be a "final *aestheticization* of human existence," in the sense that the expansion of productive forces would be brought into full harmony with human capacities. At present under capitalism, human capacities are hardly entirely positive, including as they do aggression, domination, and exploitation. Thus one cannot imagine socialism as a simple liberation of human powers latent in capitalist society or repressed by it. The careful discrimination of which human powers should be emancipated requires a particular consideration: the preferable capacities are those involving individual realization through the similar free self-realization of others, in a dialectic between individual and collective. The aesthetic nature of interpersonal communication, finally, lies in drawing together both theory (the totalizing power of intellectual abstraction) and value (judgment based in everyday experience and feelings) in emancipatory knowledge (or critical thought). The result should be an aggressively discontented *and* "theorizing" subject (as described in chapter 1). This final aestheticization "cannot be prematurely anticipated by a reason which surrenders itself wholly to the ludic and poetic, to image and intuition. Instead, a rigorous analytical rationality is needed" as well, if action upon "sensuous" experience is to play a political role, rather than remaining the province of a minority aestheticist cult, whether in academia or bohemia (1990:220–28). This movement constitutes the dialectic described by Benjamin and Brecht, a dialectic between affective, sensuous response to cultural forms and articulated connection of them with social experience.

Given the present situation, though, one should probably start not from such utopian objectives, but from the simple, fundamental fact that an intuitive urge to freedom, especially in the young, can develop despite the present cultural-political nexus of authority. The crucial objective is to combat the authoritarian attitude inculcated in youth, many of whom are quite receptive to such challenges, and bring into focus the frustration of elders not necessarily amenable to authority, but unfocused in their discontent. This effort must include a purposeful, not merely playful crossing of borders like those between literature and mass culture—between the aesthetic and the political, in general—that authoritative specialists have traditionally so doggedly enforced. The anarchist artist or critic—Benjamin's "destructive character"—offers "insights that cannot prove other than destructive to the traditional view of art." The most important of these insights is that forms branded grotesque by dominant institutional judgments might very well be, in reality, "an expression of the exuberant health of an age." From this view, the crudities of art in so-called decadent epochs, like that of mass culture, "actually arise from the nucleus of its richest historical energies." Intellectual work cannot become politically useful until the separate spheres of theory and practice have been combined in a praxis that, "instead of competing against the newer means of communication, tries to apply them and to learn from them" (Benjamin 1985b:362, 366; 1969:237; 1973:95, 99).

To this end, both students and a wider audience should sense in neglected forms—old as well as new, literature and popular culture alike—the search for a noise authentic to their discontent, a noise to pit against the chain of alienating cultural commodities produced by the media of social order. Scholastic activities, in particular, must become "potential modes of resistance, celebration, and solidarity" (Batsleer et al. 1985:5). Giroux and Paulo Freire, writing on schooling, have stipulated recently that the effort to encourage a "critical literacy" requires expanding the range of cultural materials deemed to constitute meaningful knowledge. Their objective is not simple pluralism, but "social relations that legitimate popular culture, cultural diversity, and dialogue as crucial elements in the debate about citizenship and cultural/social justice" (1989:xi)—the sort of dialogue described by Eagleton, Habermas, Vaneigem, Willis, and Williams.

Though often maligned by cultural authorities as harbingers of the death of civilization (and so forth), newer aesthetic technologies, put to deviant uses, could actually prove sources of freedom. Even at the garish surface of the most incessantly "plugged" cultural forms, and especially if one looks beneath it (and not necessarily all that far beneath), artists can be found who do produce progressive texts, offering their audience models of subversive expression. Rock and roll offers numerous examples, including the ethnic and Third World musics to which some musicians and fans have turned as a source of revitalization. Hall, no real aficionado of mass culture, finds rock music itself of considerable importance, in writing on movements in England like Rock Against Racism (which grew out of racial strife in and around the punk scene), Red Wedge (which campaigned for the Labour Party), and Geldof's antiracist, internationalist Band Aid/Live Aid projects. The ubiquitous presence of rock music "in the lives of young people gives it an unparalleled mobilizing power. When politics makes contact with this culture, it finds itself in touch with the cultural language which, for the majority of young people today (and for many not-so-young people, too), most authentically expresses how they experience the world" (1988:253; see Garofalo 1992).

Rock music, of course, may now in large part set the tone for conformity as much as rebellion. But for every enormously hyped, mindless celebrity, there exists a subcultural artist with humane, antiauthoritarian designs upon his or her audience. For every Bon Jovi, a narcissist who disdained writing songs about the Vietnam War because his audience didn't know anything about it, there exists at the same time an angry, unadorned D. Boon (the late leader of the Minutemen), who sang in "The Price of Paradise" of Vietnam and "men who die very young / afraid to see that their cause is unjust."[22] Although cynical cognoscenti lament the loss of any social significance in commercial popular music (see Frith 1987c), the 1980s saw some of the strongest political efforts to date in rock and roll and allied musics like rap (a politicization subsequently expanding into the work of groups as diverse as Deee-Lite and L7), and not necessarily by lesser-known performers: DJ Afrika Bambaataa and John Lydon's "World Destruction" (recorded under the name Time Zone), the Clash's "This is England," Little Steven's "Sun City" project, N. W. A.'s "Fuck the Police," the Ramones' "Bonzo Goes to Bitburg," the Soft Boys' "I Wanna Destroy You," and X's "The New World," as well as the corpus of notables like Public Enemy and Queen Latifah. Rock music has understandably come under attack, in an authoritarian era, in indictments (by the Parents' Music Resource Center [PMRC] and others) that condemn not just immorality, but political deviance.

The contrast between Bon Jovi's (bad) quietism and D. Boon's (good) agitprop is to some extent a false problem, however, first of all because it tends to privilege lyrical content over music (though the political songs above are cited because of their visceral power, not just their politics). For a properly dialogic criticism, moreover, taking into account the social and historical context of a music's use as well, the political problem "is not whether rock music is oppositional or co-optive, but rather how it arbitrates tensions between opposition and co-optation at any given historical moment" (Lipsitz 1990:102). Rock is less a text than a context, or an "open field of reference for the most varied cultural activities." Listeners do not have to be aware of any express politics for a music or song to be politically effective, particularly since the everyday contexts in which they use music seldom take the form of direct political consciousness or protest. Whether conformist or dissident, the politics (if any) expressed in the lyrics only form—with the music—a medium of which listeners make active use for better and for worse, in the middle of cultural and ideological conflicts. If the significance of a song thus resides "*far beyond* the material nature of the music," political evaluation focusing on the musical text is foredoomed to a futile obsession with "alternative text production" and with authenticity in anticommercial terms, neither of which guarantees political significance. For whatever the results of the production process, the audience persistently produces "meanings, values, significance, and pleasure" in its own right, however dilapidated and exploited rock and roll, as a musical form, may seem in the nineties (Wicke 1990:ix, 25, 147, 181–82).

Other recent rock critics, however, have affected a fashionable postmodernist cynicism concerning popular music. The insurrectionary avant-gardism of punk in the late 1970s has only led, presumably, to a static radicalism, "a set of concepts—'subversion,' 'rebellion,' 'counterculture,' 'underground,' even 'youth'—that no longer plausibly apply to rock or pop culture in general" (Carson 1988:21). This is true enough if one speaks of rock and roll in isolation from other cultural productions and activites. But the realm of cultural anarchism is hardly one of texts, musical and otherwise, alone: the ultimate question concerns how those productions are reorganized with other artifacts in lived cultural ensembles. If the most important question in cultural studies concerns whether a release of desire occurs, in terms of questioning and even surpassing existing social relations, then music matters only in its use, its social outcome, and not as a text that somehow does the lion's share of the listener's work for him or her. "Poetry makes nothing happen," W. H. Auden once wrote; rock and roll, in and of itself, makes nothing happen either.

Hence in cultural studies the text "is no longer studied for its own sake, nor even for the social effects it may be thought to produce, but rather for the subjective or cultural forms which it realises and makes available" in its social life (R. Johnson 1986/87:62). Audiences respond with varying degrees of commitment to pop songs, often with none at all; the "best" songs are those that prove useful to their listeners in situating themselves socially. Such songs should be judged historically, for their use value, rather than by some timeless ideal like that of rebellion. Just as musical texts themselves "are volatile, contradictory, and collective in their effects," musical consumption is dynamic as well (Frith 1988a:79; 1980:54). In defining the "popular" song, Gramsci distinguished songs composed by and for the people, however politically correct, from those that they adopt because they find alternatives to the official conception of the world, ones better suiting their own way of thinking. The latter are truly popular (A. Ross 1989a:10; Sinfield 1989:40). It is important, therefore, not to conclude with "the fallacious belief that changing the commodities," or the nature of texts and their production, will necessarily change popular culture, or habits of consumption (Fiske 1989:186).[23]

Whether the commercial source is large or small, furthermore, it always remains true that an *asymmetry* can exist between "the short- and long-term interests of an institution" like a music company, when the immediate opportunity for profit outweighs the potential of a particular production to provoke dissent (Sinfield 1989:32, 304). (Rap, the most recent music to emerge from independent record companies into the mass media, strikingly illustrates such contradictions.) Art historian T. J. Clark, a former member of the Situationist International, asserts that producing the popular, especially music, always remains a risky business for commercial culture "because the 'popular' is not simply a commodity made from dead, obedient materials," but in part from forms generated independently in everyday life, which "are always capable of recapturing the apparatus of production.... There is always the chance that a line or phrase will be used by the singer to enforce fleetingly the kind of attention—the kind of collective vehemence—that . . . censor[s] fear" (1984:236; see Marcus 1989:149).

Subcultures

Cultural studies considers youth subcultures formed around music with the same attention to collective vehemence. To understand them in this light, as forms of cultural anarchism, helps first to counteract criticism that the study of youth subcultures does not supply any immediate political utility, given their past failure to link up with conventional politics. Second, if, as a number of critics have claimed, the class structure in England makes the original work on youth subcultures unsuitable for importation into the United States, this objection might be laid to rest by understanding them not just in terms of class tensions, but as expressions of contumacy, often in parody of authoritarian discourse.

The first major study to emerge from the Centre for Contemporary Cultural Studies, *Resistance through Rituals,* read subcultural styles by considering commodities as cultural signs, with "no 'natural' meaning as such" (Hall and Jefferson 1976:55). The commodity is real enough, but also laden with ideology, or its own specific connotations and, more generally, its place in the larger commodity system, the whole process of production and consumption reinforced every time one buys something. This semiotics, or study of signs, was derived in large part from Roland Barthes's *Mythologies* and *Elements of Semiology.* But it was ultimately felt that Barthes treated "bourgeois ideology" one-dimensionally and ahistorically, as something of an irresistible force. For the same reason, *Resistance through Rituals* prefers Gramsci's theory of hegemonic struggle in social discourse, rather than Althusser's account of a virutally omnipotent "ideological state apparatus." The Centre instead inflected semiotics, or structuralism, with Williams's culturalism. The work on youth subcultures reflects two of his arguments in particular: first that the structures of feeling running through a wide range of textual and lived practices find a common denominator in the literary term *style;* second, that the reality of emergent cultural activity is undeniable, making it crucial to find new forms or adaptations of form as models for such efforts (Williams 1977:126, 131).[24]

One member of the Birmingham group, John Clarke, employed Claude Levi-Strauss's anthropological concept of *bricolage,* as a means to mediate between structuralism and cultural studies. Through semiotics, Clarke read subcultural styles as unacknowledged forms of oppositional expression, coherent, meaningful assemblages of cultural objects in rituals of consumption. Just as Levi-Strauss had demonstrated the complexity of presumably primitive cultures, cultural studies redeemed the leisure activities of working-class youth.[25] In Clarke's view, "The major developments in commercial Youth

Culture have [relied on] innovations originating *outside* the commercial world"—in popular culture, that is—at a "grass-roots" level of local interactions and needs (1976:187). Hebdige, in analyzing punk, relies heavily on Clarke's description of the bricoleur, who "re-locates the significant object in [an] overall repertoire of signs, ... a different total ensemble, [in which] a new discourse is constituted, a different message conveyed" (1979:104).

The Centre found in postwar working-class youth cultures that it was quite evidently possible for subordinate groups to actively construct a subcultural, oppositional style out of mass-culture forms. They did so by

> subverting and transforming ... the social meanings which [commodities] seem "naturally" to have: or, by combining them with something else, ... to change or inflect their meaning. [N]either money nor the market could fully dictate what groups used these things to *say* or *signify* about themselves. The new meanings emerge because the "bits" which had been borrowed or revived were brought together into a new and distinctive stylistic ensemble: but also because the symbolic objects—dress, appearance, language, ritual occasions, styles of interaction, music— were made to form a unity with the group's relations, situation, experiences. (Hall and Jefferson 1976:54–56)

The effect of the Centre's work was to turn subcultures themselves into texts, radically revising the whole relation between text and context (or audience) in cultural analysis—including that between individual creators and collective experience, traditionally esteemed and ignored, respectively. The "definition of what constitutes a text broadened dramatically," not only including the generation of meanings through social practices, but sociologically grounding "these meanings in those who participated in the practice, rather than the practice itself" (Turner 1990:112).

The stylistic ensemble constructed by younger subjects, from this view, closely resembles the montagelike practice, in everyday life, envisioned by the avant-garde. In a description of montage that now seems prescient, Benjamin found that "the world is full of the most unrivalled objects for *childish* attention and use." In using presumed "waste products"—like mass-culture forms—the young "do not so much imitate the work of adults as bring together, in the artefact produced in play, materials of widely differing kinds in a new, intuitive relationship" (1985a:52–53). He finds the avant-garde essentially allegorical (as chapter 6 discusses at length), in its attempt to link cultural materials with larger social meanings; subcultural style also makes considerable sense as an allegory of this sort, as a codified commentary (more and less conscious) on the ideological climate in which the insubordinate group finds itself. As in Benjamin's theory of the mimetic faculty, furthermore, the creation of allegorical "similarities" is brought about by the sparks created by technological forms, so often dismissed for their inauthenticity and pacifying effects (see McRobbie 1992).

The similarities with public discourse, in the subculture's parody of it, emerge out of a milieu with some technologically enhanced popular music, such as rap or rock and roll, at its center. In the form of records, mass industrial products, rock music is hardly a spontaneous popular product, yet it has proven immensely useful nonetheless. The immediate meaning of a music, therefore, is far less significant to the subculture than a general "sensuous identification" with it, through "patterns and images of *movement*" (just as the avant-garde would have it). This second system of meaning is not contained in songs, but is not independent of them, either. Such patterns of movement, most apparent in dancing, are assimilated into "a more comprehensive system of meaning, combined with other materials such as clothes, hairstyles, gestures, ... and styles of speech," also placed into *motion* by their transformation in that ensemble (Wicke 1990:68, 87–88).

The ultimate "functional transformation" is effected not by artists, but by audiences, who act as a collective force to transform (to some degree) the apparatus of consumption. Without an emphasis on such transformations, says Hebdige, cultural studies becomes a "truncated amalgam of textbook 'tendencies' and 'traditions' which some people are currently purveying" (1988:12). Befitting Benjamin's concept of avant-garde activity, the results of the subculture's dynamic reception of commodities and texts include not only new ideological meanings, but also "progressive moments in the production of corporeality," or alliances based on similar affective sensibilities. The expropriation of artifacts and texts in punk, in particular, was "a refusal to let the dominant culture encode and restrict the meaning of daily life," a form of resistance linking pleasure and play with the reconstruction of meaning (Giroux and Simon 1989:13).

Since the original work of British cultural studies, the concept of the subculture has advanced by taking more into account the mobility of social relations within and outside the subculture, especially considering the numerous commodities and cultural forms available, and their uses with different investments of intensity. Insubordinate subcultural styles can rarely be attributed to a single unamiguous source like social class, in particular, but must be seen as a complex network of connections and contexts instead (Chambers 1986:207).[26] Abandoning the description of discrete subcultural styles in his first book, Hebdige prefers theories of affective alliances that occur across a heterogeneous field of aspirations and desires. The concept of the affective alliance was popularized by Grossberg, but through his emphasis on the fleeting, even unconscious nature of the relationship, as well as its often authoritarian basis, it serves to confirm the postmodern fragmentation of cultural and social experience. The function of popular music, he says quite explicitly, "cannot be reduced to or equated with the lived experience of its fans [since] we live and act in ways over which we have no control and about which we may be unaware" (1986:54–55).

To Hebdige, in contrast, the affective alliance designates the continuing possibility of coalescence even among widely dispersed persons and groups, as in Rock Against Racism or Bambaataa's Zulu Nation. In listening to rap music, in the latter case—a seemingly characteristic postmodern pastiche of fragmented sounds—audiences both black and white certainly "feel affinities across national, ethnic and cultural divisions," and may share even at some distance a sense of connection to and responsibility for the reality out there and its terrors, and bond together accordingly, discriminating "when it really matters what is real and what isn't." Thus, if cognizant of the multiple social positions every individual occupies (including their shifts over time), analyses of expressive ensembles, of creative, oppositional forms of consumption remain viable. Collective resentment is a perfectly sound basis for cultural and political organization, but it needs to recognize the varied sources of that attitude: people undeniably can get "some joy and pleasure and good cheer out of the whole exercise, moving along together though in different times to different rhythms." Hebdige continues to discern practices befitting the avant-garde sense of montage, moreover, finding that audiences as well as artists continue to appropriate new cultural technologies, and assemble new meanings and sensibilities through them (1988:205, 211–12, 215, 219, 221, 241).[27]

With respect to the question of oppositional uses of cultural artifacts and texts, finally, a "postmodernism of resistance . . . will always have to be specific and contingent upon the cultural field within which it operates," or else one inevitably succumbs to gloomy generalizations about contemporary culture. Andreas Huyssen, whom Angela McRobbie has cited along with Hebdige as a solitary example of a positive theory of postmodernism, argues that such concreteness is the only way "to abandon th[e] dead-end dichotomy of politics and aesthetics" (1986:220), in which subcultures, for example, are derided if they do not expressly enact a political doctrine. The best critic or teacher knows from personal experience that he or she receives unexpected moments of revolt not at all with complacency (as many theories of postmodernism would have it), but with the intensity of the ravenous—and with the faith that people change, that someday "renunciation of authority shall have replaced faith in authority and the political catechism" (Proudhon, qtd. in Guérin 1970:15). That critic or teacher encourages the search for the contumacious moment, informing his or her audience about moments either less conspicuous or misrepresented in our culture because they challenge dominant beliefs and values. This search, as in cultural studies, turns up the "breaking of codes" in both texts of all kinds and the audience's use of them, emphasizing in the process "disrespect for previous authorities, boundaries and rules." One exposes "what was previously subordinate and hidden. Different histories become available, their languages . . . producing unexpected encounters" everywhere in everyday life, from the classroom to the experience of music, with high culture just one more option for use in everyday life (Chambers 1986:193–94). The second part of this book will supply the specificity, as Huyssen and others such as Hebdige, McRobbie, and Williams would have it, necessary to fulfill and validate such a quest.

Part 2

CHAPTER **4**

The Fifties: The Angry Decade and Responses to Affluence

The following three chapters trace the interrelation of literature, popular music, and working-class youth subcultures in postwar England. Much like contemporary authoritarianism, postwar English culture has revolved around demagogic arguments about the irrelevance of social class, in the "affluent" society; also irrelevant, presumably, are politics on the left, even any "ideology" whatsoever, since proponents of the status quo only defend what is natural and commonsensical, inevitable and universal, and thus "nonideological." The turn from a focus on theory and contemporary American culture, therefore, to concrete events in English culture over the past thirty years or so, is intended to suggest possibilities for contemporary and future subcultural resistance, and not so much the precise forms it might take, as the tasks and problems its practitioners must face. Examining the relations between "many and diverse human activities [within] whole historical situations," including creative forms and their social locations, holds a contemporary use value if it contributes, in the final analysis, to the conviction that the present is changeable (Williams 1989:164, 174–75).

Though the introduction to this book expresses uncertainty concerning this political purpose, claiming more specifically to volatilize aesthetic judgments on "high" and "low" culture, it must be said at this point that the two ends are inseparable. Dick Hebdige ascribes a good deal of political significance to any "cartography of taste," in terms resembling Raymond Williams's theory of "patterns" that would "reveal unexpected identities and correspondences in hitherto separately considered activities" (qtd. in Brantlinger 1990:57). By "pursuing a limited number of themes and images across a fairly wide range of discourses," says Hebdige (which sometimes requires "the reiteration of histories . . . already familiar to the reader," as portions of the following chapters may be), one can modify the received wisdom concerning different cultural forms. But recharting conventional assumptions about different expressive forms, like literature, rock and roll, and youth subcultures, ultimately has real political implications. By "outlining the connections and breaks between groups of separate but interlocking statements," not only are historical conditions and their lost languages reconstructed, "but also the social conflicts and shifts in power which were registered inside" those languages (1988:48). A synthesis of literature, in particular, with those cultural practices and social activities from which it has traditionally been detached is crucial to overthrowing specialist judgments and tastes, so that a significant range of cultural forms might help in the larger process of political transformation. Cultural studies, in other words, should emulate the purposeful use of montage described by avant-gardists such as Walter Benjamin, Bertolt Brecht, and the Situationist International.

In the historical period under consideration, each of the areas of English culture to be examined made extensive use of the others in grappling with the ideology of "affluence"—in its original, strongest form, the notion in the 1950s that class distinctions were eroding. As economic reality set in, a reversal in the location of the most powerful cultural resistance occurred, culminating in the punk subculture. In the fifties, the literary drew on the music to launch what was in fact a conservative critique of the new England and its mass culture; in the 1970s, with punk, a musical avant-garde well versed in the work of the Situationists drew on literature, in part, to express its alienation under a failed economy. The major figures in this transition include Colin MacInnes, "castrato-rock," and the teddy boys; Anthony Burgess, the Rolling Stones, and the mods (in the 1960s); and Graham Greene, the Sex Pistols, and the punks. These subjects will be the focal points of each of the next three chapters. What follows, then, is not a comprehensive cultural history but a succession of *moments,* in the sense of Walter Benjamin and Henri Lefebvre (discussed in chapter 3). For each decade, roughly speaking—more like the years 1956–58, 1964–65, and 1976–77—something like a structure of feeling is described, a succession of moments of emergence when new forms, or new adaptations of extant forms, were realized. Literature, as much as any other cultural form, is "moved about incessantly" in such initiatives, "shuffled with forms which originate in other contexts, . . . and, in the process, made the bearer of different and often contradictory functions, meanings, and effects" (Bennett 1980:22, 24). There is no special privilege for it in the complexity of leisure experience; "events without prestige," in Lefebvre's terms, have all along explored just as profound a vein (Chambers 1985:2).

The linkages here, it should be emphasized, are not meant to suggest a direct correspondence between imaginative activities and economic and political pressures, but a deeper, not always conscious connection (also described in chapter 3). Directly or indirectly, various creative efforts responded to the structure of feeling or ideological tone between 1956 and 1977, which followed the shift of the state and the mass media from a celebration of consensus to the reassertion of authoritarian coercion, as the English economy steadily declined. In the fifties, the ambiguities and contradictions of claims for the "affluent" society immediately bred "a diffuse social unease, [experienced] as an unnaturally accelerated pace of social change," eroding reference points in both class and morality. The anxieties of that decade seized "on the hedonistic culture of youth," in particular, and its presumed verification of the disappearance of the class structure. By the late sixties, the counterculture and student movements had prompted an extension of that anxiety to "the permissiveness of social life" in general. Rhetoric about disruptive, extremist minorities, originally aimed at militant unionists, began to expand into a larger law-and-order ideology. As full-blown economic crisis arrived in the seventies, and conflict and dissent assumed once again, as before World War II, a "clearly delineated class form," widespread anxiety permitted a far more coercive politics, in the forceful regulation of trade unions. But in keeping with the obsession with youth culture dating from the mid-fifties, that coercion was also directed against the young, in near-hysterical invocations of "the threat of anarchy, riot and terrorism," terms dating from the sixties (Hall et al. 1978:218–19, 263, 321; see Bennett 1982:20–26).

The responses of youth subcultures to the tensions of each decade now appear increasingly acute, and distinctly more so, at every stage, than literary responses. As English subcultural sociology has shown, working-class youth subcultures, through an ensemble of commodities and musical allegiances, articulated quite successfully the limits of affluence throughout the postwar period. The increasing sophistication of youth subcultures, as a diachronic trajectory, presents an absolute reversal in the relations of "high" and mass culture. Literature—most notably MacInnes, in *Absolute Beginners*—initially incorporates rock and roll and related youth subcultures; the latter subsequently give literature a use value either unintended, as in Burgess's case, or lost to scholarly obscurantism, as in Greene's. Each synchronic stage in the presentation of this reversal between high and mass culture, accordingly, will itself move through literature, music, and youth subcultures.

The foremost concern is the degree both of resistance and submission, in each area, to the prevailing or *hegemonic* consensus about English society. Antonio Gramsci's concept of hegemony, described below, evolved from study of the radiation of innovations, or the competition between different groups' uses of language in various forms of communication, through which some speakers influence others (see Gramsci 1988:355–57). Ideology, from this view, is understood as a struggle waged between different, more and less powerful "accents" and meanings to articulate the most plausible accounts of self and society. Because hegemony is continually renewed and modified, "forms of alternative or directly oppositional politics and culture [always] exist as significant elements" in a lived social process. And if the limits on expression of experience effected by hegemonic domination are internalized ones, then "many different forms of struggle, including those not easily recognizable as and indeed not primarily 'political' and 'economic,'" might be grasped with "a much more profound and more active sense" (Williams 1977:109–12). In postwar England, popular culture has been a key site "in the struggle for hegemony, rather than being merely a 'superstructural' reflection of that struggle" (Bennett 1982:26).

Rather than some absolute triumph of a dominant ideology, hegemony describes a shifting, dynamic cultural process, in which material social experience continually reminds people of their genuine grievances. Emphasizing a positive orientation to the future, Gramsci insists that analyses of hegemony must not be ends in themselves, but acquire significance only in practical activity by indicating "how a campaign of political agitation may best be launched, what language will best be understood" (1971:185). The sensuous textures of popular culture are particularly important to him, for their potential use to contest authority with more convincing social alternatives, which take seriously and engage directly with the popular in its own language (Hebdige 1988:203–4).

The dialogical theory of Bakhtin dovetails with Gramsci's recognition of the continual struggle in the hegemonic process, and the significance of every area of the culture in that struggle. Bakhtin shares "the premise that cultural processes are intimately connected to social relations, that culture, as the site of social difference and contradiction, is deeply involved with power." Bakhtin, in his concept of *heteroglossia,* emphasizes the continual presence of languages and discourses competing for ascendancy, each marked by its own tonalities and meanings. This materialist concern with *tone,* with the "confrontation of differently oriented social accents" (Stam 1988:120–22), usefully focuses attention on the affective as well as the ideological, and is thus the fundamental basis of comparisons and contrasts here between literary, popular, and subcultural forms. Colin Mercer, arguing for analysis of pleasure in popular cultural experience, also brings Bakhtin and Gramsci together. From reference to the persisting circuit of consent and contumacy in Bakhtin's carnival, a shifting duality of tone, Mercer moves to terms more of hegemonic struggle: popular complicity with power in "beliefs, 'gut feelings,' common sense" is always "transacted in an unstable medium of dialogue in which the response might not fit with the original mode of address" (1986:61).

In every instance in the following chapters, from the age of affluence to punk, the concern is the success or lack thereof with which voices in different cultural forms resisted the influence not just of prevailing ideas, but of prevailing tones of voice. Recorded are not just ideological successes and failures, but also affective ones. In postwar English culture, the central aims of the avant-garde were realized to a significant extent, as cultural studies has documented: the audience and its use of cultural texts in everyday life became as significant as the producers of the texts themselves; and other hoary dichotomies, especially that of high and low culture, were swept away as well. Though the focus is on England, avant-garde revolt of this sort has recently begun to make "political sense" in the cultural context of the United States as well. If the institution of art was long negligible in its influence in that country, since the onset of cold war (as chapter 1 indicates) the arts have become increasingly significant in legitimizing capitalist domination (Huyssen 1986:167, 193), and hence to resisting it as well.

Hegemony and Affluence

The Birmingham cultural studies group made its first use of the theory of hegemony to explain the ideological situation in England between the midfifties and early sixties (if not longer). That period saw the achievement of true hegemonic domination (Hall and Jefferson 1976:40; Hall et al. 1978:319), with the ideology of affluence defusing working-class resistance and delivering a spontaneous consent to the Conservative party, in numbers sufficient for it to maintain power for thirteen years, 1951–64. It is important to note that the argument for an incipient classless society offered a future understood to have yet to arrive. The signs of social class did not actually disappear for anyone, regardless of the extent of subscription to the propositions based on affluence.

Consent of this sort is won not through the imposition of some closed system, or a prefabricated conception of the world. It requires instead a process of formation, condensing and connecting different discourses, and through them, drawing together subjects with heterogeneous interests (Hall 1988:10). Such leadership thereby wins active, not passive consent; people have to believe consent is in their best interests. If ideology were the result of simple manipulation, such a practice could simply be stopped at some point in time, and thus society would be much easier to change than it ever has been in reality. Hegemony refers instead to "a whole body of practices and expectations; our assignments of energy, our ordinary understanding of the nature of man and of his world" (Williams 1980:37–38).

Gramsci describes in the hegemonic process a conflict of ideologies, in which one or a combination of them tends to prevail, and propagates "itself throughout society—bringing about not only a unison of economic and political aims, but also intellectual and moral unity." In capitalist societies, the dominant alliance would in particular have "all the questions around which . . . struggle rages [cast] not on a corporate [or class] but on a 'universal' plane" (1971:181). Discourse *within* the "universe" of the dominant culture, minimizing or denying the injuries of class, contrasts with negotiations that fully acknowledge the culture and grievances of subordinate groups (Hall et al. 1978:155). The attempt, in other words, is to limit public discourse, what is thinkable and sayable, to questions that do not entail conclusions violating the existing parameters of common sense. This containment of common sense works when it "appears as natural as the air we breathe. It is simply 'taken for granted,'" a success every ideology hopes to achieve by naturalizing itself "out of History into Nature, and thus [becoming] invisible" (Hall 1988:8). The hegemonic bloc succeeds to the extent that even critics of the social system confine themselves within the framework of the prevailing common sense (like the Labour party in Britain or liberals in the United States).[1]

At the level of the *conjuncture*, or quotidian politics without apparently far-reaching significance, the ruling bloc, especially the state and the mass media, in general "seek to demonstrate that the necessary and sufficient conditions *already exist* to make possible . . . the accomplishment of certain historical tasks" (Gramsci 1971:178). Faced with the *organic* (deep, long-term) contradictions of capitalism, however, the dominant groups must make a larger effort as well, but still within limits, to preserve the existing social system. Those limits lie in restructuring political forces, ideological discourse, and the state (with the general effect recently, for example, of centralizing power even more in the chief executive)—anything rather than altering profoundly the fundamental distribution of economic resources. These efforts cannot be merely defensive and conjunctural, finally, but must be *formative*, constructing the crisis and representing it as it is lived (Hall and Jacques 1983:23). Gramsci, says Stuart Hall, recognizes "that every crisis is also a moment of reconstruction. [T]he disruption of the old economic, social, cultural order, provides the opportunity to reorganize it in new ways." Authoritarian populism, for example, was a form of "regressive modernization," simultaneously transformative and regressive, in the accompaniment of arguments for radical economic restructuring (or flexible accumulation) by appeals to nostalgia (1988:164–65).

The election of Labour in 1945 marks one distinctive sort of crisis described by Gramsci, occurring after a "major political undertaking for which [the ruling class] has requested, or forcibly extracted, the consent of the broad masses (war, for example)." The English "masses" considered wartime sacrifices to amount to a guarantee of a new society after the war, and unsentimentally voted out Churchill. Thus, just as Gramsci describes it, they "put forward demands which taken together, albeit not organically formulated, add up to a revolution" (1988:218). What happened, in point of fact, was more of a compromise defusing the situation, with the right settling for the welfare state and the left only a modification of capitalism along the lines of Keynesian management of the economy. Along with reforms in education, health, and housing, then, a distinctive ideology of welfare capitalism was a chief product of the moment, a project legitimating the state by claiming to be what the people wanted. Social democracy, however, with some state direction of the economy, provision for the social welfare, and mediation between capital and labor, "is not socialism, but an attempt to rescue capitalism" (Sinfield 1989:16; see also Hall et al. 1978:227–35).

In the characterization of postwar social change that dominated the fifties, the

> key terms [were] 'affluence,' 'consensus,' and 'embourgeoisment.'
> Affluence referred, essentially, to the boom in working class consumer spending (though it entailed the further, less tenable proposition that the working classes not only had more to spend, but were *relatively* better off). 'Consensus' meant the acceptance by both political parties, and the majority of the electorate, of all the measures—mixed economy [between public and private ownership], increased incomes, welfare-state 'safety net'—taken after 1945 [and Labour's stunning victory] to draw people of all classes together, on the basis of a common stake in the system, [with] a broad consensus of views on all the major issues [marking] the end of major political and social conflicts. . . . 'Embourgeoisement' gathered all these, and other social trends (in education, housing, redevelopment, . . . etc.), together with the thesis that working-class life and culture were ceasing to be a distinct formation in society, and everyone was assimilating rapidly towards middle class patterns, aspirations and values. (Hall and Jefferson 1976:21, 40)

The myth of an impending classlessness effectively delimited public discourse by fixing attention on the most conspicuous indications of significant change—higher employment and wages (relative to the Depression, though), and the accelerated consumer culture, symbolized by the teenager. The ideology of affluence thereby suppressed the economic facts that remained unchanged, at base the persisting relative inequalities in income.

A comparative affluence was indeed tangible for everyone, after the Depression and the sheer physical deprivation of rationing under wartime and postwar austerity measures. The actual lack of change in relative wage rates and the general distribution of wealth was "experientially overridden" by emphasis on increases in wages alone (S. Laing 1986:24). The higher wages and levels of employment enjoyed by the working class, as a result, permitted an unusually high degree of consensus on suggestions that the class war was ending, an argument focusing on "local shifts and transformations while concealing the essential continuity of the 'outer boundaries'" of social class. And besides the persisting gap in incomes, the ideology of affluence obscured even more disastrously the decline in the economic infrastructure. In retrospect "British economic growth had looked impressive [only] in isolation" and was merely temporary and fortuitous. The narrow focus on the comparative difference from the England of the thirties obscured the dire need for long-term planning and restructuring (Hill 1986:7, 9–10).

The real economic backwardness of England is indicated by the fact that the ideology of "consumerism," concocted in the United States in the 1920s (see Ewen 1982), was only feasible in England in the fifties. With higher wages, "Workers were recast not just as those who subsisted by the sale of their labor, but as a group with significant purchasing power. In a word, more than ever before, the English working class became defined and interpellated as *consumers*." Though there was never any empirical data to support suppositions about embourgeoisment, "'affluence' seemed to be producing an 'I'm all right, Jack' individualism" (Hitchcock 1989:22–23). The Conservative Party regained power in 1951 on the basis of accepting a reformed capitalism, and subsequently bribed voters with a short-term expediency in economic policy, promoting private consumption at the public sector's expense, especially in the inflationary "give-away budget" of 1955. Tax cuts in that year brought a predictable inflationary halt to postwar prosperity, but also an end to rationing, and won the election for the Conservatives. The 1955 victory, finally, enabled particularly bald talk of a classless society (S. Laing 1986:59). Prime Minister Harold Macmillan famously proclaimed, in 1957, that "most of our people have never had it so good," and in 1959 that the class war was over (adding, according to some accounts colored by hindsight, "and we have won it," by persuading so many it had ended).

Subsequent descriptions of a "bread and circuses" politics, employing the classical metaphor for social control by a combination of both economic manipulation and mass spectacle, indicate the extent to which the the success of "affluence" was bound up with the unprecedented ascendancy of mass culture, especially television, as well as the youth culture centered on rock and roll. "What was really new about rock," in the history of popular music, lay not in its African-American roots—already present in England in a number of forms, such as jazz—but "in the fact that it was so much a part of the mass media," and the general evolution of leisure and consumption into the primary field of personal development and fulfillment (Wicke 1990:4, 10).

The dramatic increase in the ownership of televisions by the midfifties was not only the primary symbol of affluence and embourgeoisment, but the main material proof of it. Plausible but unverified observations on the significance of television included Labour Party Leader Hugh Gaitskell's conclusion that the class basis for the historical strength of Labour had been sapped by "the new way of life based on the telly, the frig., the car and the glossy magazine." Changes in leisure opportunities and consumption, then, not just in wages, were for many "decisive indicators" of a "New England" (S. Laing 1986:3–4, 13–17, 29, 141). Williams was one of the few critics in the fifties to argue that simply enjoying a higher standard of living, in the consumption of cars, television sets, washing machines, and better clothing and housing, did not at all advance the working class into the bourgeoisie (1983:323–24).

The many contradictions of the period hardly passed unnoticed, but were contained in common sense as a "moral unease" (just as concern over a general moral "permissiveness" constricts the social agenda in the 1990s). Despite Macmillan's celebration of consensus, invoking the Edwardian sunset of the Empire, it did not escape attention that he extolled a "highly un-Edwardian world of supermarkets and motorways, juxeboxes and jets, jeans and guitars, scooters and televisions." The reaction to youth culture in particular embodied this moral dilemma. Youth served as an index of social anxiety at the same time it was a metaphor for social change, seen as both the "vanguard of the Golden Age and [of] the new hedonism," an ambivalence apparent in the moral panic over the teddy boys (Hall et al. 1978:233–34).

The situation in the United States at present differs somewhat in its details, but the general hegemonic argument takes a form quite similar to the ideology of affluence. In the United States in the 1980s, in the face of a similar decline due to imperial overreach and neglect of the economic infrastructure, an ideology of supposed "revolution" in free enterprise was declared (the "Reagan Revolution"), though what occurred was brutally reactionary, exacerbating existing economic inequality. Authoritarian populism in the United States advanced, in particular, essentially the same arguments as those put forward in England in the fifties, about the irrelevance of class politics. (These arguments seemed to increase in insistence, not surprisingly, in direct correlation with the increase in the actual social injuries taking place.) At the same time, the tensions of the eighties and nineties, as in Britain in the fifties, have been registered to a considerable extent in moral disquiet over the young.

But if "a situation like the fifties in Britain [seems] the dominant mode in the U.S." at present, in a consensus "that everybody in America [is] middle class now" (Irving 1988:167), the very different historical background to the American situation should be remarked. The suppression of discourse about class, in the United States, has long deformed its politics: the failure "to acknowledge the sweep and power of class in conditioning our fates is the single most terrible obstacle we face in constructing a polity less cruelly unjust" (Smoler 1991:67; see DeMott 1990). When George Bush, for example, chastised Michael Dukakis in 1988 for breaking "with the American tradition of entrepreneurship and free enterprise," the specific basis of his denunciation was his opponent's "increasing appeals to class conflict.... Good heavens, this is the United States of America. In my view, there is no place in American public life for philosophies that divide Americans one from another on class lines and that excite conflict among them" (Warren 1988:A3). By the next year official

Washington had embraced a neoconservative's argument that the end of history had been reached, just as the "end of ideology" had been declared three decades earlier (by Daniel Bell). The "end of history" line was based in the ludicrous, unexamined premise that "the class issue has actually been successfully resolved in the West. [T]he egalitarianism of modern America represents the essential achievement of the *classless* society envisioned by Marx" (Fukuyama, qtd. in Hitchens 1989:302). This rhetoric traveled back across the ocean in 1990, when the new Prime Minister John Major announced the objective of a "classless society." Such a society, he stipulated, would be one in which the *attitude* that class and its injuries are significant has been eradicated, not the material reality of inequity. In England in the fifties, pundits similarly declared that the "fantastic growth of the economy [has] rendered obsolete the whole *intellectual* framework within which Socialist discussion used to be conducted" (Hogg, qtd. in Hill 1986:6). Anthony Crosland wrote in 1956 that the Labour Party needed to follow the American model: eradicating the sense of class on the "socio-psychological plane" by providing not actual economic equality, but an ideological belief in something like the American " 'office-boy to president' mythology" (qtd. in Sinfield 1989:253–54).

The literary preoccupation with mass culture did reflect a modest resistance to notions of classlessness, a suspicion that affluence was an ideology of the dominant culture, directed at the working class through the media, political speeches, and so forth (Allsop 1964:37).[2] Williams, however, distinguishes such mildly alternative or oppositional productions—ones remaining within a specific hegemony that limits, neutralizes, or incorporates them—from works that remain more independent of adaptation or conformity (1977:113–14). On the one hand, the popularity of the so-called Angries in the fifties can be attributed in part to a widespread disappointment at the return of the Tories: "The optimism of 1945 had changed in the decade to Osborne's sad reflection that 'the old gang are back.'" Such anger, on the other hand, did not have overtly political consequences because it remained an expression of disappointment at "what the return of the Tories symbolized," in general "the apparent *immutability* of social and political life," a sense of futility distinctly colored by notions of the end of ideology and social class (Cooper 1970:276).

The generation of writers who emerged in the fifties, in the final analysis, were quite susceptible to arguments about the diminishment of the class structure. Nigel Dennis's novel *Cards of Identity* (1955), for instance, is not so much an early postmodernist tract on the frailty of the subject as a document of fears of mass persuasion. The novel's play with identity seems to underwrite the sense that traditional moorings in social class were breaking up; for some characters, changes in identity entail shedding "old memories of class differences," which seems to be a relatively easy matter. The country-house setting, established as a symbol of prewar social relations by Evelyn Waugh's *Brideshead Revisited,* appears in Dennis's novel as "one of the last relics of an age of established identities." John Arden's play *Live Like Pigs* (1958) shares this ambiguity. A rough working-class family, descendents of sixteenth-century "sturdy beggars," terrorizes the other residents of a public Housing Estate who aspire to the middle class, until the latter become an angry mob, itself an atavism of working-class history. But Arden, as is his wont in other works, offers little by way of judgment, besides the uncertainty of a policeman's summation on the "law-abiding neighborhood. Least it has been for the last year or two, once the folk got settled down; and we don't want your lot"—the throwbacks to the sturdy beggars—"stirring it up again." The implication here is ambiguous: is Arden satirizing the engineering of consent, or does he accept the view that class strife is an anachronism?

The Angries and their immediate predecessors, the Movement, seem to have genuinely felt themselves cut adrift from older causes of social discontent. Products of educational opportunity for the most part, moreover, the leading young English writers were steeped in traditional elitist belief in the primacy of literary expression. Thus the so-called Angries remained well away from the cultural and ideological battlefront manned by the likes of the teddy boys. The literary preferred F. R. Leavis's description of a small, discerning minority pitted against mass culture; Doris Lessing, for example, set the "small personal voice" of the novelist against the "barrier of financiers, actors, producers, directors" facing anyone who would work in film and television (1958:201). Given this literary default, from about 1963 the best young English minds from the lower middle and working classes have gone into rock music.

The Angry Young Men/The Movement

Distinction between the Movement and the Angry Young Men has been dealt with at length in Blake Morrison's *The Movement*. It will simply be noted here that Morrison and others cite substantial similarities between the two groups, though the only members of the Movement identified with the Angries were Kingsley Amis and John Wain, and no one after John Osborne, such as John Braine and Alan Sillitoe, wished to be labeled an Angry Young Man. One similarity between the groups, in this respect, is the common complaint that their identification was a purely journalistic phenomenon. But the Movement was already widely identified as such when *The Spectator* attempted to boost its circulation by running articles on the group in 1954, and the poets featured on Wain's radio program *First Reading,* in 1953, certainly represented a self-selected grouping (see Morrison 1980:42–54).[3] In retrospect, the clear development subsequent to the Movement is not Angry Young Men, but a "new phase of fictional representation of working-class life," a relocation of the postwar genre, established by the Movement, "of the young male hero on the make in the fluid social situation of a new Britain." Braine's *Room at the Top,* in this regard, was the crucial linking text between Movement novels and the working-class fiction of Sillitoe, David Storey, and Keith Waterhouse (S. Laing 1986:61–62).

Both the Movement and the Angries "considered themselves enemies of the old order, but one can tell that their nonconformism was based on an emergent conformity," especially in the Leavisian denunciations of mass culture and cultural leveling, as well as the adjustment to the perceived insignificance of social class. The essential acceptance of the ideology of affluence is recorded continually in the ease and impunity of hypergamy, in particular. Marrying above one's class is heavily laden with a sense of compromise with that ideology: Wain overtly declaring his neutrality, in *Hurry on Down* (1953); Amis asserting in *Lucky Jim* (1954) that "luck" is the only social force (in the absence of class). The collection of essays entitled *Declaration,* published in 1957, had no difficulty conflating "Movement neutralism," in the person of Wain, with "Angries activism," since the perspectives on affluence scarcely differed (Hitchcock 1989:31). Wain, for example, advises young writers to ignore elders "who jeer at them" for their caution and compromise, a reversal of the usual terms of generational conflict, symptomatic of the distortions of the time. One contemptuous passage, in his contribution to *Declaration,* exemplifies in a single stroke the Movement's elitism and capitulation to the ideology of affluence and consensus: "nearly three decades further on, . . . the English working class have never been less Red in their history; all they are interested in is wringing higher and higher wages out of the bankrupt industries that employ them, with never a thought of altering the social structure in any way" (1958:74–75, 88).

When the Situationist International set out to create a genuinely revolutionary movement in the midfifties, based in part on subverting mass culture or "the more advanced material means of the modern world," it defined its initiative against not only a now-respectable, decrepit surrealism, but also the "utter innocuousness" and "reassuring flimsiness" of its contemporaries, the Angry Young Men. The Angries, says the first issue of the journal *International Situationniste,*

> discovered, thirty years behind the times [after surrealism and the original avant-garde], a certain moral subversiveness that England had managed to completely hide from them all this time; and they think they're being daringly scandalous by declaring themselves republicans, . . . indicative of how tepidly literary their perspective is. They have simply come to change their opinions about a few social conventions without even noticing the whole change of terrain of all cultural activity so evident in every avant-garde tendency of this century. ("The Sound and the Fury" 1981:41–42)

The Situationists were wrong in a number of respects, however. Not unlike the original avant-garde, first of all, nearly every English writer in the fifties was very much bound up with the change in cultural terrain marked by a newly ascendant mass culture. The English literary response, however, was scarcely republican, but bitterly elitist and thus far from tepid (though ultimately quietistic in acceptance of affluence as a reality). The culture of postwar England was felt by the literary to mark a precipitous decline into pacification, attributable to television, rock and roll, and working-class youth conditioning the taste and values of a new youth culture—all linked to the perceived new affluence for the working class. The Situationists correctly found a reactionary attribution of a privileged, redemptive value to literature, in English writers of the fifties, but failed to note the distinctive frequency and intensity of literary inspections of mass culture.

In presenting mass culture, members of both the Movement and the Angries (particularly Wain and Osborne, and, in their wake, MacInnes, Waterhouse, and Stan Barstow) tend towards disapproval of the Americanization of English culture, specifically its technological standardization. Leavis's essay "Mass Civilization and Minority Culture" (1930) helped establish the Americanization thesis, which he subsequently promoted in the journal *Scrutiny*. Complaints about Americanization can be traced back even earlier, to Rudyard Kipling, for example; American film and dance music were well established in England by the 1920s. In the fifties, the indictment of Americanization reflected in part the economic boom in the United States and its rise in international prestige and imperial outreach, while the decline of England's strength became painfully apparent. More importantly, the Americanization thesis served the myth of classlessness, by masking the fact that concerns over cultural decline directly involved fear and loathing of the working class. If commercial culture threatened the authority of cultural institutions, it did so precisely because its attention to mass consumption "was bound to lead to a shift in cultural processes towards the needs and lifestyle of the working class" (Wicke 1990:59)—an apprehension that could not be directly expressed when class antagonism had supposedly waned.

The complaint of Leavis and his epigones obviously concerned not so much America as the perceived effect of mechanically reproduced art—moral and aesthetic leveling—which undermined from below the traditional arbiters of taste and their cultural capital (Chambers 1985:4–5). What was really at stake was the cultural prestige of the literary in particular, both creators and critics. In his 1930 essay, Leavis found that the "few who are capable of unprompted, first-hand judgment" on culture were under an assault by the loss of "inherited codes of habit and valuation, . . . a breach in continuity" (1933:14, 17) that writers of the fifties found even more pressing. Like him, they worried over the perceived conformity induced by the "automated society," and the resulting corruption of the authentic emotions of "felt life." The language of excellence and quality, directed against newer cultural forms like rock and roll and streamlined design, reflected a crisis in cultural continuity and social stability, at least for the traditional arbiters of moral and aesthetic absolutes. The old critical languages confronted the rhythms and participatory possibilities of languages made possible by new forms, especially popular music, and "were right to perceive that what was at stake was a future—their future" (Hebdige 1988:52–54, 71, 73).

The recourse to Leavis's elitism was consistent with the generally hostile relationship to the leftist literary movement of the thirties, writers such as Auden and MacNiece, or Christopher Caudwell and Ralph Fox, who took an enlightened interest in mass culture as well as radical politics. But the persistence of Leavis's suspicion of popular texts also reflects the fact that generations of schoolchildren, in England, have been trained in a literary criticism based directly in his work, a criticism "built to withstand the supposed weakness and errors of popular materials" (Cunningham 1988:279). As late as 1964, Denys Thompson, a Leavis cohort from the thirties, produced *Discrimination and Popular Culture,* a collection of pessimistic essays growing out of the 1960 National Union of Teachers' meeting. The NUT project, in Thompson's vague, idealist Leavisian terms, was the teaching of "discrimination" through "the first-rate in art, literature and music,... to provide children with standards... against which the offerings of the mass media will appear cut down to size" (qtd. in S. Laing 1986:213).

Williams (1958) was one of the few dissenters, criticizing in the essay "Culture Is Ordinary" both how widespread the diagnosis of a new mechanized vulgarity in culture had become, and the failure to acknowledge the hoary basis of that diagnosis in Leavis's longstanding ideas. (Wain does cite Leavis in his essay in the *Declaration* collection.) Williams, in *Culture and Society,* was one of the few voices to challenge the general denigration of mass communication, pointing out first of all that there are no masses, but "only ways of seeing people as masses," and second, given the essential neutrality of communications techniques themselves, that their effect depends upon their uses by their owners (1983:300–301). Art critic Lawrence Alloway, who coined the term *pop* in arguing for an audience-oriented sociological model for understanding mass art, made the same point a year later: "The audience today is numerically dense but highly diversified.... Fear of the Amorphous Audience is fed by the word 'mass'" (qtd. in Hebdige 1988:124–25, 142).

Hall, however, found it difficult to break at the time with the NUT paradigm, though he and Paddy Whannel, in *The Popular Arts* (1965), "defined a stance distinct from both the militant hostility of the NUT position and the 'opportunist' approach which, patronisingly, refused to make any evaluative distinctions" (S. Laing 1986:214–16). Hall and Whannel eschew Leavis's original distinction of folk and mass culture, specifically disavowing his mystified concept of organic culture. But their own category of preference, the "popular," merely represents an intermediate phase inserted into Leavis' original dichotomy. Popular art derives from folk cultures, in essence, and remains entirely opposed to mass culture (Turner 1990:74). Hall and Whannel are actually much closer to conventional equations between the "popular arts" and "hand-crafted folk arts" than to Alloway—and his compatriots in the Independent Group at the Institute for Contemporary Arts, including Richard Hamilton—who "felt none of the dislike of commercial culture standards [common] amongst most intellectuals." Alloway believed that pop culture should be treated "with the seriousness of high art," along the continuum of a "unifying but tolerant aesthetic." The enthusiastic consumption of leisure culture, as well as its production, embodied "the same dimensions of skills as work which once stood alone as serious [artistic] activity," and thus no "social critic in his right mind should simply reject [mass culture] as being a load of rubbish or even the opium of the people" (qtd. in Whiteley 1987:37, 48, 50, 67).[4]

The New Left's perpetuation of Leavis (and even Matthew Arnold), epitomized by the NUT, actually helped buttress the notion of class mobility "by entangling it with the acquisition of superior culture, [a] way into a fuller humanity" no longer facing the encumbrance to education posed by class barriers. This elite left culturalism reflected a grudging acceptance of claims for the affluent society, a sense that working people were indeed happier thanks to increased consumption, but that mass culture "was destroying their dignity and resistance. It all seemed a failure at the level of culture [to develop] the spirit that should accompany socialism." Working-class culture in the fifties was continually represented, as in Richard Hoggart's work, "either negatively or as quiescent; or, if positively, as something that is being lost" (Sinfield 1989:243–45, 257).

In Hall and Whannel's *The Popular Arts,* high culture is defined pretty much in Leavis's own words: the "really creative work..."

bears the stamp of an original imagination; its power depends upon its capacity to force us 'out of ourselves' and to attend to the range and quality of someone else's mind." Popular culture, to Hall and Whannel, is an acceptable counterpart to high culture because it deals with familiar situations, in a direct relationship between performer and audience. Historically it provided a significant source of adhesion in "organic" communities (the repressed Leavis returning here), both rural and urban. The Edwardian music hall, in which some repartee still went on between stage and stall, exemplified popular culture, or a transitional phase between folk culture and the corrosiveness of the mass media (1965:50–53, 60). As a symbol of the ostensible transition from folk to popular art in late Victorian and Edwardian culture, the music hall had for some time, in fact, been employed by writers like Osborne, nostalgic for the social certainties of the Edwardian period. (The music hall became the subject of a book by MacInnes, for the same reason, as late as 1967, as the next chapter details.) In *The Entertainer* (1958), which attributes the death of the music hall to rock and roll, Osborne laments the passing of "Some of the heart of England, [of] something that once belonged to everyone, for [the music hall] was truly a folk art. . . . Its contact is immediate, vital, and direct." In this light, all Hall and Whannel appear to have done was substitute *popular* for *folk*.

Popular art like the music hall and jazz, according to them, still "has in common with folk art the genuine contact between audience and performer: but it differs from folk art in that it is an individualized art, the art of the known performer." It has its redeeming features—its contact with its audience's values, attitudes, and experiences—and is sharply distinguished from the mass media, which have no personal quality. Mass art, on the other hand, is universally manipulative, destroying "all trace of individuality and idiosyncrasy which makes a work compelling and living." The popular artist still found individual stylization necessary, but mass culture relies solely on formulae: "In mass art the formula is everything—an escape from, rather than a means to, originality" (1965:66–69). Hall and Whannel's authorities for this claim, not surprisingly, include Theodor Adorno and Dwight Macdonald (a disciple of both Adorno and Leavis), as well as Hoggart.

The Situationists likewise found mass culture stultifying in the fifties: "raging and ill-informed youth, well-off adolescent rebels lacking perspectives but far from lacking a cause—*boredom* is what they all have in common." But contemporaneous English writers, in contrast, could not sufficiently let go of the conventional conception of literature, as a practice autonomous from the inauthenticity of mass culture, to "execute the judgment that contemporary leisure is pronouncing against itself." That would have involved exploring dissident uses of mass culture. English writers retained archaic elitist attitudes, instead, foredoomed to irrelevance with the further success of television and pop music. "The Angry Young Men," the SI concluded, "are in fact particularly reactionary" in their privileging of literary practice, "defending a mystification that was denounced in Europe around 1920" by the avant-garde (Debord 1981d:24; "The Sound and the Fury" 1981:41–42). Given the Angries' fairly ready inclination to jettison the old politics of class, finally, anger was apparently excited less by political issues than by cultural ones: the idea of a homogenized culture rankled more than that of a classless society, political issues taking a back seat to cultural ones. In this respect in particular, "anger was more selective, occasionally more unpleasant, and certainly more conservative than is generally acknowledged" (Hill 1986:22, 24).

The Situationists were right in still another respect: a seemingly innocuous change of mind about a few social conventions shows up in the content of the Angries' work, in a consistent, though usually troubled subscription to the myth of affluence. The novel of class may be revived in questioning the new status of the class structure, but it betrays a pronounced "lack of assurance about what the man or the society is really like" (Gindin 1962:4). Kenneth Allsop characteristically attributes the Angries' solipsistic dissidence to a sense of detachment from social identity. They presumably "feel unassimilated," like "a new rootless, faithless, *classless* class—and consequently, because of a feeling of being misplaced and misprized, also often charmless—who are becalmed in the social sea,...strangers to their own sort" (1964:27). The uncertainty and frustration described here were the product of the formative hegemonic moment when, to paraphrase Osborne, everything had changed and everything had stayed the same.[5]

Affluence did have limits and contradictions that left Movement writers ill at ease, though they had difficulty pinpointing what was troubling them, apparently because of the dominance of "affluence" in social discourse. Thom Gunn's first volume of poetry, suitably entitled *Fighting Terms* (1954), can only chide the socialist half measures of Labour: "Security a fraud, and how unwise / Was disembarking on your Welfare State." His next collection, *The Sense of Movement* (1957), would raise, more profoundly than any other literary production of the fifties, the difficulties of a dialectic between intellect and action, a common predicament for his uneasy yet antipolitical generation. The university boys who first enlivened literature in the fifties—in chronological order, William Cooper, Wain, and Amis— evoke primarily their disaffection from the dullness of material austerity and its concomitant culture, especially their vapid academic experience. The subsequent chroniclers of school-leaving age (or just after) and non-U(niversity) rebels—Braine, Waterhouse, and Barstow—close out the decade in bathetic resignation. Arnold Wesker, at the end of the fifties, devoted a dramatic trilogy to the decline of the commitment of the thirties into the pathos of the fifties, a decline he links directly to mass culture.

Gunn, in *The Sense of Movement,* vividly embodies the difficulties inherent in attempting to promote action by literary means alone. He was even labeled a poet of violence, and an acute psychological violence is certainly possible in literature. But Gunn's critique of intellectuals and their passivity (see "Lines for a Book") is limited by the fact that they make up most of his audience. And if he aims to "hurt / The pale curators and the families / By calling up disturbing images," the image of his leather-jacketed motorcyclists, celebrated in "On the Move," holds only a fleeting shock value. Asked, furthermore, "if he had been fascinated by the aggressive power of working class boys," Gunn replied that "I was quite a self-inclosed middle-class boy. . . . So I never had any notions about class other than that it was something to be disregarded as much as possible" (Bold 1976:8). Here one finds the elemental contradiction of the fifties: a burning desire to shake up a dull, presumably homogeneous culture, undermined by a disinclination to challenge the minimizing of class relations, the fundamental source of that sense of stasis.

Gunn, however, did describe quite presciently the connection of revolt and style, both the literary and lived senses. Style, as a disruption of passivity expressed through a variety of forms, frequently marks the basis of identity in *The Sense of Movement*. His equation of *style* and *movement* not only suggests earlier avant-garde theory, but anticipates as well the subsequent arguments of cultural studies concerning the significance of youth subcultures. George Melly very fittingly took the title of his study of British rock music, *Revolt into Style,* from Gunn's poem "Elvis Presley":

> The limitations where he found success
> Are ground on which he, panting, stretches out
> In turn, promiscuously, by every note,
> Our idiosyncrasy and our likeness.
> We keep ourselves in touch with a mere dime:
> Distorting hackneyed words in hackneyed songs
> He turns revolt into a style, prolongs
> The impulse to a habit of the time.
> Whether he poses or is real, no cat
> Bothers to say: the pose held is a stance,
> Which, generation of the very chance
> It wars on, may be posture for combat.

The poem's politics are vitiated by the fiction of a nascent classless Youth Culture; Gunn underestimates the really original, unsettling power of Elvis's music in his initial, quite class-based incarnation, as an unredeemed hillbilly performing a racial crossover. But Gunn does realize that the limitations of what are commonly considered hackneyed, even manipulative forms require only a style of negation and contradiction, a distorting, discomfiting, rejuvenating voice, to transform their possibilities. Beyond this astute defense of technical mayhem in music, he credits even more assuredly the possibility of style to the audience as much as the artist, just as cultural studies would. Elvis's stance has the pall of commercialism hanging over whatever authenticity, musical, social, or sexual, it may appear to possess, but it has its use value as well. Simply Presley's attitude represents a potential weapon for the expression of desire, in the hands of his audience.

Gunn's realization that the mass audience can matter as much as the performer makes him unique in the fifties: "far from placing bike-boys, Presley, leather jackets and juke-boxes with thoughtful detachment in terms of art, individualism, seriousness, and 'good' culture, Gunn presents and justifies the social construction of subcultures." Otherwise, his quest to surpass literary, intellectualized classification of emotion in poetic language does not find a means of expression much past leather fetishism, though in this respect as well, he differed from the rest of the Movement, undermining its "'blokeish' ethos . . . with intimations of unorthodox sexuality" (Sinfield 1989:168). The Boys, in "On the Move," represent something like a subcultural style: their motorcycles create a "dull thunder of *approximate* words," such that one can "almost hear a *meaning* in their noise" (italics added). Of all the Movement and Angry writers, Gunn is unique in recognizing that the affective appeal of newer, despised cultural forms might have a productive relation with making meaning. The confinement of others to conventional literary prejudices left their own expression sheerly splenetic, a limitation they found in young hooligans like the teds, who in fact were far more successful in giving their anger meaningful form.

The hyperbolic rage of John Osborne's *Look Back in Anger* (1956), though, not Gunn's insight into stylistic revolt, established the mythical "Angry Young Man" (Hewison 1981.135). (Colin Wilson's *The Outsider* appeared at the same time, but its blunt, neofascist extolment of the worst elements of modernism, especially Nietzsche, provides only the narrowest of antipolitical stances.) The year 1956 is often described as a critical one in the postwar era, with Britain's humiliating debacle in the Suez crisis, when the United States intervened to rein in the invasion, signifying the demise of the Empire. The Soviet invasion of Hungary, in addition, seemed to confirm the bankruptcy of what vestige of left politics remained in the cold war. Though Osborne's play was first performed in May, and the Suez invasion occurred in November, the two events have often been linked in depicting an annus mirabilis. American rock and roll first reached Britain in 1956, as well. The combined effect of Suez and Hungary "was to exacerbate dissatisfactions and tensions. . . . What was needed was a myth" to embody those feelings, hence the Angry Young Man (Hewison 1981:127, 139).

But *Look Back in Anger,* in retrospect, seems a reflection less of these more profound cultural and political events than of another development in which 1956 was a key year, "the consolidation of [the] image of an affluent Britain undergoing embourgeoisment." A series of articles appearing that year in *Encounter* recite the usual litany of proofs of affluence—suburban housing estates, car and television ownership, the end of political grievances—while the *Spectator* published articles identifying increasing consumerism and the new housing estates "with a new social and political 'estate' or class" (S. Laing 1986:17–18). If Osborne captured any of the notable developments of 1956, it was this last one, and it might better be said to have captured him. At the beginning of the play, Jimmy reads his weekly posh paper, in which the Bishop of Bromley angrily "denies the difference of class distinctions. 'This idea has been persistently and wickedly fostered by—the working classes.'" Despite Osborne's clear recognition of this contradiction on the subject of class, however, on the whole he accepts the entire range of arguments associated with affluence, out of antipathy towards presumably concomitant cultural changes. This mixture, combining uncertainty about social changes with conviction about cultural ones, epitomizes the younger writers of the fifties.

Notwithstanding the immediate connection of Osborne's character Jimmy Porter with Amis's Jim Dixon (in *Lucky Jim*), Porter does present one very large difference, in pouring out all the venom Dixon kept internalized. Writers belonging to the earlier Movement, in fact, felt uneasy about Osborne's stress on emotion and rebellion, the explosive charge of his aim "to make people feel." Perhaps one great difference in this regard is that Osborne had not actually attended a university, though his character Porter attended the redbrick university highlighted by Amis and Wain in their portraits of scholarship boys, educated out of the working class into a social limbo (see Worpole 1985). In his disorientation and resentment over an apparently realigned, banal classless society, though, the one recourse Porter has pursued is the same as Dixon's—hypergamy. In the theme of marriage above one's class, Osborne, like the Movement, seizes on the presumably eroded barriers of class, in sexual relations, to confirm the scholarship boy's sense of social dislocation. Jimmy describes himself riding up on a white charger to do battle with Alison's mother, who conducted a holy crusade against him, "a young man without money, background." But in the conclusion to this soliloquy, for no discernible reason other than acquiescence to the ideology of affluence, Jimmy declares his "poor old charger," or class warfare, "all tricked out and caparisoned in discredited passions and ideals! The old grey mare that actually once led the charge against the old order—well, she certainly ain't what she used to be."

The sentimentality of the play's romantic conclusion, which features much cooing about bears and squirrels, especially appalled Movement writers. But to dismiss the sentiment too quickly is to miss its real significance in Osborne's general cultural schema, consistent with other writers. The "feminizing" of Jimmy at the end represents a quite harsh, despairing conclusion on the debilitating effects of the new mass culture. The play's general montage of mass-culture forms, employing all sorts of old and new cultural languages, did supply much of its impact. Osborne, therefore, captures very well the contradictions of an uncertain, socially and culturally confused, yet static milieu; unfortunately, he can only resolve those contradictions by scapegoating women. Had critics "been less spellbound by its surface rhetorical outpourings[,] they could not have helped but notice that the real subject of the play was neither social injustice nor hypocrisy but the debasement and degradation of women" (Hill 1986:25). Lessing did notice: with no good brave causes left, according to the play, "there is nothing for it but to stagnate and submit to being sucked dry by women. I think I quote more or less correctly" (1958:200).

Osborne is particularly influenced, in this regard, by the ideological capital made of female consumption, of the housewife who had perfected the "art of continuous consumption," an important symbol of affluence (Hill 1986:17–18). The television was always accompanied in popular periodicals and politicians' speeches by reference to domestic appliances, such as the refrigerator and the washing machine. If, therefore, the widespread attack on effeminacy in literature of the fifties is often couched in its conventional association with class privilege (including pettiness, snobbery, superficiality, and so on), this attack also represents an equation of the feminine with pacification by the consumer society and mass culture. Osborne's exceedingly blatant misogyny, in this respect, makes clear his capitulation to the ideology of affluence, especially supporting arguments citing cultural changes.

Critics such as Andreas Huyssen (1986:44–62) and Tania Modleski (1986) have pointed out fairly recently the long-standing, virtually reflexive tendency in negative assessments of mass culture (particularly those of modernism) to express its inferiority and pacifying effect in feminine terms. A gross example is Adorno's dismissal of jazz: "'Give up your masculinity, let yourself be castrated,' the eunuchlike sound of the jazz band both mocks and proclaims"

(1981:129).[6] Now that it has been denaturalized, the formulation equating pacification by mass culture with feminization, whatever its origin, becomes fairly glaring in *Look Back in Anger*. Jimmy Porter's general complaint about English culture and society in the fifties concerns passivity, or the absence of "ordinary human *enthusiasm.*" Osborne, from the opening stage direction, contrasts Jimmy's restless cruelty with the well-bred malaise of his wife Alison, indicted as Lady Pusillanimous ("Wanting of firmness of mind"), who leads her husband, the once-virile Sextus, to "the Games"—described in terms of a Hollywood film scenario, with "beefcake Christians" cuckolding him "in the wonder of stereophonic sound." Osborne, in other words, links contemporary mass culture directly with Rome and Juvenal's "bread and circuses," the classic negative metaphor for mass entertainment, and has a woman as its agent. (In this respect, Alison's upper-class background, the usual focus of critics, becomes distinctly secondary, further indicating that social class has become a dead issue.) Tory policy in the fifties has been summed up as a modern form of bread and circuses, of course, and thus the really reprehensible element of the Angries' failure becomes apparent here. Their misogyny, the sexist reduction of women to possessions, reflects quite directly an incomprehension of the actual hegemonic forces at work; Angry writers give up serious effort, in a sense, by confining their concerns over the new cultural and social order to more easily managed sexual preoccupations. Osborne is unusual in that he actively punishes women, through Jimmy's physical and verbal brutality, for the perceived changes brought about by mass culture.

Those changes, in the play, are also summed up in the classic Leavisian terms of Americanization. The threat of mass culture and consumerism to the singularity of British culture was often associated directly with scapegoated symbols of decadence like teenagers, but especially with " 'feminisation' of the national stock." For Hoggart and Osborne, as for Orwell in the late thirties, the American influence lay particularly in the "soft" and "streamlined"—that is, feminizing—qualities of new commodities and materials (Hebdige 1988: 9,58). One of the play's larger contradictions appears here: although Osborne laments the committed politics of the thirties (in the portrayal of Jimmy's father), his cultural perspective is based in Leavis's conservative work of the same period. At the core of Jimmy's "look back," a nostalgic yearning for the bygone social certainty of the

Edwardian class structure and good causes like the Spanish Civil War, is the feeling that "it's pretty dreary living in the American Age." Regretting language that has "bite, edge, drive," or that precious commodity enthusiasm, he frequently satirizes the new media of banality, writing pop songs like "You can quit hanging around my counter Mildred 'cos you'll find my position is closed," which reduce hard living to stereotyped emotions: "I'm so tired of necking, / of pecking, home wrecking, / of empty bed blues— / just pass me the booze. I'm tired of being hetero / Rather ride on the metero / Just pass me the booze / This perpetual whoring / Gets quite dull and boring." Besides Tin Pan Alley torch songs and their formulae for engineering tastes, Jimmy also parodies Madison Avenue, doing a Charles Atlas bit (in mocking religion, itself associated with the temptations offered by Alison and her upper-class friend Helena): "I was a liberal skinny weakling. I too was afraid to strip down to my soul, but now everyone looks at my superb physique in envy."[7]

Despite the critique of Americanization, Jimmy is also an advocate of "real jazz," which was just as much an American export; the Movement also assigned a positive "symbolic status to the jazz enthusiast" (Sinfield 1989:158). This contradiction in the tastes of the Leavisians is resolved by reading jazz as a more authentic "folk," or at least intermediate "popular" form (à la Hall and Whannel), though its importation required essentially the same commercial processes, differing only in scale, as Hollywood film. Jazz had long received an exemption from the Americanization thesis by English intellectuals, including members of the Movement such as Philip Larkin, a noted jazz critic, and Wain. In an articulated quest for authenticity based in race, "the 'dissenting' British use of black American music only makes sense in terms of middle-class ideology" revolving around jazz (rather than working-class uses of rock and roll) from the thirties through the early sixties. By the 1930s, English jazz criticism had already established oppositions that must have filtered through to Osborne (and certainly have to rock and roll criticism): as "a matter of feeling, expressive of personal not social identity"—terms used by Jimmy Porter himself—authentic/black/"hot" style was preferred to inauthentic/white/popular music. From this view, jazz was at its best when close to its racial "origins among the common people," and "lost its expressiveness and integrity" and power of protest with commercial diffusion. This elitism or connoisseurship, in the obsession with authenticity, fairly quickly passed to the aspiring lower middle class from which Osborne emerged (Frith 1988:47, 56–61). On Leavis's model, "exclusive, earnest commitment is preferred to the unthinking 'good taste' of a leisure class that takes its culture for granted." Thus the "intellectual jazz fan disdained the prevailing notion of the artistic," yet simply redeployed it on new ground. Rock and roll was intolerable, as a result, because it suggested the commercial and racial contradictions of drawing any American music, including jazz itself, into an intellectual apparatus still committed to traditional high-culture values. Wain, in *Strike the Father Dead* (1962), treats jazz not as the opposite of parental "high culture, educational attainment, tradition and respectability, but an additional way of expressing them" (Sinfield 1989:160, 167–68).

Bourgeois and/or literary jazz fans in England, furthermore, were actually devotees of relatively sedate, traditional ("trad") New Orleans jazz from the turn of the century, and "revival" jazz, associated with Chicago jazz of the 1920s, and groups such as Louis Armstrong's Hot Five. The stronger stuff of postwar modern jazz—Charlie Parker, Thelonius Monk, Dizzie Gillespie, Charlie Christian—was in fact "never considered" in England (Chambers 1985:47–48); there was never any English equivalent to the American Beat poets and writers. Larkin, for example, loathed modern jazz, questionably lumping Parker with Picasso in *All What Jazz,* as part of the modernist privileging of technique over human life; *Strike the Father Dead* likewise "suggests that jazz should have stopped at 1948" (Sinfield 1989:167). As opposed to the American Beats, who declared modern jazz the music of orgasm, Larkin actually believed that the tension went out of jazz when black musicians tried, through bebop, to distance themselves from the white audience. (But if his taste is questionable, in finding more "tension" in trad, at least he could take a hint from bebop where the patronizing Beats, self-styled White Negroes, did not.) Trad became a quite popular if sickly commercial form by the late fifties—even, briefly, the leading commercial opponent of rock and roll—indicating an extremely fine line in this case between a connoisseur like Larkin and popular tastes he would have considered insipid. Given the tepidness of English literary taste in music and its actual closeness to popular taste, finally, it is not surprising that in *Look Back in Anger,* for all Osborne's invocation of authentic "feeling," jazz in the final analysis serves precisely the mood of indolence and escape the literary connoisseur disdained in other white appropriations of the music. If jazz had an anti-institutional appeal for writers who wished to offend Mandarin literary taste (Hewison 1981:114–15), those younger writers' tastes were hardly much more liberal.

Apparently just preceding the importation of Beat and hipster styles from America, *Look Back in Anger* itself makes no strong association between jazz and race, as did the American Beat writers and MacInnes.[8] In the simple Leavisian association of the music with "feeling," Jimmy says that "anyone who doesn't like real jazz hasn't any feeling either for music or people," lionizing jazz largely because of its supposed independence from the marketplace. Hall and Whannel likewise pronounce jazz infinitely richer than other popular musics, both aesthetically and emotionally, employing terms such as "inner musical life" and "quality," typical of Leavisian abstractions. *The Popular Arts* derives from the attentive listening demanded by the subtleties of jazz from Leavis's practice of close reading while the praiseworthy aim of individual players, a "sound and tone which are characteristic of their personalities and feelings," is directly extrapolated from his literary strictures. Jazz presumably resides somewhere between his poles of "the folk arts and the commercial assembly line" (1965:307–11), though it does so less definitely than the music hall, the other "popular" form privileged by Leavisians.

Osborne writes in his contribution to *Declaration* that Jimmy's rhetoric about English culture and society is not to be taken as his actual belief, but as hyperbole resulting from the "texture of ordinary despair" (1958:51), a not altogether satisfactory distinction. Jimmy's pessimism over class and commitment, in any case, results in more of "a personal splurge of nostalgia" than "a one-man insurrection against the Establishment," as Allsop puts it. Jimmy hates his wife Alison, Allsop says, specifically because she totally misunderstands him in saying that he is "hurt because everything is the same." Her father Colonel Redfern, on the other hand, whose recent return after leaving England in 1914 makes him a perfectly preserved relic of the Edwardian period, is "hurt because everything is changed." In fact, Jimmy himself actually secretly regrets "that everything isn't the same"; though he professes to despise the Colonel's "self-discipline, certainty and courteous gentleness," Allsop finds that Jimmy yearns for it, at heart (1964:112, 117)—especially the Edwardian certainty of social position. Jimmy hardly dismisses the Edwardian period altogether: "The old Edwardian brigade do make their brief little world look pretty tempting.... Always the same picture: high summer, the long days in the sun.... What a romantic picture. Phoney, too, of course. It must have rained sometimes. Still, even I regret it somehow, phoney or not. If you've no world of your own, it's rather pleasant to regret the passing of someone else's." Osborne closely resembles Movement writers, in this respect, criticizing "the more blatantly unacceptable aspects of the 'old order' while maintaining an underlying respect for many of its values" (Morrison 1980:75). He describes his socialist attitude, in *Declaration,* in terms of his oft-declared "experimental attitude to feeling," terms less evocative of socialism than of the liberalism he rescues in the same passage from T. S. Eliot's scorn (1958:65), and features prominently in the play, in the entirety of the Charles Atlas bit.

Out of despair at English society, the conclusion, which has Jimmy a teddy bear (not teddy boy) and Alison a woolly squirrel, closes the play on a wretchedly maudlin note, confirming the earlier linkage of cultural degeneration and femininity. The bear-and-squirrel dialogue throughout the play has an explicitly mood-altering effect on Jimmy, turning him into a simp, as Alison coos, "You're a jolly super bear.... A really soooooooooooooooooper, marvelous bear." She expresses a desire to escape the "pain of being human" by becoming "little furry creatures with little furry brains"—like television viewers, one speculates—and "to be a lost cause. I want to be corrupt and futile!" She beguiles him into accepting this futility himself, just after he has asked if he was "really wrong to believe that there's a—a kind of—burning *virility* of mind and spirit that looks for something as powerful as itself." A sufficiently virile bear, he says, has "no herd to comfort him," but he wavers: "that voice that cries out doesn't *have* to be a weakling's, does it?" His voice does come out that way, though, in his last speech, reduced to puerility by a whimpering woman: "we'll live on honey, and nuts—lots and lots of nuts.... I'm a bit of a soppy, scruffy sort of a bear.... [pathetically] Poor squirrels!" Finally, then, Jimmy himself is rendered "pusillanimous," a victim of the cultural effeminacy despised and despaired at by Osborne. Robert Hewison seems quite wrong in his general conclusion on the fifties, that "anger, however confused, is a more positive response than nostalgia or despair" (1981:198)—his terms are inseparable in Osborne's case.

Rock and Roll and the Teddy Boys

The endemic literary revulsion at mass culture, youth culture in particular, is not entirely reprehensible, when one considers the ersatz rock and roll produced in England at the time. As Nik Cohn says, "British pop in the fifties was pure farce" (1970:53). The term subsequently applied to that music, *castrato-rock,* signifying close commercial control as well as musical and vocal vacuity, certainly suggests the traditional critical association of mass culture with emasculating effects. But as an allusion to actual commercial practices in music, it is not entirely inappropriate.

One might also detect in the process of "feminization" a somewhat positive development, though: rather than a decline in rock and roll, the shift to romantic ballads (and to girl groups by the early sixties) reflected the importance of girls in the rock audience, if their use of music was less public. Even with the resurrection of rock and roll by groups like the Beatles and the Rolling Stones, harder rock was mixed with softer ballads, an implicit recognition of the feminine audience (Frith and McRobbie 1990:383). Girls were involved in pop music from the start, often exercising a determining influence on the music through romantic attachments to pop stars, though they did so within "domestic space that was permitted rather than the public areas of streets, clubs, coffee bars and amusement arcades." Public visibility of that sort would have brought untenable moral condemnation (Chambers 1985:42–44; cf. McRobbie and Garber 1976:212–13). Thus there were no teddy girls to speak of; an extradomestic subcultural life for young women only gradually evolved over the next twenty years.

Hall and Whannel's description of fifties pop music reflects the absence of any challenging style. Generalized expressions of the yearning of nobody-in-particular for anyone-at-all, they found, resulted in a "hollow cosmos" effect (in Hoggart's terms). J. B. Priestley, in the collection *Thoughts in the Wilderness,* a critique of "Admass society," describes youth in terms of an air of conformity, loutish, sullen acquiescence, and absence of open rebellion, and uncritically reads responses to English pop off the music itself. But his sense of that music's passivity is accurate enough. Along with other mass media, the music waits "to pounce on the boys and girls as they come out of school," offering the "smooth and easy. . . . No effort must be required. . . . [N]obody is challenged, disturbed, asked to reflect or feel deeply," with everyone "kept by sinister magic in a closed circle of false mass culture" (1957:9–11, 13, 225, 241).

A representative collection of British pop from the late fifties and very early sixties, *Roots of British Rock* (see Shaw 1975), follows blow-by-blow George Melly's *Revolt into Style* (1970). The songs are definitely dreadful, with the exceptions of one number by Cliff Richard, whose backing group the Shadows had the salutary long-range impact of legitimizing groups, as opposed to individual singers; the tough rhythm and blues of "Shakin' All Over," by Johnny Kidd and the Pirates, a genuine anomaly; and later instrumental songs like the Tornadoes' "Telstar," important for their early experiments with electronic devices and effects. Skiffle music, too, represented by Lonnie Donegan, was important to the sixties and rock and roll, as the first do-it-yourself music. Mostly, however, one finds unlistenable ballads by "pretty-boy" singers, covers of the most wretched, contrived American hits, and hideous trad New Orleans jazz by the likes of Acker Bilk, in his bowler hat a "mixture of Edwardian dandy and rural bucolic," who married an "increasingly dull noise" with the Edwardian music hall (Melly 1970:60). It seems fitting that trad jazz, the favorite music of the Movement, would in its death throes invoke the Edwardian period, seemingly confirming how wrongheaded the literary were about both popular music and English society. (By the late seventies, former trad jazz stars Kenny Ball and Chris Barber played benefits for Margaret Thatcher, their politics consistent with the conservatism of that music's proponents, literary and otherwise, in the fifties.) The nadir of the collection, though, is fourteen-year-old Laurie London's sickly gospel hit, "He's Got the Whole World in His Hands." That song led MacInnes to declare, at the outset of *Absolute Beginners,* that the teenage thing was dead, in the hands of children.

In a typically banal song from the *Roots* collection, Marty Wilde's "Bad Boy," each element devotes itself to the essential formal quality, languor, from the soothing, barely projected vocal to the lazy, sliding, country-and-western guitar. The guitar supplies just the sort of ornamentation, of otherwise blank repetition, described by Adorno in the essay "On Popular Music," which has always remained valid in evaluating the worst of popular music (see Gendron 1986). The lyrical content of "Bad Boy" makes the whole aim abundantly apparent; Wilde begs to differ with parents and members of the public-at-large who might find him threatening. The girl involved is abstracted, peripheral, addressed only in the chorus, just as in Barstow's and Waterhouse's literary parodies of pop songs in *A Kind of Loving* and *Billy Liar,* respectively: "If only they knew how I love you / They'd say a bad boy / Could be a good boy / Who's just in love."[9] The denial here seems symptomatic of the fifties, even of the Angry Young Men's distillation of disaffection into sexual relations. Both literary and mass culture in the fifties are best characterized by "bad boys" who only really amount to mildly vexed romantics. Hoggart may be disputed on other subjects, like the teddy boys, but his description of the popular music of the late fifties seems fair enough, though once again antifeminine: "there is always love, as a warm burrow, as a remover of worry; love borne on an ingratiating treacle of melody" (1961:189).

In Cohn's terms, English pop in the fifties had all the "white sentiment" of American rock and roll, and none of the "colored beat" (1970:1). When Cliff Richard, with his newly scrubbed, radiant cleanness and presentable manners, moved to ballads like "Living Doll" in 1958, "it killed rock stone dead" in England: "No rage, no farce, no ugliness left. We have mass-produced faces with mass-produced voices on mass-produced songs." It all "reflected the extraordinary smugness and optimism of that time perfectly: the British never had it so good" (Cohn 1970:61). With Richard's decline and Laurie London's ascent, the first British pop explosion was effectively "castrated," but it had three crucial, sustained effects. The first dates from the career of Tommy Steele, who in 1956 was "the first British pop event" (Melly 1970:4). Subsequently made over into the English Elvis Presley, though much nicer, and then "an all-around family entertainer" (Cohn 1970:55–56), Steele was discovered in the 2I's coffee bar, a center for skiffle music. The coffee bar, in its emulation of Continental style and bohemianism, was an important symbol of "a strong desire, at least on the part of the younger generation, for something new" (Hewison 1981:59).

Skiffle itself established several precedents that would underlie each successive resurgence of challenge to prevailing pop music, from the Beatles and Rolling Stones to the Sex Pistols. Skiffle was simple; any standard required only three chords, and the instruments besides the acoustic guitar(s), such as the single-string bass and washboard were virtually homemade. By 1957, as a result, "it seemed that every kid in England was playing in a skiffle band." Skiffle allowed virtually anyone to express himself (not herself at that point) through popular music, including the blues idioms that would be so significant in the sixties. Thousands of British teenagers (including future members of the Beatles) were introduced to the democratizing "notion of being in groups, singing and playing guitars," and to "the excitement and novelty associated with rock and roll" (Shaw 1975; Chambers 1986:157–58). Skiffle's "American folk song mix of white and black," furthermore, weakly but significantly approximated the musical miscegenation in American rock and roll, appropriating various possibilities in "American popular music that were not drawn directly from the US charts or show business." Even in the puerile fifties, then, the stage was being set for probing the possibilities of popular music. In the early sixties, with skiffle having established the centrality of the guitar, skiffle groups would shift to electric guitars and rhythm and blues (Chambers 1985:45, 47).

The real movers of the era, in the final analysis, were the popular singers' managers, not any artists. Larry Parnes, for example, groomed singers "to fit [his] image of what the public wanted in a teen idol"; Julien Temple's film of *Absolute Beginners* (1986) makes quite overt the managers' sexual interest, as well, in their young men. The result was safe and gutless, flimsily and exploitatively packaged in "contrived, wishfully descriptive names" like Steele, Wilde, Fury, Faith, Eager, Power, Gentle, Storm, Pride, and Quickly (Shaw 1975); Melly finds the English system of naming rock stars positively Dickensian. None of these singers was aware "of the explosive [racial] combination that rock'n'roll rested upon," and thus they could only imitate a barely understood American style, with Americans continuing to produce the few rock and roll hits that made the English charts. But even those hits were "drawn from the more assimilable American developments," and yoked "with the existing patterns of the British music industry." In the case of original American music, as a result, Pat Boone's puerile reworking of black sounds outsold Presley in England (Chambers 1985:34, 38–39).

Cohn, who grew up in the fifties, does give credit to one manager, Jack Good, for creating "total anarchy" with his talk of pop as "the product of real social change, . . . a big help in getting rid of rock's built-in inferiority complex" (1970:59). From the beginnings of rock and roll, therefore, a conflict existed between different sectors of capitalism. Against the already self-conflicted "political apologists of a commerce-led consumer society who were complaining about the reality [or cultural and moral results] of such commerce," the music industry had an "equally direct interest" in promoting rock and roll, "whether this suited the official model of a uniform [or orderly] consumer culture or not"—hence Good's impunity. This conflict within the power structure has continued ever since to provide the background to the "spectacular significance" of British rock music, to the more immediate conflict between the tastes of alienated youth and the exponents of orderly consumption (Wicke 1990:62–63). Good, in his rhetoric at least, was a mild harbinger of the Rolling Stones' Andrew Loog Oldham and the Sex Pistols' Malcolm McLaren.

The early managerial types more certainly had the virtue of overthrowing the dormant Denmark Street publishers, who still controlled popular music in the early fifties. Colin MacInnes, in his 1962 essay "Socialist Impresarios," lauds "loud-mouthed hucksters ... obsessed by the whole enterprise of promotion, themselves emotionally involved in the adventure whatever their other motives" (qtd. in Frith 1981:100–101). Melly, however, points out that Good himself was responsible for cleaning up Cliff Richard, a major disaster for late fifties pop. In general, if each pop music explosion in the fifties and sixties came "roaring out of the clubs in which it was born like an angry young bull," proclaimed "dangerous, subversive, a menace to youth," it was the entrepreneur, desperate for publicity and acceptability, who persistently defused them. But Melly ultimately tempers the attribution of complete musical control to the manager: "what has proved beyond even the most determined and knowledgable entrepreneur is the invention of a group or artist to lead a pop revolution." Regardless of the machinations of the entrepreneurs, "Sooner or later a new generation of teenagers will adopt some form of music with its accompanying lifestyle to symbolize and reflect their revolt." This cycle in pop music has gone on for thirty-five years now, often abetted by the petit-entrepreneur. An initial proposal of revolt is converted, by mass production and promotion, into "the illusion of that revolt" (1970:39, 43–44, 222), but fresh voices or sounds always take its place.[10]

Gunn's "Elvis Presley" proves the strongest literary document from the fifties, in the long run, because it recognized early on the use value of musical revolt, in the further stylization of resistance by the music's audience. In this regard, the first sensational subculture of the postwar period was the teddy boys, who preferred American rock and roll—Eddie Cochran, Buddy Holly, Jerry Lee Lewis, Presley, Gene Vincent—a harder music than any produced in England. The teds preexisted rock and roll, but when the latter appeared in 1956, it immediately seemed their aural equivalent, likewise providing "an exciting declaration with which you could reject your subordination ... in the rigid prospects of British life" (Chambers 1986:154). Though the ted style had waned in London by that time, it continued to spread through the rest of the country along with rock and roll, furthering the perception that their origins coincided.

Whatever the chronological relation, an inversion of the conventional relationship between popular music and its audience occurred, which set the stage for the subsequent history of youth subcultures and rock and roll. Music was "to be used rather than listened to: a banner to be waved in the face of 'them' by a group who felt themselves ignored or victimized" (Melly 1970:36). A secondary system of meaning emerged, in which the music was "taken as material for expression—by the young audience now." The use of rock and roll, furthermore, was the expression not of the so-called generation conflict and a classless youth culture, but of working-class youth and "the class-specific experience of the changing face of British capitalism" (Wicke 1990:62, 66–67). Thus BBC radio, not surprisingly, did its utmost to ignore and resist rock and roll and its class connotations, while the popular music press extolled the authenticity, quality, and taste of forms like trad jazz. In preferring an utterly alien alternative to BBC programming designed for the model middle-class listener, the teds' musical taste therefore violated authoritarian aesthetic boundaries, and the myth of classless culture they served. At a time when the injuries of class were minimized in public discourse, working-class teenagers understandably seized upon a form entirely outside the British media, to give voice to their experience.

In its early incarnations, American rock and roll was very much a working-class form, made by virtual hillbillies in many cases, a class basis enhanced all the more when passed through English awareness of "Them and Us." British listeners, however, first experienced a "real strangeness" in American rock and roll, "the exciting disturbance of an explicit, almost bacchanal emphasis on the body in the singing voice" (Chambers 1985:21, 24, 26). But the energy of rock and roll proved quite class specific, in its appeal to a "longing for something 'real,' . . . beyond the oppressive ordinariness of life." As for the lyrical content, furthermore, the more it addressed largely irrelevant American experiences like high school, the more open the songs were to articulation with British experience. Thus the affinity for rock and roll hardly constituted a hazy longing for America, as many critics believed (Wicke 1990:55, 61, 66, 69). From a retrospective view, at least, the teds highlighted for both countries the social origin of rock and roll; if one looked closely, there was "a clear connection between pop preferences and class background" in England (Murdock and McCron 1976:16).

As it did for the incipient pop artists of the midfifties, especially Richard Hamilton and Eduardo Paolozzi, America functioned for the teds "as a repressed, potentially fertile realm invoked against the grain" of forces like the numerous Leavisian voices in criticism, education, and the media. Between rock and roll and Hollywood, "images of crime, disaffected youth, urban crisis and spiritual drift [became] anchored together around 'popular' American commodities," which "served to accentuate rather than annul class differences." Far from a homogenizing influence, American culture instead provided "a rich iconography, a set of symbols, objects and artefacts which [could] be assembled and re-assembled" (Hebdige 1988:57, 70, 74, 128). In the general discourse about the destruction of the British way of life by Americanization, as a result, the teds were "understood to be symptomatic of these social alterations" (Pearson 1984:19).

The teddy boys, in their head-to-toe outsider appearance, "weren't quite like any movement that had happened in earlier decades. . . . [R]ight through the '50s, the teds held command; they were the only action going" (Cohn 1970:6–7). Melly believes that the "ted spirit, in a diluted form, did affect a great many teenagers" (1970:34), an important point about any subcultural style, for the inclination to resistance inspired by a particular subculture is internalized on a more widespread basis than the actual number of teenagers wearing, for instance, a Mohawk haircut. The teds "offered stylistic suggestions to young males who did not directly participate, . . . new horizons [that] promised an alternative sense of youth culture from that suggested by official agencies." This leadership had the important effect of establishing and diffusing the two major expressive forms employed by every subsequent youth subculture, pop music and clothes (Chambers 1985:28).

Cohn's recent autobiographical work documents the impression ted style made on him, at the age of eleven, living in Londonderry, Northern Ireland. In his discovery of rock and roll, the teddy boys

> came to embody everything I sensed, everything that I still couldn't spell.
>
> In their daytime incarnations, I understood, the Teddy Boys were...the delinquent flotsam and jetsam of the Bogside. As such, their life prospects were nil. Foredoomed, dispossessed,...they had no work, no home, no hope whatsoever....They were, in every common sense, non-persons. And yet, here on The Strand, in the neon night by Rock'n'Roll, they were made heroic. In every flash of flourescent sock or velvet cuff, every jive-step swagger for Chuck Berry, every leer and flaunt of their greased pompadoured ducktails, they beggared the fates, made reality irrelevant.

Elvis himself, with his famous sneer, actually seemed "a direct extension of the Teddy Boys," rather than the other way around (Cohn 1988:175–76).

The teddy boys, benefiting from the postwar increase in employment and wages, had come up with an amalgam of Edwardian-revival fashion—the long drape-jacket (to which drainpipe trousers were added)—and the attire of the Western Gambler in Hollywood films, including wide satin lapels, shocking colors, and bootlace ties. Relatively unintentionally, the teds subverted the former's designs on an upper-class clientele, while more deliberately employing the latter, symbolic of the outsider. The influence of American films and music merged with an earlier expropriation of the attempt by fashionable tailors on Saville Row, in 1950, to cash in on disapproval of the Labour government through the Edwardian (hence ted) suit, a combination of "the dangerous male dash of [both] the Regency Buck [and] the Western desperado" (Melly 1970:35). The style also reflected other domestic and American influences, those of the Spivs (among the last of the zoot-suiters) and gangster movies, respectively.

However unconsciously, the teddy boys were more acute than

any literary figure in their stylistic response to the ideology of affluence, having made laughable, as early as 1953, Edwardian nostalgia like Osborne's. A newspaper story on a murder case in that year was headlined "Edwardian Suits, Dance Music, and a Dagger"; early on the "flagrant finery of these working-class youths suggested . . . those who bucked authority and betrayed the civic duty of austerity and restraint" (Chambers 1987:232). Ted style had nothing to do with the inclination of others, like the literary, to look back to "the last golden moment for the British upper classes, the long Edwardian summer" (Melly 1970:35) and more to do with the self-definition of the working-class adolescent as an outlaw, the image provided by Westerns and rock and roll.

In the latter instance, the Americanization of European culture, begun in the 1920s, became fully material (Frith 1981:184)—but with a positive function inadmissible in the Leavis school, the symbolic expression of dissent. Hebdige attributes the American influence to the remoteness of film images from the "drab routines of school, the job and home" (1979:50). Rather than the "dull reflex of a group of what Hoggart called 'tamed and directionless helots' to a predigested set of norms and values," the fairly deliberate attribution of meaning to American forms, in actuality, was an attempt at gaining some sense of control of one's circumstances (Hebdige 1988:74). The slick gambler had the specific appeal of a high social status, grudgingly granted "because of his ability to live by his wits and *outside* the traditional working class mores" (Jefferson 1976:86). This display of status in spite of deprivation also asserted a form of control, setting off work experience by reclaiming some pleasure for one's body.

An oft-noted irony of later work on subcultural sociology, at Birmingham, is that the Centre was founded in 1964 by Hoggart, who excoriates the teds in Leavisian terms in *The Uses of Literacy,* lamenting the passing of the working-class culture in which he grew up. He does have the merit of standing Leavis upside down, at least: "the displaced or damaged culture was not high or elite, as it had been for Leavis; it was proletarian" (Brantlinger 1990:46; see also Turner 1990:47–51). But Hoggart very conventionally presents the "Juke Box Boys" as a prime example of pacification by Americanized mass culture, and the "sensation without commitment" it offered. Even the Juke Box Boys' *posture* suffers from American influence, in their affectation of an "American slouch." Entirely reversing actuality, he describes as "spiritual dry-rot" their "myth-world compounded of a few simple elements which they take to be those of American life." It was, of course, precisely the use of American film and music, and their very distance, that enabled the teds to express at least a symbolic resistance, not acquiescence, to their working lives—they would seem to have escaped the suasion of "you've never had it so good." Like Leavis, who unblinkingly linked "the machine" itself to Americanization, Hoggart proves a technophobe in fixing the contemptuous adjective "mechanical" to the record player, surely a benign piece of technology if there ever was one. And, like Adorno, Hoggart despises the "doctored" music emanating from the record player, decrying its emphasis on beat.

The abysmal leisure pastimes of the Juke Box Boys presumably form a perfect fit with the oppression of their labor: "Most of them have jobs which . . . encourage no sense of personal value. As compensation, "society gives them an almost limitless freedom of the sensations, but makes few demands on them—the use of their hands and of a fraction of their brains for forty hours a week. For the rest they are open to the entertainers and their efficient mass-equipment." To Hoggart, there is no distinction to be made between labor and leisure, and the result of the teds' degradation, presumably, is an abdication of the traditional sense of "Them and Us." In keeping with his disdain for the new youth culture, he concludes that though at bottom "the [class] division is still there, and little changed in its sharpness," young people "often seem simply to be ignoring it, to have 'contracted out' of any belief in its importance; they have gone into their own worlds, supported now by a greater body of entertaining and flattering provision than their parents knew" (1961:65, 202–4).

The new consumerism of ted style, however, "fertilized by the big money from dead-end jobs" (Melly 1970:3–4, 35), actually captured the contradictions of affluence. Consumption, first of all, became emblematic of the gap between having discretionary income and the "largely manual, unskilled, near-lumpen real careers and life-chances" that provided it (Hall and Jefferson 1976:48). The teds "visibly bracketed off the drab routines" of labor (Hebdige 1979:50); Hoggart could not have been more wrong in assuming that their leisure experience was identical to that in labor. They embodied in their leisure pastimes the contradiction between a modest degree of affluence and the absence of meaningful opportunity (a contradiction even more pronounced in the mod subculture of the sixties). The teds, moreover, also obliquely represented the fact that relative deprivation still persisted in teenage consumption, as in incomes generally: "Far from being a casual response to 'easy money,' the extravagant sartorial display of the ted required careful financial planning." In that acute awareness of just how dear an economic commitment they had made, in particular, the teds were "remarkably self-conscious [in] going against the grain" (Hebdige 1988:69–70).

Like subsequent subcultural styles, ted style worked not through direct invocation of social class,[11] but through offense against one of the main assumptions about affluence, concerning "consensus." If the teds were far from some developed political discourse on the nature of the class system, the usual complaint about subcultures, they most certainly were the one group who suffered no illusions about consensus—as opposed to academics, artists, or almost all of their supposed betters. Ted style was a gamble that behind "a nullifying common sense there must be something else" (Chambers 1985:33). The scapegoating of the teds for violating consensus, like present-day assaults on rap music and other outrages in youth culture, encouraged "moral panic" over "folk devils," as Stanley Cohen puts it in his work on the mods and rockers of the sixties. Whether teds or rappers, a "group of persons emerges to become defined as a threat to societal values and interests, ... presented in a stylized and stereotypical fashion by the mass media; the moral barricades are manned by editors, [clergymen], politicians and other right-thinking people" (1972:28). Such moral panics help contain at the conjunctural level the real crisis at hand, in the fifties the shakiness of the myth of consensus: "Troubling times, when social anxiety is widespread but fails to find an organised public or political expression, give rise to the displacement of social anxiety on to convenient scapegoat groups." Youth, then, became the displaced focus of English society's "quarrel with itself" (Hall and Jefferson 1976:71–72; see Pearson 1984:12–24), of the anxiety, so to speak, over contradictions between the discourse of affluence and actual experience.

The mass-media account was therefore quite authoritarian, the ted serving as "a model to be held up before society, so that right-thinking people could avoid his behavior" (Cohen and Rock 1970:294). The Edwardian suit all by itself, rather than the grievances it might symbolize, was blamed as the cause of all the trouble.

Cohn recounts how, in Ulster newspapers, "the Teddy boy riots over *Blackboard Jungle* and Bill Haley in England" were cast not simply as teenage rebellion, understood to be classless, but as an even more generalized moral threat to "civilization as we know it" (1988:177). The riots during Haley's film performance of "Rock Around the Clock," a staple historical memory from the fifties, were in fact a fiction of the popular press. Overreacting to a single incident of "good natured larking" after a showing at a South London theater, when "a few hundred boys and girls danced and chanted 'Mambo Rock' on Tower Bridge, holding up traffic," the *Daily Express* reported a pitched battle between the police and thousands of rioting teenagers (Whitcomb, qtd. in Wicke 1990:58). All delinquency, any incident of hooliganism, was subsequently attributed to teds, and John Osborne was even labeled "an intellectual Teddy Boy." As a farcical result of this diffusion and demonization, just as the ted style faded out entirely in London, in 1958, "in the public mind their image had just jelled" (Cohen and Rock 1970:307).

Without the precursor they would provide later, more deliberate subcultures, the teds did not immediately define themselves as outsiders at all, but accepted to differing degrees the mantle assigned by sensationalist news media (see Cohen and Rock 1970). Every subsequent subculture, though, has agreed with as well as contested the dominant culture's definition of it in somewhat the same way, negotiating unconsciously as well as consciously. The "hostility to one's life being determined," as Williams put it in the fifties, certainly characterizes the teds, who shared in the chafing of "felt life against the hands which seek to determine its course" (1983:336–37). If some teds understood themselves as outsiders only when execration in the media led to their banning from dance halls and so on, the delinquent attitude nonetheless represents a response to vilification by Them. Because there was no indigenous music through which other youths might exercise a more diffuse and vicarious, less precise symbolic allegiance with the ted style, their assuming it required "wholeheartedly adopting and defending the immediate signs of an uncompromising dress and attitude" (Chambers 1987:233). But contrasted with the sophistication of punk, the teds seem primitive ancestors, simply representing the first striking moment in postwar subcultural style. They would in fact return to the public spotlight, in the late seventies, as aging patriots, now cheered by the press for attacking punks (see Pearson 1984:23–24).

Hebdige's summation of the whole history of disaffected adolescent, urban subcultures pertains as much to the teds as anyone, though. When they "resort to symbolic and actual violence, they are playing with the only power at their disposal: the power to discomfit," to pose a threat. As a condition of their entry into public debate, they must first offend the symbolic order of common sense, drawing down the attention and/or wrath of media pundits and sociologists, and getting "talked about, taken seriously, . . . arrested, harrassed, admonished, disciplined, incarcerated, applauded, vilified, emulated, listened to" (Hebdige 1988:18). Their success in all these respects lies in the public refusal of consensus. The "threat" they pose is to trouble people to no end, whether at the most immediate or the most reflective levels, in the mass media or in academia. As a symbolic form of dissent, the teds brought down heated reproach on themselves, as have subsequent subcultures, but the teds' "exposé" lay simply in the fact that the same institutions minimizing the class structure were provoked to denunciations marked, self-contradictorily, by the traditional fervor of bourgeois contempt (like the complaint of Osborne's Bishop of Bromley about those in the working class who denied the reality of classlessness).

A subordinate group's adaptation of what cultural capital it possesses to the end of social transformation, furthermore, "depends little on volition (indeed, declared intent often becomes a hindrance)." Working-class writers may be most frustrated precisely when they succeed, given their willing participation in the milieu of established cultural capital (Hitchcock 1989:35). A group like the teds, one might infer, appears as the greater success in the long run because it never cared about that milieu and was actively despised by it. This is the real strength of the imaginary, symbolic, if nonpolitical activity described by subcultural sociology. The subculture's negotiation of everyday tensions goes on entirely outside constricting institutional discourses, like those revolving around literature and the arts. The teds obviously did not seek to displace extant "epistemological categories and 'regimes of truth'" with ones of their own; they represent instead an irruption "through the agency of *real* objects, a new range of material commodities—of another message, written, so to speak, in a quite different 'language'" (Hebdige 1988:71). In the search for objects defining a stance, subcultural style is thus fundamentally allegorical, even avant-garde, in putting flesh on "experience operating in 'the gap between art and life'" (Murdock and McCron 1976:20, 25).

The last chapter in the history of the teds, the race riots of 1958, has left them, somewhat unfairly, with a tarnished reputation. Cohen and Paul Rock, however, referring to the Notting Hill (actually Notting Dale) race riots as the last dull bang of the teds, point out that their behavior resulted not just from xenophobia and racism, but also from being swamped by the "teenage image," with the exclusion of teds from the activities of their peers. Banned from cinemas and dance halls, the teds held "enough latent hostility to make the object of [their] aggression irrelevant," but, not surprisingly, they wound up serving "as a scapegoat for respectable British society to cover up its own failures and prejudices in dealing with its immigrant population" (1970:313–14).

Black immigration, from the West Indies and Africa, had been encouraged in the early fifties, in the belief that as England's affluent society achieved full employment, immigrants from the Commonwealth would have to fill out the labor force—at the bottom end, of course, and without any governmental planning for the influx. Although the black West Indian population grew tenfold between 1951 and 1961, the total black population in the latter year was only around 350,000 (Hill 1986:27). England, in other words, had barely begun to assimilate a significantly large black population before the riots of 1958. The fuel for the trouble was the economic hopelessness of both blacks and whites, belying the ideology of affluence: "That large numbers of working class adults [joined in] demonstrates that it was not only the young 'lumpen' who were experiencing a worsening of their socio-economic position. But, in an age of 'affluence' the real structural causes could not be admitted, and, predictably, were not" (Jefferson 1976:83).

With the ted style actually already in decline, it was a "dark fringe" of diehards who "swarmed in on Notting Hill to mix it during the race riots of 1958" (Melly 1970:57). Occurring during the writing of *Absolute Beginners,* those riots became the focus of the novel, which conspicuously excoriates the teddy boys' role in them, though MacInnes observes that things grew far uglier with the involvement of older people, including racist organizations like the Union Movement and the League of Empire Loyalists. (Temple's film of *Absolute Beginners* presents the teds in an extremely ugly, vicious light, clearly in the interest of an allegory about skinheads and contemporary racism.)

MacInnes also represents at some length in his novel the combination of racist goading and ted scapegoating that occurred in the press, though this perception does not soften his opinion of the teds, conditioned more fundamentally by his abhorrence of any vestiges of workingclassness. The news media's scarcely veiled racism helps fuel the violence by suggesting that black immigrants were the cause of "a slight, though of course temporary, recession"—not that MacInnes entirely disagrees with the discourse about the affluent economy he records here. After invoking black criminality, the threat of miscegenation, and so on, the "Mrs. Dale daily" (a reference to a television character living in London's suburbs) proceeds to blame the teds for racist violence. Yet MacInnes depicts another mass medium, television, as putting a stop to the London race riot, as if some virtue inheres in the newer medium and its more immediate visual images of the event (and though elsewhere he questions the veracity of TV reports on cultural matters). Ray Gosling (1980), in contrast, believes that the Nottingham riots, which immediately preceded those at Notting Dale, were directly attributable to the inflammatory presence of TV cameramen expecting trouble.

Paul Gilroy confirms much of the rest of MacInnes's account, though. Race was associated with "sordid sexuality" as well as impoverished squalor, before the riots, with miscegenation actually emerging "ahead of crime as a theme in the popular politics of immigration control." When politicians and the media later attempted to account for the origin of the riots, the main emphasis "fell on the issue of law and order . . . as the appropriate response to the hooliganism of the Teddy boys." That youth, as much as race, was invoked to explain events makes sense when "it is appreciated that the Teddy boys and their urban community were described almost as a 'race' in their own right" (1991:80–81)—a logical result of confining the subject of class to indirect reference. The end result of the 1958 riots was thus to blame all the victims, both the scapegoated teds, for their violence, and black immigrants, for "the bad habits . . . which had caused the tension" (Hall et al. 1978:158).[12]

Given the newness of a sizable black presence in England, the ted subculture had no other relation with West Indian culture than this linkage by authority, unlike virtually all later working-class youth subcultures. And if the teds perhaps heard class overtones in American rock and roll, they certainly did not hear the music's roots in black rhythm and blues:

> in the early days of rock . . . a symbolic alliance [between black and white working-class youth] was by no means assured. The music had been taken out of its original context where the implications of the potentially explosive equation of 'Negro' and 'youth' had been fully recognized by the parent culture and transplanted to Britain where it served as the nucleus for the teddy boy style. Here, it existed in a kind of vacuum as a stolen form—a focus for an illicit delinquent identity.

But by the early sixties, it was already apparent that Notting Dale was an exception to an otherwise relatively peaceful coexistence between youths of different races, and to broad cultural exchanges, first evident in the mods, between West Indian and white youth subcultures, a relationship "strengthened by time and a common experience of privation." MacInnes, for one, could hear black roots in rhythm and blues (though he dismissed the music as an anachronism), sharing the American Beats' pretension to racial sensitivity. But in England middle-class Beats always remained "literally worlds apart" from working-class teds. The Beat, from "a literate, verbal culture, . . . affected a bemused cosmopolitan air of bohemian tolerance," while the ted "was uncompromisingly proletarian and xenophobic" (Hebdige 1979:40, 49–51).

Colin MacInnes

MacInnes, in *Absolute Beginners* (1959), buys into the moral panic over the ted, pitting the regressive aberrance of the teds against a utopian, classless teenage culture. His abhorrence of teds is savage: the allegorical character Ed the Ted belongs to a gang of four hundred—MacInnes swallowing a media fiction about sophisticated Ted organization—led by a cinema-wrecking sociopath named Flikker, who has "no grasp at all of what being bad really *meant*." This

extended ted organization is seen carefully preparing for racist attacks, instigating the Notting Dale riots single-handedly. Ed the Ted
is himself crude and repulsive, a "goon" and a "primitive," beaten
and beleagured even by his own mates. MacInnes singles out Ed's
speech for phonetic rendering, to emphasize the moronism of anyone
bearing traces of the traditional working class, the "full-fledged
Teddy-boy condition" consisting mostly of "words of one syllable":
" 'Yer'll be earing frm me agen, an ver lads. . . . You fink I'm sof, or
sumfink?' "

Above all, Ed hates the teenager, just as Cohen and Rock believed teds in general did, but MacInnes seems to think this reflects
an idiotic, that is, class-conscious impairment of stylistic sensibility.
In the novel he lingers over Ed's unsanitary and scabies-ridden state,
right down to his "dirty fingernails"; in an essay entitled "Sharp
Schmutter," he castigates the ted's "grubbiness, awkward uncouth
energy, [and] built-in self-dissatisfaction, like monstrous ingrown toe-
nails." The new, presumably less class-oriented Italian style that appeared by 1958 (developing later into the mod subculture), as the ted
subculture waned, has the "enormous virtue" of encouraging cleanliness (1961:150, 157). He assigns the style to the narrator in *Absolute
Beginners,* a point that says more about MacInnes's psychopathology
than anything: his "bourgeois preoccupation with cleanliness" and its
sexual repression—understandable in his case, with homosexuality
still illegal in the fifties—is expressed in "myths of working-class
squalor" (Wood, qtd. in Hill 1986:136).

MacInnes shared the conventional belief that the teenager was a
harbinger of the classless consumer society, and already part of a
"class" in its own right, youth. The new insignificance of the class
structure was heralded by "the coming of the new Teenager, who
was anyway partly [MacInnes's] own creation" in England (Gould
1983:136). (The teenager had been invented several years before by
a young American advertising entrepreneur, Eugene Gilbert, so it was
not the coinage that MacInnes introduced to England, but the associated argument for classlessness.) The notion that class divisions had
been replaced by generational ones, however, belied evidence of "the
continuing centrality of class inequalities in structuring both the life
styles and life chances of adolescents" (Murdock and McCron
1976:10, 17). In the influential *The Teenage Consumer,* Mark
Abrams exemplifies schizoid deferrals to the ideology of affluence,

contradicting his own statistical evidence by emphasizing generational difference and dissociating the teenager from social class. *Absolute Beginners* appeared the same year as Abrams's work and shares the same assumptions. MacInnes, as a result, is well-intentioned, but also a pace-setting mythologist, and his primary value ultimately lies in a rather traditional conservative appraisal of audience manipulation by mass culture. Given his quietism on the subject of class, he naturally found a wide audience, pretty much defining the teenager for England, a nation seemingly inundated by such youthful beneficiaries of affluence as teddy boys, Angry Young Men, and nouveau riche pop stars (Hill 1986:10).

The teenage revolution, with its economic and social basis in the upsurgence of the working class, leads to styles that are "really classless," MacInnes pronounces in "Sharp Schmutter." His notion that "the transformation of the working-class to power and relative affluence means that . . . styles are no longer 'working-class' in the old sense at all" was, of course, deluded. But according to him, history itself had changed, supposedly: the vast sweep of rich youth comprise a new international "classless class"; "teenagers have become a power," blessed with wealth as well as energy. *Upper* and *working* class are thus old-fashioned terms, replaced by adult and teenager in the real postwar social revolution, which was not the welfare state but the dramatic rise in teenage economic power. Teenagers effortlessly step outside class, not caring about it at all, and are "blithely indifferent to the Establishment" (MacInnes 1961:11, 47, 54–56, 153).

Outside MacInnes's work, however, the phenomenon of the teenager not only served as an indication of new possibilities in consumption, but also received a negative construction, serving condemnations of cultural philistinism, sexual immorality, and violence. Youth thus appeared simultaneously as a positive "avant-garde" force and as the underside of affluence, "slavish devotion to consumerism" and the "absence of 'authentic' values." This ambivalence reflected the widespread anxiety concerning consumerism and mass communications. But focus on youth helped channel and contain that anxiety, negative discourse about the teenager serving a hegemonic function, in this respect, as much as positive themes did. In either case, "The dominant representations of youth in the 1950s tend to tell us more about the social groups producing them than they do about teenagers themselves" (Hill 1986:11–13, 15). This is particularly true of adult concern about teenage delinquency, which in essence represented a fear of working-class adolescents, despite a discourse about "unaccustomed riches" (rather than poverty) causing moral decay and supposedly new forms of juvenile crime, rebellion, violence, and so on (Pearson 1984:16–17). Denial of the persistence of class required that *delinquent* and the classless *teenager* become associated terms. Concern over working-class delinquency was nothing new; the teds' "aggressive and exclusive sense of youthful style," however, did contribute a new inflection to the fear of teenage corruption (Frith 1981:184, 186).

MacInnes's emphasis on the positive view of the teenage consumer, defending teens against straight society, reflects his Beat perspective, found most clearly in his importation of American intellectual mythologizing of the black jazz musician (e.g., by Jack Kerouac and Norman Mailer).[13] The American hipster, as opposed to the middle-class Beat, shared the impoverished origin of the jazz player, but given the historical absence of a large black population in England until the midfifties, "it should hardly surprise us that the Beat subculture alone, the product of a somewhat romantic alignment with black people, should survive the transition from America to Britain in the 50s" (though the Americans' association with modern jazz did not survive the passage, of course). The English Beat, finding his own culture stifling, lived an "imaginary relation to the Negro-as-noble-savage," who ostensibly persevered in existential fashion between "constant humility" and "everthreatening danger," rage and joy, despair and orgasm, as Mailer put it in his essay "The White Negro," which MacInnes admired a great deal (Hebdige 1979:48–49). Unlike other fairly young intellectuals in postwar England, however, MacInnes took up the cause of pop culture without desperate intellectualizing. MacInnes was one of those, in Melly's terms, for whom pop in the broadest sense, including jazz, "seemed the justification ... for a style of life we had been trying to live," for whom "the division between pop culture and traditional culture was at most arbitrary." At the same time, though, even the more astute Beats shared in a will to classlessness, thinking that pop culture had weakened the class structure (Melly 1970:19–20). The liability of the Beats in this regard reflects their continuity with the "personalistic vein of romanticism," the priority on alleviating "spiritual nakedness" rather than "social justice" (Graña 1964:180–81).

But if *Absolute Beginners* succumbs almost completely to the hegemony of affluence, at the same time the novel constitutes "an astonishing feat of empathy" with teenagers and pop (Melly 1970:51), based in a common sense of rejection and a mutual attraction to a manic state. MacInnes grasped the fact that music, around which the other industries geared to teenagers' spending money revolved, "was the key to understanding the teenage revolution" (Gould 1983:127, 143). The teenager, he says in *England, Half English,* "is a key figure for understanding the 1950s," and "song is, and always has been, a key indication of the culture of a society." As an anthropologist as well as a mild enthusiast, he finds deplorable "the abysmal ignorance of educated persons about the popular music of the millions," when there's "no doubt which . . . voices penetrate and mould more English hearts and brains," and provide the best "clue to what lies behind those myriad [young] faces." Though his advocacy is ambivalent—"pop music, on its own low level, can be so good"—he also chides the way "in England, pop art and fine art stand resolutely back to back." He believed that adults were hostile to teenagers for "undermining not so much culture itself, as their hitherto exclusive possession of it." Whatever their political persuasion, he correctly points out, those who disapprove of enjoyment, condemning pop music, always turn out not "to know anything whatever about it" (1961:45–46, 55). "I do not believe," MacInnes wrote, "you can 'improve' anything unless you are, in some sense, fond of it"; Melly would eulogize him for being "always on the side of feeling" (qtd. in Gould 1983:170).

In all this, however, "MacInnes wanted to believe that the class war was obsolete," envisioning a solidarity between right-minded and patriotic people from all classes, with aristocrats and teenagers alike joining in an antiracist crusade (Gould 1983:136). This vision supplies the utopian resolution of *Absolute Beginners,* in which upper-class Hooray Henries, the ex-Deb, and TV personality "Call-me-Cobber" lend their notoriety to making the Napoli riots "big stuff," publicizing, along with hip declassed teenagers, the atrocities committed by teds and other hooligans. To counteract "a sort of conspiracy in the air to pretend what was happening in Napoli, wasn't happening," the narrator's solution, publicity, is hopelessly apolitical, not surprisingly, limited to the same media he criticizes for playing down the riots. After the Notting Dale riots, exercising his faith in publicity,

MacInnes went around the riot area stuffing a newssheet (*What the Stars Say*) in mailboxes, and claimed to have "prevented a second Notting Hill race riot—and said it in all seriousness" (Musgrave, qtd. in Gould 1983:137).

His willfulness and political naïveté regarding the ideology of affluence are abundantly apparent in *Absolute Beginners,* in describing Napoli during the riots. MacInnes points out the containment of the "blood and thunder," the division of the middle-class "world of Mrs. Dale and What's my line? and England's green and pleasant land" from the Napoli "concentration camp; inside, blue murder, outside, buses and evening papers." But he refers in a simile to a national (i.e., international) frontier, rather than a class one. Elsewhere he offers acute, detailed descriptions of the Napoli slums: "huge houses too tall for their width cut up into twenty flatlets, and front facades that it never pays anyone to paint, and broken milk bottles *everywhere* scattering the cracked asphalt roads like snow . . . and diarrhoea-coloured street lighting—man, I tell you, you've only got to be there for a minute to know there's something radically wrong." Despite the existence of continuing economic misery, however, MacInnes seems grotesquely compelled to deny the existence of social inequity: "my Lord, how horrible this country is, how dreary, how lifeless, how blind and busy over trifles!" he writes, in a revealingly empty conclusion to his own contrast of "glamour people" at the airport with "peasant masses" at the bus terminal. The denial is extraordinary, and undermines the novel throughout—testimony not just to the power of the hegemonic milieu, but also to MacInnes's bohemian mania to escape, as the narrator says, "what I am, or what I do, or where I come from, or whether I'm educated."

The narrator's most negative moments are antipolitical ones, dismissals not only of any concern over the H-bomb, but especially of the thirties, in keeping with the general literary tendency of the fifties. The worst instance in the novel occurs when the narrator ignores as irrelevant blather his father's memories of the Depression. MacInnes renders that historical memory quite compellingly, but only to signal all the more its anachronistic pathos: "You've simply no idea what the pre-war period was like," the father says. "Poverty, unemployment, fascism and disaster and, worst of all, no chance, no opportunity." The narrator's response is "Hard cheese." He knows that that's all in the past, musing on his half-brother Vernon's generation, "one of the last ... before teenagers existed"; Vernon himself resents "kids getting all these high paid jobs and leisure." MacInnes's assumptions about money and leisure lie at the heart of his apolitical stance. Though members of subcultures like the teds in reality scrimped and saved for their finery, "the boy's time is his own [and] money problems miraculously disappear," leaving the impression that consumption "can cut you free from other allegiances: that if you listen to jazz, dress snappily and stay cool, then the rest of it needn't bother you." Taking up a style, however, "is a response to class, gender and racial pressures, not an alternative to them" (Sinfield 1989:170).

Analysts of the new youth culture, like MacInnes, could repress its class basis by concentrating sheerly on texts, like music and fashions, and not their use, seeing no "dialectic between youth and the youth market industry," or no reciprocal process of appropriation. Thus they tend to couch matters "almost exclusively in terms of the commercial ... manipulation and exploitation of the young" (Hall and Jefferson 1976:15–16). The narrator of *Absolute Beginners,* accordingly, may believe that "youth has power, a kind of divine power," and if teenagers and children "only knew this fact, namely how powerful they really are, then they could rise up overnight and enslave the old tax-payers." But he finds that youth has been bought off, made insipid by the likes of Laurie London. The "adult mafia" rules the Soho streets, one large teenage shopping mall, stocked with every conceivable music- and style-related commodity; teenagers have been turned into mindless, identical butterflies, fluttering "round exactly the same flowers." The "show business pop song pirates ... despise us—dig?—they sell us cut-price sequins," culled from the coffee bars, which are no longer an "authentic big event," but fishbowls "just as real as nothing, made for mugs." Pop music, having suffered castration, is rejected altogether in favor of jazz, MacInnes seizing the opportunity to promote Beat tastes.

In his historical situation, he couldn't realize that the "decadence" of Laurie London was part of a cyclical, built-in obsolescence in pop music, which, it seemed to him, was finished for good: "these elderly sordids bribe the teenage nightingales to wax, [an e]xploitation of the kiddos by the conscripts." In *England, Half English* he declares rock and roll "mercifully in decline," and in *Absolute Beginners* parodies the manufacture of castrato-rock singers in names like "Strides Vandal," "Rape Hunger," and "Soft-Sox Granite." Apart from the dire conclusions that could fairly be drawn from castrato-rock, though, he had no affinity for rock and roll. This is apparent everywhere, whether in his mourning the loss of the music hall and English song to American idioms—though he did envision rock and roll being given English themes and voices, a development not fully realized for twenty years—or lauding Steele's smarminess: "he is Puck.... Mums adore him too" (1961:13, 15, 49–50, 56–57). In the novel the narrator, revealingly, is assigned a deep affection for Gilbert and Sullivan, despite his insistence on songs "about the scene."

The biases in MacInnes's musical taste and attribution of tastes to others correspond quite directly with his general quietism. His facile rejection of the blues, which would be the source of the rejuvenation of rock and roll in England and America alike in the sixties, is based on its social connotations. He ridicules the "ballad-and-blues movement," represented by the Marxist Ron Todd, for seeking to prove that all folk music (in this case Mississippi jail songs) is an art of protest. The narrator's point is actually well-taken, in part: Todd's insistence on authenticity, or "source music" as opposed to "period music, that feeds on it," and disdain of the slightest tinge of commercialism are excessively purist and elitist. But the blues is presented as an anachronistic preoccupation not only with folk cultures, but with class authenticity as well, and is thus associated with a Marxist. (MacInnes seizes the opportunity to deliver an addled version of Marxism as a theory of historical disengagement and irresponsibility.) More forgivably, MacInnes doesn't see that the expression of racial resistance in the blues, often couched in more universal terms of sexual desire, would be transplantable to England and would overthrow the prevailing, much more harmless purist form, trad jazz, by 1963. His purism, though, is not actually much different from Todd's, in that both studiously avoid the potential link between rock and roll and the urban electric style in the blues. Todd appears to share to some extent the music establishment's tendency to identify "acoustic not electric, 'human' not mechanical" sounds with authentic folk music, with regard to the blues as well as jazz (Chambers 1985:20), but MacInnes occupies the even narrower ground of the jazz purist.

In placing Ella Fitzgerald ("Maria Bethlehem") in the foreground, with similar musicial attributes, MacInnes unwittingly echoes some of the most reactionary screed in midfifties criticism of rock and roll: when Presley's "Hound Dog" was released in 1956, *Melody Maker* denounced its "sheer repulsiveness," asking, "How much further can the public be encouraged to stray from the artistry of Ella Fitzgerald?" (qtd. in Chambers 1985:30). MacInnes does recognize a schism between modern and trad jazz, but given the effective suppression of modern jazz in England—and his invocation of Count Basie and Fitzgerald, which suggests his taste ran to swing—it isn't clear that he knows much about modern styles. Though MacInnes knew Kenny Graham, who had imported bebop sounds and combined them with African drums, Graham says flatly that his erstwhile friend "couldn't understand Negroes and jazz musicians, their total disrespect for everything" (qtd. in Gould 1983:140). With regard to subcultural style rather than music, the character Dean Swift does fairly accurately represent the earliest exponents of the Italianate "modernist" (later mod) style, middle-class dandies who took their name from modern jazz (Barnes 1979:8).

The narrator's musical "university," in any case, has been the jazz clubs, presumably oases of withdrawal from social conflict. Jazz is, to him, above all else properly classless: "no one, not a soul, cares what your class is, ... so long as you ... have left all that crap behind you." When the teenage thing fell "into the hands of exhibitionists and moneylenders," he turned to jazz, "a heavenly sound, ... strong and gentle, just like it would carry you right up on its kind notes to paradise." The virtue of jazz, then, is twofold: it is both *classless* and *euphonious,* intimately connected qualities for MacInnes. The music of Basie ("Czar Tusdie") and Fitzgerald "just makes you feel happy" in a very simple way; the fans, admirably, "will all sit and listen," feeling that "it's absolutely wonderful to be alive and kicking, and that human beings are a dam fine wonderful invention after all." If the salient quality of jazz and its audience is, in other words, *passivity,* one wonders why Laurie London is objectionable. Given this fundamental quietism, it is no wonder that the narrator seems so aghast when law and order—"the one great English thing," in his naïve belief—fails at Napoli.

MacInnes, describing the emotions in pop songs as synthetic, did realize that the voice mattered most, that the art of the individual singer, the use of the larynx, could "acquire an obsessive power," but MacInnes couldn't inject such power into his writing. He aimed for "a language for 'coloured people' or for teenagers, that was almost

entirely an inverted one, more 'real' and therefore timeless," to avoid
the "period dialect" naturalism would yield (1961:13–14, 147–48).
The results, Burgess concludes, indicate that MacInnes had a dull ear
for the language of disreputable London, and thus had to make up
dialects out of his head (1970:146).[14]

Sillitoe realized in style what MacInnes could not, simply by
eschewing cultural contemporaneity, and drawing on his own working-class background to find an unassimilable voice. Rather than the
sense of a dilettante dabbling in safe, mild criminality, Sillitoe conveys
a genuine "out-law" attitude, in early works like *The Loneliness of
the Long-Distance Runner,* published the same year as *Absolute Beginners.* The "perfection of form" of *Loneliness,* says Burgess, in a
reductive though accurate comment, lies in our learning "what makes
juvenile delinquents tick." Sillitoe's style, what Burgess calls his "poetry of the body" (1970:148–49)—summed up by Sillitoe himself as
"absolute untamable rhythms"—embodies not just contumacy, but
class consciousness itself, that supposed anomaly in the affluent society. The voices of Sillitoe's characters bear a visceral *ressentiment*
more immediate than any English rock and roll of the fifties, to be
sure. In the short story "Loneliness," the narrator vividly execrates a
generic "Tory telling us about how good his government was going
to be if we kept on voting for them—their slack chops rolling, opening and bumbling, hands lifting to twitch moustaches and touching
their buttonholes to make sure the flower hadn't wilted, so that you
could see they didn't mean a word they said." In the end, the governor
of Smith's Borstal, another voice of consensus, "is going to be
doomed while blokes like me will take the pickings of his roasted
bones and dance like maniacs around his Borstal's ruins."

Saturday Night and Sunday Morning (1958) and *Loneliness,*
however, were widely read without offending the common sense of
consensus to anything like the extent the teds did. MacInnes, of
course, illustrates very well that the hegemonic success of myths
about affluence was so great as to induce a virtual schizophrenia, in
which a writer or reader could deny the evidence of an unchanged
class structure in front of his or her face. Thus, "A lot of people
'heard' Arthur's voice when *Saturday Night* was first published, . . . although many simply did not know what they were hearing—for this is how the 'other' is often constructed and marginalized
in the same act of consumption" (Hitchcock 1989:73). But there are

two facets of the fiction itself that may explain why it was received not only without outrage and scandal, but with outright warmth. First of all, Sillitoe's politics are as much anarchist as Marxist, and anarchist not on a collective basis, but on that of a radical individualism as solipsistic as the far more conservative Movement writers. Though he fully invokes class antagonism and its politics throughout his work—Arthur Seaton finding it merely dormant, in *Saturday Night*—his characters disavow any political identification, Seaton liking the Communist party only as an isolated underdog like himself. Sillitoe's early stories, furthermore, sometimes suggest a nostalgia for clear-cut class consciousness, particularly for that of the thirties, perhaps enabling a reading of the work as a whole on that basis.

If one wished to read his fiction in the late fifties as relatively consistent with the parameters of affluence, it would not be impossible to do so, reassured by assertions that it's "every man for himself" and "I don't believe in share and share alike, Jack," not inconsistent with bourgeois individualism. Writing on *Saturday Night* in 1961, Sillitoe made it clear that "those who see Arthur Seaton as a symbol of the working man and not as an individual are mistaken.... I try to see every person as an individual and not as a class symbol, which is the only condition in which I can work as a writer" (qtd. in Hill 1986:203). Given this fundamental commitment to individualism, *Saturday Night* ends up with Arthur fishing, alone; *Loneliness* with Smith betrayed by the one person he trusts; and Sillitoe himself in the throes of existentialism by the midsixties, after dismissing the English working class as the dupes of television.

Bogdanor and Skildelsky, in *The Age of Affluence*, speculated in 1970 that the period of Conservative rule, from 1951–1964, "will be looked upon as the last period of quiet before the storm, rather like the Edwardian age which in some respects it resembles" (1970:7, 13). At base, and in a number of more superficial, cultural respects, they were correct—the English economy subsequently went on the skids; along with it, malaise among youth has continually intensified. But the fifties hardly seem as becalmed a period as the Edwardian age (in its mythical status, at least); the decade, with the close connections between traditionally antipathetic cultural forms, was downright volatile.

With the rejuvenation of pop music by black rhythm and blues, however, its increasing cultural dominance, along with television, quickly made worrying over mass culture in literature passé. Once recognized as voices of resistance in their own right, and acquiring some artistic and literary pretensions in the process, the music and an ascendant pop culture assisted in the diminishment of literary involvement at the cutting edge of culture. If the Angry Young Men were "the first pop stars of literature" (Hill 1986:22), they were also the last; as a creation of the mass media in the first place, the ostensible movement inevitably fell prey to built-in obsolescence. But only some larger cultural change, like the displacement of literature almost entirely from popular attention, can explain why there have been virtually no attempts, let alone any of notable achievement, at something like *Absolute Beginners*. "Lesser men," says Gosling, nonliterary "experts and maharishis, took the later limelight" as elder statesmen of pop culture, "and the potential of Colin MacInnes was never fulfilled" (1980:72)

Beyond these explanations, the transience of the Angries might simply be ascribed to their one indisputable function, the relief of the dullness of English literature immediately after the war. The new writers were popular in no small part on account of the freshness of their literary excesses, and the shock value of "angry" style quite naturally wore off. The power and violence of their engagement with their period remain readily apparent, however, no matter what their failings in coming "to grips with the essential problem of the society they attacked" (Cooper 1970:284). But the teddy boys, free of the literary baggage and cultural elitism the Situationist International condemned in the Angry Young Men, were smarter. If "pop's 'vulgar' sonorities were generally considered only fit" for working-class youth, "a general weakening of more traditional forms of cultural consensus" was actually occurring, opening up "the construction of new possibilities" in popular culture (Chambers 1985:28–29). Those possibilities would entail a considerably more progressive transformation of the relations between high and profane culture than Hewison's sparse conclusion suggests: "The word was giving way to the image, and the old-style man of letters was losing ground." It was the teds and skiffle and blues players—not the literary, as Hewison thinks—who "opened up the possibility of future cultural change"

(1981:198–99). Subsequent musical and subcultural voices would put literature itself in their service, with stronger, more effective results than the literary employment of popular music and subcultures in the fifties achieved.

CHAPTER 5

The Sixties: A Sort of Avant-Gardism

A literary critic writing in 1970 found it difficult to date the end of the Angry Young Man in literature, but could say this much with assurance: "The concept of Britain as the fertile breeding-place and deserving object of attacks by passionate young men has given way to the concept of Britain as the dynamic leader of popular culture." He goes on to assert that "the images could not be more different" (Cooper 1970:254), a questionable judgment. The dynamism of British popular culture in the 1960s rendered passion or "anger" more lucid, if anything, in both popular music and subcultural ensembles, with literature becoming the object of expropriation that popular culture had been for the literary in the 1950s. What took place throughout the sixties and seventies was a leveling of cultural hierarchies, a transfer of power from the literati to the popular realm. The end result, in punk, owed something to both faces of the sixties: the increasing power of youth culture and the popular myth of Swinging London, during the years 1964–67; and the more radical bohemian elements of the counterculture associated with the volatile year of 1968 and its aftermath (Hewison 1987:xiii).

The explosion of British pop music around 1963 was fueled by black rhythm and blues, which emphasized timbre, "rhythm, vocal expressivity, and participation" (Gendron 1986:31)—a music eminently suited to the expression of resistance, whether that of race, class, or generation. If there were obvious discrepancies between the

235

culture from which the blues emerged and that of white Englishmen trying to play the music, the contradictions served all the more to produce an "'outsider' style destined to encounter social disapproval," particularly through the shock effect of "proposing music as the direct extension of the sexual body" (Chambers 1987:236; 1985:67). The urban, electric variety of r & b produced by Chess records of Chicago—home of Chuck Berry, Muddy Waters, Howling Wolf, et al.—provided a "bottomdog consciousness" that allowed white musicians in the sixties "to articulate youth's collective feelings of frustration and aggression and rebellion and lust" (Frith 1981:20; 1988b:125). Pete Townshend of the Who has described in r & b a feeling of kinship with exploited people (in the notes to the album *Who's Missing*), indicating that the bohemian appeal of authenticity and emotional truth had shifted from jazz to blues (Frith and Horne 1987:88–89). With "beat" music generally accepted after the emergence of the Beatles, the critical outrage over rock and roll characteristic of literature in the fifties "was no longer in vogue." A decisive shift occurred in the "public imagery surrounding pop music, [which] became the central symbol of fashionable, metropolitan, British culture" (Chambers 1985:52, 57), rendering the traditional cultural hierarchy, privileging literature, irrelevant in an instant.

At the same time that rock and roll began to explore the politics of refusal, English literature was moving away from the close involvement of the fifties with mass culture. R & b–based music, distinctly noncerebral in its devotion to a heavy beat, was not at all to the liking of writers like Colin MacInnes and John Wain, who held a traditional esteem for the qualities of melodic and harmonic complexity. With the sudden, overwhelming ascension of the new music and its attendant culture, by 1964 "the desperately 'contemporary' novel, with its bright identikit trappings"—that is, the paraphernalia of mass culture, like rock and roll—had disappeared. In its place appeared a different sort of social realism, represented most notably by Alan Sillitoe, David Storey, and Edward Bond. This working-class fiction and drama was presented "from a very different angle" (Allsop 1964:8), one of intense inwardness, in a preoccupation with the individual proletarian's psychology. Postwar affluence for some part of the working class had continued into the sixties, and thus writers like Sillitoe and Storey, in their introspection, seem to have felt a commensurate luxury in approach, in a social situation apparently free of reasons for open conflict. But both seem out of sorts with the comfortable working class as well; their acceptance of the arrival of affluence, implicitly registered in the more exclusively literary, technical concern with internalized exploration, is quite clear in their disdain for the results of the new consumerism and leisure, the effects of which were only really beginning to be a strong presence at the beginning of the sixties (Hewison 1987:3). In Sillitoe's *The Death of William Posters,* with the television "wank[ing] people's brains off every night," the hero, Frank Dawley, takes off for a mystical experience in the war-torn Algerian desert, while extolling the "waters of illumination" found in literature, especially "Conrad, Melville, Stendhal—the giants." Just as John Fowles dismissed the working class as culturally limited, in comparison with "more complex" middle-class people (qtd. in S. Laing 1986:78), Sillitoe's Dawley yearns to catch up to his middle-class lover's wide reading.[1]

At the same time that the working class was being put on the analyst's couch in literature, however, a quite material discovery about it was being made: in the midst of affluence, poverty continued to exist. Poverty was "rediscovered" in the early sixties; with the relative positions of the classes virtually unchanged, the "shaky economic foundations [of] Britain's affluent 'miracle'" were inevitably exposed. Studies by the Titmuss Group and John Westergaard demonstrated great inequalities in wealth, and the fact that it "had been only nominally redistributed and that the main beneficiaries of the Welfare State were, in fact, the middle classes." The social structure, the distribution of life chances, was hardly fluid; clerical jobs had increased, but the status of white collar occupations, more heavily rationalized and automated, had declined (Hall and Jefferson 1976:22–25). The notion that power had been diffused in the general consensus was also under fire. Westergaard argued that the age of affluence was simply and "noticeably blind to the sources of actual opposition and latent dissent [against] the institutions and assumptions of the current social order." A common tendency was to confuse the institutionalization of conflict—in union activity, for example—with universal consensus (qtd. in Hall and Jefferson 1976:26).

One area of continuing conflict was the housing situation. Some sections of the working class found it necessary, through a community politics, to resist "incursions into the localities by property speculators and the redevelopers, and steadily rising rents" (Hall and Jefferson 1976:26). In his memoir *Personal Copy,* Ray Gosling (originally a disciple of Colin MacInnes) describes a "battle for the slums" in which he took part in 1965, in the St. Ann's district of Nottingham. Poverty, if one looked very close at all, was evident: "The streets were crowded with life at night, poor and low life: apron-tied mothers, bawling out at their child [*sic*] among a squad of squawking kids, scruffy and arrogant as street commandos. They didn't need adventure playgrounds in those days: the whole district was a combat zone, a battlefield. . . . Conditions were terrible, and these sewers were used, these condemned houses were lived in." Affluence, consensus, and so on, in this light, existed solely in the mass media; in reality, the affluent society's philosophy of redevelopment seemed to be that "plans for your eventual transportation to paradise mean life now must be a hell. . . . And the future planned becomes rosier the longer the wait." The mass media did discover St. Ann's poverty, but in the process, predictably, swept away Gosling and his activist combine of students and working people. A pair of sociologists wrote up the district, and, "like the discovery of life on an uninhabited planet, let loose all hell and the ballyhoo of public opinion. . . . The sociologists—'poverty mongers'—first produced their pamphlet, then a booklet, then a best-selling Penguin paperbook. Then there was a television film." When the shouting stopped and St. Ann's was obliterated, the people were just as poor, but had "nothing spectacular any more to show" it. After waiting for housing at a time presumably of "increasing affluence and increasing freedom," once "done," St. Ann's, "our new world, our council-house estate under one almighty authority, [was] in danger of being forgotten again" (1980:143, 155, 164, 193–94, 210, 219).

In response to such conditions, the Labour party, from 1961–64, produced only a vague "social-democratic variant of the Conservative consensus ideology." But it was inflected "with a particular stress on the need for modernisation and reliance on technology" (S. Laing 1986:21), a need to which the aristocratic Conservatives and their cult of amateurism began to seem ill-suited. Like the admixture of concern and vicarious excitement over the moral effects of the affluent society, triggered by the Profumo scandal that brought down Harold Macmillan in 1963 (see Hewison 1987:35–36), the theme of modernization accorded with the assumption of general affluence— still real enough for many, but clearly not for everyone. As in the fifties, the contradictions of the sixties, as recorded by Gosling, were best articulated not in literature but in popular culture, which developed in ways prompting serious challenge of the myth of a classless youth culture (Hebdige 1979:75).

Swinging London, "a false image that disguised the reality of economic and political decline," was essentially an extension of the myths about youth culture that originally permitted the perception of affluence. The image's use to verify England's vitality, if more short-lived, is also comparable to the function served by the Angry Young Men. Like the Angries' moment, Swinging London had a self-reinforcing resonance in the national imagination, despite the absence of a basis in fact (Hewison 1987:76–78, 272). Christened by the American *Time* magazine at the late date of 1966, Swinging London's actual social milieu hardly bespoke a new classlessness, composed as it was of the affluent and titled, pop artists and photographers—such as David Hockney and David Bailey—and a few working-class film stars, like Michael Caine. But pop art, following the Independent Group at the Institute of Contemporary Arts, had been challenging distinctions between high and popular art since the midfifties, creating a climate conducive to acts like the Rolling Stones' expropriation of Anthony Burgess's *A Clockwork Orange* (1962). Pop encouraged a more anthropological attention to the audiences for mass culture, as well; thus the mod subculture, Carnaby Street fashions, and r & b clubs were a significant part of the popular picture of Swinging London, and, in fact, its material basis (see Hebdige 1988:116–43; Platt 1985; Wicke 1990).

The mods, many stuck in low-echelon white-collar and service jobs, emphasized the appearance of affluence, which they effectively subverted simply by the apparent incongruity of the caricature. Their opulence implicitly belied the dead-end clerical jobs that funded their finery, an irony explaining the seeming paradox that their well-groomed appearance caused so much offense. The mods thereby handled the sixties more lucidly than any contemporaries, taking into simultaneous account both affluence and social inequity, or the contradictions of a system riding high without resolving the continuing economic disparity between classes. Once again, then, popular culture, in the specific form of a youth subculture, seems more acute than the literary, even the new wave of working-class writers—one of whom, Bond, at the time found working-class youth grotesquely inarticulate.

The crucial development in the sixties, finally, setting the stage for the eventual alliance in the punk movement between working-class youth and middle-class bohemians, revolves around the popular association between the Rolling Stones and *A Clockwork Orange*. The Rolling Stones were understood, in midsixties England, to represent a working-class voice, and thus were an early focal point of the mod subculture; at the same time, their interest in Burgess's novel reflected their actual bohemian roots. What happened to *A Clockwork Orange* now appears a first vague step towards the "revolutionary" use of literature defined by Terry Eagleton: the reinsertion of a literary text into the whole field of cultural practices, with relation to other forms of social activity. The Stones expropriated Burgess in an untheorized but astute act of montage, employing his "nadsat-talk" on record sleeves and living out something of an "ultraviolent" life-style for a brief period. The significance of this use of the novel lies in Burgess's own thorough antipathy to everyone involved. His satire on youth culture and devotion merely to philosophical abstractions, worked out through a deeply conservative ahistoricism, leave the novel's teenage argot a sheer contrivance. But in subcultural hands that language found a power Burgess never intended for it.

A Clockwork Orange

Graham Greene's *Brighton Rock,* later appropriated by punk, figures prominently in Burgess's criticism, in terms that sound like a treatise for *Clockwork*. He finds that Greene "adheres to the Jansenist heresy ... brood[ing] more on man's inborn depravity than on his ability to be regenerated. . . . [H]e is more interested in presenting evil than good." Greene's character Pinkie Brown, exactly like Burgess's Alex, "is dedicated to evil—betrayal, violence, murder, . . . with a full awareness of the eternal—or eschatological—meaning of his acts." In a sense, says Burgess, "It is better for one's soul to pursue evil rather than right. It is a dangerous paradox, but it produced a superb novel" (1970:60–61). *Clockwork*, however, recapitulates only this theological theme; if *Brighton Rock* wins his praise for not portraying sin as a matter for cool intellectual discourse, he does just the opposite, conveniently ignoring Greene's association of corruption with material poverty and social injustice. Burgess, not surprisingly, thinks that the "furniture" of English culture and society is a distracting irrelevance in *Brighton Rock,* merely a stage for the enactment of spiritual drama alone. But this is true only of his own novel, not Greene's.

In relation to more recent literature, from the fifties, *A Clockwork Orange* closed out literary attention to rock and roll (indicating how much the novel differs from *Brighton Rock,* and Greene's interest in popular music); pop music at the beginning of the sixties no doubt seemed bankrupt, in light of castrato-rock. In this foreclosure and in his blunt conservatism, Burgess represents the endpoint of the Movement, a group with which he is not commonly identified, given the Malaysian setting of his first novels, and the futuristic bent of his novels in the early sixties. In 1963, the year after *Clockwork* appeared, the separation of pop music and literature was clinched from the other direction by the ascension of the Beatles. The mainstream would no longer look to literature for its "pop stars," nor pay as much attention to elite opinion on the popular.

In 1962, in *Strike the Father Dead,* Wain had already eulogized jazz, some vague ideal strain in-between modern and trad, now "choked with a particularly noxious weed they called rock'n'roll." It hardly seems lamentable, considering the dull, abstracted prose devoted to it: "An insistent, sharp-angled sound; discontinuous, and yet indicating continuity as it pushed forward into the air." Sharing a program with Rod Tempest and his Lightning Conductors shows Jeremy Coleman, a curmudgeonly jazz pianist, the writing on the wall: "In the world of popular entertainment these adolescents had the adults in their power. . . . But, Christ! That *this* should be the result!" A mass of glassy-eyed, dancing teenagers resembles "a giant machine, . . . oiled with sweat and money, [in] the middle of a huge assembly line. . . . Someone had discovered a formula that would suck money out of these youngsters' pockets." Jeremy discerns only "conditioned reflexes" and gross repetition, believing that the "stuff . . . just goes round in a circle, with no way out." Wain at least has him admit "that I simply didn't understand them. I had no clue whatsoever to their feelings or motives." The proof of this befuddlement is the description of Rod Tempest's show, unintentionally the most exciting portrayal of a musical performance in the novel. Wain captures the essence of Tempest's appeal much as Thom Gunn did Elvis Presley's, not as a matter of musical quality, but of style: "he wasn't exactly a singer, nor exactly a player: he just projected his personality out in front of the band, [a] solid wall of noise behind him." To Wain, however, this merely fed a cult of personality.

MacInnes had long since abandoned the subject of pop music by 1967, when he published *Sweet Saturday Night,* a nostalgic history of the English music hall. It turns out that in "diving into teenage cellars," he had all along been "in search of the modern equivalents of the Halls" and their charming innocence. No wonder he fell away from the rock and roll scene, considering not just this nostalgia, but also his aversion to English interpretations of black blues singers. He continued to operate, as well, from the same highly subjective preconceptions about social class: the music hall vanished, he claims, along with the proletarian world. He might have attributed the decline of the halls, however, to his own observation that they basically accepted the established social order, not to the mythical demise of working-class self-assertion. MacInnes dates the decline at World War I and the immediate postwar years, which included, for example, the General Strike of 1926, a period of increasing working-class militancy. *Sweet Saturday Night* seems to incorporate directly the Leavisian description of the music hall's virtues found in Stuart Hall and Paddy Whannel's *The Popular Arts,* which was going out of date when it was published; all of MacInnes's analytical terms are contained in that book. The music hall, according to him, bridged "a historic gap between a folk song that was quickly dying, and a commercialized pop which has attained . . . its mechanized apotheosis." In "impersonal" pop music, "Idea and emotion, such as they are, have become generalized. . . . A direct contact between artist and audience has gone." The new music lacks the capability of revealing and teaching via a message, or an intellectual, moral component (though it may make an emotion "clearer and more explicit," MacInnes is fair enough to admit).

Particularly in *Clockwork* and *The Wanting Seed* (also 1962), Burgess epitomizes the quietism endorsed by MacInnes, which displaced the historical "discussion of society and social change into *moral* terms, in which youth was a central metaphor [for] the consequences of affluence and the growth of the mass media" (J. Clarke 1976:157). In the ahistorical schema central to Burgess's work, English culture and society change only in cyclical shifts between Augustinian (pessimistic) and Pelagian (optimistic) phases in the moral judgment of human nature. Like his immediate predecessors,

Burgess had only contempt for the young, popping up everywhere in the sixties to denounce the ignorance and "cowering innocence" of layabout youths. The abstract moral contrast drawn in *Clockwork,* between absolute behavioral conditioning and absolute freedom, removes the novel not only from history (and the reality and possibility of change), but also from any real concern with youth and its culture; in this respect the novel marks the waning of literary interest in pop music and youth culture. Kenneth Allsop thought the "futuristic trappings" in Burgess's work barren and half-baked, and wondered at their "rather mysterious vogue" (1964:8). Burgess's popularity makes sense, though, as an extension of the Angries' popularity, given both the disparagement of youth culture and the conservative moral allegory. When he first laid into England in *The Right to an Answer* (1960), after his Malayan trilogy, he went after mass culture immediately and from a classically elitist perspective: "I tried to settle down with Anthony Trollope, but the siren voice of the modern world kept calling me, luring me to submit to the blue hypnotic eye and the absence of the need for thought or sodality." With Burgess's subsequent notoriety, he was able to pronounce publically the verdict, via the presumably malignant medium of television, that pop music could not even be discussed in terms of "real" music.

MacInnes bitterly resented, and not without some reason, the fact that *A Clockwork Orange* was made into a highly successful film. (Julien Temple's film of *Absolute Beginners* appeared in 1986, ten years after MacInnes's death.) Gosling reports that MacInnes "was terribly hurt his three London novels were not made into films—*A Clockwork Orange* by Anthony Burgess was, with its violence and fantasy, make-believe sex, drugs, and rock'n'roll, but not Colin's straight, wide-eyed look at social phenomen[a] and reality with modest affection" (1980:75). Burgess has essentially acknowledged the influence of MacInnes's attempt at a teenage argot—the two novels represent a period of conception no greater than 1958–1960—which Burgess realizes more successfully by not even attempting authenticity, instead creating his nadsat-talk out of derivations from Russian. He also profited from the strong example of Sillitoe's young, anarchistic narrator in *Loneliness of the Long-Distance Runner* (1959); Sillitoe's "poetry of the body," as Burgess described it (see chapter 4), informs both Alex's voice and the content of his statements.

MacInnes might instead have resented the fact that his own relatively sympathetic parody of the pop music scene becomes, in Burgess's Tory hands, an entirely contemptuous satire of its subject. In *The Novel Now,* Burgess finds *Absolute Beginners* to be "psychologically accurate, very enlightening, and full of a real (and quite unsentimental) compassion" (1970:147), but he seems to have absorbed more enlightening material than compassion. His youthful subject is a mere pawn, and popular culture an excrescence. Burgess's descriptions of the music, performers, and audience, unlike those in MacInnes's novel, emphasize only one quality, "yarbleless"-ness, or castration, an accurate enough characterization, though only barely preceding the revival of rock and roll in Liverpool and London. The Dickensian tactic of assigning pop stars hyperbolic descriptive names is parodied much as it is in *Absolute Beginners,* the "MELODIA disc-bootik" in *Clockwork* featuring "eunuchs" like "Johnny Burnaway" and "Lay Quiet Awhile with Ed and Id Molotov." In a milkbar (the milk now spiked with drugs), Alex finds the nadsats listening to Jonny Zhivago sing "Only Every Other Day," and some other "very sick electronic guitar vesch."

The singers' names also typify the russification of England, to Burgess the logical end of the social-welfare state, along with the cultural leveling visited by its excessive tolerance of a more pervasive mass culture. The pop stars have taken literary names, "Goggly Gogol" and "Luke Sterne," and when Alex's droogs don masks before a robbery, one resembles Elvis Presley, while another—worn by Dim, who is "like his name"—resembles "a poet veck called Peebee Shelley," a presumably grotesque intermixing of high and popular cultural levels. In *The Right to an Answer,* Burgess laments the "postwar English mess ... that's made by having too much freedom, ... the great democratic mess in which there's no hierarchy, no scale of values, everything's as good—and therefore as bad—as everything else." He excoriates notions of equality in cultural and educational entitlement, insisting on the necessity of both cultural and social hierarchies, which are associated much in the manner of T. S. Eliot's *Notes Towards the Definition of Culture.* But Alex's highbrow taste in music—Beethoven, not rock and roll—though it sets him off from nadsat culture so Burgess can sympathize with him, is hardly unsuitable to the violence of *A Clockwork Orange,* as Burgess is fully aware. The Nazi atrocities Alex is forced to watch in undergoing behavioral conditioning ("Ludovico's Technique"), accompanied by a soundtrack including Beethoven, were themselves committed to the background of classical music. Thus Alex rightly mocks an article suggesting that "Modern Youth would be better off if A Lively Appreciation of the Arts could be like encouraged. Great Music, it said, and Great Poetry would like quieten Modern Youth down and make Modern Youth more Civilized. Civilized my syphilised yarbles. Music always sort of sharpened me up." When he plays Beethoven's Ninth Symphony, he imagines his victims "lying on the ground screaming for mercy," while he's "grinding my boot in their litsos."

The novel's primary thesis, as well, is conveyed through classical music, when the Ludovico therapy inadvertently makes Beethoven's symphonies unbearable to Alex, suggesting that the loss of the capacity for evil eradicates the possibility of choosing the good, as well, dehumanizing the subject. In *1985*, Burgess explains that the "unintended destruction of Alex's capacity for enjoying music symbolizes the State's imperfect understanding...of the whole nature of man.... The State has committed a double sin: it has destroyed a human being, since humanity is defined by freedom of moral choice; it has also destroyed an angel," since music—classical music—is a "figure of celestial bliss" (1978:95–96). Thus, to Burgess's mind, does any social planning inevitably destroy the individual, leaving the mechanical (the clockwork) while eradicating the natural and organic (the orange). (This mechanical/organic binary, it should be noted, is also the traditional basis of elitism like his toward mass culture.) To the psychotherapists, in *Clockwork,* the Ninth Symphony is only "a useful emotional heightener," rather than a "glimpse of heaven," as Alex (and Burgess in a number of his works) puts it.

Though Burgess dissociates himself at length from *Clockwork* in *1985,* he devotes a section entitled "Clockwork Oranges" to "irresponsible people who spoke of aversion therapy, the burning out of the criminal impulse at the source," in connection with juvenile delinquency. His first motive in writing *Clockwork* was to defend the individual against society, specifically against the use of behavioral conditioning to render antisocial acts impossible. (The concluding story in Sillitoe's *Loneliness,* "The Decline and Fall of Frankie Buller," raises the same issue.) The discussion of aversion therapy in *1985* affords a clear-cut example of Burgess's limitations as a commentator on youth culture, when he misremembers writing *Clock-*

work to counteract talk of drugging or otherwise conditioning mods and rockers, which he dates at 1960: "respectable people began to murmur about the growth of juvenile delinquency and suggest, having read certain sensational articles in certain newspapers, that the young criminals who abounded—or such exuberant groups as the Mods and Rockers, more playfully aggressive than truly criminal— were a somehow inhuman breed and required inhuman treatment" (1978:94). The mods and rockers did not, in fact, appear together in the popular press until just before their seaside battles of 1964, two years after the novel was published. What Burgess actually recalls is the reaction to the teddy boys recorded by many in the fifties, including Allsop and MacInnes (the latter, in *Absolute Beginners,* not at all averse to subjecting teds to the direst of treatments). When American doctors lauded the drug chlorpromazine in the fifties as an aid in curing juvenile violence, they specifically noted that "it soothes Teddy boys and makes them co-operative for treatment" (qtd. in Cohen and Rock 1970:307–8). More than one English newspaper suggested that teddy boys, suffering from psychosis, "need rehabilitation in a psychopathic institution" (qtd. in Brake 1980:73). Burgess's mistake suggests just how little interest he had in the issue at the time, as it pertained to youth culture, and his indifference both to subcultures and to history itself—there was simply a philosophical point to be made.

According to Burgess's philosophy of history, elaborated in *The Wanting Seed* and *1985,* Alex lives in a period known as Pelphase, one of three continually, cyclically revolving historical phases. The others are Gusphase and Interphase, the latter the period of transition between the two dominant views of the world Burgess reads off the Pelagian heresy.[2] Briefly put, Pelagius believed man had a free will, and thus could achieve salvation through his own efforts; St. Augustine insisted on the inherent depravity of mortal man, and the mystery of divine grace. The ideal of Gusphase would more than likely be laissez-faire capitalism, as opposed to the social-welfare state, let alone the vaguely socialist, apparently Soviet-dominated society in *Clockwork.* In *The Wanting Seed,* Augustine is explicitly tied to English Conservatives, Pelagius to "liberalism and its derived doctrines, especially socialism and Communism," the latter compression of ideologies indicating just how simplistic Burgess's system is. A Conservative government supposedly exercises less extensive control because of a benign if "gloomy pleasure in observing the depths to which human behaviour can sink." Liberals view the individual as perfectible, and thus intrude the state into his or her life, while Interphase involves the brutal totalitarianism that sets in with the liberals' disappointment. The conservatism in this account is quite conventional, that is, hypocritical: the liberal or social-welfare state is execrable because it lacks a proper moral and cultural authority, yet is seen to verge on totalitarianism in politics. By the same illogic, a laissez-faire conservative state combats deviance and difference, maintaining a moral catholicity and cultural hierarchy, yet somehow better preserves individual freedom—in reality, of course, only for the plutocrat, and the aesthete in control of cultural capital.

Pelphase occurs when a society tries to engineer, to any great degree, social cooperation and community, or even simply to help its subjects. In *1985*, Burgess is chiefly nettled by Pelagianism that blames criminal impulses on the social environment rather than the person, a familiar conservative attitude. Burgess's whole argument is window dressing for attacking social democracy; he appears in retrospect a mundane Tory. His views present an absolute contrast, therefore, with his ostensible predecessor Greene, who explicitly attributes the crimes in *Brighton Rock* to social deprivation. And in general, as with all cyclical theories of history—such as that of James Joyce (based in Vico), a frequent subject of Burgess's criticism—social activity is implicitly futile. *A Clockwork Orange,* in sum total, is a highly derivative satire on contemporary England and its youth culture, rather than an exercise in futurism.

Thus Alex only apparently participates in a youth subculture, but in the final analysis seems quite solitary from it. He is clearly distinguished by his love of classical music, use of Elizabethan speech ("Come, gloopy bastard as thou art"), and theological meditations ("the not-self cannot have the bad, meaning they of the government . . . cannot allow the bad because they cannot allow the self")—all of which render him quite superior to nadsat culture. The nadsat-talk, which at times has considerable energy—"tolchock some old veck in an alley and viddy him swim in his blood"—is a mere contrivance, a style disjunct from the novel's content. Burgess, in fact, has very recently disavowed not only the novel, but specifically and even more disingenuously its style as well, as the mere "curtain of an invented lingo, . . . intended to muffle the raw response we expect from pornography." His novel has long been distasteful to him because of its reputation as a quasi-anarchist text. His sympathies never lay with his "thuggish young protagonist," whom he compels to "grow up" to recognize "that human energy is better expended on creation than on destruction" (1986:vii, x).

In this last choice of phrase, he is clearly the polar opposite of Walter Benjamin and Greene, who in the essay "The Destructive Character" and the short story "The Destructors," respectively, both revived Bakunin's thesis that the urge to destruction is also the creative urge. This "destructive" form of creativity appears precisely in the appropriation of A Clockwork Orange into Swinging London, which gave the visceral style in the novel—a curtain or muffler to Burgess—a life he apparently never intended for it, and would never have conceded a youth culture could create. In 1985, published during the heyday of punk in 1978, in a section entitled "Bakunin's Children," Burgess describes youth cultures in terms redolent of an anachronistic obsession with sixties counterculture (very much as Allan Bloom has more recently), concluding that they offer only a "bland sense of alienation,... with no need of stressing [that] alienation through aggression." He believes that the "important thing is to sit about and be young together. There are activities on the verge of doing nothing, such as taking mild narcotics or hallucinogens and listening to rock music—both substitutes for art and learning." Like Hoggart's analysis of the passivity of the teddy boys, Burgess's elitist blindness leads him to a conclusion, on the ignorance of youth, diametrically opposed to reality. He argues that "the experience of others... contained in books" is at least as important as direct experience, condemning an unnamed, "brutish" British pop singer who insisted that "Youth don't need education. Youth susses things out for itself like" (1978:73, 75). Yet, among other things, it sussed out Burgess's book.

Burgess is also on shaky ground in treating "youth" as a universal condition, a point that should be made about MacInnes as well. "The youth-age conflict is a time war," according to Burgess. "Youth is time's fool, youth's a stuff will not endure, ... but it becomes important to the young that it be represented as a quasi-permanency" (1978:73). This may indeed have been a fallacy in the counterculture, and its pronouncements about not trusting anyone over thirty, but Burgess errs badly again in confining his attention to the sixties. Celebrants of the counterculture like Theodore Roszak made great claims for the unity of youth, but the counterculture was a small minority of young people, emerging primarily from disaffiliated sections of the middle class. John Muncie makes this point in concluding that the notion of an abstract, homogeneous youth culture, used on its own, obscures and mystifies the real bases of youthful experience. The young actually share a good deal of psychological and social ground with adults—many of the same anxieties, and the same class identifications. Thus "there is nothing 'natural' about 'adolescence' at all. It has only existed in socio-psychological literature for the past eighty years or so. Adolescence is a social construction, a recent invention of certain western, industrial societies," especially their efforts to create markets specifically directed at young people. As opposed to Burgess's simplistic mockery about aging, youth is not based solely on "biological determinants, but rather is socially determined by particular sets of relations between home, education and work, [and is] perhaps not that dissimilar from other stages in life." Thus Burgess's construction of youth and maturity could not be more addled in holding, in essence, that young people behave in strange ways, "but the phase is temporary, and sooner or later they will emerge as respectable adult citizens" (Muncie 1982:36, 38). In particular, many people remain angry at injustice, and energized against it, throughout their lives.

The paradoxical transmission of A Clockwork Orange as a document of rebellion, finally, clearly has nothing to do with Burgess (though he once traded considerably on his reputation as "the godfather of punk," as he put it in lectures in the late seventies). Its reputation has come about in part because of the notoriety of Stanley Kubrick's film, which has continued to show up in various forms in British subcultures. Burgess largely disavows Kubrick's work, seemingly unable to stomach his own subject given any kind of flesh—which certainly explains his minimizing of the novel's style as a muffler—though the film is in actuality extremely faithful to the novel. To a lesser extent, the novel's reputation wasn't hurt by the excision, until 1986, of the last chapter from the American edition, which has Alex settled down in front of the television. (One might question why, if Burgess despises mass culture, "growing up" into "creativity" entails the passivity of watching television—the contradiction makes quite evident his notion of the appropriate leisure pastime for the model worker.) The persisting misconstruction of *Clockwork* can also be attributed to its appropriation by the Stones, finally. After describing his novel's style as a curtain of "linguistic adventure" drawn between the reader and the anarchic content, Burgess seems to bely the presumed muffling of raw response, in claiming that "people preferred the film because they are scared, rightly, of language" (1986:x). He has matters half-right: in Swinging London, soon after the novel's publication and well before the film, the linguistic adventure had already proven a harrowing one—not for people in general, but for those scandalized by the youth culture that embraced and enacted it.

The Stones and the Mods

Art colleges, since the early sixties, have had a continual, pervasive influence on British rock and roll, fueling its enactment of weaker and stronger bohemian traditions, or both Romantic and avant-garde aesthetic theories, respectively. The prominent role of the art schools in British rock, in this respect, and in drawing together bohemian students and peripheral working-class youth as well, has been the primary reason for the international power and success of that music. Many of the principal figures in Swinging London's music scene came from art-school backgrounds—Townshend, John Lennon, Keith Richards of the Rolling Stones, Ray Davies of the Kinks. The melting down of literature, music, and everyday life into a combustive mixture, in the case of *A Clockwork Orange,* appears to have been relatively spontaneous and untheorized. But the groundwork was clearly laid for the more sophisticated punk epoch, in the meeting of bohemians and working-class youth. Two previously separate worlds came together around r & b, with "the new generation of art school musicians, who straddled both worlds, develop[ing] an ideology of music-making that kept both groups of fans in play together" (Frith and Horne 1987:88). The Rolling Stones, in particular, "took the Bohemian tradition of non-conformism and self-expression," and a concern with musical authenticity, "to a mass youth audience of a scale and immediacy hitherto unseen, and unreckoned" (Savage, qtd. in Chambers 1985:237).

This sort of intersection occurred in symbolic fashion with the expropriation of *A Clockwork Orange* by the Stones in 1964, at the high point of the mod subculture. Returning to accounts of the Stones from the sixties reveals that the group's class-conscious song lyrics, generally slovenly appearance and behavior (by pop music standards at least), and Mick Jagger's mock-cockney accent had distinct working-class connotations, as odd as that role seems in light of their subsequent career as jet-set millionaires. Accounts of what they meant in England in the midsixties present a striking contrast: "There is a great deal of hate in the Stones' best records," Melly found, actually invoking Lautréamont in calling Mick Jagger pop's Maldoror (1970:89). Anthony Bicat thought the Stones exemplars of disgust with "the general emptiness of the affluent life" and its lack of "solidity" or veracity. They seemed "the most obvious example of the young turning against a whole society in their music," but, moreover, they also invoked the politics of class; Bicat points out a consistent theme concerning the degradation of upper-class women by working-class males. He labels Jagger an Angry Young Man, in fact, on the basis of the analogous interest in hypergamy, "beside whom the writers and dramatists [of] the Fifties dwindled into insignificance. After all, they never actually tried to put John Osborne in gaol," as they did Jagger and Richards in 1967: "It was as if the English language had gained a new swear word" in the sixties—"Bloody Mick Jagger!" In light of the vehemence of this response, something more than the Angries' misogyny was clearly involved: "'Bloody Mick Jagger!' made the pop song a battlefield [not only] between young and old, [but also] between *them* and *us*" (1970:326–29).

The most pronounced class overtones occurred in the Stones' skein of misogynist hit songs in the midsixties, taken in England as an expression of a class revenge of sorts. Songs like "Play with Fire" (1965) directly associate their female antagonist with extreme wealth, with chauffeurs, diamonds, and fancy clothes. The lyrics caustically describe the fashionable open marriage of the girl's parents, their social milieu specifically demarcated by the geography of Swinging London. The mother, an heiress, has scorned the father's bribe of jewels, preferring a fast life moving across Knightsbridge and St. John's Wood in the west of London, to Stepney in the east. "19th Nervous Breakdown" (1966) likewise chides a spoiled debutante with too many toys provided by her wealthy parents. It is not just the woman whom Jagger attacks, in other words, but her whole class, both her mother, who owes a million to the taxman, and her father, who manufactures banal commodities like floor wax.

Nik Cohn provides a sense of why the middle-class Jagger, who agonized for a time over leaving the London School of Economics for music, would adopt a cockney voice (more like a mumble). Linking the downfall of Macmillan and the myth of the affluent society with the emergence of the Beatles, Cohn recalls that for some "there was a sense that times were turning tough again, that not all life was a fairy tale, and the need now was for something earthy, something halfway honest" (1970:62). But the Liverpudlians seemed "essentially childlike, androgynous, pre-pubertal" (Hall and Whannel 1965:282, 312), particularly to the mods. Bicat would later find that the Stones' revolt against the affluent society, the most striking to "have ever appeared in any medium whatsoever, was much more obvious than that of the Beatles," though the Stones' music was not nearly as revolutionary (1970:327).

Both groups, in the beginning, played straight derivations of black r & b, but the Stones, based in London, were more responsible for deposing the "nostalgic archaism of [trad jazz], which reassured those in authority." The Beatles were not central to teenage revolt in England for very long, in Melly's estimation, because they were too willing to accept the accolades of the Establishment, such as MBEs arranged by Prime Minister Harold Wilson. But their provincial origin worked against them, too. Jagger, on the other hand, in his cockney pose, tapped into "the feel of the working-class with its non-forelock tugging approach to the bourgeoisie and determination not to be kicked about" (1970:61, 67). The Beatles' increasingly experimental music flew away altogether "into limbo," in Cohn's view: "And there are maybe a million acid-heads, pseudo-intellectuals, muddled schoolchildren, and generalized freaks who have followed them there." The Stones, however, were "committed," in a distinctly political sense: "The dominant fantasy had the singer as randy working class, surly and always dissatisfied, cold, entirely ruthless, who picked up debs like dust, loved to make them break." (Thus Jagger, to return to Bicat's contrast, went way beyond Osborne, who has Jimmy Porter succumb to his upper-class wife.) The perceived political component in the Stones' music was a matter of form as well as content, in its "chaos, beautiful anarchy, [and] murderous mood"

(1970:129, 138). The Stones, therefore, not the Beatles, supplied "the decade's sonorial metaphor for white metropolitan youth rebellion" (Chambers 1985:68). Margaret Thatcher was quite correct, in 1988, when she blamed the sixties for displacing "courtesy and good manners" with "aggressive verbal hostility" (qtd. in Sinfield 1989:296), a development that appears a virtue from a less authoritarian view.

If none of these attributes of the Stones seems even remotely genuine, in retrospect, they did add up to an influential style, founded at least on the aggression, scruffiness, and "post-beat bohemianism" of art students, if not actual working-class aggression. Thus the Stones expressed quite convincingly "the voice of hooliganism" (Cohn 1970:132), though they were uniquely able "to attack" English society precisely because of their education (Melly 1970:89). The hooliganism, in other words, was an astute calculation. Their manager, Andrew Loog Oldham, had a great deal to do with this early, less theorized fusion of bohemian and working-class sensibilities, which would be more fully developed in punk. The "most anarchic and obsessive and imaginative hustler...British pop has ever had," Cohn says (before Malcolm McLaren appeared), "he loathed slowness and drabness, age and caution" (1970:133). Melly seconds all of this, stressing Oldham's hatred of conformity, an assault on boredom via outrage from which McLaren directly descended.

At first Oldham tried to clean up the Stones, in the interest of commerciality, but he quickly discovered that "revolt in the crudest, most vicious style possible" held a far greater appeal to the young. The Stones "were loved like that"—ugly, wild, nasty, foul, and cretinous, unmistakably a working-class caricature. Jagger, Cohn believes, was Oldham's disciple for some time: "Jagger on-stage wasn't like Jagger off-stage, but he was very much like Andrew Oldham." Managers as a rule are more "image-obsessed than the singers they handle, and then they use the singers as transmitters." At Oldham's urging, Jagger "trampled the weak, execrated the old, poured out a psychotic flood of abuse against women" (1970:134–36; 1975:24). A significant part of the hatred the music industry felt towards Oldham and the Stones, as a result, involved the way they made "money through outrage," rather than cooperation and conformity, the bourgeois approach (Melly 1970:86). It was Oldham, then, who first proved "that you didn't need to soften up to make it." The Stones established a rule of thumb in rock music, that "each pop generation must go further than the one before," in giving offense to orderly commerce by being "arrogant and vain and boorish" (Cohn 1970:136–37).

These assessments of Oldham's role were all written before punk; more recent accounts of Oldham clearly read his practices in light of the provocations offered by McLaren and the Sex Pistols. The "pioneer of an 'artistic' approach to marketing," Oldham helped the Stones ride "to fame in a series of gleeful games with the media" that openly exhibited the role of commerical promotion in popular music. The Stones were the first pop group to draw attention to the pop process, to expose the fact that music rarely if ever achieves widespread popular success without proper marketing, which only a major company can organize. Their image of authentic rebellion, accordingly, resulted largely from the ironic fact "they were clearly in charge of their own selling-out process" (Frith and Horne 1987:101–2).

Another precedent set by Oldham occurred in drawing literature into pop, a relation which had previously operated only in the opposite direction. In his general effort to distinguish the Stones from the Beatles, as offensive rather than respectable, "revolt began to change into a conscious stance, . . . ablaze with vengeance and mockery," the point at which he made the Stones

> read *Clockwork Orange*, . . . and soon they began to live out its style. They broke up restaurants, . . . howled obscenities and abuse at random. Instead of jeans and denim jackets, they began to wear frilly shirts, high-heeled boots, even make-up. In interviews they went out of their way to slag off everyone and everything, and, when they were photographed, Andrew would pose them in drag, or dressed up as Nazis, or kicking over a baby carriage. (Cohn 1975:13)

Those pictures of the group demolishing baby carriages may have influenced Bond's notorious play *Saved*, first produced in 1965, in which a baby in a carriage is stoned to death by degraded working-class youths. Cohn's own imagery, however, appeared well after the film of *Clockwork* had established a somewhat similar picture of the novel brought to life, and, more significantly, shortly after he collaborated with artist Guy Peellaert on *Rock Dreams* (1974), which depicts the Stones as Nazis (though only Brian Jones, in actuality, had posed in Nazi garb). Whatever the accuracy of Cohn's memory of 1964–65, it might safely be said nonetheless that *A Clockwork Orange,* published at the same time the Stones began to play London clubs, not only gave sharper form to the group's hooligan voice, but also helped shape its overall image, the milieu of outrage beyond the music. If Burgess's mean-spirited satire of pop music was rendered obsolete almost immediately, by beat groups like the Stones, it is fitting that his novel, in the process, would actually be expropriated and put to better ends by the culture he held in contempt.

Burgess himself repeats in lectures the legend that that he actually sold the Stones the film rights to *Clockwork* for $1,000, during the famous period of rapid output in which he mistakenly believed he was terminally ill (the timing of which fluctuates with different recountings). They supposedly made a quarter-million dollars on the resale of the film rights to Kubrick. According to Oldham, however, in 1978, the group never actually owned the rights to *Clockwork:* "I believe if you lie enough it becomes a reality. That was all during the *Clockwork Orange* period. Eventually, though, we had to face the fact that we didn't have the rights to do it. I wouldn't have done all those great sleeve notes without Anthony Burgess," though (Schulps 1978:18). In light of Oldham's admission that he made up the whole story, this particular matter serves to highlight, once again, Burgess's indifference to history and to the subject of youth culture.

A Clockwork Orange, in any case, became a prominent "literary equivalent for the Stones' ethic...of teenage violence" (C. Ehrlich 1975:40). Burgess's brutal language was first imitated by Oldham in the liner notes for the Stones' British album of 1964, *The Rolling Stones No. 2,* which were revised for *Now!,* released in the United States in 1965. The second version, below, includes a more graphic depiction of violence, suggesting some further immersion in the *Clockwork* ethos, or, more likely, the same commercial calculation that led Burgess's American publisher to excise the last chapter of the novel—the assumption that Americans like more violence. The clearest, most widely known indication of the Stones' *Clockwork* period, the notes mimic the novel's style with just as much malchick threat:

It is the summer of the night London's eyes be tight shut all but twelve peepers and six hip malchicks who prance the street. Newspaper strewn and grey which waits another day to hide its dirgy countenance the six have been sound ball journey made to another sphere which pays royalties in eight months or a year. Sound is over back eight visions clear and dear. Friends, here are your new groovies so please a-bound to the sound of THE ROLLING STONES.... This is THE STONES new disc within. Cast deep in your pockets for loot to buy this disc of groovies and fancy words. If you don't have bread, see that blind man knock him on the head, steal his wallet and low and behold you have the loot, if you put in the boot, good, another one sold! (Oldham 1965)

Richards confirmed in the seventies that the Stones went through a *Clockwork Orange* phase in both their private and public behavior: "There was a time when Mick and I got on really well with Andrew. We went through the whole *Clockwork Orange* thing. We went through that whole trip together. Very sort of butch number. Ridin' around with that mad criminal chauffeur of his" (C. Ehrlich 1975:40). The Stones apparently didn't indulge for long in the *Clockwork* phase, but they did help very much to fix the reputation of *A Clockwork Orange* as pop literature.

Considering the conspicuousness of this use of Burgess, and the prominence of the Stones in the mod subculture, it seems fair to assume that the mods were well aware of the novel. Swinging London in general certainly was, and the Stones were popular with the mods in 1964, according to Melly. Richard Barnes minimizes their significance for mods, but his account must be qualified by his friendship with the Who, and by his own description of the importance of the *Ready Steady Go!* television show, on which the Stones frequently appeared (1979:12–13, 123–24). The group understandably traumatized adult England, but to its fans the *Clockwork* period was one of a "total vision": "They were freedom, release, true independence. Quite simply they were *revolution*" (Cohn 1975:13). In 1967, however, they discovered Flower Power and LSD, and when Jagger and Richards had celebrated drug convictions overturned after the intervention of the *Times* of London, they lost for good, in England, their status as outsiders. The void left by the Stones' mostly voluntary abdication of their role as pop music's revolutionaries wasn't filled until the Sex Pistols arrived in 1976. Though the Pistols' career mirrored almost exactly the Stones' early tactics of outrage, the punks made a point of vilifying their predecessors, who had let down a large number of young Englishmen long before becoming jaded junkies and jet-setters. Johnny Rotten, echoing McLaren, said that the "Stones should have quit in 1965," an astute dating: "I absolutely despise those turds" (Young 1977:72). They were a sad lot by the seventies, in their cynical profit taking, if one measured "the whole sense they're putting across now against what they once meant" (Bangs 1973:74). The Stones had been, in the sixties, "quite major liberators, [stirring] up a whole new mood of teen arrogance, and the change was reflected in the rise of Mod. . . . For the first time, England had something like a private teen society going" (Cohn 1970:137).

The mod subculture, not unlike the Stones, represented an indirectly coded workingclassness, in its feverish consumption of high-fashion Italian suits, Chelsea boots, motor scooters, and amphetamines. The Stones were models, in a sense, for the linkage of black r & b to the life of English "teenagers with a certain amount of money and no sentiment. Where [the Stones] were remarkable is that they . . . never suggested that their determination to live like this led to happiness or fulfillment" (Melly 1970:89). The mods shared this sensibility, while exploiting the discovery that in leisure activity "you were under no limitations and nobody controlled you" (Cohn 1970:176–77). In this respect, they also represented "a caricature of traditional capitalism" (Melly 1970:87), more specifically a parody of the rhetoric of consumerism directed at the working class. Their drug of preference, speed, was a metaphor as well as a necessity for the freneticism of their life-style, the sixty-hour weekend.

The mods' well-publicized seaside battles with the rockers, on bank holidays in 1964, were less of a threat than the way the mods looked and moved. In their commitment to style, in the conviction "that leisure is the only part of life that matters," the mods, though largely working-class, touched on traditional bohemianism (Frith 1981:223). The union of working-class youth and bohemia, only an analogy here, would eventually come to life in punk. The mods, through "an imaginary relation [with] the conditions of existence of the socially mobile white-collar worker," dealt with the impact of the new ideology of consumption on the working class in a dual manner: "While their argot and ritual forms stressed many of the traditional values of their parent culture, their dress and music reflected the hedonistic image of the affluent consumer" (P. Cohen 1980:83).

These teenagers were aware as well, at more and less conscious levels, that the consumer's life was an empty one, yet, all the more subversively, at the same time they took a great deal of pleasure in it.

The calculated subversiveness of mod style—exceedingly well-groomed but all the more threatening—lay in the contradiction the mods expressed, allegorically, in their very persons: "Everything about them was neat, pretty, and *creepy:* dark glasses, Nero hair-cuts, Chelsea boots, ... gleaming scooters and transistors" (Melly 1970:152; see Whiteley 1987:99–104). The apparent conservatism of the mods' suits and short, clean hair "enabled them to negotiate smoothly between school, work and leisure," while concealing "as much as it stated. Quietly disrupting... the conventional meaning of 'collar, suit and tie,' [they pushed] neatness to the point of absurdity." The mods, in their intense leisure pastimes—imported black music, amphetamine abuse, scooter transport, and fanatic grooming—created a " 'secret identity' ... beyond the limited scope of the bosses and teachers." In the alternative order of the mods, focused on the weekend, "work was insignificant, irrelevant; vanity and arrogance were permissible" (Hebdige 1979:52–54). Their finery belied their actual social status, however; the implied, quite glaring contradiction lay in the fact that their money came from dead-end employment in service jobs, such as clerical work, and also, like the teds, that the style required a total financial commitment, not frivolous discretionary spending. As Tom Wolfe described the situation in New Journalese, "What the hell is it with this kid? Here he is, 15 years old, and he is dressed better than any man in the office.... All—those—straight—noses up there have better jobs than he does, ... but he has ... *The Life.*" In fairly traditional terms of class, "Hardly a kid in all of England ... harbors any sincere hope of advancing himself in any very striking way by success at work." Thus the mods' clothes "symbolize their independence from the old idea of a life based on a succession of jobs" (1969:77–78, 81).

The mod subculture, an embodiment of contradiction, could therefore handle quite successfully the simultaneity of discourse about a new consumerism and the reality of continuing social inequity. While affluence was coming into some question, as in the rediscovery of poverty, "its public iconography was triumphant, ... far from over. None knew this better than the mods," whose "furious consumption ... pushed consumerism to the point of parody" (Chambers

1985:78; 1986:12); Barnes recalls an outright grotesque parody of parental aspirations. Working at low-level jobs, both manual and white-collar, the mods' "experience of the world was characterized by the recurrent themes of working-class youth—routinized domination and control by others,... an experience intensified by the disjuncture between it and the promises of the 'Golden Age' of affluent consumerism." The mod was particularly acute in seeing "commodities as extensions of himself, rather than things totally independent of their maker or user" (as in commodity fetishism), and through a collective, active consumption pitched class conflict on "the terrain of a struggle for the control of cultural as well as material resources" (J. Clarke 1976:152–54, 157). In transforming "records, clothes, dance, transport, drugs" to fit the particular realities of their time and place, the mods enacted what Benjamin termed "market-orientated originality" (Chambers 1986:7–8).[3]

By mining leisure as a form of resistance against the drudgery of labor, the mods followed in the footsteps of the teddy boys. Like the teds, they mined the "exotic elsewhere" of American music—in this case black r & b and soul—sufficiently distant from any British context to be made to resonate exclusively with working-class experience. The mods also extended that imaginative exploration to Italian fashion and motor scooters, the cool sophistication of Continental style (Hebdige 1988:9, 75). But the most significant historical evolution beyond the teds was the influence on mod style of black West Indian culture, which appeared to live, through some sleight of hand, "outside the white man's comprehension." The essential thesis of Dick Hebdige's *Subculture* holds that white working-class youth subcultures, beginning with the mods, must be understood as "a succession of differential responses to the black immigrant presence in Britain." Though contacts with blacks were part of everyday life for many mods, and West Indian ska music and related styles like the porkpie hat were directly adopted, the influence remained more at the level of an emotional affinity with black people, including American blacks via soul music. This difference in musical taste, in itself, marks the evolution beyond the teds in race relations. The mods sought their own "imagined underworld" through a detailed, brilliant, but opaque appearance, a highly visible but still "private code" like that of West Indians (Hebdige 1979:29, 53–54).

Along with West Indian subcultures, the newly up-scale "indigenous gangster style," which emerged in public attention with the liberalized gaming laws of 1963 (immortalized by a recent film about the Kray twins), also offered the example of a dressed-up outsider, a further caricature of conventional capitalism. The opening-up of the West End of London by gambling increased the opportunity for adventure, too, in Soho and Westminster. This new impunity in movement, facilitated by the scooter, is reflected in the geographical subject matter of songs like the Stones' "Play with Fire." But the mods' emphasis on movement and speed also "clearly corresponded to the way they used music" (Wicke 1990:80), that is, to the frenetic formal energy of British beat groups. In this respect, the mods directly embodied musical movement in a style of living—more so, perhaps, than any subculture before or since.

Unlike the world in the Stones' music, however, the mod subculture did allow some positive visibility for women, primarily because the mods, in their preoccupation with style and appearance, manifested a certain femininity. The mod ethos of well-groomed "individual 'cool' could be more easily sustained by girls," therefore, whether at home, school, or work, "without provoking direct parental or adult reaction" the way a more aggressive style would have (Garber and McRobbie 1976:215, 217). The autonomy of women in the mod subculture did result in part from the boys' disinterest to some extent in girls, the result of amphetamines removing the sex drive, and of dating costing money necessary for personal upkeep. But the space opened up allowed the women to explore stylistic options of their own in clothing and dance, most significantly in the adoption of men's clothing, such as slacks, which marked "the beginnings of a new style for girls generally. . . . As the boys got more feminine, so the girls got more masculine," throwing off the traditional paraphernalia of femininity (Barnes 1979:15–16). London was the international center of youth fashion, by 1964, thanks to these innovations in women's apparel. The mini skirt, though a development that held as much or more appeal for men, evolved out of London fashion, hailed as "a victory for the girl in the street against the couturiers." The trouser suit, more significantly, was held at the same time to liberate the woman from short skirts, so as to participate "fully in her all-action life" (Whiteley 1987:98–99, 104).

As "pure, unadulterated STYLE, the essence of style," finally, mod declined fairly quickly because it was eminently susceptible to commercial diffusion. But in their amphetamine-driven devotion to "action, risk and excitement [in] the endless round of consumption" (Hebdige 1976:89, 91, 93), the mods briefly brought the pace of *A Clockwork Orange* to life. The novel suits very well the noonday and weekend underground described by Wolfe in *The Pump House Gang*. Though *Clockwork* is only minimally futurist, the memory of its linkage with Swinging London persists in a recent description of the mods' scooters looking "like apparitions from science fiction stories, . . . a harmless means of transport [changed] into an outwardly menacing, futuristic symbol." It would be more accurate to describe Burgess's Alex, rather than the scooter's rider, as "both the victim and caricature of a fascination with everything technical" (Wicke 1990:80).

But if the Stones and the mods brought the novel's ethos of destruction to life, they did so more in the constructive form of style than the packhunting for trouble and battles with the rockers depicted in the film *Quadrophenia* (1979), based on the Who record of the same name. The mods' bank holiday excursions to seaside resorts only became riotous when hangers-on, looking for violence, were attracted by characteristic exaggeration in the news media of minor vandalism in Clacton. The occasional violence in *Quadrophenia* must be qualified by Barnes's testimony that his "own strongest memory of Mods was how gentle they were. When I was running a Mod club they were incredibly helpful and friendly. Not aggressive or loutish at all" (1979:127). Such testimony indicates again how willfully misleading the demonizing of youth subcultures by the mass media has been in the postwar period. The real threat is never violence, but the expression of refusal, even just in symbolic fashion.

The new working-class literature, namely Bond's *Saved*, seems to have understood youth subcultures about as poorly as a rank conservative like Burgess. Though *Saved* unflinchingly presents bitterly disaffected working-class voices, it remains most striking for the moral and theatrical taboos it aims to violate, not unlike working-class fiction of the same moment, also exploring the new permissiveness. (From a Brechtian view, the linguistic shock in *Saved* seems mere formalism: theatrical experience is under assault far more than social perspectives beyond the theater, and the social content is entirely implicit.) Bond, in other words, looks on youth essentially from the traditional literary position on high.

His perspective is also affected by his Marxism, apparently incapable of appreciating more imaginative, symbolic expressions of refusal such as subcultural style, just as some subsequent commentators on the left privilege only direct political expression. The play was quickly closed because of the torture and murder of a baby in its carriage, the incident reminiscent of the Stones' *Clockwork* phase. The murder is anticipated in the shock of the play's laconic but charged dialogue: "Rock a bye baby on a tree top, / When the wind blows the cradle will rock, / When the bough breaks the cradle will fall, / And down will come baby and cradle and tree / an' bash its little brains out an' dad'll scoop 'em up and use 'em for bait." In an angry, ironic introductory note, Bond says that "the stoning to death of a baby in a London park is a typical English understatement," considering that beside "the cultural and emotional deprivation of most of our children, its consequences are insignificant." The young, rough working-class murderers are the greater victims, disfigured by a common fury "kept under painful control." He demonstrates that fury in a moral bankruptcy most evident in words, in a moral illiteracy. Therein lies the problem: the youths in his play embody the everyday violence of capitalism, but they do so entirely out of "unidentified discontent" (1977:10–15, 310–11). To write during the heyday of the mods and find, however empathetically, that working-class youth are frighteningly inarticulate seems a rather conventional elitism, from both a cultural and a political standpoint.

Conclusion: The Counterculture

If "youth culture" in the fifties, in England, was largely a working-class phenomenon read into terms of classlessness, by the early sixties it more genuinely transcended class, in a "gradual middle-class adoption of the trappings of working-class teenage life," or values amenable to opposing one's parents (Frith 1981:190). In terms of the music around which youth culture revolved, the white blues of 1963–65 or so had yet to evolve into the subgenres that would allow affiliation with class-specific tastes. Thus in the early and midsixties "rock'n'roll and teenage pop got mixed up with blues and soul and folk and protest." By the late sixties, however, black music had come to seem a limiting source, as white musicians acquired essentially bourgeois artistic pretensions, valuing self-conscious reflection, individuality, and technique over immediate emotional expression. "Rock" music (no longer rock and roll) preferred deliberative, intellectual, literary effects; as in Kant's definition of the aesthetic, pure art required a distinction of mental from bodily experience. Rock music's bourgeois aesthetes were also much like literary ones in their antipathy to any sort of ideology, preferring a Romantic individualism to the point of self-indulgence. Meanwhile working-class "hard" mods and the skinheads into which they evolved turned to Jamaican ska (and later reggae), a music unambiguously identifiable with blacks and delinquency. It was not until the late seventies that the formative punkrockers and/or their managers, "a self-conscious, artful lot with a good understanding of both rock tradition and populist cliché," actually "demystified the production process itself," joining bohemia and the working class by spawning "a people's version of consumerism" (Frith 1981:21, 77–79, 158–59, 190, 213).

Through the midsixties, youth in the form of the mod and rocker subcultures continued to embody, for mainstream culture, its uneasiness about postwar social change (S. Cohen 1972:192), but when the middle-class counterculture took the stage, in 1968, the sense of moral crisis was exponentially exacerbated. The two faces of the social reaction to youth already established in the fifties—"patronising publicity and imitation versus moral anxiety and outrage"—began more clearly to have

> their roots in a deeper social and cultural crisis in the society.... Above all, as the first flush of economic "affluence" gave way to crisis and stagflation, the bloom faded. Whenever the "Law and Order" society went campaigning—as it did with increasing frequency in the late 1960's and 70's—some section of youth was never very far from the centre of social concern, and of social control.... The whole collapse of hegemonic domination from the 1950's to the 1970's...was written—etched—in "youthful lines." (Hall and Jefferson 1976:74)

As the ideology of affluence and consent began to deteriorate, a moral panic occurred over public morality, caused by a "perceived breakdown in 'values'... connected to the jamboree of consumerism." Mrs. Mary Whitehouse and Malcolm Muggeridge led the charge against permissiveness, juxtaposing youth with consumerism and sexuality (Chambers 1985:59). From within, the counterculture appeared "a seemingly bewildering and diverse scenario of intense activism, lacking cohesion, theoretical clarity or tactical perspective," but from the outside the counterculture looked like "a hydra-headed conspiracy against a whole way of life" (Hall et al. 1978:251, 253). Such fears were unfounded; the counterculture's defense of private pleasure did not provide a basis for any lasting political organization, and class differences remained intact in youth culture.[4]

The use of music changed in a genuinely radical way, however, as "fantasies of community (drawn from images of the street and lower-class city life) were sold to the suburbs, fantasies of creativity to the street." The street, for the powerless, is the only location of resistance "on which 'them' and 'us' is made visible"; the middle class understands this in theory, the working class in practice. The fusion of these two components in praxis, in England at least, has been supplied by individual entrepreneurs, local hip figures crucial since the sixties as "the link between the culturally adventurous of all classes. They provided the continuity of bohemian concern that runs from the beats to the punks." Rebels such as Oldham and McLaren aim to disrupt the cycle of work and leisure, reading all manner of cultural productions, from rock music to literature, "for alternative values" (Frith 1981:192–93, 217–18, 224, 263), and instigate others to do so as well. A continuity exists, then, between the sixties and the seventies, as much as concentration on working-class subcultures tempts some to dismiss middle-class hippie counterculture as fatuous, to the extent "that there appears to be a belief that nothing really happened in the 'sixties." But the counterculture "covered several types of groups, some deferential and some highly political" (Brake 1980:159), and some of the latter, such as the neo-Situationists, never went away at all.

The Centre for Contemporary Cultural Studies helped disseminate the negative view of the counterculture, describing disaffected middle-class youth in unflattering contrast with working-class subcultures: "Middle-class counter-cultures are diffuse, less group-centered, more individualised"—classically bourgeois in outlook. But the Centre also noted that the counterculture of the late sixties took widely varying directions, generally following one of two courses, "via drugs, mysticism, the 'revolution in life-style' into a Utopian alternative culture; or, the other way, via community action, protest action and libertarian goals, into a more activist politics." At the level of ideology and culture, the counterculture attacked such institutions as the family, education, and the media, "the very apparatuses which manufacture 'attachment' and internalize consent." The more political strand sought to push its parent culture's contradictions to extremes, to foster negation through "systematic inversion...of the whole bourgeois ethic." (In the early seventies, in work revising his position in *The Popular Arts,* Hall cites Situationist rhetoric in a very favorable light—see Turner 1990:75). But because middle-class counterculture operated *within* that culture, it presents contradictions of its own, oscillating "between two extremes: total critique and—its reverse—substantial incorporation" (Hall and Jefferson 1976:60–62).

A few decades before, Antonio Gramsci had already linked concern over a "wave of materialism" in the younger generation with a crisis of authority for the ruling class, a crisis actually brought about by the detachment of the general populace from traditional ideologies (qtd. in Hall 1988:137). Though traditionalist forces were indeed mustered in defense of the old order, they actually served more to contain than to counteract a dramatic general change. They made sure the horizon of rising expectations remained limited to consumption—or focused on moral unease about it, that is—and thus did not entail expectations of significant change in the social organization. Confined this way, the erosion of traditional mores was a positive boon to advanced capitalism, which required "not only new social and technical skills,...but a more repetitive cycle of consumption, and forms of consciousness more attuned to the rhythms of consumption." The productive system, not the counterculture and the new permissiveness, was the real source of the disturbance of the gospel of work in the middle class, and of the self-repression represented by frugality. The apparent hedonism of the new permissiveness may have been experienced as a threat, but in reality "in its own traumatic and disturbing way, [it was] profoundly adaptive to the system's productive base," which had increasingly appealed to self-gratification throughout the postwar period. The counterculture was ambivalent from the outset, then, in actually helping to develop "the new ideas, techniques, attitudes and values which a developing society requires" (Hall and Jefferson 1976:64–65). The bourgeois virtue of deferred gratification had become a hindrance to the necessity of intensified consumption; the counterculture actually helped advanced capitalism to pass the crisis of legitimation provoked by the evolution from Fordism to the accelerated economy of flexible accumulation. With the uneven development of economic and ideological transformation, the rupture within the dominant class in large part involved ideology, morality, and educational institutions that needed revolutionizing anyway, and countercultural innovations were fairly readily incorporated.[5]

In retrospect, an extensive portion of the counterculture was engaged merely in a rush to enjoy the ever-greater bounties of consumerism: "The 'cultural revolt' of the 1960s, ... a revolution that took place in an era of economic expansion and increasing living standards ... was a *radical consumerism,* aimed at the authoritarian figures (parents, police, politicians) who barred the way to new kinds of consumption (clothes, drugs, sex)" (D. Laing 1978:128). Hence some yippies later became yuppies, having actually succumbed from the start to the phenomenon defined by Herbert Marcuse in the influential *One-Dimensional Man,* "repressive desublimation." The increasing moral permissiveness in "partial and localized," commercialized sexuality (1964:78) and other forms of immediate consumer gratification, he believed, depletes social dissatisfaction by offering a closely administered libidinal compensation. This modicum of freedom served as a distraction, as a spurious proof of genuine political freedom even as that freedom diminished, a point now frequently made about the consumer society. Many in the counterculture, though, merely used Marcuse to construct "a philosophical rationale for a hippie, rather than more directly political counterculture" (Wexler, qtd. in P. Smith 1988:61). If a modicum of liberation was actually an advanced means of control, they could conceive of no better response, in essence, than intensifying the quest for libidinal stimulation. The concept of repressive tolerance, in other words, was not used to identify real repression, but merely to redefine the counterculture's "own relative affluence as a kind of alienated, spiritual poverty" (Hall, qtd. in Hewison 1987:292), sometimes explicitly invoking the roots of that sensibility in Romanticism. The withdrawal of some into extreme self-gratification thus represents a far less lucid breaking of the bounds of permitted consumption than that found in working-class youth subcultures, which bore an edge based on experience of real oppression in education and labor. The mods may have taken speed (methamphetamine), but they did so in the face of authority, courting surveillance or reaction as much as they evaded it, expressing an antiauthoritarian energy that posed the more genuine threat. Julie Burchill and Tony Parsons go so far as to describe speed as a "proletarian drug," one spurring the "confidence to flaunt sharpness in the faces of those who would have dismissed you because of your background, the confidence to look down on *them*." In contrast with the counterculture, the mods, "aware not doped, . . . used their drugs instead of letting their drugs use them" (1978:78).

In relation to institutional art as well as popular culture, the counterculture presents a contrast very much like that between modernism (as well as Romanticism) and the avant-garde. The modernist strain may be found in work like Steve Strauss's "A Romance on Either Side of Dada," which shares Marcuse's veneration of European modernism and regret for the loss of the "second dimension" of aesthetic autonomy. That the counterculture could embrace the gross elitism of *One-Dimensional Man*—which condemns general education, paperback books, and American literature (Faulkner and O'Neill)—indicates that part of the movement was located well within the dominant order. As Alan Sinfield says of the 1965 Poetry International in London, there is "something traditional to be recognized in the image of the bohemian romantic poet appealing to transcendent and authentic values" (1983:164). Strauss ties his version of the counterculture to modernist icons like Baudelaire, Nietzsche, Rimbaud (whom Eagleton recently called every leftist's favorite hippie), and the Symbolists, praising their aversion to the supposedly repressive "embrace of other men and of life itself."

The dandy (or hippie), estranged from society and history, instead re-creates his own world in the "freedom of a creative existence" (a phrase reminiscent of the enlistment of modernism in the cold war a decade before, discussed in chapter 1). Strauss lauds a movement away from explicitly political activities "to mythical folk-art themes," in a "withdrawal from the crushing problems of an impersonal civilization." Where modernists present considerable complexity, however, the motivation in this retreat is merely self-gratification, given a literary veneer: "If dope has helped us to do anything, it has helped us to see the world the dandy saw. [W]e surrender a sense of our privacy to an idea of a general will, until, returning, we take that privacy back again" (1969:118–20, 134). (In a similar vein, Roszak, an American popularizer of Marcuse's synthesis of Freud and Marx, proclaimed social conflict merely a derivative case of individual psychological conflict.) Strauss's account of drugs reproduces that moment in the mid–nineteenth century when Baudelaire extolled hashish for feeding the insatiability of the artist's solipsitic "hurricane of pride," leading the mind only "to that glittering abyss in which it will gaze upon the face of Narcissus," the embodiment of self-absorption (qtd. in Graña 1964:146).

In an ironic invocation of 1968 and its revolutionary spirit, this Romantic narcissism reemerged in the neoconservatism bolstering Reagan and Thatcher, and their celebration of "untrammeled capitalism as a personal quest for autonomy [and] self-realization" (Marcus 1989:136). Robert Pattison, for example, in *The Triumph of Vulgarity: Rock Music in the Mirror of Romanticism,* celebrates ad nauseam the "pantheistic universe of the self," or "selfhood militant" (1987:89, 126). Expropriating rock music to literary tradition even more extensively than Strauss, Pattison neglects other more direct traditions in rock, especially its avant-garde and/or bohemian sources, because "he is reluctant to find deliberation in its practices and wants to demonstrate that its arguments were reached 'intuitively'" (Frith 1987b:406). Thus he rules out any social element in rock, whether history, politics, race, or social class—in the last instance declaring British rock homogeneous with American—and lauds rock and roll as an important part of the global supremacy of American capitalism.

His own agenda hardly seems apolitical, however, given his obsession with burying not just Marxism, but the whole anachronistic "European" concern with social class. Pattison has a typical "rocker" declare to the Old World that he will liquidate "European politics in a sublime act of American selfhood, . . . eradicating the conflicts you study with such avidity by eliminating the concepts out of which they arise" (the familiar ambition of ideologies of affluence). Pattison's rocker "will do away with classes and conflicts by the destruction of history and consciousness," a revealing neocon confession, in the midst of the Reagan-Bush era. With the triumph of the American way "has come the promise of fun and prosperity." One sees every day, of course, the fun and prosperity the United States brings to other nations, like Grenada, Iraq, Nicaragua, and Panama. Pattison is aware of this irony, but explains that "rock is not a force in opposition to but completely in accord with the nation's political mythology" (1987:173). This may be true of the most trite corporate rock and roll—such as Whitney Houston's lip-synching patriotic hymns while military jets boom overhead—but it is hardly universally the case, as Pattison wishes, in either the music itself or its reception.

With this sort of work informing critical hindsight, the disastrous effect of countercultural pretensions and utopianism on rock and roll has been widely noted. "When the countercultural dream died, it turned all that visionary artiness," like the Beatles' *Sergeant Pepper,* "into pure sludge." The first half of the seventies, before punk, represents "a long tunneling out from the wreckage of the sixties, . . . among the worst years in rock'n'roll history, as smugly reactionary as the void between the apostasy of Elvis and the arrival of the Beatles," the epoch of castrato-rock (Carson 1990:445). Rock and roll became not only the more stately *rock,* but, still worse, progressive or art rock, "a thinking person's music" (Chambers 1985:84). A radical countercultural community was somehow supposed to be realized through music enacting, conversely, the musician's exceptional individual creative talents. This contradiction in what is now referred to as the "ideology of rock" led to the result evident in Pattison, Roszak, Strauss, and so many others: the Romantic emphasis on the individual artistic consciousness converted the problems of the world into the problems of the individual. Liberation presumably lay in reminding the individual of his or her inner potential; creativity "meant removing the barriers which imprison man from within. [Hence] musicians' self-perception was dominated by the idea that music was the direct result of . . . a creative baring of man's inner psychic forces" (Wicke 1990:97–99, 107, 109).

Oldham had deliberately placed the importance of commercial promotion in popular music fully on display, but the Romantic conception of art as unique individual expression forestalled development of that revelation for another decade, when McLaren did the same thing to even greater revilement. In replaying, instead, the self-contradicted notions of Romanticism and modernism about their autonomy from the marketplace (discussed in chapter 1), the counterculture fed delusions "that stars and fans were somehow in alliance *against* the business that actually mediated between them" (which some in punk would continue to mistake as the upshot of the Sex Pistols and the Clash). CBS happily employed the prevailing rhetoric:

"The man can't bust our music!" read many music sleeves. Utopia turned out to be hip capitalism, Crosby, Stills, and Nash (the first prepackaged supergroup), and, in general, an unchallenged regulation of the "urge to be different" (Harron 1988:181, 191, 193). If market strategists, during the late sixties and early seventies, continued as they had since Elvis to find rock music incomprehensible, thus "most successful when they simply gave musicians a free hand," this only "nourished the musicians' illusion that . . . they were in control of the production and distribution of their music" as well (Wicke 1990:93). The corporate structure, however, had not changed one iota.

But the confused, uneven picture presented by the counterculture does contain oppositional elements, quite distinct from the revolutions in life-style that were "nothing so much as a looney caricature of petit-bourgeois individualism," and hence a raging commercial success. The more politically acute products of the counterculture, in contrast, "went forwards into a harder, sharper, more intense and prolonged politics of protest, . . . and, finally, the search for a kind of convergence with working-class politics," evident in punk (Hall and Jefferson 1976:66–68). The coexistence and subsequent detachment of romantic-individualist and radical strands, in British countercul-ture, is particularly clear in the evolution of "art-school ideology," prevalent in British rock since the Beatles first appeared. In the milieu of the art schools, the Romantic emphasis on autonomy and creativ-ity commingled with the influence of earlier political avant-gardes, the result casting the narcissism of the aesthete and the avant-gardist's concern with formal shock into one style. The late sixties, in essence, saw the beginning of a divergence between these Romantic and avant-garde strands: between "the first wave of art school musicians, the London provincial r & b players who simply picked up the bohemian *attitude* and carried it with them into progressive rock [e.g., Eric Clapton], and a second generation, who applied art *theories* to pop music making," as McLaren did (Frith and Horne 1987:100). This schism simmered for almost a decade, until exploding in the punk attack on the ideology of rock.

The radical vestige of the counterculture would continue to try to exploit and expose the consciousness-forming industry, recogniz-ing the economic changes underlying the increasing power of the mass media: the association of the increasing regulation of the private world—a world narrowed to in "possessive individualism"—with the increasingly interventionist state and the more rapid, flexible accumulation of capital. Situationist theory in particular, Hall and his cohorts believe, was directly germane to confronting new forms of power, particularly the power of consumerism's stress on private wants and needs at the expense of participation in the public sphere (left to the operations of the state and its corporate clients). The Situationists left a "profound trace in the revolutionary culture. [Their] targeting in on the 'revolution of everyday life' was not irrelevant," given their recognition that the consciousness-forming industry "had a real material base in the productive technologies . . . of the new capitalism," particularly the electronics and information systems necessary for the rapid circulation of capital (Hall et al. 1978:242–43, 254–58).

The Situationist influence was pervasive before and during the May Revolution in France, beginning at Strasbourg and the Sorbonne and spreading to young workers who frequented the latter. The Situationists believed even after 1968 that the temporary union of students and workers remained portentous. Together the two groups read Guy Debord's *Society of the Spectacle* and Raoul Vaneigem's *The Revolution of Everyday Life:* "Those who doubt this need only read the walls" of Paris (photographed and published by Walter Lewino in *L'Imagination au pouvoir;* see also Rohan 1988). Offering a new spirit in debates on spectacular society, culture, and everyday life, the Situationist International was at the center of a "recognized desire for dialogue. . . . If our enterprise struck a certain chord it was because the critique without concessions was scarcely to be found. . . . If many people *did* what we *wrote*, it was because we essentially wrote the *negative* that had been lived by us and by so many others." Though the capitalist order won out—preserved by the news media, unions, and subsequent academic analyses—"the movement was already a great historic victory." The occupations movement of May 1968 marked "the sudden return of the proletariat as a historical class, [and] an awareness of the possibility of intervening in history [through] spontaneous revolutionary improvisation" (Knabb 1981:225–27, 241), the sort of discovery of the unexpected championed by anarchism.

Situationist theory and practice, which have continued to migrate internationally, represent best the radical branch of the sixties revolt, as opposed to the solely hedonistic disposition. The lesson in action was not lost on McLaren, who only in legend witnessed the events of May 1968, but who certainly preserved the Situationist pride that the term "*situ*...tended to evoke an image of a vandal, a thief or a hoodlum" (Knabb 1981:249). The more radical strands of the counterculture first provoked, in the early phases of political polarization in the midsixties, the rhetoric concerning a crisis of authority and moral order, which led to the "law-and-order" campaigns of the seventies (Hall 1988:137). Thus the authoritarian backlash to which punk responded had its roots in 1968–69, when the threat of "anarchy" was first articulated (Hall et al. 1978:258). The punk subculture included a number of the sixties student radicals, like McLaren, who had prompted that response and never relented on their earlier aspirations and tactics.[6]

Given their contact with less compromising vestiges of the counterculture, the punks understandably professed to hate hippies in particular. Johnny Rotten of the Sex Pistols denounced everything from long hair and flared trousers (or bell-bottoms) to the lethargy of drug users (Rotten preferring amphetamines, like the mods). Hippies, he said, "were so complacent. They let it all—the drug culture—flop around them. They were all dosed out of their heads the whole time. 'Yeah man, peace and love. Don't let anything affect you. Let it walk all over you but don't stop it.' WE say bollocks! If it offends you, stop it. You've got to or else you just become apathetic and complacent yourself" (qtd. in Coon 1978:47). Though the punks disdained "the sloppiness of the late hippy era," they did remember the belief in the late sixties that youth culture could change the world. If the corporate structure colonized every level of rock and roll in the 1980s, ensuring no spontaneous eruptions like those in San Francisco, in 1967, and London, in 1977 (Harron 1988:174–75, 184, 195–96), there remained less thoroughly scouted areas of popular life, such as inner cities left to rot, which could still surprise (so to speak) the conglomerates with forms like rap music.

CHAPTER **6**

The Seventies: The Fusion of Avant-Gardism and Youth Subculture

In the career of the ideology of affluence in England, the moment of punk appears, with hindsight, a critical turning point. Just as Walter Benjamin, Henri Lefebvre, and others believe, it illustrates how profound a particular moment can be, and how persistent in its instructive significance, as continuing interest in the Sex Pistols attests. Punk rock and its related subculture do not simply mark the ultimate, bitter recognition of the completed decline of the English economy. Description of a new Depression was quite widespread, and hardly a unique insight. Punk responded instead to a broader rhetoric of crisis, which invoked not only the economic situation, but also the accompanying ideological construction of a "crisis of authority," which would soon bring Margaret Thatcher to power. The punk subculture, like its predecessors, resisted and undermined the prevailing common sense, but did so, notably, at a time when hegemonic discourse revolved specifically around the terms of *authority* and *anarchy*.

In Stuart Hall's analysis (1988) of the hegemonic forces at work, the 1970s saw a widely restructuring transition from a benign forging of consent, based on affluence and consumerism, to the brute coercion of the law-and-order society. With the failure of social-democratic consensus, labor militancy came increasingly into the open in the early and midseventies, exemplified by the miners'

273

strikes and the ensuing political and media rhetoric concerning authority and anarchy, conspiracy and the enemy within, and so on. The move from collaboration to coercion began some time before the economic crisis in 1976, when postwar economic confidence proved once and for all a delusion. In that year, with the Callaghan-Healey government attempting to control the money supply while maintaining "a 'social contract' with trades unions in the face of rising unemployment," welfare capitalism was stretched to its limit. The attempt "to create sufficient growth to maintain a social system that would produce an enthusiastic workforce fell to pieces," as a result (Sinfield 1989:281–82; see Hall et al. 1978:273–323; Harvey 1989:166–68). Raymond Williams, looking back in 1975, wrote that the period from the 1950s through the early seventies had clearly been "a time of evasion of all the structural problems of the society.... The evasion was systematic, and the communications institutions were one of its central agencies," offering a lively but deeply flawed "series of short-term definitions and interests" (qtd. in Hewison 1987:271), such as those bound up with Swinging London, before finally declaring a crisis.

Punk captured and parodied that rhetoric of crisis, produced by the mass media in the initial stage of authoritarian populism. At the unconscious edge where social discourse works on the subject, at the very least, the pressure of an increasing authoritarianism was clearly felt. Whether "consciously or involuntarily," the punk invocation of anarchy "existed on the obverse side of the public representations of 'crisis' and political emergency" (Chambers 1985:184). Yet Thatcherism proceeded apace, and many of those who came of age with punk have since come to see its promise as a fluke. The general sense seems to be that postmodern culture has obliterated the possibility of an avant-garde.

But at least two prominent scholars on the left, Terry Eagleton (1981) and Jürgen Habermas (1983), have suggested that the so-called Benjamin-Brecht position, developed in the 1930s, has not yet even begun to realize its potential. Many others,[1] though, have perpetuated the Frankfurt School's excoriation of "technologism," most forcefully expressed by Theodor Adorno. From this view, Walter Benjamin and Bertolt Brecht were foolishly optimistic about techniques opened up, in mass and popular culture, by electronic reproduction. Far from holding any emancipatory possibilities, according to this scholarly common sense, technology in culture can only serve the purposes of ideological domination. To Richard Wolin, Benjamin's essay "The Author as Producer" is a "calamity" (1982:160), a misguided manifesto on literature's learning from new media such as film and recorded music. This ostensibly calamitous essay appears in a very different light, however, in examining actual material events, like the appearance of Graham Greene's *Brighton Rock* (1938) at the center of English punk rock. Though the novel appears only briefly in a prose-montage biography of the Sex Pistols, the use of *Brighton Rock* affords a glimpse of "high art" finding utility in subcultural hands. The rediscovery of the novel, moreover, confirms Williams's assertion that an alternative aesthetic tradition can be found in neglected work of this century like Greene's—an avant-garde tradition counterposing the dominant versions of modernism and postmodernism.

In enabling the reconstruction of a chain of avant-garde theories and practices with an encouraging continuity, the recovery of *Brighton Rock* reaffirms the continuing potential of the Benjamin-Brecht position. A contemporary avant-garde, following in their footsteps, would do well to understand not only Greene's original significance, but especially the general aims and methods of the punk bohemians who restored him to the avant-garde tradition. Both his assimilation of everyday life and their reciprocal use of *Brighton Rock* exemplify Benjamin's essential proposal, the functional transformation of one's own medium by learning from other techniques. Just such an interest in mass culture suffuses *Brighton Rock,* which exemplifies the original interest of the avant-garde, in the thirties, in mass culture. The novel's palpable contumacy also offers a strong reminder of the lost relation between the avant-garde and anarchism.

The critical question of cultural studies, however, ultimately concerns the use value or outcomes of lived cultural forms, like subcultural styles: whether they "permit a questioning of existing relations or a running beyond them in terms of desire" (R. Johnson 1986/87:72). In this regard, punk remains significant in verifying the continuing possibility of antiauthoritarian resistance. The connection between Greene and the Sex Pistols is less important in itself, then, than in its suggestiveness for future avant-gardists seeking a similar, vibrant critique of authoritarianism, through the integration of "art, literature, music, style, dress, and even attitude," specifically the attitude of negation (McRobbie 1986:108). Such volatile moments confirm Williams's belief that "it would be wrong to overlook the importance of works and ideas which, while clearly affected by hegemonic pressures, are at least in part significant breaks beyond them, which may again in part be neutralized, reduced, or incorporated, but which in their most active elements come through as independent and original" (1977:114). In the face of nihilistic portrayals of postmodern apathy and stasis, the recovery of Greene by the Sex Pistols' entourage clearly represents a more than partially "significant break."

Detournement: *Brighton Rock* and the Sex Pistols

The Situationist International, the first link in the avant-garde chain here, formed out of the Lettrist International and the Cobra movement, eventually shedding all but those committed to the complete supersession of art (see Marcus 1989:245–405; Maayan 1989; Wollen 1989). The SI reached its apogee in the May Revolution of 1968, when its slogans prominently decorated the walls of Paris.[2] George Woodcock, in his history of anarchism, cites in particular the slogan "Imagination is seizing power!", commenting approvingly: "Not men seizing power, or parties seizing power, or even students seizing power, but *imagination*! This, surely, is the only seizure of power that could take place without corruption!" (1986:272). The Situationist critique of everyday life under late capitalism coupled this anarchist "prescriptive vision" with a "descriptive method" derived from Marx (Ward 1985:147), and from Georg Lukács's work on reification. The Marxist diagnosis of social conditions was not an end in itself, therefore, but led onto an aesthetic "program for their transformation.... From the Dadaist vanguard of the teens and twenties [the SI] took an urge to destroy art; from the surrealists, an aim to reconstitute it at the level of everyday life" (Ball 1987:24).[3] A subsequent English translation of Situationist texts, Christopher Gray's *Leaving the 20th Century* (1974), was a primary inspiration for avant-gardists involved in punk rock, most notably the Sex Pistols' manager, Malcolm McLaren; the manager of the Clash, Bernard Rhodes; and the group Gang of Four. In 1975 (as the Sex Pistols first came together), John Berger predicted quite accurately that the "revolutionary hopes of the 1960s, which culminated in 1968,... will break out again, transformed, and be lived again. . . . When that happens, the Situationist programme (or anti-programme) will probably be recognized as one of the most lucid and pure political formulations of that earlier, historic decade" (qtd. in Knabb 1981:389).

Given the appropriation of their theory into the rock and roll scene, it is important to note that the Situationists did not excoriate the technology of mass communication, but the concentration of its control. The SI sought to broadcast new uses of cultural commodities (Vaneigem 1983:206), not to reject them out of hand.[4] In targeting the whole of culture, the SI had an " 'aesthetic' strategy in the sense that [their] opposition was raised on the terrain proposed by consumer capitalism itself, the terrain of the commodity and of reified daily experience. . . . [I]f a revolution of [economic] production is no longer in reach, one can begin with a revolution of consumption. The premise: politics is in part the problem of the use or reading of objects" (Ball 1987:31–32). (This is a problem with which English youth subcultures, by the seventies, had long been engaged, if on a less theoretical basis.) The unified environment envisioned by the SI required that art, or the poetry of revolt, and technology become one. If the society of the spectacle is organized as appearance, it "could be contested on the field of appearance; what mattered was the puncturing of appearance—*speech* and *action* against the spectacle" (Marcus 1982:16).

Scholars, however, particularly theorists of postmodernism, frequently acknowledge only Guy Debord's negative critique of mass culture in *Society of the Spectacle* (see Jamceson 1979; 1984). The other significant component of his book, its description of *detournement* (translatable as "diversion" or "hijacking"), has largely been suppressed. Debord actually emphasizes praxis, explicitly insisting on the unity of theoretical critique and social practice.[5] Lautréamont, in *Poésies* (1870), first introduced a systematic, iconoclastic use of plagiarism (*plagiat*); the SI, which renamed the practice detournement, thought it had remained scandalously undeveloped. Debord announced that Lautréamont's slogan " 'Plagiarism is necessary, progress implies it' is still as poorly understood, and for the same reasons"—especially scholarly obfuscation—"as [his] famous phrase about the poetry that 'must be made by all.' " Detournement became an overtly politicized form of montage in the SI's hands: not just a testimony to the wearing out of older cultural spheres (as in earlier avant-gardes), nor an irreverent, playful reassembly of existing artistic elements (as in postmodern pastiche), but a blow that specifically undermined cultural hierarchy, or "the previous organization of expression" represented by the "literary and artistic heritage of humanity" (Debord 1981b:9–10; 1981a:55). The distinctive priority of detournement, in relation to other species of montage, lies in its assault on institutionalized valuations of "high" and "low" culture that obscure their potential social utility. Judging mass and popular culture degraded has traditionally justified insistence on high art's autonomy and antiutilitarianism, in essence assigning high and low a dialectically interdependent uselessness. In detournement, artifacts and texts "frozen solid in a hierarchic array" would instead undergo "an all-embracing re-entry into play," simultaneously "a 'devaluation' of art and its 'reinvestment' in a new kind of social speech" (Vaneigem 1974a:150–51; Marcus 1989:170). The resulting rediscovery of fluidity should disrupt the hoary dichotomy drawn between art and everyday life, and thereby expose "past critical conclusions which were frozen into respectable truths, namely lies." The ultimate objective, though, is to upset the general authoritarian monologue of the social order, not just authority in art (Debord 1983:#205–6, 209).[6]

Eschewing conventional privileging of the artist and aesthetic autonomy, the SI officially dropped the creation of art from its program, taking "a step no literary or artistic avant-garde had taken before: it denied revolutionary value to cultural innovation," or the "original" work of art (Maayan 1989:52). In their theses on the Paris Commune, the Situationists ask whether artists, acting as specialists, were "right to defend [Notre-Dame] cathedral in the name of eternal aesthetic values—and in the final analysis, in the name of museum culture—while other people wanted to express themselves then and there by making this destruction symbolize their absolute defiance of a society that ... was about to consign their entire lives to silence and oblivion" (Debord et al. 1981:316). The destruction of museum culture would have been the genuinely creative act, in other words. The inherent poetry of the Commune, therefore, was one necessarily without poems: "Realizing poetry," both then and now, "means nothing less than simultaneously and inseparably creating events and their language"—not creating works of art. But if poetry in its old forms is obsolete, it might "return in effective and unexpected forms" ("All the King's Men" 1981:115, 117). Detournement, for example, should interrupt "everyday experience and expectation in such a way that people are forced to confront the familiar from an altered perspective" (Ward 1985:150). Art in general is often theorized in terms of defamiliarization, but the new perspective in this case should be a *useful* one, too, a less common position on art, given the traditional loathing of utility (discussed in chapter 1).

With a similar sense of strategic purpose, Benjamin describes montage as an effort to prompt some analysis of social relations, not just to interrupt familiar cultural contexts. The "melting-down" of conventional distinction between art and mass culture, exemplified by Brecht's use of new media to generate the alienation effect, should help compel "the spectator to take up a position towards the action." Facilitating astonishment, by disclosing the real "conditions of our lives," constitutes a "situation" (1973:99–100), just as it does in Situationist theory. In essays like "Karl Kraus" and "The Destructive Character," as well, Benjamin describes the creation of situations through quotation and juxtaposition destructive of received cultural assumptions. Debord would likewise have the former spectator drawn "into activity by provoking his capacities to revolutionize life," in part by subverting his or her expectations of art and leisure (Debord 1981d:25). This is not a matter of purely formal shock, but of some dialectic between surprise and articulation.

To Debord the negation of boredom means "scandal and abomination in terms of the rules and corresponding tastes of the dominant language." This shock effect in various languages—musical, sartorial, verbal—was precisely the virtue many later cited in the punk subculture. The Sex Pistols and their bohemian cohorts constructed a situation very much like Debord's own description of momentary ambiences of life, while the audience entered the tumult with its own less theorized but equally impassioned initiatives. Such transformative moments of "superior passional quality" involve a fraught interaction between the material environment—like London in 1976, with the English economy ravaged, a crisis of authority declared, rock and roll bankrupt—and "the comportments it gives rise to." The ultimate result, if such situations could be realized with some frequency and continuity, would be a "unitary urbanism," defined "by the use of the ensemble of arts and technics as means contributing to an integral . . . milieu."[7]

The ensemble created in unitary urbanism first of all volatilizes the acoustic environment, revitalizing language by setting up a disruptive noise and breaching traditional aesthetic categories. That ensemble, furthermore, is also dynamic in the specific sense of cultural studies, in its "close relation to styles of behavior," to a broad "series of clashing ambiences"—much like the contradictory iconography Dick Hebdige (1979) describes in punk style. Debord even singles out clothing as an example of the material on which "ultradetournement," the outright conversion of signs, operates in everyday social life (1983:#205; 1981d:22–23; 1981b:13). Constructing a situation means not only bringing together different artistic techniques, as the avant-garde would have it, but also realizing "a unified pattern of behaviour... formed of gestures contained in a transitory decor"—a neat if unintentional summation of subcultural styles. And, most importantly, that temporary field of activity must be considered not with pessimism over its momentary, transitory life, but with optimism that such moments are favorable to the further development of desire, whether by the current actors or future ones (Gray 1974:13).

With regard to the future, it has been suggested that detournement, "as a technique of popular agitation,... has even now hardly tapped its available reservoir in newer media" (Ward 1985:149). Outside academia, Greil Marcus, in particular, has maintained in popular memory the Situationists' quest for a new language of action, for the situation in which the spectacle stands exposed. Not unlike Williams,

> They understood, as no one else of their time did, why major events—May 1968, the Free Speech Movement, or, for that matter, Malcolm McLaren's experiment with... the politicization of consumption—arise out of what are, seemingly, the most trivial provocations and the most banal repressions. The reason such events developed as they did was what the Situationists said it was: people were bored, they were not free, they did not know how to say so. Given the chance, they would say so. (1982:16, 18)

This understanding echoes traditional anarchism as well: Mikhail Bakunin believed that revolutions, when they explode, are "often precipitated by apparently trivial causes" (qtd. in Guérin 1970:34).

One such apparently trivial moment occurred when *Brighton Rock* was "detourned" in a 1978 biography of the Sex Pistols, put together by Fred and Judy Vermorel, long-time cohorts of McLaren. *The Sex Pistols: The Inside Story*[8] makes the connection of sacred and profane art forms characteristic of detournement, but its practice of montage has gone unremarked. The book's liberal use of quotations from Greene creates a parallel between his sociopathic hero, Pinkie Brown, and Johnny Rotten, the Sex Pistols' singer. At a literal level, the Vermorels juxtapose definitive remarks by and about Johnny Rotten, equally applicable to Pinkie Brown, with Greene quotations:[9]

> Greene: ... a face of starved intensity, a kind of hideous and unnatural pride.

> *Sounds* magazine: His [Rotten's] eyes look so glazed, his menace so unbelievably disturbing [*sic*], that you seriously wonder if there isn't some pathological monster straining inside him to get out.

> Greene: ... a Catholic is more capable of evil than anyone. I think perhaps—because we believe in Him—we are more in touch with the devil than other people.

> Rotten: Roman Catholic schools have an even worse way of destroying you. . . . They don't like people who stick up for themselves. And they tend to be the ones who turn out the most violent. Most crooks, criminals, they've all got suss up there. (Vermorel 1978:128–29, 131)

The passages from *Brighton Rock* serve a deeper function, however, by illuminating the Pistols' own stance, especially catchwords like *anarchy* and *vacancy*. In the anger behind the lines cited by the Vermorels—"a dim desire for annihilation stretched in him: the vast superiority of vacancy"—Greene's text hardly eschews political and theological commitment, just as the Pistols were scarcely vulgar nihilists, though invoking vacancy.

The new significant whole created by detournement, therefore, "confers a fresh meaning on each element," but "their old senses and new, immediate senses" do coexist (Gray 1974:150; Debord 1981a:55). The use of *Brighton Rock* is an excellent example of what Debord calls the "premonitory proposition detournement... of an intrinsically significant element" from an honored radical predecessor like Eisenstein or Saint-Just, an element "which derives a different *scope* from the new context" rather than a new meaning (1981b:10; italics added). The juxtaposition of Greene and the Pistols clarifies not just their original significance independent of one another, but especially, with the new historical scope, the "propositions" about the class structure and popular culture that make Greene genuinely "premonitory" in relation to punk (a prescience often ascribed to him regarding international events, but not youth cultures). Prompted to return to *Brighton Rock,* with regard to the ethos of vacancy, one finds that the early stages of the novel frequently describe Pinkie in terms of his vacant eyes, at various points dangerous and unfeeling, ageless or "young ancient," and heartless "like an old man's in which human feeling has died."[10] That "soured false age" is attributed directly to slum life; the lines used by the Vermorels appear when Pinkie stares at the spot where his parents' tenement used to stand. Those eyes directly invoke Greene's theological concerns as well, touched as they are "with the annihilating eternity from which [Pinkie] had come and to which he went." Thus they draw together, in microcosm, Greene's general suggestion—a political as much as theological one—that material poverty is a form of hell.

The juxtaposition of the novel with punk's own invocation of vacancy, by amplifying the theme, should also prompt reconsideration of punk's presumed nihilism. On closer examination, the Sex Pistols' song "Pretty Vacant," generally thought to evoke a predictable moronism ("Don't ask us to retain 'cause we're not all there"), contains at its heart a denial of spectacular images of depraved youth: "I don't believe illusions / When too much isn't real / So stop your cheap comment / 'Cause we know what we feel."[11] Comparison with the Pistols corrects critical conclusions about Greene, as well, such as Anthony Burgess's assertion that Greene's concerns are purely theological. False ideas of this sort are replaced with the right ones (Debord 1983:#207), by providing an opening onto Greene's political leanings, specifically his anarchism, which a similar anarchism in punk serves to highlight. His dissident poetry is thus "effectively rediscovered, ... placed in the context of particular events [that give] it a largely new meaning" ("All the King's Men" 1981:117)—but one that includes the original meaning, long suppressed. Greene, like the punks, aimed to delve below the middle class into the life of materially and emotionally degraded youth, and thereby explode the insular fantasies of everyday life. As guitarist Steve Jones put it, "Working class living is what life's all about, middle class is just fantasized living" (qtd. in Vermorel 1978:162), an explicit observation in *Brighton Rock* as well (concerning Ida Arnold).

Published in 1938, *Brighton Rock* makes sense in conjunction with the Sex Pistols for historical as well as thematic reasons. Comparisons of the Great Depression with the late seventies were widespread. The Birmingham collection *Resistance through Rituals,* for example, suggested that the decline and fall of postwar affluence had brought England right back to a conscious social polarization last experienced during the prewar economic crisis (Hall and Jefferson 1976:40). Such comparisons with the Depression were especially prominent not only in the sociology of subcultures nominally led by Hall, but also music criticism. Dave Laing, paralleling Hall's characterization of recent English history, found that punk signaled a transition from consumption to desperation in the basis of youth cultures. If the sixties counterculture was at base a radical consumerism, in the midseventies a very different economic situation prevailed (see chap. 2), one in which "teenage frustration is caused not by fuddy-duddy parents, not by easily-shocked adults, *but by an intractable economic situation.*" Thus punk rock reflected a "transition between the period of increasing consumption and one where the expectations of that phase have been frustrated" (1978:128). Punk and that intractable economic situation, the onset of something like a new Depression, are widely considered to have gone hand in hand. Hebdige describes how "the old mythology of doom and disaster was reasserted with a vengeance," during the heat wave of the summer of 1976. "Last Days imagery began to figure once more in the press. Economic categories, cultural and natural phenomena were confounded with more than customary abandon. . . . Apocalypse was in the air" (1979:24–27).

Incorporating all the postwar subcultural styles at one point or another, as the ideology of affluence and consensus that spawned them collapsed once and for all, punk threw youth style back to a prewar attitude of economic hopelessness. Music writer Caroline Coon (1978) dourly recounted the decline of industry and education, the rehousing of urbanites in concrete tower blocks, and the doubling of prices, and linked the social situation to the anesthetization of the rock audience by supergroups with classical pretensions, stadium concert/spectacles, and the like. Among all the explanations of its emergence, punk most certainly marks a profound disgust with the state of rock and roll in the midseventies, "when leisure-service conglomerates had concentrated record sales in the hands of corporations hardly more numerous than American auto manufacturers." Aging rock stars "now found themselves granted the dispensation to purvey their wares forever and, what is more, to celebrate the act as a moral triumph, a triumph that devalued any effort to pursue adventure and risk" (Marcus 1989:42). The capital-intensive nature of recording in sophisticated studios, as well as the increasing pretensions of musicians and critics to the status of art—or "rock"—entailed an "aesthetic of artistic excellence, . . . opulence and grandeur," which punk rock savaged (D. Laing 1978:124). Coon, however, like many critics, found the Sex Pistols' desire to shock people out of apathy rooted still further in the social contradictions in London, "where the contrast between the promise of a better future and the reality of the impoverished present is most glaringly obvious. Drab, Kafka-like working-class ghettos are a stone's throw not only from the wealth paraded on Kings Road, but also from the heart of the banking capital of the world" (1978:48).

Beyond the overt social protest, though, punk was a parody of public representations of political emergency, of a generation in crisis; the basis of authoritarian populism had already been established in the cultural and political arenas by 1976. With British capitalism in a state of unstoppable decline, calls for law and order and social discipline had led to "a dramatic deterioration in the ideological climate generally" between 1972 and 1974. Hall attributes this movement toward reaction to the unresolved contradictions of affluence in the postwar period. The arrival of economic crisis caused the manifestation first of "an unlocated surge of social anxiety," fastening on phenomena including "the hedonistic culture of youth [and] the threat of anarchy." The tutoring of public opinion "in social authoritarian postures by the method of sponsored 'moral panics'" was especially pronounced in the period when punk emerged (1988:23–24, 34–35). Thus punk must be understood to have deliberately exaggerated and parodied this threat, mocking the rhetoric of the mass media and the state.

The net result of that rhetoric was a tilt in the exercise of hegemony from *consent* to *coercion,* "a response, within the state, to an increasing polarization of social forces (real and imagined)" (Hall 1988:33; see also Hall et al. 1978:278, 287, 300). With the old consensus breaking down, authoritarian measures were presumably required. Official language in the late seventies acquired "a shriller tone, and the public consensus, increasingly sensitised to unwelcome change, was easily shocked into rigidity" by the media. The response to punks, as a result, was to present them as "the shock troops of an advancing wave of chaos." In this atmosphere, punk was quite prescient, with regard to Thatcherism, in proclaiming "the necessity of violating the...everyday script of common sense" by making a mockery of discourse about crisis, and refusing to be defined, as in "Pretty Vacant" (Chambers 1985:184–85; see also Pearson 1984:3–11). The centrality of the Sex Pistols and their cohorts resulted precisely from their articulating and enacting most conspicuously the collision with authority, and the rhetoric of anarchy. They "appeared as an embodiment of the general situation, [providing] the crisis with a cultural symbol which pushed this society's pathological nature to monstrous heights" (Wicke 1990:141), an act of parody so astute and uncompromising, at such a critical historical moment, that interest in the group has continued unabated to the present.

Graham Greene and the Thirties

In her early, on-the-spot account of punk's origins, Coon may exaggerate the socioeconomic basis of punk, but in the protest against extremes of wealth and poverty, her genuine outrage is unquestionable. To find a similarly unequivocal, angry drawing of lines before the midseventies, one would have to return to the 1930s, to a work like J. B. Priestley's *English Journey.* Priestley's could be a contemporary description of industrial England,

> a cynically devastated countryside, sooty dismal little towns, and still sootier grim fortress-like cities.... It is not being added to and has no new life poured into it.... What you see looks like a

debauchery of cynical greed. . . . I felt like calling back a few . . . sturdy individualists simply to rub their noses in the nasty mess they had made. Who gave them leave to turn this island into their ashpit? (1934:399–400)

Left-leaning writers of the thirties weren't simply the last unaffectedly "angry" English writers, either; some had a good deal in common with the continental avant-garde, particularly in their employment of popular music. Bernard Bergonzi does find contradictions in even the most friendly uses of popular song by the Auden generation, in the accompaniment of their sharp observation by a "difficulty of responding, of understanding and judging." But "the first literary generation in England to have to face mass civilisation directly" engaged it with alacrity (1978:143).[12]

With the arrival of sound in film in the thirties, and the wide ownership of radios, popular song became more fully a part of social consciousness. Despite others' interest,[13] though, only Greene uses popular music in a manner that fully refutes Samuel Hynes's depoliticizing account, in *The Auden Generation,* of literary interest in popular culture. Hynes, who generally recasts social concerns as moral ones more appropriate to literature, argues that there never was a movement "toward popular forms for explicitly political reasons" (1977:166). Greene's employment of popular song, however, leads directly onto his political anger, highlighting a steadily intensifying alienation. The teenage hired killer Raven, for example, in *A Gun for Sale* (1936), "bore the cold within him as he walked, [as] the words of a song dropped from . . . the scrape of a used needle." When popular song appears in Greene's thirties fiction, it does so virtually always in tandem with the expression of bitter, vitriolic resentment, with both a keenly felt personal edge and a society-wide aim. In *Brighton Rock,* popular song has a distinct resonance in Pinkie's experience. As a film crooner sings, the music's moan "was like a vision of release to an imprisoned man. He felt constriction and saw—hopelessly out of reach—a limitless freedom: no fear, no hatred, no envy." The novel's use of popular forms also fleshes out, more generally, intertwined conflicts pitting Catholicism against empty liberalism, in theology, and Us versus Them, in society. This avant-gardism was apparently long unassimilable in scholarship, or suppressed, as in Hynes's account. Forty years later, Bergonzi would express surprise at discovering that Greene's "pre-war fiction is much more impressive than it is often given credit for being, [combining] exact observation with a maximum of individual, even obsessional response" (1978:145–46).

Those personal preoccupations, which developed at the Berk-hamsted public school headed by his father, carry his public material far beyond the pale. At the age of thirteen, Greene was shifted from home to an adjacent dormitory, and seems to have been emotionally scarred by a sense of betrayal by his parents, to the extent that his dire, lifelong perception of childhood's despoilment by the evils of experience might be traced to this episode. Due to Greene's own adolescent trauma, he "began to believe in heaven because one be-lieved in hell, but [like Pinkie] for a long while it was only hell one could picture with a certain intimacy" (qtd. in Sherry 1989:68). Greene's early works, furthermore, based predominantly in "the memories of flight, rebellion and misery during those first sixteen years when the novelist is formed," consciously enact a form of re-venge on adolescent tormentors at Berkhamsted. He wonders "if I would ever have written a book had it not been for [his schoolmates], if those years of humiliation had not given me an excessive desire to prove that I was good at something" (1971:84, 226). It is remarkable, says biographer Norman Sherry, "that a relationship between a few boys at a public school should have had such repercussions, bringing Graham Greene to...sympathy for the outsider [and] the hunted man (for he had felt hunted);...he would have a profound interest in, and compulsive love for, the down-trodden everywhere" (1989:89, 91).[14] The obsession with personal revenge became an an-tiauthoritarian social vision. In *Brighton Rock*, Sherry notes, Greene compares the pain of the razor attack on Pinkie with a stabbing by dividers (the measuring instrument), experienced in school by Greene himself.

As in the case of many thirties writers, the debilities of Greene's personal life make up the infrastructure of the social and theological themes in his fiction. During the Depression, when he found it was impossible not to be politically committed (1980:37), he arrived at a sympathy with collective experience and popular consciousness latent in his personal experience. One of the most important discoveries in his life was that "I belonged on the side of the victim, not of the torturers" (1971:65; see 1980:72). It is hardly surprising that *Brighton Rock* anticipates the punks and other contumacious subcultures of the future with whom Greene is uniquely in touch: "Rose stood at the bed-end and pressed a hand against her body. . . . A child . . . and that child would have a child. . . . It was like raising an army of friends for Pinkie. If They damned him and her, They'd have to deal with them, too." As these passages suggest, his politics are virtually anarchist.

It is worth noting, in this regard, that by 1937 Greene had formed a close friendship with Herbert Read, who had been writing for some time the essays on anarchism collected in 1938 in *Poetry and Anarchism* (see Sherry 616–17); Greene's later short story "The Destructors" pointedly invokes Bakunin's thesis on destruction and creation, in depicting young vandals. In his thirties fiction, Greene's anarchism seems more visceral than doctrinal, just as Bergonzi notes an absence of explicitly Marxist politics. Later in life, however, Greene would write that "it has always been in the interests of the State to poison psychological wells [and] to restrict human sympathy," and thus the artist must "elicit sympathy and a measure of understanding for those who lie outside the boundaries of State approval" (qtd. in Sherry 1989:75–76). In the last decade of his life, Greene increasingly identified with Read and anarchism. In an interview published in 1984, when asked if he was anarchist, Greene replied that "that depends on what you mean. One of my great friends, Herbert Read, was an anarchist. For him, anarchy meant reducing a system of government to its smallest possible entity. . . . In that sense I'm not an anarchist. I, like most of us, am against the abuse of power while recognizing the necessity for a minimum of power" (Allain 1984:117). But not long before his death in 1991, Greene did designate himself an anarchist, "with a certain reluctance," one who follows in Read's steps in believing that power should be exercised as close to the people as possible, with the power of the central government reduced.[15] Whatever the degrees of ideology and intuition, Greene always favored anarchs nearly choked by resentment, who keep in their hearts "the sense of justice outraged— [their] crimes have an excuse and yet [they] are pursued by the *Others*. The Others have committed worse crimes and flourish. The world is full of Others who wear the masks of Success. . . . Whatever crime he may be driven to commit, the child who doesn't grow up remains the great champion of justice."

In his own adolescence, Greene found in playing Russian roulette "that it was possible to enjoy again the visible world by risking its total loss" (1980:75, 130): along with his empathy for youthful contumacy, this fascination with the tonics of risk and danger places him on common ground with the radical bohemians who would detourn *Brighton Rock,* in their assault on the more common boredom of everyday life. Concerning his own effort to conquer boredom, in fact, Greene cites the avant-garde, in the person of André Breton: "I insist on seeing what lies on the other side of boredom" (qtd. in Greene 1971:158).[16] Bergonzi, while not the first to write on Greene's use of popular music, does insightfully place him squarely (if vaguely) in a tradition of radical aesthetic practice:

> Critics have dismissed [*Brighton Rock*] as a confused mixture of thriller, a realistic story of Brighton low life and a theological fable; but these multiple dimensions now seem to me a source of strength rather than weakness. It may be that we had to wait to get accustomed to the fiction of *deliberately mixed genres* that emerged in the sixties and seventies before we could learn to read *Brighton Rock* properly. (1978:122; italics added)

What he describes, given Greene's political anger, is something more radical than pop art (in Bergonzi's terms), something much like avant-garde montage. Though rarely if ever discussed in terms of the avant-garde, Greene actually defined his early work against high modernism: "I've reacted against the Bloomsbury circle. . . . I think to exclude politics from a novel is excluding a whole aspect of life. . . . Virginia Woolf, I mean, certainly wouldn't have introduced politics. I began to get a little tired of Virginia Woolf," and reacted against her "by being a storyteller," writing a sort of high popular fiction, in the form of entertainments or thrillers (MacArthur 1991:27–28).

His use of popular music, at least, has been directly compared with Brecht, in their common concern to draw on " 'the directness of popular songs' [and] their ability to open up language" (Frith 1988b:121). In the novels Greene wrote before *Brighton Rock,* from 1934–36—*It's a Battlefield, The Shipwrecked* (or *England Made Me,* its more pointed American title), and *A Gun for Sale*—he increasingly adopts popular song as the correlative of an ever-mounting rage in alienated, socially displaced young Englishmen and women. In

Greene's novels, song serves at base to represent typical cultural experience, but also consistently summons up profound despair and indignation in the central character. Popular music is not part of the social brutality suffered by working-class youth, but prompts what articulation of alienation the belabored characters can manage. Jules Briton, the young outsider in *It's a Battlefield* (1934), feels that "only a gramophone playing . . . could save him then from sinking back, back into himself. Shout, sing, be in a crowd; . . . that was better than searching in the dark to feel himself for ten minutes . . . part of London, *part of a country*" (italics added).

The irony of Greene's self-penned song lyrics lies in their coupling of such brutalization with romance. While an industrialist's henchman beats a young worker in *England Made Me,* the pathos is reinforced by song: "I'm waiting, dear, / Leave off hating, dear, / Let's talk of mating, dear, / I'm lonely." In *Brighton Rock,* the promise of love (the birds and the bees) is falsified by rather violent social experience (the cacophany of drills, taxis, and trains):

> Music talks, talks of our love,
> The starling on our walks, talks, talks of our love.
> The taxis tooting,
> The last owl hooting,
> The tube train rumbling,
> Busy bee bumbling,
>   Talk of our love.
> The west wind on our walks, talks, talks of our love.
> The nightengale singing,
> The postman ringing,
> Electric drill groaning,
> Office telephoning,
>   Talk of our love.

In his characters' reactions to music, though, he is not at all inclined to treat popular music as an intrinsical false promise. The bittersweet love songs of the thirties, "fantasies of courtship set in the pragmatic context of working-class marriage, . . . lacked the passion or 'realism' of, say, the blues, but they did not lack cultural power" (Frith 1981:34). Greene reads that power as negative, emotionally, but ultimately a positive virtue in its evocation of bitterness and resentment.

In a period characterized by conventional romantic themes in song, the songs themselves could not realistically contain that rage; the context in which Greene continually places them is what matters.

In addition, Greene's montage specifically deflates the target of the original avant-garde, institutionalized art, namely William Wordsworth's *Ode: Intimations of Immortality.* The most optimistic lines in the Ode, on the Platonic doctrine of preexistence (the idea that the child still recollects heaven), were selectively taken as the gospel on childhood throughout the nineteenth century (see Garlitz 1966).[17] Thus the Ode makes a perfect foil for Greene's obsession with childhood's ruination. *A Gun for Sale* says of Raven, "If his immortality was to be on the lips of living men, he was fighting now his last losing fight against extinction. The cloud was blown away; it evaporated.... What a joke it all was, 'trailing clouds of glory.'" *Brighton Rock*'s social, cultural, and theological concerns all might be centered on its own transmogrification of the Immortality Ode: "He trailed the clouds of his own glory after him: *hell* [rather than heaven] lay about him in his infancy."[18] The novel's many ludicrous references to flowers ridicule their employment as a metaphor for both the child and heavenly preexistence by Wordsworth and his much more sanctimonious successors. Greene's savaging of high culture, finally, completes a triple-faceted allegory in *Brighton Rock,* the evident contrast with mass culture indirectly supplementing the clashes between theologies and social classes.

The novel's narrative concerns the skein of hideous crimes and sins Pinkie Brown commits while pursued, for a murder he didn't actually commit, through the seedy arcades of Brighton. An atheistic, promiscuous, self-appointed avenger and sleuth, Ida Arnold, prating of petit-bourgeois Right and Wrong, hounds both him and Rose, the innocent he eventually marries in order to silence her. Greene has regretted the relentlessness with which he contrasts Ida's secularity (ouija boards, séances, and so forth) with the adolescents' sense of the "stronger foods" of Catholicism, Good and Evil. Rose's Goodness also complements Pinkie's Evil for quite material reasons, though; the very obsessiveness of Greene's theology, as recourse to Benjamin will amplify, is essential to the incendiary social allegory. As a product of the Nelson Place slums, like Pinkie, Rose too resents secular comfort: "You can tell the world's all dandy with [Ida]." Ida could represent the "great middle law-abiding class" of any period, having "no pity for something she didn't understand," namely the poverty from which Pinkie and Rose spring, and thus "no more love for anyone" than the rest of the middle class had.

The weight of the secular material in *Brighton Rock* makes it a political novel more than an exercise in Jansenism; talk of hell always directly concerns Nelson Place. If Greene is a Jansenist, though, he has radically reversed the theology in a material social direction. Because Jansenism characteristically dismisses the corrupt physical world, it rejects the significance of historical activity, which Greene most assuredly does not. A line of Marlowe's Mephistopheles, " 'Why, this is Hell, nor are we out of it,' " presides over the novel for a secular reason—being poor in England is damnation. Depravity does indeed originate at birth, as a Jansenist would have it, but as a result of birth into the pernicious English social structure. As late as 1979, Sherry reports, Greene wrote that "I don't think that Pinkie was guilty of mortal sin because his actions were not committed in defiance of God, but arose out of the conditions to which he had been born" (1989:638–39). (Sherry, however, immediately dismisses Greene's own priority on social conditions.) When Pinkie, returned to Nelson Place, thinks that to find spiritual innocence one must go all the way back to "the ugly cry of birth," Greene's Jansenist tendency is fully fused with the locale. Rose, accordingly, perceives through her Nelson Place eyes "murder, copulation, extreme poverty"—commingled with "the love and fear of God." Both Pinkie and Rose define themselves against conventional society through their Catholicism, making it an oppositional, virtually subcultural emblem. They wear their conviction of evil like a safety pin in the nose.

Thus the secular world, particularly Brighton and its arcades, matters very much in the novel. Brighton presents a dialectic, a contrast between the irrelevant ideals of Wordsworth and the entertainments through which basic, primitive emotion struggles to manifest itself. The cultural struggle always invokes the social antagonism. Music continually torments Pinkie through both its musical and lyrical suggestion of sexuality; he suffers over sexuality because he witnessed, in psychoanalytic terms, the primal scene, his parents having sex; he saw them as a result of poverty, of being forced to live in one room with them. Brighton culture especially overlaps with the novel's interest in social inequity in the figure of Colleoni, the boss of Brighton crime. He functions as the representative of Greene's successful Others, or Them, making even a life outside the law impossible for Pinkie. Colleoni looks like he "owned the whole world, the whole visible world that is, the cash register and policemen and prostitutes, Parliament and the laws which say 'this is Right and this is Wrong.' The visible world was all Mr. Colleoni's." Immediately after suffering the horrific razor attack ordered by Colleoni, Pinkie spots him driving by in a limousine: "Or perhaps it was not Mr. Colleoni at all, ... but any rich middle-aged tycoon returning to the Cosmopolitan" (which serves elsewhere as an allegorical emblem of the upper class).

Mass culture, the profane, is redeemed when it provokes resentment of the Colleonis of the world. Popular music has a positive function in provoking Pinkie to confront his personal devils, while high culture appears inept in contrast. Music not only contributes to the novel's malignant tone, but also reiterates the conflict between Pinkie and Ida by gauging their divergent reactions to their surroundings, with Ida's taste in song astutely tied to the Victorian music hall (and romantic ballads), just becoming an object of nostalgia in the thirties (see Consolo 1962). Among the numerous instances of music augmenting the view of Pinkie's sexual plight is a scene in which he meets Rose. Waiting on Brighton's West Pier, he hears a band playing—"the music made him uneasy, the cat-gut vibrating in his heart"—while fondling a bottle of vitriol, "his nearest approach to passion." Popular music, in such passages, especially refracts the viciousness of the Brighton underworld. One "love" song leads him to reminisce about "all the good times he'd had ... with nails and splinters: the tricks he'd learnt later with a razor blade"—"Gracie Fields funning, / The gangsters gunning, / Talk of our love." The rather violent imagery suits perfectly Pinkie's anxiety over the remoteness of love, or sex, the "experience" he sorely lacks but also finds revulsive. (Greene at several points suggests a priestliness corrupted by material deprivation.) More than an ironic reflection of the debasement of love, music excites "anger like a live coal in [Pinkie's] belly," provoking despair, rage, and, potentially, *action*.

The cultural, social, and theological conflicts in *Brighton Rock,* finally, serve a single, primary allegorical function as well, in which negation (in keeping with Bakunin) proves a source of redemption. Because allegory is often fundamentally dialectical, in a "radical opposition of two independent, mutually irreducible, mutually antagonistic substances"—like Ida's secularism and Pinkie and Rose's Catholicism—in radical political uses its general function coincides with that of the avant-garde: "When a people is being lulled into inaction by the routine of daily life, so as to forget all higher aspirations, an author perhaps does well to present behavior in a grotesque, abstract caricature. In such a way he may arouse a general self-criticism, and the method will be justified." Greene similarly works as both an allegorist and an avant-gardist, sacrificing mimetic naturalness in order to force his reader into a critical frame of mind. An interpretative code like his matters more than accuracy and fairness, fetters propriety would place on "a straight-line movement that is obsessive" (Fletcher 1964:22–23, 107, 156, 222–24). Sherry's description of Greene's method in *Brighton Rock* suggests more specifically how excess succeeds in allegory: Greene projects the pattern of his obsessions onto his character's circumstances, but at the same time understands their plight as the result of both careful research and, most crucially, a "sympathetic interchange . . . between his emotion and experience and that of his characters." Though no real-life Pinkie would utter the theological meditations and so forth expressed by the fictional one, Greene does uncannily find an entirely convincing tone (1989:627, 637).

Greene's achievement as an allegorist can only be fully grasped by turning to Benjamin's *The Origin of German Tragic Drama,* an allegory in its own right, which uses German baroque tragedy (or *Trauerspiel*) to present a treatise on the avant-garde.[19] *Brighton Rock,* like baroque tragedy, leaps forward from death and damnation to the idea of redemption. Greene's own highly subjective, obsessive practice matches perfectly the transformation Benjamin finds in *Trauerspiel*'s negative theology: "a restoration of meaning through the 'miraculous' transfiguration of hideous and profane material content . . . into a parable of redeemed life" and salvation. Allegory is dialectical in this redemptive transformation as well as in the conflict of opposed principles (Wolin 1982:70, 72). An allegory, by definition, carries a second, more abstract meaning, derived from one particular set of ideas, often political or religious. That second level of meaning may profoundly alter understanding of the work's materials, even entirely reversing their valuation into their dialectical opposite, negation, for example, becoming a positive virtue. Even Pinkie's commission of murder takes a different cast, in *Brighton Rock*'s social allegory. Understood at an abstract secular level of meaning, it emerges as an act of class revenge, not simply a mortal sin; Greene later suggested that Pinkie's "crimes have an excuse" (1980:37). This is not to say that one forgives Pinkie because the victimizer is also a victim, nor even simply that one should, in contrast with Ida Arnold, understand the social origin of his crimes. The point instead is to grasp the novel's anger at the general economic violence of capitalism, the ultimate implication of the allegory.

Greene's own negative theology is clear: the conclusion of *Brighton Rock* raises the question of whether Pinkie, who avidly courts damnation, might not be saved because his devotion to evil was a form of faith, clearly preferable to Ida Arnold's jolly atheism. Pinkie is not simply the allegorical personification of evil, though, since he also embodies the profane elements of English culture and society found in the microcosm of Brighton. The corrupt leisure amusements of Brighton and the poverty of Nelson Place are also emblems of Pinkie's merit of salvation, not as a Catholic, but as a victim of social oppression. Benjamin describes the ultimate meaning of evil in *Trauerspiel* in terms of a similar shift from the theological to the social: "Evil as such exists only in allegory, is nothing other than allegory, and means something different from what it is. . . . The absolute vices as exemplified by tyrants and intriguers [like Pinkie] are allegories. . . . By its allegorical form evil as such reveals itself to be a subjective phenomenon" (1977:233). Evil, in other words, arises only in the mind of man himself, and thus very much in relation to the secular realm. This reading of spiritual abstraction into material social terms represents an assault on reification, on any eternalizing description of human experience, whether social (as in capitalist versions of "human nature") or theological. One can easily see the contrast between Greene and Burgess: Greene recognizes the considerable social basis of evil whereas Burgess, indifferent to social injustice unless the state takes too active a role in remediating it, treats evil in traditional metaphysical fashion, as some spiritual miasma that settles in certain individuals for no particular reason.

In the social context of the allegory, evil (or negation) is dialectically transformed, emerging as a legitimate desire like Pinkie's for "judgment" against the force that always presents itself as the good, in the sense of the positive and natural: authority. From the obsessive, arbitrary rule over things of an allegorical conception of good and evil, according to Benjamin, emerges a fundamental, dialectical vision of struggle, both social and spiritual. And in the negative judgment on authority contained therein, an "unconcealed subjectivity triumphs over every deceptive objectivity of justice," whether the specious objectivity of seventeenth-century Counter-Reformation Christianity or twentieth-century capital.[20] Negation thereby swings dialectically into a positive virtue. In evil the allegorist's subjectivity "grasps what is *real*" (1977:234), or the social realm; for all the invocation of the eternal, as in Greene's case, the artist's mind never leaves the injustices of the here and now. Discussing Lautréamont's *carriere du mal* in the essay "Surrealism," Benjamin calls evil a *political device*—something with use value—linking it with insurrection, spontaneity, and independence (1978:187–88).[21]

In a contemporary avant-garde, the profane materials necessary for an allegory redeeming destructiveness and disenfranchisement could be culled from mass culture and from everyday life, rather than crime and gang life. These sources would be elevated and redeemed in the allegory's movement from surface narrative to a larger set of analogous meanings—precisely the sort of work that goes on within subcultural styles. If an audience perceives the recontextualizing effect of montage, whether in a text or in the audience's own or another lived culture, "the joining of fragments and the positing of meaning" imbues the materials in play, however disturbing, with a new value, including a new use value (Bürger 1984:70).

The Sex Pistols

As Rose predicts in her meditation on Pinkie's descendents, *Brighton Rock* only found its apotheosis a few generations later. At the end of 1976, the Sex Pistols shook English spectacular culture—or provoked it to shake itself—after the sensationalist English press headlined the group's vulgarity on a television talk show. The Sex Pistols thereby solidified their position as the catalyst for punk rock until they broke up in 1978. The Sex Pistols' lyricist and lead singer, Johnny Rotten, had in myth at least a rough working-class childhood, in which "violence is about the only feeling strong enough to survive." Rotten, who attended Catholic schools, tended to think in theological terms, much like Pinkie—"They'd take your soul if they'd got the chance"—and was especially sour on romance and sex: "There's no love at all. I don't believe in love" (qtd. in Coon 1978:55, 59). In performance, he snarled "lyrics as though they tasted of his own piles, dancing like a rotting corpse,...glassy eyes burning,...amphetamine-parched lips turned back in savage contempt as he went for the jugular" (Burchill and Parsons 1978:34). For all the apparent nihilism, though, Rotten's noticeably Cockney singing voice actually embodied a desire to change the world, based in both contemporary economic collapse and a long-standing avant-garde "demand to live not as an object but as a subject of history." Unprecedented in postwar popular culture, that voice denied, in its visceral negation, both ideological constructs and received cultural assumptions: "Nothing like it had been heard in rock'n'roll before, and nothing like it has been heard since— though, for a time, once heard, that voice seemed available to anyone with the nerve to use it." The musicianship likewise turned rock and roll against itself; writing off the prevailing "professional cult of technique, it was a music best suited to anger and frustration, focusing chaos, dramatizing the last days as everyday life" (Marcus 1989:2–3, 5–6, 17, 57).

The lyrical content of the music, as in punk rock generally, introduced specific political topics into rock and roll to an unprecedented extent. The antimonarchism in "God Save the Queen," inserted to foment outrage during the jubilee year of 1977, is much less significant than the description of social hopelessness; the song's original title is found in the anthemic chorus, "No future for you." The song's critique of consumption—"Don't be told what you want / And don't be told what you need"—reflects Debord's exposé of the "choice already made" in commodity production (including entertainment) and admonitions to consumption. Other lines conjure up two of Greene's own themes, the social justification of sin and the degradation of "flowers": "When there's no future, how can there be sin? / We're the flowers in the dustbin." The song is widely considered the most effective political effort in the history of British rock music, for managing to be both ideologically scabrous and a meteoric number-one hit. (Some record charts, though, felt compelled to manipulate sales figures when the record reached number one, not at all ironically, at the height of the jubilee.) "Anarchy in the U.K."—a "blistering, nerve-bruising paean to anarchy as self-rule" (Burchill and Parsons 1978:36)—has the same grounding in political critique. Disdaining a society whose "future dream is a shopping scheme,"

Rotten rejects orderly consumption under the rule of the spectacle: "Not many ways to get what you want / I use the best / I use the rest."[22]

Beyond the music, McLaren and his cohorts succeeded precisely in creating situation out of spectacle, by provoking cultural and political authorities. Even when "operating on a chaotic series of intuitions, [McLaren] was the first manager to use the subversive possibilities of hype" by exposing how the music industry worked. Vile, wildly amateur, and offensive, totally unlike respectable rock stars, the Sex Pistols turned the industry's publicity machine against itself and made it a mockery. Yet at the same time they used it to "disseminate a disruptive, rebellious attitude," putting it to anarchist ends (Harron 1988:201, 205). In bringing into glaring relief the traditional role of promotion in producing pop hits, McLaren (like so many avant-garde predecessors) paraphrased Bakunin: "destroying record companies is more creative than being successful"; "I felt that negativity was absolutely creative, . . . a fabulous notion of disorder in a world that profited by order" (qtd. in Wicke 1990:140; Hoare 1991:14).

As their name suggests, the Sex Pistols presented an image of unrelenting raunchiness, calculated to go well beyond the bad boys of the sixties, the Rolling Stones. Anecdotes about Rotten's green teeth and a group member vomiting in Heathrow airport became, extraordinarily but quite predictably, front-page news. The use of the word *fuck,* however, on Bill Grundy's "Today" program, a teatime family show, galvanized national hysteria overnight. Spectacular culture's fury, at first predictable, soon turned dangerously ugly, tapping into the already established discourse concerning the crisis of authority. "God Save the Queen" was a "Jubilee Shocker," according to the *Sunday Mirror:* "Such is the new-found and disturbing power of punk," it raved, "that nothing can stop the disc's runaway success. Punk Rock—the spitting, swearing, savage pop music of rebellious youth—is sweeping teenage Britain" (qtd. in Vermorel 1978:96). The repugnance, outrage, and incomprehension went well beyond the usual calculated manipulation of readers. The real vehemence of spectacular culture's reaction to the Sex Pistols is borne out not only by the physical violence committed against them, virtually assured by the hysteria of the popular press, but also by the unprecedented, near-universal banning by local councils of the group's 1976 "Anarchy in the U.K." tour (largely because of the Grundy incident). The banning of the group from radio and television was hardly surprising or unprecedented, but the refusal of record company packers to handle "Anarchy in the U.K." suggests the unusual degree of media exhortation.

Finding the right chemistry of dissent, the Sex Pistols caused English society to reveal its true nature through its repressive as well as its ideological apparatus: "cops, vigilantes, and other thugs were practising [the anarchy] Malcolm preached, and it wasn't society toppling on the precipice of annihilation—it was McLaren and his lads" (Burchill and Parsons 1978:41). Reaching its apogee the week group members and their bohemian cohorts were assaulted, beaten, and razored, when they could not go out in public except clandestinely, "the polarization in England was beyond belief. It was a *crunch*" (Browne, qtd. in Marcus 1989:459). Rotten actually denounced violence repeatedly; one critic found "that contrary to almost all reports published everywhere," British punks were "basically if not manifestly *gentle* people" (Bangs 1987:229). But the punks, especially the Pistols and their entourage, suffered at the hands of loyal subjects and the police, all the while punk was denounced in the media for its supposedly sinister violence. In a ludicrous mélange condemning punks for wearing "stinking sneakers" and not giving "a damn what anybody thinks of them," rather minor offenses, the *Sunday Mirror* leapt to the utterly specious claim that punk "songs cause violence. Fans are injured in riots" (qtd. in Vermorel 1978:97).[23]

Not everyone understood punk as a provocation and revelation of repression, obviously, but this is less a failure of avant-garde intent than a strategic problem for subcultural shock tactics. "There is such a thing as expected shock," Peter Bürger points out. He does not mean simply that shock is therefore minimized, but that the dominant culture is quite capable of redirecting the impact of provocation against its perpetrators. Violent reactions to the Dadaists and the Cabaret Voltaire in 1916, for example, were fueled in large part by newspaper reports (1984:81). Nonetheless, as Benjamin says in "The Author as Producer," the avant-garde does what it can within the limits of the possible, however much "the bourgeois apparatus of production and publication is capable of assimilating, indeed of propagating, an astonishing amount of revolutionary themes" (1973:93-94). No one avant-garde moment settles the score with authority, obviously; if that moment wanes, even if it blows up in one's face, one moves on. Jamie Reid, the graphic artist for the Sex Pistols, remained optimistic a decade after their moment. Although new ideas "are plundered and pillaged, especially by the media," he comes to no more negative conclusion than "it's a constant battle, and you need to be on your guard" (1987:127, 142).

Sociologist-cum-music critic Simon Frith quickly recognized the importance in the punk movement of avant-gardists like Reid and McLaren, qualifying hasty treatises on "dole-queue rock" with an emphasis on the "punk bohemians." Rather than some working-class ground swell, punk was

> another art school demo... with a firm place in the history of radical British art.... The special interest of art-school ideology for punk derived from the role of manager Malcolm McLaren in the articulation of the Sex Pistols' style and stance,... in his art school past [and] 1960s experience of the brief but passionate fusion of political, aesthetic and cultural revolution [in] the Situationist International. (1978:535)[24]

But if punk was not a direct reflection of working-class misery, "neither was it merely a glib commercial ruse, a vulgar con dreamed by the Sex Pistols' manager Malcolm McLaren, [who] was only one of the 'authors' of punk. Between the subculture and the Situationists there existed less personalised links, brought together in a common programme to subvert the passive society of 'boredom'" (Chambers 1985:181).

In other words, though punk techniques may have represented "a strident expression of the traditional bohemian challenge to orderly consumption," punk was, significantly, also a "working-class bohemia that rejects both the *haute bohemia* of the rock elite and the hallowed bohemian myth of classlessness." On this specific basis, it would have "more dramatic and more public success than any other conceptual avant-garde artists have ever achieved" (Frith 1978:536; Christgau, qtd. in Frith 1981:266). The phrase "working-class bohemia" describes quite well the combustive meeting between a genuinely alienated appendage of the dole like Rotten and an older art-school product like McLaren, who had long hawked deviant clothing (from ted suits to bondage apparel) on the King's Road, London's traditional parade for youthful fashion. The injection of real anger into the bohemian sensibility made the enterprise avant-garde: the "tension of something sincere (Rotten's rage)" balanced McLaren's "own ironic parodic stance" (Carr 1988:40).

The point here is not to canonize McLaren, who has already been rendered canonical by institutional art and mass culture alike, as the subject of museum retrospectives and accompanying fashion-magazine paeans (see Bishop 1988; Chua 1988).[25] But the praxis of everyday life he preached—realized in actuality to some extent, though limited at times to more grandiose, self-serving claims[26]—remains essential to any subcultural initiative. Indisputably in the interest of shock effect, he exploited the Sex Pistols' excesses to the hilt:

> One tried to create a situation in which kids would be more interested in . . . creating havoc than in going out and buying the records. [T]he politics of boredom is really a wonderful weapon to use against the music business because that is the one thing they often try to sell. . . . When Rotten wrote the song 'No Future,' I was only concerned . . . to make those kids proud of that future, and to do that was to make them become as violent as possible against it, . . . creating [through the media] every kind of event that inflicted that hatred. (qtd. in Watts 1979:50)

Out of chaos, he said, should come a sense of purpose, a refusal of prepackaged leisure culture—the power to think. Whatever the degree of opportunism, McLaren's work with the Sex Pistols served, as the SI would have it, "to turn spectacle (the passively experienced structure of reality that we live with, as consumers) into situation (the structure blown up, its rules made clear, the possibilities for action and desire exposed)" (Frith 1978:535–36). Reid, whose earlier Situationist work helped define many Sex Pistols stances, wanted his audience to "think for themselves, always with that element of questioning the status quo and what is considered normal" (1987:105).[27]

As a "subversive comedy, a satire upon the 'depravity of modern youth'" (Watts 1979:37), the Sex Pistols certainly succeeded magnificently (with dire physical consequences, of course). In "dramatizing what had come to be called 'Britain's decline,'" the punk subculture, spearheaded by the Pistols, "appropriated the rhetoric of crisis which had filled the airwaves and the editorials throughout the period and translated it into tangible terms." In the apocalyptic atmosphere of the midseventies, the punks presented themselves as "'degenerates,' as signs of the highly publicized decay which perfectly represented the atrophied condition of Great Britain" (Hebdige 1979:87). McLaren and Reid declared, on a Sex Pistols record sleeve, that "the media was [sic] our lover and helper and that in effect *was* the Sex Pistols' success" (qtd. in Taylor 1988:52).

In using a generally available language, the punk subculture (or its more avant-garde sector, at least) was in effect satirizing and exposing the hegemonic framing of common sense by the dominant media and the state.[28] No subculture, says Hebdige, "has sought with more grim determination than the punks to detach itself from the taken-for-granted landscape of normalized forms, nor to bring down upon itself such vehement disapproval" (1979:19). It openly invited demonization by political authority and did, indeed, elicit the full force of law-and-order demagoguery concerning moral crisis. The arts chairman of the Greater London Council raved in 1977 (before the left took over the G.L.C.) that "I will do everything within the law to stop them from appearing here ever again. I loathe and detest everything they stand for and look like. They are obnoxious, obscene, and disgusting. The Sex Pistols are scum." The Tory shadow minister for education denounced the group's music as "a symptom of the way society is declining. It could have a shocking effect on young people" (qtd. in Young 1977:75; Stevenson 1978:60; see also Pearson 1984:5–6). The Sex Pistols thus managed the transformation of the negative and profane into a positive, genuinely disruptive force—the destructive becoming the creative. In their simultaneous creation and parody of spectacular culture's image of depraved modern youth, the Sex Pistols revealed the gross, superficial stereotypes that fill everyday life under the spectacle.

The Shock Effect

McLaren's quasi-Situationist practice (however self-aggrandizing) demonstrates the continuing significance not only of the SI, but also of the Benjamin-Brecht position. The Situationists' description of detournement and situation projects the possibility of mastering new media—learning how they have been used against oneself and others, and then how to turn them to better use—just as Benjamin associates the shock effect with a heightened presence of mind. Benjamin's formulation implies a genuine dialectic between formal stimulus and content. He refuses cultural hierarchies because he experiences style, in every form, as a tactile stimulus occurring in a social exchange, the producer's provocation of critical response. The audience's own activity would then be tantamount to the producer's employment and/ or emulation of the various media at hand.

Shock alone, however, is obviously purposeless, as Benjamin points out about Dada in his essay on art and mechanical reproduction. The shock of new techniques—new ways of singing and playing, in rock music—should place the audience in a critical frame of mind such that the content will be confronted. The most revolutionary content, presented in a familiar form, is easily appropriated by the market and audience alike, as "The Author as Producer" argues. Why does the widespread popularity of rock music with political themes, like the music of Bruce Springsteen, Sting, and U2, march hand in hand with conservative, authoritarian attitudes among the young? Less digestible sounds in rock music may prompt attention to the reasons for their development—alienation, antiauthoritarian fury, and so forth—even when those reasons are not clearly indicated in the lyrical content (as in the case of Nirvana). These aesthetic concerns, of course, should not lose sight of the fundamental sociological issue, the actual reception and use of any particular music. That social experience generates meanings well beyond those borne by the music itself. But if the politics of any particular work are less decisive, in evaluating its success, than the social uses to which it is put, it would be foolish for criticism not to concern itself with the production of the most radically useful texts possible. This section, therefore, focuses on artistic production; the following section complements and grounds this one by turning to reception.

Marcus describes the significance of the Sex Pistols' music in terms striking an appropriate dialectic between form and content, aesthetics and politics. The fact that he virtually recapitulates Benjamin's thesis makes one wonder why Marcus doesn't care for Benjamin's work:

The Sex Pistols made a breach in the pop milieu, in the screen of received cultural assumptions governing what one expected to hear and how one expected to respond. Because received cultural assumptions are hegemonic propositions about the way the world is supposed to work—ideological constructs perceived and experienced as natural facts—the breach in the pop milieu opened into the realm of everyday life. . . . Judged according to its demands on the world, a Sex Pistols record had to change the way a given person performed his or her [everyday activities]— which is to say that the record had to connect that act to every other, and then call the enterprise as a whole into question. Thus would the record change the world.

The Sex Pistols were in sum total, in self-presentation as well as their music, "a carefully constructed proof" that received propositions about the way the world works "comprised a fraud so complete and venal that it demanded to be destroyed" (1989:3, 18).

Benjamin's theory of shock, however, indicates that this dual dialectic—between form and content in a work, and subsequently between art and social experience—is necessarily a momentary success, requiring continual further movement. "Interruption" is not a practice that can be concretely exemplified and codified once and for all. A complete account of *grotesque realism,* Mikhail Bakhtin's term for visceral, contumacious expression, "must add that it is always in process, it is always *becoming,* it is a mobile and hybrid creature" (Stallybrass and White 1986:9). But the sense of the moment should not be unduly truncated. Exemplary texts and subcultural styles retain a considerable power even as commercial culture incorporates them, and spins out its replicas. Does Public Enemy cease to hold any significance because McDonald's uses rap music in its commercials? The existence of facsimiles of oppositional cultural forms does not somehow obliterate the fact of their emergence, nor their continuing usefulness.

An important conception of the appropriate relation of form and content, of the affective and the ideological, is contained in Marx's *The Eighteenth Brumaire of Louis Bonaparte.* Historical content in a genuinely revolutionary situation, says Marx, always "goes beyond the phrase," or its formal representation. The real significance of events set in motion by revolution runs beyond, for instance, the political symbolism used to articulate them. In the case of Louis Bonaparte's career from 1848–51, in contrast, his specious adoption of the mask of his uncle, Napoleon, concealed a careful containment of revolutionary forces. The form thus exceeded the content, as in the

"Reagan Revolution," which exploited nostalgia in order to advance and cement the prevailing contemporary interests, scarcely implementing the purported revolution.

Eagleton interprets Marx's formulation to mean that the opposition of form and content must be rethought, "grasping form no longer as the symbolic mould into which content is poured, but as ... a ceaseless self-production [or] self-excess" (1976:184). These terms of ceaseless mutability do not suit a "static, classical paradigm of an equilibrium of form and content," but they do suggest nonetheless a simultaneous, dialectical attention to affect and ideology. Marx expressed two perspectives on the relationship of form and content, which Eagleton finds not wholly incompatible. Marx's aesthetic ideal was a classical one, a harmonious interfusion of form and content, while the *Eighteenth Brumaire* describes a "good" version of the sublime (or unrepresentable), unanticipatable process in which form adequate to historical content would be ceaselessly sought out. Eagleton asserts that one can envision "some blending of the two—by a process which has all of the sublime's potentially infinite expansiveness" but retains some formal law within itself, yet would not amount to a "'predetermined yardstick' of forms and standards extrinsic to the 'content' of history." This relationship of form and content entails something very like Benjamin and Brecht's functional transformation: a break beyond mere exchange value in cultural production that releases a variety of genuine use values, a circuitry of dissident production and creative reception.

Brecht's formal experimentation, the inspiration for Benjamin's theory, depended on content in two ways: "First, form must change to reflect changing realities; [second,] political theater is a theater of possibility—a theater showing that life doesn't have to take on only the forms it generally does" (Polan 1987:352). These terms, however, do not sufficiently indicate the necessary supersession of art, by the poetry of actual social events. The SI's conclusion on the Paris Commune echoes Marx's on the 1848 Revolution and the poetry of social revolution in general. If, in the revolutionary situation, the "old world retains strongholds (ideology, language, morality, taste)"—in expressive forms, in other words—"it can use [them] to recapture the territory it has lost. Only active thought [or thought-in-acts] can escape it forever" (Debord et al. 1981:73).[29] Avant-garde artists have to work with a constant attention to both formal devices and content, maintaining them in a fluid, ongoing process of innovation that never loses sight of the concrete social purposes to which it wishes to do justice. In terms quite similar to Eagleton's understanding of *The Eighteenth Brumaire,* Williams describes the process of emergence as "a constantly repeated, an always renewable move beyond a phase of practical incorporation:...it depends crucially on finding new forms or adaptations of form" (1977:124, 126).

The key in this process is not to eschew altogether the past, and some degree of repetition of forms. One should not to seek to "make it new," in other words, in some entirely unprecedented fashion. Revolutionary repetitions are not necessarily parodic and regressive, like Louis Bonaparte's, but sometimes expressions of solidarity with the discontent and insubordination of radical ancestors, whose voices remain significant sources for insubordinate forms in the present and future. Benjamin's concept of a *constellation* refers specifically to a practice like montage that expropriates and recombines different forms, through which a politically electrifying connection between past and present can be realized (Eagleton 1990:210–17). A "revolutionary nostalgia" of this sort combines recovery *and* innovation in the same process. In popular music, for example, various styles undergo commercial defusion, but can be mined nonetheless by new musics, in the rejuvenation of older styles by groups like the Pooh Sticks and Teenage Fanclub, and in the now-familiar practice of sampling. In these and other cultural commodities "which have only recently gone out of fashion," one can discover "something useful and important about the conditions of their historical production [and] the dynamics of the moment of their creation." That discovery, Benjamin stipulates, is fueled specifically by discontent with the present (McRobbie 1992:160–62). The SI similarly believed that cultural forms recuperated by the dominant culture held the potential for subversive reuse, that commercial caricatures of rebellious expression might become vessels for a resurgence of genuine feelings of discontent (see Plant 1992).

Brighton Rock provides a significant illustration of Benjamin and Brecht's aesthetics: an antiauthoritarian attitude suffuses form, or style, and content alike; as the novel's employment by the Sex Pistols illustrates, that negation has resonated through further productive use of the text (if its proper relation to social practice took forty years to discover). The formal practice of montage, in this process—the interruptions created first by Greene's own style and subsequently by the appropriation of his text—has at each step been offered as "a stimulus to change one's conduct of life" (Bürger 1984:80). *Brighton Rock* in its own right realizes something like Benjamin's dual sense of montage, not only integrating snatches of popular music, but also discovering its own bitter style through immersion in Brighton's extraliterary culture. Greene's avant-gardism, in other words, lies less in the juxtapositions of song lyrics with prose than in deriving from popular life, in particular the misery of the Depression's victims, a palpable anger simultaneously innervating form (or tone) and informing content. The deepest legitimation for drawing together literature and popular forms, accordingly, will never lie in demonstrating superficial resemblances in content,[30] but in realizing further their sensuous affinities. "To raise cultural theory based in rock and roll strictly in terms of lyrics," says Marcus, "is the equivalent of raising a cultural theory based in Impressionism strictly in terms of Monet's occasions for painting (i.e., by discussing bridges, cathedrals, and ponds, not the paintings themselves)" (1986:79). Rather than concentrating on similar images and themes, it is necessary to account for both the sensuous and ideological impact of different expressive forms, considered on the common stylistic ground of language (or signs, to include partially or entirely nonverbal media).

Eagleton provides a useful lead for such an approach, in linking the avant-gardism of Benjamin and Brecht with Bakhtin's dialogical theory of language. Bakhtin shares the avant-garde's desire to explode the "authoritarian solemnities of monologue," through an everyday cultural praxis with a sensuous, somatic root (1981:149–50). He takes a "broad view of 'text' as referring to all cultural production rooted in language," which "has the salutary effect of breaking down the walls not only between popular and elite culture, but also between text and context," or work and audience. He refuses to dissociate literature from everyday life, including the mass media, or from larger social processes, believing that the linguistic sign "is material, multi-accentual, and historical; it . . . lives in dialogical interrelation with other material signs" (Stam 1988:118–20).

More fundamentally still, Bakhtin's colleague V. N. Volosinov points out that the acoustic, tactile accent given the linguistic sign by its social use is inextricable from some portion of its meaning. That "evaluative accent" bears a content in its own right, something like an attitude, generated by the "interaction between speaker and listener . . . via the material of a particular sound complex." That material "is like an electric spark, [with] a meaning quite independent of the semantic composition of speech, . . . implemented entirely and exclusively by the power of expressive intonation." To identify in language a particular emotive quality, in other words, is to express a meaning that inheres in the use of a signifier (or acoustic image), belying the abstracted Saussurean notion that meaning results only from leaping the gap between the signifier and the signified (or the concept arbitrarily connected to a sign). Given the inherent evaluative (or attitudinal) function in every use of signs, finally, they represent an arena of ongoing struggle open to inflection by subordinate as well as dominant groups. The electric spark borne by the sign, furthermore—a metaphor used by Benjamin as well—occurs even in the printed word, understood as a social exchange (1986:23, 103–4). Literary language can transpose into its own form, to some extent, the language of sensuous forms in carnival: not just its anarchic voices, but even nonverbal materials with which the "language of artistic images [nonetheless] has something in common, [namely] the carnival sense of the world," or its attitude (qtd. in Lachemann 1988/89:139–40).

Benjamin, in his *Trauerspiel* study, quite similarly takes some pains to elaborate the actual electricity of the "tense polarity" between print (considered part of material social experience) and sound. Literature, just as Bakhtin experiences it, actually gives rise to a dialectic between its plastic form and its content, or form and meaning (1977:213–15). Style, to Benjamin, is the means by which a writer "seeks a suitable relation between materiality and meaning that alludes to their subtle complicity, while stopping just short of conflation" (Eagleton 1981:77). The spoken word, the written sign, and the signified (or meaning), he says in "On the Mimetic Faculty," are all tied together by the flame or flash that always occurs in the use of signs, or the semiotic element. These elements of language (disjunct in the various structuralist and poststructuralist theories) correspond in "nonsensuous similarities." Such similarities are nonsensuous not in a literal sense, but in the increased distance of language from things since humankind's original, directly embodied imitations of nature like dance, associated directly with physical objects. Language, in fact, is now the medium into which those earlier powers have passed. The mimetic faculty, he wrote elsewhere, had shifted from the eyes to the lips, and thus in what he called nonsensuous correspondences, in actuality "the medium of *sound* is preeminent" (Wolin 1982:244).

Both Benjamin and Bakhtin ground their linguistic theory in examples of antiauthoritarian dissent, in which the somatic impulse fuses, as one, sound and meaning in language—spoken, sung, or written. Benjamin's portrayal of historical stasis in seventeenth-century Germany reflects his understanding of Lukács's theory of reification, while Bakhtin allegorizes the conditions of Stalinism in his Rabelais study. Thus the "bombast" of discontent in *Trauerspiel,* and the "billingsgate" directed at authority by carnival, suggest the contemporary possibility of negation. Benjamin finds that negative judgments on authority, as in *Trauerspiel,* generate the tactile force in a work's language, placing abstract knowledge in touch with the concrete elements of language. This early philosophy of language, in his own view, was quite compatible with his later Marxist materialism (Roberts 1982:6); his linguistic theory leads naturally to his openly Marxist essays on the shock effect in mass culture (so often treated as an aberration in his career). Literary language and the amplified rage of Johnny Rotten, from this materialist view, have in common "language so plain the very act of speaking it would grind one's teeth down to points" (Marcus 1989:195). In lived culture as well, particularly subcultural styles, one can find examples of a collective "affective engagement in which there is no great disjunction or interruption between the act and its meaning" (Giroux and Simon 1989:12). If meaning can be slippery, the articulation of emotive outrage at human misery is not.

Benjamin's concern with the dialectic of form and content in language connects directly with his insistence on "melting down" form and content in art. Given his stress on a material element in literary style, Benjamin posits *music* as the "antithetical mediating link" between oral and written language (1977:214), metaphorically if not literally the role served by the Sex Pistols in revivifying *Brighton Rock.* In the essay "Caution: Steps," Benjamin describes three highly material steps in creating prose, the primary one a musical stage of composition. Bakhtin's terms, such as accent, intonation, and polyphony, also "have simultaneous verbal and musical connotations" (Stam 1988:124, 128).

Benjamin's qualifying term *antithetical* must be acknowledged, however: many vain attempts to compare literature and music have already been made. The content of popular songs usually does not seem as rich as that of poetry, nor is the song's compensatory quality, the further control of tone of voice, fully available in print. The printed word obviously bears nothing like the rhythms and tonal ranges available in song. But that word does share, to use terms derived from Benjamin, the quality of "fundamental emotive enunciations, . . . the language of wishing, cursing, fearing, denigrating, celebrating and so on." The relation between text and social experience, says Eagleton, "is a question of form and force, of finding the very language of [literature] alive with electric currents"—that familiar metaphor—"that spring from a more-than-literary source" (1981: 124; 1988:xiv).

Williams similarly derives from Bakhtin the assertion that even written language is a constitutive element of material social practice. All forms of communication comprise active relationships between the intention of the author or speaker and the response of the reader or listener. (This is not to say that the intending author in literature is entirely present, but that he or she has certainly left some traces affecting the reader's activation of the text.) Aesthetics cannot remain abstracted, remote from that sociality: the "ebb and flow of feeling from and to others, [and] the relationships implied or proposed within the immediate uses of language are always present and always directly significant." On this dialogical basis, he finds that "the true effects of many kinds of writing are indeed quite physical: specific alterations of physical rhythms, . . . experiences of quickening and slowing, of expansion and of intensification" (1977:131–32, 154, 156, 165–68, 170). One might compare this with Frith's description of the sign of the voice (or the accent) in song, which works through nonverbal devices such as changes of tone, emphases, and hesitations, as well as verbal ones (1988b:120). Benjamin, in writing on mimesis, similarly describes a fusion of materiality and meaning in the literal rapidity of writing and reading. To Williams, literary style as much as any other cultural practice may share in and even help provoke changes in structures of feeling, or the broad sweep of material social experience.[31]

The primary principle of style in the avant-garde, says Williams, is the "language of the cry, the exclamation." That cry, much as

Bakhtin puts it, emerges from "sharply polarized states of mind, angrily polarized social positions, whose conflict was then the dynamic of truth." The clear subversiveness of Dada's otherwise nonsense phonetic poems offer a "reminder of how deeply constituted, socially, language always is, even when the decision has been made to abandon its identifiable semantic freight." In Brecht's work in particular, the cry "is a consciously liberating, indeed revolutionary moment: the cry can become a shout or [even] the *still inarticulate cry a protest.*" The latter instance seems a very apt description of Pinkie's voice in *Brighton Rock,* as well. The angry shout could be a means to collective action, an effort "to intervene in the social process and to change reality by struggle" (1989:69, 74–75; italics added). Marcus offers a striking illustration of Williams's avant-garde linguistics, in writing on the Sex Pistols' "Anarchy in the U.K." What amounts to Dada-like sound poetry, bereft of actual words, is nonetheless as replete with meaning as a more discursive critique of social life:

> Reduced to a venomous stew, . . . you heard not woe but glee.
>   'Is this the em pee el ay / Or is this the yew dee ay / Or is
>   this the eye rrrrr ay / I thought it was the yew kay / Or just
>   / Another / Country / Another council tenancy!'
>   It was the sound of the city collapsing. In the measured, deliberate noise, . . . you could hear social facts begin to break up— when Johnny Rotten rolled his *r*'s, it sounded as if his teeth had been ground down to points. This was a code that didn't have to be deciphered. . . . It *felt* like freedom. (1989:7–8)

In *Brighton Rock,* a novel full of music, Greene's great metaphor for such negation is *vitriol,* the material in which style and content melt down. Vitriol is obvious enough in the novel's narrative, even occupying a subtle centrality. Pinkie frequently fondles his bottle of it precisely when listening to music; in the end, having lived by vitriol, he dies by it. But when popular song suggests to Pinkie that "life held the vitriol bottle and warned him: I'll spoil your looks," Greene anticipates not only the angry assertion of "no future" by the punks, but also the tactile shock of punk's sputum. The *rock* in the novel's title refers to stick candy, but the novel's style bears a grain of embitterment not that far removed from punk voices: "An awful resentment stirred in him—why shouldn't he have had his chance like all the rest, seen his glimpse of heaven if it was only a crack between the Brighton walls." As Bergonzi demonstrates, Greene frequently uses colons to link clauses and phrases into verse, if not song. He often highlights in the process his darkest lines: "He was like a child with haemophilia: every contact drew blood."

Pinkie, in fact, *cuts a record,* containing the most chilling spiel of fury in *Brighton Rock.* The novel closes as Rose walks towards "the worst horror of all," the recorded (now posthumous) message "God damn you, you little bitch, why can't you go back home for ever and let me be?" This is not sheer misogyny; Pinkie sees not Rose, as she stands outside the glass walls of the recording booth, but Nelson Place. However repugnant this meanness seems, Greene, like Benjamin's allegorist, indicates throughout the novel that this resentment has a justifiable social basis.[32]

The reference here to resentment reflects an important source of Benjamin's work on negation in *The Origin of German Tragic Drama,* namely Friedrich Nietzsche, whom Benjamin stands on his head.[33] *Ressentiment,* synonymous with negation in Nietzsche's *Toward a Genealogy of Morals,* has traditionally been a ruling-class ideological device, used to derogate any radical impulse as irrational, self-centered embitterment. *Ressentiment* still reappears through the television darkly, whenever the news covers protests by antimilitarists, environmentalists, labor groups, women, and so forth. In Nietzsche's work, the person full of *ressentiment* is ostensibly paralyzed with feeble rage, confined to unenacted moral judgments on his or her rulers. The revenge of the slave lies in getting the master to take seriously those morals, particularly by embracing Judeo-Christian values, thus handicapping the presumably superior person who would otherwise act without circumspection (a view quite similar to social Darwinism, and blaming the victim, in the Gilded Age). An avant-garde must thus recast resentment as a positive virtue, with an emphasis on collective, not individual contumacy. As opposed to Nietzsche's ideal—a nihilistic, solipsistic, aristocratic barbarian—negation "assumes the existence of other people, calls them into being" by making it "self-evident to everyone that the world is not as it seems." When McLaren described "Anarchy in the U.K." as "a statement of self-rule, of ultimate independence, of do-it-yourself," whatever he meant, "it *wasn't* nihilism" (Marcus 1989:9). Vaneigem could be describing Rotten, in particular, when he says that the "man of *ressentiment* is a potential revolutionary, but the development of his potentiality entails his passing through a phase of larval consciousness: he first becomes a nihilist." Nihilism is only prerevolutionary if it takes an *active* form: as opposed to a passive nihilist simply watching things fall apart, an active one "criticizes the causes of disintegration by speeding up the process" and thereby sabotaging it, much as the Sex Pistols induced paroxysms in the spectacle (1983:135–36).

There is, contrary to Nietzsche, also a sense of fun in a *ressentiment* with a collective cast. Nearly all the postwar youth subcultures, as caricatures, have been enraging jokes cutting right to the heart of the spectacle, exposing the whole range of caricatures and images that rule in it. For both Bakhtin and Benjamin, laughter with this antagonistic basis "is the very type of expressive somatic utterance, an enunciation which springs straight from the body's libidinal depths" (Eagleton 1990:337–38). To Bakhtin, in fact, "laughter is a vital source of social renewal." In inverting "all hierarchies as it turns the 'natural' social world upside down, [i]t restores the community to itself in physical convulsions which revive our untheorised sense of solidarity in embodiment" (Hebdige 1988:243). Resentment of social injustice is thereby transformed into something positive by its allegorical, dialectical awareness of Them and Us, of domination and manipulation, and by the pleasure and fun it takes in the process. The negative, the profane, becomes a parable of a redeemed life, an emblem of salvation; the destructive becomes the creative.

In Benjamin's description of baroque tragedy (i.e, the avant-garde), immersion in discontent acts as a vitalizing force on allegorical objects, in one about-turn redeeming both them and the emotion of *ressentiment* itself. Whether literary emblems and tropes, the lyrical and musical contents of phonograph records, or the ensembles constructed by subcultures, those vile objects through which discontent seeks a style "turn into allegories [that] fill out and *deny* the void in which they are represented" (Benjamin 1977:232–33). That void might be the oft-remarked "seediness" of Greene's fiction, the Sex Pistols' lack of musical virtuosity, or the punk subculture's presumed nihilism—superficial, reductive perceptions corrected by an understanding of their allegorical significance. The allegory of struggle presented by vile, profane materials set against the authority of institutionalized forms infuses life into the reified, the static, and keeps alive the spirit of refusal. If the "crucial necessity for political action is a felt collectivity" in popular culture (MacCabe 1986:9), hopefully the basis of that feeling will be pent-up resentment of capitalism's irrationality, brought to full articulation. In an affirmative, feel-good culture that puts a happy face on plutocracy, in the enormously positive, indisputable, inaccessible spectacle described by Debord, all the *ressentiment* and vitriol possible is needed.

Not surprisingly, popular-music criticism has understood this need much better than specialized literary criticism. Several theories of rock and roll could easily be brought to bear on literature, on the model of McLaren's yeomen and their work with Greene. In the late sixties, Marcus described the social function of rock music in virtually the same terms of fundamental emotive enunciations that Eagleton would derive from Benjamin over a decade later. The repetitive tactile element in rock music, Marcus says, belies its educative role in the listener's reaction to a situation. He finds the same connection between a style of feeling and an idea that Benjamin wished for film, in "a way of thinking that allows one to give mood and emotion the force of fact, to believe one's instinctual reaction more than someone else's . . . logical argument" (1969:20).[34]

More recently, Laing has directly invoked Benjamin's description of the shock effect and its creation of a heightened presence of mind. Punk rock, as Laing hears it, combined "an apparently artless 'natural' vocal approach [with] cockney-novelty singing [and] the chant of football fans." In asserting an uncompromising working-class voice, punk challenged "bourgeois hegemony in the cultural sphere, [which] works through *tone of voice* (Standard English and its musical-vocal equivalents) as well as through the dissemination of specific ideas." The punk tone was a form "undigested by the leisure apparatus, and unfamiliar as musical material to the audience," simultaneously underlining and exceeding any message, or content. *Ressentiment* in tone befit the lyrics, that is, but also bore a content in and of itself—and something broader than class overtones alone, namely contumacy (the reason it made sense to listeners in the United States with less sensitivity to the signs of social class). Punk vocal style, however it was heard, created a dialectical shock effect, a jolt with both cognitive and tactile aspects, which led some part of the audience to make active connections between the sound and other areas of social practice (D. Laing 1978:125–27; 1983:60).[35]

Frith, following Laing's lead on the subject of the voice in popular music, has drawn not only Benjamin, but also Roland Barthes's
essay "The Grain of the Voice" into his theory of music: "We respond
to the materiality of rock's sounds. . . . Our joyous response to music
is a response not to meanings but to the making of meanings." The
singer's voice works through an aural combination of music and
words, or "structures of sound that are direct signs of emotion"
(1981:35, 63, 164–65),[36] such that form and content, signifier and
signified, melt down. A similar, more recent theoretical import in rock
criticism is Jacques Attali's *Noise,* a materialist history of music based
in large part in Situationist theory. Attali describes the social relationship generated by "composition," the creation of new codes in sound,
and opposes it to "repetition" in commercial music, the latter term
borrowed from Debord's account of the spectacle.[37] Composition,
says Attali—"a labor on sounds, . . . a pretext for festival, in search
of thoughts—is no longer a central network, an unavoidable monologue, becoming instead a real potential for relationship. It gives voice
to the fact that rhythms and sounds are the supreme mode of relation
between bodies" (1985:143). This description echoes the terms of the
onetime Situationist ally Lefebvre, who similarly finds that "musicality communicates corporeality," socializing and binding bodies together (qtd. in R. Middleton 1986:159).

The Punk Subculture

More perfectly than any of the other postwar youth subcultures,
punk represents the fruition of Benjamin's notion that technological
reproduction (rock music, in this case) might revivify the mimetic
faculty in popular life, by sparking the impulse to create similarities
in other forms (namely subcultural style). Style in the punk subculture, like style in avant-garde literature and music, unquestionably
served for a time to disrupt conventional passive reception. Performance itself, too, was a possibility that virtually everyone involved
contemplated, with the do-it-yourself aesthetic of the music; the barre
chords on guitar, simple but versatile chord forms, were a staple of
punk. Hebdige and a number of subsequent critics have fondly cited
the "fanzine" *Sniffin' Glue* (whose editor Mark Perry went on to form
Alternative TV), in which the text "Here's one chord, here's two
more, now form your own band" accompanied a set of chord dia-

grams (for open rather than barre chords, in this case). The "d-i-y" ethos has persisted to the present in alternative rock music, and is directly attributable to punk.

But beyond the resulting music, one must consider punk's absorption by its audience; aesthetic evaluation, to reiterate, is bankrupt without some sociological scope. The uniqueness of the punk audience lies in the fairly full realization of Benjamin and Brecht's goal, a progressive relation between mass-reproduced and popular lived culture. Though punk, like preceding subcultures, operated primarily in the sphere of leisure, due to the lack of power available to the young, the punk subculture contained a much more explicit, widespread political consciousness. Its reassembly of cultural fragments, therefore, is legitimately comparable with avant-garde montage. The ensemble that made up punk style involved the appropriation of artifacts and texts regardless of their origin, and a quite purposeful courting of outrage and condemnation every step of the way (whereas previous subcultures' motives in dress and so forth could be quite benign at times). What emerges is the common ground of avant-garde praxis not only in literature and popular music, but their audience's reception and use of them: the shock effect. McLaren himself has emphasized the linkage of music and sartorial style: "Music was always important to those clothes. . . . If people don't get a sense of emergency from the music they're not going to be interested. You've got to have *attitude* or else it won't work" (qtd. in Harron 1988:198).

Hebdige, interestingly, never mentions McLaren, and suggests that the New York punk scene was more avant-garde and literary than that in England, while leaving the Situationist background of the latter in a short footnote.[38] His thesis on the collective activity involved in the punk subculture, virtually omitting the bohemian element in England, seems somewhat willful—decapitating the leading elements in order to portray a more perfectly egalitarian communal creativity. This omission undercuts somewhat Gary Clarke's charge that Hebdige creates an elitist divide between the original, authentically creative members of a subculture and the poor sods who purchase a style after its commercial incorporation. Clarke makes important points—that "the diffusion of styles cannot be classed as a simple [commercial] defusing of the signifying practice of an elite few," and that relatively straight youths not adopting the "complete uniform of a subculture" may share in its spirit (1990:93). But whether Hebdige is guilty of privileging an elite minority is highly disputable.

If he brings it less into the foreground than he could have, the alliance of bohemian, middle- and working-class elements explains in part Hebdige's observation that even emblems of workingclassness were primarily signifiers of chaos, standing "for the spiritual paucity of everyday life" (terms implicitly suggesting the presence of Situationist theory). The punk subculture, in toto, is best understood as having given a general alienation a tangible quality. The sheer number of antagonistic sources used to connote "chaos at every level," furthermore, attests to the array of contributors involved. Androgynous, deliberately grotesque hairstyles and makeup; black, leather, and/or torn clothing, including bondage paraphernalia; haphazardly produced and distributed fanzines; household commodities like the safety pin (worn in the cheek or nose) and plastic trashbag (converted to apparel); and violent antidancing like the pogo were all guaranteed to shock. Otherwise the symbols were as "dumb" as the rage they provoked—even in the case of the swastika, Hebdige argues (1979:27–28, 113–17).[39]

Punk's noisy style did hold a widely recognized coherence, however, based in the dominant political discourse in the midseventies, the rhetoric of crisis. Punk's parody of the spectacular imagery of depraved youth appropriated the generally available language of crisis into both form and content: thus in order "to communicate disorder, the appropriate language must . . . be subverted. For punk to be dismissed as chaos, it had first to 'make sense' as noise" (Hebdige 1979:87–88). As in all subcultural styles, the body in particular was the canvas, offering an allegorical commentary not so much on England's economic decline, as on its mediation through cultural and political apparatuses. Through a parodic semiotics (or sign system) made up of commonly available commodities, rhetoric, and symbolism, punk deliberately brought the wrathful official language of authoritarian ideology down on its head; its subversiveness lay in making commonsense discourse sensational, weakening that discourse's pretension to naturalness by laying bare the predictable patterns of its manufacture. The success of the punk subculture, in this regard, can be measured in its excoriation; as the case of the Sex Pistols illustrates, the response of outsiders was trauma and loathing.

In transforming "alienation from society into a *reabsorption*, if a negative one, through the reactions which it provoked" (Wicke 1990:146), punk's stylistic destructiveness and ugliness involved a creative and positive struggle with the dominant culture, in the final analysis, not the actual disengagement of nihilism. The SI, prefiguring Hebdige's terms, considered the creative incarnation of nihilism or meaninglessness worthwhile as "a moment in the contestation of the spectacle, a tactical response to a particular configuration of spectacular relations" like the rhetoric of crisis—"useful only to the extent that [it operates] with some other end in sight" (Plant 1992:147).

In Bakhtin's description of carnival, one finds the same virtue of parody assigned to subcultures appropriating discourse for their own ends. Such parody is "especially well suited to the needs of the powerless, precisely because it assumes the force of the dominant discourse only to deploy that force, through a kind of artistic jujitsu, *against* domination" (Stam 1988:139).[40] Whether in the case of the Sex Pistols or the subculture as a whole, punks served precisely the function Bakhtin attributes to clowns in carnival: "the clown sounded forth, ridiculing all 'languages' and dialects [in] a lively play with the 'languages' of poets, scholars, monks, knights, and others, where all 'languages' were masks and where no language could claim to be an authentic, *incontestable* face. [This play] was parodic, and aimed sharply and polemically against the official languages of its given time" (1981:273). Carnival in this sense affords "a glimpse through the ideological constructs of dominance," resulting in a temporary exposure of the fictive foundations of the social formation (Stallybrass and White 1986:18). Punk similarly brought into glaring relief "the dominant order's attempt to suppress all differences through a discourse that asserts the homogeneity of the social domain." This destructive effort entailed a creative dimension as well, the possibility of "a politics of democratic difference, [of] forms of resistance in which it becomes possible to rewrite, rework, recreate, and re-establish new discourses and cultural spaces that revitalize rather than degrade public life" (Giroux and Simon 1989:13). The avant-garde cry or shout, in this case the noise of both punk music and the punk ensemble, "fights to be heard above the news bulletins, the headlines, the false political speeches of a world in crisis" characteristic of England in the midseventies (Williams 1989:75).

Hebdige rightly ties subcultural style to an earlier avant-garde, describing very much like Benjamin and the Situationists how the transformation, in style, of the "order of structured appearances" prefigures more profound social transformations: "subcultural styles do indeed qualify as art, ... not as timeless objects, ... but as 'appropriations,' 'thefts,' subversive transformations, as movement. [B]oth artistic expression and [the audience's own] aesthetic pleasure are intimately bound up with the destruction of existing codes and the formulation of new ones." What can be done in art, or cultural production, can be done in life, or consumption—and the punks remain noteworthy for the extent to which they drew the two together. They altered considerably "the boundary between artist and audience [that] has often stood as a metaphor in revolutionary aesthetics (Brecht, the surrealists, Dada, etc.) for that larger and more intransigent barrier which separates art ... from reality and life under capitalism" (1979:110, 129). Punk's effect was precisely that championed by Brecht's practical avant-gardism, the creation of a more critically astute audience. The punk "iconography of disrespect [not only] served to disrupt the status quo," but also "turned the attention of subsequent youth culture to the actual mechanisms of representation: the codes themselves" (Chambers 1986:172).

Hebdige observes, however, that punk style proved to be more contradictory in its results than his original description could have anticipated. On one hand, punk topicalized "the themes of 'youth unemployment' and 'urban crisis' which were generalised as the recession deepened during the next decade, as the deteriorating, underfunded inner cities erupted in the youth riots in 1981." But it also helped to boost the British fashion industry and the medium of the rock video. Punk rock's employment of a number of strands from past popular music fueled, in general, a greatly increased diversity in crossovers between musical and visual styles (Hebdige 1988:212–13; see Wicke 1990:154–55). Thus the punk subculture, as Hebdige's original study in 1979 had already noted, proved only slightly more resistant to commercial incorporation and defusion than previous subcultural groups (see Hebdige 1979:90–99; Ewen 1988:251–53). If punk helped usher in a more intense focus on youth styles, in the 1980s, on the part of the culture industries, it must also be said that consternation over this development reflects in no small part the legacy of punk's own politics, in its deliberate effort to place commercial relations on public display. McLaren, aware that punk would inevitably be incorporated, "did at least ensure that punk had some control over its own recuperation" (the tactic established by Andrew Loog Oldham and the Stones). The recuperation of deviant cultural forms is not without danger for the dominant culture, either: "it is far from certain that artistic rebellion in the next generation will continue to be recuperable into consumable works," the Situationists predicted in the sixties, a prophecy fulfilled to some extent by their successors in punk (Plant 1992:146; qtd. in Plant 1992:85).

Other outcomes of the punk subculture are indisputably positive, such as its role in sparking confrontation of Britain's racial divisions, through "explicit interventions like Rock against Racism [RAR] and Two Tone and through the creation of hybrid musics which integrated or spliced together black and white musical forms" (Hebdige 1988:213). One of the early punk groups, the Jam, generated a nostalgia for mod style, which eventually flowered in the revival of ska (the Jamaican music of the sixties that preceded reggae) by a number of integrated groups from Coventry associated with the Two Tone label, including the English Beat, Selecter, and the Specials. (The latter's 1981 hit "Ghost Town" captures the alienation of that riotous year.) Harder working-class forms of punk (epitomized early on by Sham 69) did spawn Oi, the generally racist, anti-immigrant music that neo-Nazi groups seized on as a means to recruit latter-day skinheads. At the same time, though, more progressive punk groups like the Clash helped launch the effective response to racism of RAR.[41]

Particularly given the influence on punk of reggae—"a white 'translation' of black 'ethnicity,'" infusing a heightened sense of alienation (Hebdige 1979:64)—punk understandably provided the basis for the highly visible, by most accounts genuinely important RAR movement. "The appearance of RAR coincided precisely with the growth of punk," Paul Gilroy emphasizes, "and the two developments were very closely intertwined, with punk supplying an oppositional language through which RAR anti-racism could speak a truly populist politics, . . . something more than the simple sum of its constitutive elements," the various youth cultures. Punk style was an integral part of the movement's success, providing an "ability to be political without being boring" (1991:121–22, 126; see also Hall 1988; Cashmore 1984; Savage 1991).

Besides racism, punk also challenged to some extent the constructions of masculinity and femininity available in rock music—especially the phallocentrism of "cock rock"—and in the wider culture's "monotonously phallic and/or heterosexual structures of desire" (Hebdige 1988:213). Angela McRobbie has suggested that the element of androgyny in punk particularly facilitated the inclusion of women—"both punk women and feminists want to overturn accepted ideas about what constitutes femininity"—and has criticized Hebdige's original work on punk for treating the issue of sexual identity only in passing. (In *Subculture,* he makes brief analogies between punk and the transvestism of "glitter" rock in the early seventies, and describes bondage equipment worn by punks as a subversion of mass-mediated straight sex.) Playing with sexual ambiguity, however, is itself an activity in which each sex meets different levels of tolerance, with men credited for experiment where women are taken simply to be failures, unable to "make it in a man's world" (McRobbie 1980:44–45, 49).

If punk, as a renewal of music for everybody, did encourage a significant number of female performers, "problems for women in attendance—in the audience—remain[ed], however." Women might not have been at Clash concerts at all, if their boyfriends didn't escort them there: "Punk's legacy of music dealing with 'real life,' 'combat rock,' late-night encounters on urban streets" not only has little if any resonance for women, but also "has the added peril for women of rape" (Little and Rumsey 1989:241–42). This description of an exclusionary aura of violence, however, raises an important objection, starting with the quite literal point that in London there were complaints about how early punk shows typically closed, in order to allow people to make the last Underground train. Thus the night-life ethos was just that, an ethos, just as the hint of violence had no substantial basis other than hysteria in the media. Leslie Roman, in her ethnographic study of female slam dancers, describes a relationship between young men and women often fraught with violence, in a frequently negative ritual reenacting the violence of the home life in particular, and at best escaping rather than challenging it. (The situation—a small midwestern city in the United States in the early eighties—arguably differs considerably from London in 1977.) Though she finds her subjects conscious to differing (or "asymmetrical") degrees of both the defensive and more challenging elements of their roles in slam dancing, Roman also argues the potential of "tendential alignments" that cut across apparent conflicts like those of class and gender (1988:150). But if shared forms of resistance do exist, the complexity of the intentions within a subculture should not be reductively romanticized, either.

A prominent example of the opportunity punk's androgyny did afford women, those forming musical groups at least, is the quick move of Siouxsee Sue from the Bromley Contingent—early followers of the Sex Pistols and formative fashion provocateurs—to singing successfully right up to the present in her own group, Siouxsee and the Banshees. Iain Chambers concludes that androgynous apparel, in this case, did open up "a space for women as active protagonists within the production of [punk] music," unnatural clothing leading onto "unnatural" feminine voices (1985:179). The prevalence in punk of bohemians as much as working-class youths also helped diminish the sexism that has afflicted more purely working-class subcultures. McLaren's wife and cohort Vivien Westwood, also more a creature of the sixties, had her own notoriety as a fashion innovator, which eventually took her to the heights of continental haute couture. The access for women was due as well to punk's loathing of the mass media, as expressed in a mock-horror at conventional romantic roles (an abhorrence of sex Johnny Rotten shared with Pinkie Brown). One of the strongest female figures, Poly Styrene of X-Ray Spex (who is also black), had an early hit with the classic "Oh Bondage Up Yours!"

Punk's rejection to a significant extent of the sexism of earlier rock music, finally, was indisputably important in the long term (in some forms of rock, at least). One need only look at the number of current alternative groups, typically playing music informed more or less directly by punk, that contain men and women who participate quite equitably. Chrissie Hynde of the Pretenders has very recently praised punk's social legacy to rock music, "its non-discrimination—it was non-sexist, non-classist," and deeply informed by reggae, in her experience. "The best thing about it," though, "was that I didn't have to rely on being a female guitarist as a gimmick. . . . For the first time I could do what I wanted to do, and being a girl wasn't an issue" (qtd. in Hoare 1991:14).

Conclusion

The example of subcultural style has not been entirely lost on the literary world, since the sensation of punk. Trevor Griffiths's teleplay

Oi for England (1982), for example, documents the skinheads and the riots of 1981. Though Oi music was linked to some extent with the racist politics of the National Front and the British Movement, Frith points out that it contains above all "an us-against-the-world attitude, . . . the continuation of the tradition which has its roots in the Teddy Boys" (qtd. in LeMoyne 1981:35). Griffiths's rendering of Oi music, accordingly, is unflinching and uncompromised, not at all distanced or apologetic, and stresses class antagonism rather than racism, avoiding any cheap portrayal of the skins as proto-Nazis:

> In England's green and pleasant land
> There's some as sit and them as stand,
> There's some as eat and some as don't,
> And some who will and a few that won't.
> Oi, oi, join the few.
> Oi, oi, it's me and you.
> Oi, oi, what'll we do?
> Oi, oi, turn the screw.
> Sick of this, sick of all the shit,
> Sick of them as stand while the other lot sit,
> Sick of being treated like a useless tit,
> Sick of being shoved, sick of being HIT!

The play's language reeks of the danger in offering youth nothing but persistent boredom: " 'I'm sicker doin' nowt. Drive yer daft. Eat, sleep, sit, stand. . . . I'm eighteen an' I've never 'ad a job in me fuckin' life! . . . SOMeat better 'appen." Kicking some head, then, is a "bit o' fun." Outside the basement in which Ammunition rehearses, the streets of Manchester are a combat zone, reflected in the music: "Law and order, up your arse. / The orders are yours and the law's a farce."

But as skins, the members of Ammunition are susceptible to recruitment by the "Chocolate England" venom of the "Man," a leader of the neofascist British Movement. Thus Griffiths heavy-handedly invests Finn, the apparent guiding spirit and genuine talent in the band, with an aura of difference from his compatriots. Resistant to any racism in the group's songs or choice of venues, his Irish background becomes the subject of much comment on his loyalties. That emphasis on Finn's Irishness sets up the closing scene, in which he smashes the group's instruments in disgust, under the humanizing influence of an Irish folk song, "As I roved out." The result is "dramatically clumsy and politically retrograde. [Griffiths raises] doubts as to whether a discernible equivalent for the Finn character [who thinks for himself] really could be found in the skinhead subculture" (Poole and Wyver 1984:173, 175). Griffiths's method ultimately seems akin to Burgess's in *A Clockwork Orange:* he stomachs his subject matter, apparently, by investing one character with exceptional qualities.

Earlier, in *Comedians* (1976), Griffiths had been much more willing to present without qualification his own anger and that of the protagonist Gethin Price. Price does represent, it should be noted, the early skinhead movement, actually based in black West Indian subcultures as well as notions of traditional workingclassness (see Hebdige 1979:54–58). The irony of the skinhead's origins, with respect to race, is especially grotesque in the contemporary American situation in which skinheads are largely the tools of neo-Nazi racist groups, an irony illustrating very well the impoverishment of cultural and political discourse in the United States, bereft of the recognition of class divisions (see DeMott 1990). The skinhead subculture migrated to America during the punk movement, at precisely the same time that neofascist efforts to seize upon the harder working-class elements in punk, in England, had first caused widespread identification of the skin subculture with racism. (Penelope Spheeris's film *Decline of Western Civilization* documents the simultaneous importation of punk music and skin style into Southern California, where neo-Nazis would first recruit skinheads.) The English neofascist effort was countered in part by Rock Against Racism, but also by Thatcher's appropriation of racist appeals, rendering the far right relatively superfluous. But in the incarnation of the skin subculture in the United States, the only element of the British original most disaffected working-class youths have absorbed is racism. Long effective in dividing the working class, as historians such as Mike Davis (1986) and Howard Zinn (1980) have documented, racism was the one attitude familiar in an American context, in the absence of any politics of class.

In describing the British skinhead subculture as conscious political action, sociologist E. Ellis Cashmore has overly dignified its violence and badly exceeded the legitimate claims of subcultural sociology for the imaginative, symbolic function of style. But he does offer a suggestive, documentable caveat to the usual execration of skins. In the wake of the riots of 1981, different racial forms of working-class subcultures tended to blend, with skins, punks, blacks, and Asians presenting all sorts of cross-references in more of an anarchist, not racist politics. One skin says that in 1981, "there was this incredible feeling. We weren't fighting each other; like we weren't fighting the pakis or the blackies, 'cause they were with us doing the rioting. We were all fighting something else." Cashmore concludes that working-class youth in general, "energized [by] the tantalizing promise of consumer items and left . . . in a wasteland, . . . stopped fighting each other because of their colour or affiliation and fought for themselves." In 1981, at least, working-class youths found a common language in violence—"against society, specifically against the symbols of their entrapment" (1984:64–65, 84–86).

This resentment also finds voice in the poetry of Tony Harrison, whose own experience as a scholarship boy, plucked out of the working class, led him to a scathing, highly material reassertion of the working-class voice. In *V.* (1985), Harrison sympathetically considers the football hooligans who have spray-painted graffiti on his parents' tombstones in Leeds, finding that the "Vs" (signifying football matches) "are all the versuses of life / . . . class v. class as bitter as before / the unending violence of US and THEM / personified in 1984 / by Coal Board MacGregor and the NUM." A skin, actually that part of Harrison himself who remains ambivalent about his educational attainment, speaks articulately if obscenely, providing the poem's hard edge: "Don't talk to me of fucking representing / the class yer were born into any more. / Yer going to get 'urt and start resenting / it's not poetry we need in this class war." Harrison, throughout, has a keen sense of class antagonism revolving around the clash of vocal tonalities. Concerning a speech by a "smooth" Member of Parliament, he describes how he "hated in those high soprano ranges / . . . uplift beyond all reason." Embracing the sharply contrasting spirit of *ressentiment,* he tells the skin that "straight from the warbling throat right up my nose / I had all your aggro in *my* jeering."[42]

Greene himself took up the subject of young hooligans in the postwar period, when the teddy boys emerged in 1953–54. His thoroughly allegorical short story "The Destructors," published in 1954, recovers the same thesis from Bakunin that Benjamin employs in

"The Destructive Character": the destructive passion is the creative passion. The "Wormsley Common Gang," a worm in England's apple, is not at all disposed to self-destruction, unlike Greene's young male characters in the thirties. Instead, for the sake of social vengeance, it enjoys the destruction of a house designed by the great Christopher Wren. The gang's members are the descendents of Pinkie imagined by Rose, with a difference: they are no longer isolated and desperate, but an energetic collective. The Wren house is "beautiful," recognizes Trevor, the gang's leader, who possesses "an odd quality of danger." But the "word 'beautiful' [belonged to] a man wearing a top hat and a monocle, with a haw-haw accent." Given the class connotations of beauty, Trevor has little trouble persuading the others to destroy the house. Like England in the Age of Affluence, the house sleeps, while the interior is carefully demolished by economically obsolete young people. Old Misery, the house's owner, wants to tell young people what they can and can't do: "it's got to be regular. One of you asks leave and I say Yes. Sometimes I'll say No." All the time Old Misery orders it about, the gang is busy destroying his house behind his back. The final result seems even more plausible in light of the late seventies and early eighties than it would have in the Angry Decade: "One moment the house had stood there with such dignity between the bomb-sites like a man in a top hat [the emblem of the upper class], and then, bang, crash, there wasn't anything left—not anything." The Gang's malevolence, Greene suggests with perfect equanimity, may lead to the destruction of England from within.

The allegorical implications of "The Destructors," with regard to youth culture, manifest a very different prescience than Greene's anticipation in other works of the sites of international crisis. He essentially intuits Hebdige's linkage of youth subcultures with the avant-garde, even surpassing him in the invocation of anarchism, or Bakunin, as well. The Wormsley Common Gang's work is done "with the seriousness of creators—and destruction after all is a form of creation. A kind of imagination had seen this house as it had now become." That kind of imagination—fueled by *ressentiment,* by a desire to outrage—should be prized by any effort at a genuinely avant-garde praxis. Johnny Rotten is still active (now using his real name, Lydon) in the group Public Image Limited. The success of future avant-gardes depends on remembering the essential lesson of the punk affect: the P.I.L. song "Rise," alluding to political oppres-

sion from Northern Ireland to South Africa, unrelentingly reminds
one that "anger is an energy."[43]

In the aftermath of punk, however, "when the dust died down
and the panic was over, all that was left was rock'n'roll" (Harron
1988:204)—a rock music significantly altered for the long term, it
should be added. Worse still, punk, in the "spirit of 'fairness' which
made for pluralism," may have engendered a subsequent fragmentation of the rock music scene: "There's a hundred things to get hooked
on, everyone of them a question mark, none of them quite 'it,' that
desired totality." And even that desire for a significant movement
based in rock music may be a problem rooted in punk, in which the
ethos of inclusiveness was contradicted by a drive for exclusiveness,
for the coherence of a movement outside the mainstream. Thus rock
drifts ahead, ostensibly hamstrung by the memory of punk—a residual expectation of a new musical revolution—and "unable to offer a
crucial blow" (Stubbs 1989:268–71).

A more optimistic critic, writing on Bakhtin, argues that the
"irrepressible, unsilenceable energy issuing from the . . . provocative,
mirthful inversion of prevailing institutions and their hierarchy, as
staged in the carnival, offers a *permanent* alternative to official culture—*even* if it ultimately leaves everything as it was before" (Lachemann 1988/89:125). As Benjamin would have it, a view to the future
should have some basis in a nostalgia for the past. Such a revolutionary nostalgia would look to past moments of eruption (however indirectly), rather than expressing a regretful, pessimistic fixation on the
past accompanied by "fear of the future" (the title of the last article
on punk cited above). The example of punk retains an undeniable
instructive force; laments over the state of popular music themselves
reflect the continuing influence of avant-garde aspirations—including
an awareness of their pitfalls—that punk brought so sharply into
focus. All in all, says Marcus, punk "is the tale of a wish that went
beyond art and found itself returned to it, a nightclub act that asked
for the world, for a moment got it, then got another nightclub. In this
sense punk realized the [avant-garde] projects that lay behind it, and
realized their limits" (1989:442).

Punk thus offers perhaps the most salient example available of
the possibilities of refusal and resistance in advanced capitalist society, particularly in its highlighting of authoritarian efforts to demo-
nize difference. Williams describes some emergent cultural formations

as articulations "in solution" of the structure of feeling of an epoch—"at the very edge of semantic availability," that is, like punk in the incipient stages of authoritarian populism. If those nascent forms lead at some subsequent point in time to the discovery of more specific, successful articulations, those earlier, relatively isolated voices are "only later seen to compose a significant generation" (1977:134). The appearance of epic treatises on the Sex Pistols like Marcus's *Lipstick Traces* and Jon Savage's *England's Dreaming,* well over a decade after the group's brief career, suggests that punk's significance might very well emerge in the way described by Williams. Marcus might not exaggerate all that much in finding that "listening now to the Sex Pistols' records, it doesn't seem like a mistake to confuse their moment with a major event in history" (1989:5).

The belief that a surfeit of media coverage of a once volatile music scene has eroded the capacity of popular culture to alarm people hardly seems true, furthermore, considering the reaction against rap in the late eighties, and still more recently against a new outbreak of "rage" in rock music. The *New York Times,* for example, felt compelled to weigh in on the Lollapalooza tour organized by Jane's Addiction in 1991, which featured the industrial disco group Nine Inch Nails, the rapper Ice-T, and others. According to the *Times,* the rage of those performers' music is "as inarticulate as it is widespread," and thus the audiences "don't much care who or what that rage is aimed at. All they want is to feel that someone else is as angry as they are." Rage, supposedly, is thus merely "channeled into consumption," or buying record albums (Pareles 1991:20, 22). *Newsweek,* a month later, repackaged the same dismissive view of rage as a commodity designed for the dysfunctional, or those "reduced to often violent survivalism, . . . locked in a static battle" due to their somehow unreasonable belief that "authority is actively destructive"—in other words, literally destructive, a fact one need only look at homeless families and the environment to confirm.

But the *Newsweek* article also adds an unintentionally revealing twist. Along with the rage of Guns N' Roses and N. W. A., it cites an entirely opposed, saccharine element in popular music, represented by Mariah Carey's song "Emotions," an explicit appeal to the feel-good culture. The song's intensely banal lyrics go as follows: "I feel good, I feel nice. / I've never been so satisfied. / I'm in love, I'm alive." The article's conclusion, not surprisingly, appeals to some undefined middle ground: the "two camps—one brutal, the other unrealistically gentle—[both offer] *unreasonable* responses to the world, pulling ever deeper into their own unreason" (Leland 1991:53–54). This is a fine example of the media's continual effort to stereotype deviant youth cultures in disapproving, dismissive terms intended to reaffirm the correctness of the status quo, a tactic identified two decades ago by British subcultural sociology.

A very different conclusion may thus be entirely in order, namely that the rage of the rock and rap "camp" is in fact quite reasonable, and directed precisely and purposefully at the inane feel-good culture represented in the *Newsweek* article by Carey and Michael Bolton. Equally enraging is the fact that so many supposedly radical academics share exactly the same view as *Newsweek* and the *Times,* that they have even supplied the terms of their condescension towards musical rage. Those periodicals have clearly absorbed postmodernist theses like those of Fredric Jameson (1984) and Lawrence Grossberg (1989b) on the "waning of affect," the supposed complacency of the young even as they consume expressions of defiance. When hacks in the news media and Marxist postmodernists share the same insistence that dissent in popular culture is inarticulate, directionless, easily commercially incorporated, and thus inevitably rendered complacent, one must conclude that a different cultural politics, whether based in anarchism or not, is in order.

The achievement of Greene and the punk subculture, with specific regard to social class, suggests what outcome the articulation of anger ought to realize, but also raises a key difficulty at present in achieving a significant social coalescence based on *ressentiment.* Greene, within his novel *Brighton Rock,* managed the fusion of avant-gardism and working-class culture that the English Situationists would in life itself, with the Sex Pistols. A similar admixture of essentially middle-class, radical students and working-class youth fueled the events of May 1968 in Paris, the crucible, of course, for the Situationists, who were to a large extent the focal point of this meeting. They disbanded, apparently disillusioned by the failure of the May Revolution, but clearly out of their ashes there emerged, in the moment of punk, a profound realization of their cross-class initiative. The union of *Brighton Rock* and the Sex Pistols, then, reveals a continuing potential source of radical cultural and social action, the meeting in urban areas of bohemian and working-class youth.

Exemplars of struggle between subcultural style and the spiritual paucity of everyday life continue to appear in various cultural forms, especially in the work of marginalized groups—blacks, feminists, gays, Latinos—working in marginalized forms in music, performance art, and visual arts. And subsequent events outside music, such as repeated urban upheavals in England in the eighties, indicate that youthful working-class resentment among all races has not vanished. In the era of authoritarian populism, however, with the deliberate exacerbation of the gap between affluence and hardship, the distance between the young of different classes and races makes the prospect of such a meeting seem an absurdity, especially in the United States, with its preponderance of suburban "pods," as urban planners call them, safely insulated against the Third World of inner cities. The "desire to open up wounds seems strangely out of place [i]n a society given over to suburban subdivisions," where identical fast-foods and shopping malls "guard against surprises" (Lipsitz 1990:269). The fragmentation of social groups, however, contrary to post-Marxism and postmodernism, does not entail the hopeless fragmentation of individual identity.

The linkage of different individuals and groups, however it occurs, would logically evolve out of a common alienation from a society that places material profit and self-interest ahead of human life itself. In an essay on the American post-punk group Hüsker Dü, Frith finds that "white suburban youth in cities like Minneapolis know, secretly, that Marx was right about alienation all along. The more insistent the capitalism, the more fraught the gap between the grand language of opportunity and the mean circumstances of work and home" (1988b:93). Minneapolis has in fact seen the rise of an anarchist youth group—the Revolutionary Anarchist Bowling League (or RABL), composed in part of latter-day punks and skinheads—as have New York, Toronto, and other North American cities (Ahlberg 1988). Some groups specifically cite the Situationist International as an inspiration. Similar movements have existed in Western European nations, especially Switzerland and Germany, for some time now. The Situationists held that all these forms of resistance, "either spontaneously or in a conscious and organized way, are pre-situationist. [All have] passed through the same dissatisfaction with culture as it is, through the same acceptance of an experimental sensibility, to find themselves confronted with the objective need for this type of action.

All have passed through a specialised training and all, as specialists, have belonged to the *same* historical *avant-garde*" (Gray 1974:14). The embodiment in style of *ressentiment* is neither something to regret nostalgically nor a privileged perspective of the bohemian and the educated.

Many people feel the reality of the commodity system much as Lukács thought the proletariat alone did, in the recognition to differing degrees of "the fact that beneath the cloak of the thing [or commodity] lay a relation between men [and women], that beneath the quantifying crust there [is] a qualitative, living core." Thus he attributes a potentially revolutionary awareness of the social character of labor, both its cooperative and exploitative aspects, to those who experience the true nature of the commodity in their work. This class consciousness, recognizing relations of domination and subordination between human beings (and not just abstract relations between things, as in commodity fetishism and reification), will develop sufficiently "only when every phenomenon is recognized to be a [social] process" (1971:169, 171–72, 184). The recognition of process is also important in the sense that the proletarian's awareness of time, the labor that goes into a product, includes a consciousness of the possibilities of extended human effort. This sense of development over time presents a striking contrast with the tendency of Lukács's contemporaries, in modern art, to freeze significant experience in individual moments of epiphany, connected only through obscure artifice; and with postmodern descriptions of schizophrenia, which deny that a developed identity exists in any fashion, since each moment of experience, presumably, is utterly detached from all others. Both approaches only reproduce the fragmentation of the commodity system, and thus represent an excessively desperate form of resistance.

Though the need for productive human labor (as opposed to "services") has declined in advanced Western economies, due to automation and the exploitation of Third-World labor, people have become even better, more broadly acquainted with the commodity, thanks to the increasing significance of consumption. They know very well both the alienation and the insubordination the commodity (including creative forms) can serve. Consumption has hardly become divorced from labor, either, since Lukács wrote, given 1) the actual decrease in free time since 1973 (outside Western Europe, especially in the United States), as keeping pace with the consumer society requires increasing time at work (Schor 1991); and 2) the continuing "reproductive" function of leisure (e.g., purchasing domestic necessities) in sustaining people for work. Only with these less progressive aspects of consumerism in mind, rather than its potential for freedom alone, can it be adequately and radically connected to the world of social relationships (McRobbie 1991b:8–9).

Fully developed, organized, revolutionary class consciousness of the sort described by Lukács, however, is but one of many possible responses to the depredations of capitalism, "and a very special ruptural one at that. It has been misleading to try to measure the whole spectrum of strategies in the class in terms of this one ascribed form of consciousness, and to define everything else as a token of incorporation." English working-class youth subcultures, like many other groups in the postwar era, have constructed in the " 'theatre of struggle' . . . a whole *range* of responses" of considerable utility, out of a variety of conditions and cultural raw materials (Hall and Jefferson 1976:44–45). "Dynamic hybridizations" of this sort, employing available technologies, arguably recuperate or reinvent class and other concepts of resistance, especially those of the avant-garde. Recovering some semblance of the past, the historical record of injustice, these subcultural innovations "grapple with that unphilosophical nihilism, Baudrillardian in its cynicism but altogether devoid of rapture, which reaches from the ghetto tenements to the suburban boulevards" (Buhle 1990:171, 173).

If resistance to power can be cultivated to a wider extent along these lines, some surprising linkages might yet emerge in the resulting social network. As postmodernist theories that would marry culture and politics have emphasized, different subordinate groups do not necessarily perceive an intersection between their interests. Links between those groups, as a result, have "to be *articulated,* or bound together, from contest to contest, and from moment to moment," to use more reasonable post-Marxist terms (A. Ross 1988:xiv). The most common emphasis in recent radical politics has been on this sort of localized activity, in which such alliances definitely remain feasible. At the same time, according to the most widely dispersed Situationist slogan, one should "think globally." Local action, preserving the impulse to defiance and insurrection, creates a basis for some future, larger events. The language of contemporary society is "so impoverished by its own falsity that the smallest refusal could become a *no* everyone understood," or a more universal spirit of negation (Marcus 1989:354).

Beyond similar specific concerns or actual physical meetings, the global linkage of local actors may occur on the basis of far-flung relations necessarily mediated through mass communications. Underneath "the global domination of [communications] markets by multinational conglomerates and cartels, networks of mutual affinity and attraction [may be] grounded paradoxically in the airwaves—in the most sophisticated communication technologies available[—]working from 'the other side'... to imagine a community beyond the boundaries of the known." Hebdige's position in this case is a classic realist one, in essence raising the necessity of breaking up control of the mass media, the ultimate difficulty any progressive cultural politics has to confront. Only then will it be possible to convey, without the crippling sense of inevitability dominant at present, the real and terrible things happening somewhere else to which everyone is nonetheless directly connected (1988:216, 221). If the airwaves presented the mass slaughter in the Persian Gulf War, for example, as an exciting, sanitary video game and a corollary with the Super Bowl, the realist response must be that this had everything to do with the nexus between their owners and the state.

The "long revolution" in communications, as Williams puts it, continues to include fights in the world of art and ideas to extend "the expression and exchange of experience on which understanding depends," and to enhance the capacity of people to direct their own lives (qtd. in Turner 1990:60). In her study of the SI, Sadie Plant concludes by observing that the "networks of subversion which continue to arise in even the most postmodern pockets of the postmodern world are too numerous to detail." Aware that subversive gestures are almost inevitably disarmed, the "radical trajectory" that began with the original avant-garde has nonetheless refused to accept "the petrifying conclusions of postmodern theory," working instead "to encourage a search for irrecuperable forms of expression [such as] plagiarism, detournement, and provocation, [which] remain the hallmarks of a thriving and sophisticated world of agitation" (1992:176).

Feminism, confronting the difficulty of escaping the dominant discourses constructing gender (or sexual difference), has laid a particular emphasis on terms similar to those of subcultural theory. Teresa de Lauretis, writing on the "technologies" of gender, describes how the "practices of daily life and daily resistances... afford both agency and [an] empowering investment, [in] a movement between the (represented) discursive space of the positions made available by hegemonic discourses and the space-off, the elsewhere of those discourses." Acting locally but thinking globally means working "in the margins (or 'between the lines,' or 'against the grain')... and in the interstices of institutions, in counter-practices and new forms of community" (1987:25–26). Andrew Ross reflects this feminist interest in cultural technology (specifically that of Donna Haraway; see, however, note 12 to chap. 1) in describing a folklore of technology: "From the technofunk street rhythms generated by the master-DJs of scratching, mixing, and matching, to the neurochemical sublime of body/machine interfaces, the new appropriation culture everywhere feeds off the 'leaky' hegemony of information technology" (1989a:212).

The hiphop subculture to which he alludes, especially in its use of sound samplers for plagiarism and montage, has been lionized by many critics precisely because it fulfills the classic criterion of the avant-garde, employing innovations in cultural technologies to democratize production. The *Village Voice* recently declared rap music the "new punk," on this basis, and all the theoretical and descriptive terms developed here, especially those concerning tone of voice and *ressentiment,* can easily be applied to the *attitude* of Public Enemy and N. W. A., maligned much like punk in cultural and political institutions.[44] A more colloquial way of putting the point about technology, the local, and the global, finally, is Greene's, in "The Destructors": "We'd be like worms, don't you see, in an apple. When we came out again... we'd make the walls fall down—*somehow.*"

Any coherent appeal to both affective and ideological discernment, finally, will require a context in which "the power of image and aesthetics, the problems of time-space compression [with the new flexibility of capitalism], and the significance of geopolitics and otherness are clearly understood." Only then will "unity within difference" be possible (Harvey 1989:359). However remote such a significant change in the status quo may seem, the collective but localized, hence decentralized forms of resistance described in this book indicate the persisting health of efforts at subcultural expression, directed against an overpopulated world increasingly managed by totalitarian means, whether ideological or outright repressive.

The formation of collective identity can follow one of two tendencies in such a world, both of which address the individual's understandable sense of insignificance and powerlessness by offering identification with some larger social grouping. The aestheticized politics of passive obedience, whether Nazism, Reaganism, or Thatcherism, offer sublimation, the shedding of selfhood and its anxieties through identification with a symbolic order manufactured by someone else. Authoritarian spectacle offers at best the scant satisfaction of a meager individual recognition, the apocryphal fifteen minutes of fame for some innocuous activity (epitomized by television shows featuring home videos). Collective contumacy, on the other hand, offers the *extension* rather than the obliteration of the self. Beyond existing expressive forms among excluded groups, and the articulation of discontent on their behalf by those in dominant groups, the more fundamental political question "is that of demanding an equal right with others to discover what one might become, not of assuming some already fully-fashioned identity which is merely repressed." Respect for individual difference results from a collective process, just as the anarchists and Situationists describe the dialectical exchange between individual and federation: "To acknowledge someone as a subject is at once to grant them the same status as oneself, and to recognize their otherness and autonomy" (Eagleton 1990:414–15). In this sort of discovery, subcultural activities and other deviant forms of consumption may be destructive by conventional terms, but are nonetheless creative at the same time because each individual has been actively engaged. Each feels that his or her active expression has mattered precisely because no one involved is thought indispensable, in the sense of traditional notions of the artist's uniqueness, for example. In the second case, one chooses the enactment of desire—the desire for a human community founded on genuinely humane, egalitarian values—over resignation.

The new contestation that the Situationists are talking about is already manifesting itself everywhere. In the large spaces of noncommunication and isolation organized by the current powers that be, indications are surfacing by way of new types of scandals from one country to another and from one continent to another: their exchange has begun.

The task of the avant-garde wherever it finds itself is to bring

together these experiences and these people, that is, to simultaneously unify such groups and the coherent foundation of their
project as well. We must make known, explain, and develop
these initial gestures of the next revolutionary epoch. They are
characterized by their concentration of new forms of struggle and
a new—either manifest or latent—content: the critique of the
existing world. In this way, the dominant society that is so proud
of its modernization will find its match, since it has finally produced a modernized negation. (Guy Debord, "The Situationists
and the New Forms of Action in Politics or Art" [qtd. in Sussman
1991:149])

Notes

Introduction

1. The preeminent theorist of everyday life, Henri Lefebvre, has defined the everyday essentially in terms of leisure consumption, or nonspecialized activities outside labor and family roles.

2. David Wieck's criticism of the word *antiauthoritarianism,* as "an unhappy mode of expression," should be noted immediately: "first because antiauthoritarianism is professed by numerous and diverse political groups [such as right-wing libertarians]; second because there are forms of authority that do not entail power over persons [e.g., forms of authority, like knowledge, that may serve the common good]; third because authority is that to which power pretends and which its ideology claims for it" (1979b:140). All this will be apparent, hopefully, in what follows here.

3. Conservatives have exploited this construction in recent academic debates, claiming to adhere to a "nonideological" position, in their traditional pretense of disinterestedness.

4. For a good summary account of authoritarianism in the wake of the Persian Gulf War, see Indiana (1991).

5. This emphasis on opening up public discourse first, before worrying about new social forms, is hardly inimical to presumably more responsible leftist theory (as chapter 3 further indicates). One Marxist scholar, David Harvey, finds in the creative exploration of social contradictions "the groundwork for a [political] critique that 'brings the undiscussed into discussion and the unformulated into formulation'" (1989:345). Ernesto Laclau (1977) argues that "popular" opposition must first emerge through the recognition of antagonism between the people and power—which popular cultural forms can certainly help generate—before the more profound challenge of "populist" movements becomes possible. In actual practice, a number of groups have sought to fracture the constriction of public discourse through imaginative provocations, most notably

ACT UP, seeking more concerted action on AIDS, and the environmentalist Earth!First, as well as antimilitarists, and feminists combating indifference to forms of violence as specific as rape, and as general as the cultural objectification of women.

6. Alison Jaggar does suggest that women's subordination (along with their greater, if socially licensed, adeptness at identifying emotions) gives them a distinctive propensity for "outlaw emotions" (1989:164–65); Julia LeSage (1988) emphasizes the countervailing, inhibiting effect of the gendered construction of such emotions (specifically rage) as inappropriate to femininity.

7. Alan Sinfield not only issues the sweeping judgment that all postwar English youth subcultures have been violently heterosexist, racist, and sexist, but also condemns their failure "to build an enduring resistance" (1989:178)—that is, what they were not, as Willis puts it.

8. In concentrating on the instructive assemblages of commodities and texts identified with particular subcultures, this book will also limit debates over the coherence or discreteness of those subcultures' memberships. Subcultural sociology has been usefully criticized for privileging the objective components of a style, such as clothing, over anthropological investigation of the persons affiliated to one degree or another with it (see G. Clarke 1990). But this point quickly becomes a paralyzing preoccupation with agency, implicitly or explicitly suggesting (once again) that one won't find very much efficacious human participation, at least in terms of a political consciousness approved by academics. Ethnographic studies hardly solve all problems, either, given the necessary limitation of their scope, and the fact that individuals' accounts of their experience pose the same interpretive problems that any object or text does.

9. Critiquing academic approaches, however, sometimes leads Chambers to discount too much the intellectual activity in everyday life (1986:13), and his own work has in fact become increasingly fascinated with postmodernist theory.

10. As a number of critics have suggested, Laclau's earlier work (see n. 5, above) contains a useful theory of developing populist interpellations ("hailings" or ideological constructions of the subject) against authoritarian ones, through an antagonistic process of "disarticulation" and "rearticulation" of discourses. The terms of *articulation* (as in *Hegemony and Socialist Strategy*) come from the work of Antonio Gramsci, discussed in chapters 1 and 4; in the recent development of post-Marxism, the concreteness of Gramsci's description of ideological struggle is lost, abstracted into the ether of discursive practices that seem to exercise the only real agency (see Geras 1987; N. Larsen 1990; Wood 1986).

Laura Kipnis even relates the post-Marxist abandonment of the old class struggle, or mass *politics,* to "the emergence of mass *culture* as the privileged subject of left academia," in a form of "phantom politics which . . . marks the loss of what might be called the political subject." If mass culture has become more approachable in postmodern academic work, this development reflects in many cases a displacement of politics, such work remaining circumscribed within the domain of high theory, confined to elite specialist reappraisals of earlier elitist academic attitudes (1986:15, 34).

11. Post-Marxist attacks on class "essentialism" may also appeal to left

academics in the United States because of the long-standing, frustrating absence of any discourse about social class in that country—see DeMott 1990—making such discourse seem futile if not anachronistic.

12. A good example of the postmodern/post-Marxist pessimism described by Eagleton is Donna Haraway's "A Manifesto for Cyborgs," at base an argument that cultural theorists should move beyond traditional oppositions between technology and the organic body, such as those underlying elitism concerning mass culture (see chapter 5, on Anthony Burgess). She has described cultural studies, however, as an exciting eclecticism concerned with "everything and nothing" (qtd. in Heller 1990:A5, A8), supporting Hall's view that cultural studies has become a catchall term for just about anything the left does. Read with "A Manifesto for Cyborgs," moreover, her laudation of aimlessness also suggests the pessimistic politics Eagleton discerns in academic post-Marxism.

Haraway actually reproduces the mechanical/human binary she claims to repudiate, in asserting that the machines of multinational capital "are disturbingly lively, and we ourselves frighteningly inert," a point that does not seem so different from analyses by earlier theorists like the Frankfurt School's Marcuse, and his colleague Theodor Adorno. There is no real innovation on her part besides the familiar postmodernist evacuation of the subject, or the human side of the binary with technology. She goes so far, in fact, to argue that postmodern microelectronic machines have become "invisible" to their human subjects, citing the "technobabble" employed by multinational corporations in naming themselves, an extremely ephemeral sort of evidence. ("Genentech," "Repligen," and all the others may wish to convince the public of their anonymity, but there is absolutely no reason to concede it to them.) On the basis of that purported impenetrability (or the sublimity often discerned by postmodernists), she proceeds to present the post-Marxist argument for fragmented, "permanently partial identities and contradictory standpoints," assuming that gender, race, and class offer no "basis for belief in 'essential' unity." This observation, typically, rests on an almost nihilistic sensibility: "None of 'us' have any longer the symbolic or material capability of dictating the shape of reality to any of 'them.' . . . Abstraction and illusion rule in knowledge, domination rules in practice." The multinationals' organization of culture, daily life, and imagination seem an interlocking if disparate fait accompli (Haraway 1989:176–77, 179, 181–82, 188–89).

As long as academics persist in promoting such a framework, the "human" can not be rescued, "for it is set up as the necessary and weaker term" in relation to the political economy (or the organization of technology) that alone, presumably, enables the subject to know itself. To undermine any concept of subjectivity, in this way, leaves "unexplained how a person might achieve political understanding" (Sinfield 1989:28–29, 87).

13. Jauss approves, it should be noted, taking Adorno's view that the "pure work of art," disengaged from any social utility, constitutes the appropriate negation of modern experience. Baudelaire did condemn the *l'art pour l'art* movement of his own day, as Jauss points out, but such condemnations served primarily to enhance the artistic aristocrat's distance from lesser hangers-on.

(Baudelaire's advice to refrain from insulting the "mob," for example, is likewise hardly progressive; the point is to avoid positions in which bourgeois philistines could join, as false admirers.) When Benjamin refers to *l'art pour l'art,* in any case, he has in mind a longer train of poets influenced by Baudelaire himself, particularly the Symbolists.

14. While a member of the Lettrist International, Debord (with Gil J Wolman) wrote in 1956 that Duchamp's moustache on the *Mona Lisa,* once treated as a work of art, became no more interesting than the original painting.

Chapter 1

1. On Benjamin's anarchism, see Löwy (1985).

2. Proudhon's own aesthetics, however, go to an opposite extreme in their utilitarianism.

3. The English literary journal *Encounter* was also funded by the CIA (see Hewison 1986; Sinfield 1989).

4. See Calinescu (1987:95–97, 124–25, 140) for confirmation of this rebuttal of Anglo-American criticism, though Calinescu's deeply conservative study—endorsing the concept of kitsch, for example—distinguishes the avant-garde on a purely negative basis, indicting its supposed nihilism and antihumanism. He also provides a detailed history of the term avant-garde (1987:97– 120).

Although Astradur Eysteinsson is far less dismissive of Bürger than many scholars of modernism, he does not accept distinction of the avant-garde from modernist aestheticism. A distinction based on the express purposes of artists and works, he claims, or on sociopolitical assumptions—attributing historical pessimism and cultural despair to modernism, and a progressive interest in integrating art and life to the avant-garde—"can only be a lame one" (1990:159, 161). Eysteinsson persistently dismisses the significance of artists' intentions, though the modernists' attitudes and aesthetic theories have been just as influential as their creative works, if not more so.

His tactic, instead, is to note similarities that might be discerned in the formal techniques of a range of modernist works. His formalist argument ultimately leads him to claim that Benjamin "does not seem much troubled" by the differences between Brecht and Kafka (1990:231); Benjamin, however, hardly thought they were the same thing. Eysteinsson treats all aesthetics of "interruption," in particular, as essentially identical—attributing the same view to Benjamin—and conveniently omits the emphasis in Bürger's conclusion on Brecht's "practical" avant-gardism. Bürger strongly contrasts Brecht with Adorno's more conventional theory of modernism (and also distinguishes different theories of montage, or interruption). But Eysteinsson emphasizes Bürger's discussion of Adorno, concluding like Adorno (while citing Adorno's successor in key respects, Habermas, and Kristeva) that the "aesthetic-formalist project" of modernism can be "a culturally subversive force," opening up critical space through a liberation from rationality (1990:238). Interruption in Brecht's theater, if opposed to cathartic identification, is hardly antirational, nor antirealist as Eysteinsson's treatment suggests. Brecht called his effort to lay bare existing social relations a "popular realism"—a different kind of realism, not a rejection of it.

5. The Museum of Modern Art's recent exhibition "High and Low: Modern Art and Popular Culture" reflects the problematic nature of those points at which modern art did mine mass culture for materials. Though dedicated to demonstrating the porousness of distinctions between high and low culture, the show confines itself to the visual techniques of commercialism as they were "hoisted by fine artists for more purely aesthetic objectives," very much a top-down perspective. Celebrating "each artist's creation of poetry where once there was only 'public visual prose,'" the exhibition aestheticizes the 'social' right out of existence," essentially reconfirming aesthetic alienation from commerce and everyday culture (Deitcher 1990:99).

6. Trilling reproduces this view in defining modernism as a quest for a secularized spirituality (1967:64).

7. Cf. Herrnstein Smith (1988:64–77). For an iconoclastic lineage drawn between Kant and postmodern theory, see Hebdige (1987; or 1988:181–207). On the current relationship of corporate America and art specialists' ideas about the "social neutrality of art and its alleged universal essence," see Schiller (1989b).

8. This inability to describe feeling and reason in a dialectical manner has resulted in numerous distortions. Reference in aesthetics to affective or emotional experience has been condescendingly associated with the feminine (see Jaggar 1989; P. Middleton 1990), or emphasizes individual pleasure over collective, shared experience (see Lovell 1980). In musicology, Susan McClary points out, the association of music with the body has sometimes led to its relegation to a "feminine" realm, with male musicians responding by defining music as the most ideal and rational of the arts (a "glimpse of heaven," as Anthony Burgess often puts it). "The mind/body split that has plagued Western culture for centuries," as a result, "shows up most paradoxically in attitudes toward music: the [ostensibly] most cerebral, nonmaterial of media is at the same time the medium most capable of engaging the body" (1991:17, 151).

When attention to materiality does occur, it often becomes a fetishization of the body as opposed to meaning, and typically continues to abstract texts from their material social contexts. Peter Stallybrass and Allon White find that when scholars decide to acknowledge the body as well as intellectual experience, bodily experience winds up mystified (or fetishized)—not only detached from sense, meaningfulness, or content, but entirely opposed to rationality, as pure corporeality (1986:192). This is no improvement on the "narrow and modified meaning" assigned materiality and the body, when treated by criticism as matters of thematic content, which Mikhail Bakhtin complained about some time ago (1984:18); more recent scholarship merely goes to the opposite extreme. Oddest of all, poststructuralism, in the work of Roland Barthes and Michel Foucault, displaces close attention to the body into, ironically, an abstract, "less immediately corporeal politics," or the theoretical playground of "a privileged, privatized hedonism" (1990:7). The divorce of the sensuous from meaning, of form from content, in every case abstracts the body out of the realm of social utility, by failing, for instance, to discriminate among specific affective results. The utilitarian realm of the everyday may be one in which the body is evidently reduced into an instrument, its desires either subconsciously repressed, commercially exploited, or actively policed—but it is also the realm where this condition has to be resisted, if it is going to be changed. In the long train of European aesthetic theory since Kant, only the avant-garde, in its concern with a dialectical relationship between affect and intellect, and between the individual and the collective, has operated from a genuinely radical cultural politics.

9. On the continuities between romanticism and modernism, see also Moretti (1983).

10. Neil Larsen argues that modernism reflects the transformation of free-market capitalism into monopoly capitalism and imperialism, in which "capital in its real abstraction [broke] free from certain specific political—and in this sense, representational—relations and structures, . . . and, thereby, [appeared] to take on the attributes of a superordinate social agency with no fixed political or cultural subjectivity." A general "crisis of representation" occurred, a difficulty in perceiving human agency—hence the modernist preoccupation with recording internal individual experience and ensconcing it away from the ravages of society, a desperate attempt to transcend the seeming disappearance of agency through a "pure" practice of representation (1990:xxiv–xxv, xxxi). For negative theories of postmodernism, which inform Larsen's theory to a considerable extent, this crisis has only deepened.

11. Leighten (1989) and Sonn (1989) have reminded art history of an Anarchist Symbolism, but (as in Picasso's case) anarchism was used by fin de siècle artists primarily to extol a creed of extreme individualism. Sonn does not find the relations between anarchism and most of the Symbolist movement particularly close, and points out the contradiction in writings that equated "art for art's sake," or freedom for artists, with political doctrines advocating liberty for all. The problems with Anarchist Symbolism are virtually identical with the rest of modernism, in the assumptions of autonomy—that "a work could be radical within its aesthetic context," without any social engagement—and of formalism, "that form more than content determined whether a work was anarchistic" (1989:6, 187).

12. On Pater's influence on Joyce and Woolf, see Meisel (1980; 1987).

13. Studies of the "politics" and of "popular culture" in Joyce's work do exist (see MacCabe 1978 and Eysteinsson 1990, respectively), but such approaches usually concern the content of his texts (and highly allusive content at that), when the formal practice is more the actual cultural and political statement. As Lukács says of *Ulysses,* "Technique here is something absolute; it is part and parcel of the aesthetic ambition informing *Ulysses.*" Thus he goes so far as to find aimless and directionless the novel's "perpetually oscillating patterns of sense- and memory-data," which "give rise to an epic structure which is *static,* reflecting a belief in the basically static character of events" (1964:18–19, 34). Lukács himself, however, reduces style to a secondary quality determined by social content, one which ceases in his view even to be a formal category. Brecht

observed that Lukács, in his esteem of the historical novel, in fact merely substitutes one formalism for another.

14. The aestheticism of Woolf's actual textual practice in her novels, as Toril Moi (1985) and Pauline Johnson (1987) argue, renders claims for Woolf's feminism problematic. The fluidity of her stylistic innovation certainly represents an attempt to undermine what she experiences as the rationalist, oppressively objectifying operations of the masculine mind. But the basis of that style, at the same time, is a highly mystified opposition of the sort expressed in "Modern Fiction," between some timeless realm of spirit and the presumably degraded realm of the material. Along similar, conventionally modernist lines, Woolf denounced the "middlebrow" corruption of high culture and good taste as an effect of commerce (much as Dwight Macdonald later argued that "Midcult" tastes were even more corrosive than those of mass culture; see Rubin 1992).

15. Moi (1985) likewise finds excessively formalist Kristeva's opposition pitting the unconscious realm of the semiotic, or the rhythmic pulsion of language, against the symbolic order, that of meaningfulness. Laura Kipnis (1988) criticizes French feminism's psychoanalytic basis for reproducing literary modernism's priority on an ahistorical form of resistance, based solely in textual production of internal processes.

16. See Brantlinger (1983:184–210) on T. S. Eliot and José Ortega y Gasset's work on mass culture.

17. Other critics find the defects in Baudelaire's politics of 1848 less clearcut; see Clark (1982:171–82).

18. Fascism and long-standing conceptions of the natural (artistic) aristocrat shared Nietzschean doctrines of the superior, self-created man; the rigid social hierarchy of fascism seemed to promise a corresponding cultural hierarchy. The sympathy for fascism, therefore, could persist in some cases (such as Pound's) even after modernism's own practices came under attack by the Nazis, who professed to loathe its elitism and cult of the new (for regressive reasons like offense against militarism, morality, nation, and religion—much like current censors in the United States), though they were happy enough to confiscate valuable artwork.

Eagleton's conclusions on the modernist penchant for order and its affinity with fascism echo those of Frank Kermode, in *The Sense of an Ending* (see also Harvey 1989:33–35).

19. It should be clarified that subsequent institutional accounts of modernism, to some extent, prompt Bürger's argument that aesthetic production is placed in the foreground when the form (or stylistic and structural innovation) becomes the content in modernism. Just as Williams distinguishes modernism from its subsequent canonization, Leighten points out that the later academic divorce of form and content primarily informs Bürger's theory: many artists' own statements often express a conscious politics, however flawed in practice, with regard to both style and content (1989:111–12).

20. In its reading through postmodernist theory, one of the most astonishing recent developments in cultural studies has been Ian Hunter's argument for the

cultivation of autonomous aesthetics. He attacks British cultural studies for its basis in Gramsci's description of the whole of culture as a process of negotiation, if not struggle, between dominant and subordinate groups. It is misguided and irrelevant, says Hunter, to theorize culture, as do the avant-garde and cultural studies, in any totalizing terms that suggest an integration of art and other social activities. The basis of this view seems to be yet another rehearsal of Michel Foucault's attribution of virtually total power to institutions in the abstract— never the human beings running them, who are surely fallible—and their discursive practices. People can only work with, in Hunter's view, the "delimited norms and techniques" proffered by the "normative and technical regimes [of] legal, medical, educational, political, sexual, and familial institutions." Thus he recommends *withdrawal* from such a culture, a supposedly impenetrable "patchwork of institutions," into an autonomous aesthetic realm on the model of Kant's immediate successor, Friedrich Schiller—who also provided Marcuse's basis, which Hunter has merely dressed up through reference to postmodern theory (indicating yet again its continuity with modernism). He lauds Romantic aesthetics for not being "a *theory* of culture and society, but an *aesthetico-ethical exercise* aimed at producing [only] a local [or individual] practice of ethical self-problematization" (1988:109, 113, 115).

Schiller may have revised Kant's rigid separation of the rational and sensuous, but, as Eagleton indicates, Schiller nonetheless served the purposes of "bourgeois hegemony" by describing a kinder, gentler harnessing of sensuousness by reason, in the aesthetic realm. Hunter's stern valorization of withdrawal into an autonomous sphere of self-formation, as in Foucault's own recommended physical regimen, is ultimately difficult to distinguish from the old "public school virtues," as Eagleton puts it. In the case of Schiller, the "brave effort" to reconcile matter and spirit in aesthetic autonomy "can turn at crisis-point into an aestheticizing away of th[e] whole degraded domain" of society: "the aesthetic would seem less to transfigure material life than to cast a decorous veil over its chronic unregeneracy." Hunter privileges Schiller because he is not transparently an idealist, utterly alienated from the material, but one finally cannot overlook Schiller's attribution of "active social remaking" in culture, as Eagleton puts it, to "a universal community" that can, revealingly, "be located 'only in some few chosen circles'" (1990:117, 394-95).

21. In the avant-garde practice defined by Benjamin and Brecht, in contrast, cultural innovation should militate against easy exchangeability (the characteristic repetition of commercial entertainment), but that effort hardly entails impenetrability and uselessness. A concept of use value like theirs, unafraid of the active, pleasurable process of apprehending art, seeks to rejoin the sensuous and the rational, and eliminate any opposition between the practical and the aesthetic (Eagleton 1990:204-7).

22. The next chapter further discusses the continuities between modern/ "Fordist" and postmodern/"post-Fordist" economies, as well as the fact that Henry Ford and his ilk explicitly linked "consumerism" with social control shortly after World War I, long before anyone diagnosed that association, and/or resistance to it, as postmodern.

23. Jameson's avowed adherence to the Frankfurt group—including a con-comitant, underlying nostalgia for modernism and repeated dismissals of Benjamin and Brecht—undercuts knowing references to socially engaged forms like "British working-class rock." The residue of traditional elitism, clinging to an impossible ideal of authenticity outside the marketplace, is clear: "Still, in modernism, the hermetic text remains, not only as an Everest to assault, but also as a book to whose stable [and compensatory] reality you can return over and over again. In mass culture, repetition effectively volatilizes the original object, . . . so that the student of mass culture has no primary object of study." Jameson has no interest, like Adorno and Marcuse, in the "secondary" question of the audience's use of mass texts, elaborating only the absolute ideological pacification presumably at work in mass culture. Thus he criticizes popular music for the repetition in its use, which in his view makes the first-time hearing inconsequential, as opposed to a complicated classical piece that requires real attention at every audition, such that listening to it is a developmental experience (1979:137). (Note the privileging of difficulty over simplicity; see R. Middleton [1981] and Gendron [1986] for useful defenses of the repetitive rhythms of popular music, against Adorno's modernist assumptions about the necessity of harmonic and melodic complexity.) But where Jameson finds only "sheer repetition," an insensible absorption of the pop song, others find the exact opposite: the best pop songs remain events "even after they become texts," or undergo repetition. Their value includes *both* use value and exchange value, their social consequence or use mattering as much as their formal essence as either a text or a commodity (Frith 1988a:79).

24. By *anti-art* Marcuse means modernism, which he conflates with the avant-garde, believing that poets like the Symbolist Mallarmé practice negation by *denying* the world of "things." Brecht's alienation effect, not surprisingly, is elsewhere reduced to the Russian Formalist concept of estrangement.

25. The appropriation of Brecht by the British film journal *Screen,* which cultural studies battled in the seventies, is therefore highly inappropriate, in its "conviction that the text itself . . . constructed the subject position from which the viewer made sense of it" (Turner 1990:109). Brecht in no way discounted the expansive, interrogatory activity of the audience.

26. Huyssen argues that Benjamin differs from Brecht in seeing the shock effect, a matter of form, "as essential to disrupting the frozen patterns of sensory perception, not only those of rational discourse," while Brecht "remains instrumentally bound to a rational explanation of social relations which are to be revealed as mystified second nature" (1986:14), a matter of content. But Huyssen registers a difference not so much in their aesthetic theories as in the expression of those theories. Benjamin records his admixture of Dada and Brecht as abstract principles of interruption, seemingly removed somewhat from direct concern with social relations; Brecht presents a concrete method for the theater, clearly embroiled in them. Benjamin nonetheless clearly links shock with further rational, social ramifications—a "heightened presence of mind"—while Brecht writes continually of techniques for sensory disruption, often stressing an *emotive* response.

27. On Debord's rejection of psychic automatism, see Wollen (1989:81–82). The bourgeoisie, the SI acknowledged, was quite correctly aware of a danger in surrealism. But "now that it has been able to dissolve it into ordinary aesthetic commerce"—the montages of advertising, MTV, and so on—"it would like people to believe that surrealism was the most radical and disturbing movement possible." The quietist function of the intelligentsia comes into play here, in the cultivation of "a sort of nostalgia for surrealism at the same time that it discredits any new venture by automatically reducing it to a surrealist déjà-vu, that is, to a defeat which according to it is definitive and can no longer be brought back into question by anyone" (Debord 1981d:20).

28. For distinction of the avant-gardist montage from other uses of the concept, including those of Picasso, Eisenstein, and Heartfield, see Bürger (1984:73–78, 80–82).

29. Modernist texts like *The Waste Land* have been described in terms of montage, but actually create "organic wholes from experience while [only apparently] enacting its actual fragmentation, . . . listlessly mim[ing] the experience of cultural disintegration, while its totalising mythological forms silently allude to a transcendence of such collapse." What emerges from the poem's numerous literary and mythological allusions is simply further construction of Eliot's highly elitist Tradition, a self-contained idealist whole rendered socially impotent by its aim of autonomy (Eagleton 1976:148– 51).

30. It should be noted that other theories of "defamiliarization," "disconfirmation," and so forth, identified with Russian Formalism and reception aesthetics, virtually never question the autonomy of the literary realm—the supposed organic unity or wholeness of the text, and a presumed closed circuit between the text and the reader. The Russian Formalists merely secularized the Symbolists' "new emphasis on the intrinsic value of the poetic word [as an] ideoglyph of mystery or of myth. . . . What was being proposed instead was still a specific 'literary language,'" and a rejection of social processes (Williams 1989:67–68, 75). In general, not much actually happens within this narrowly construed literary process, as in much reader-reception theory, in which the "doctrines of the unified self and the closed text surreptitiously underlie [its] apparent open-endedness" (Eagleton 1983:79–80).

31. At the same time as his association with Brecht, Benjamin wrote "On the Mimetic Faculty," concerning the revivification of the human power to create "similarities" through a new kind of reception of different forms and their languages.

32. See Kipnis (1986) for contemporary reemphasis on functional transformation.

33. A useful clarification of this sense of avant-gardism derives from the art critic Max Raphael, a thoroughgoing materialist. Through "a consideration of skill, technique, and formal [material] properties of art," says Michèle Barrett, in summing up Raphael's view, "we can escape romantic and mystificatory assumptions about art and move towards a different understanding. In this context an emphasis on aesthetic skills is in fact democratizing rather than elitist—for skills may be *acquired,* whereas the notion of an artistic 'genius' forbids the

aspirations of anyone outside the small and specialized group" (1987:85). This is not to say that skills alone make an artist; they do, however, help create a critically astute audience. This empowerment is what Benjamin, Brecht, and Bürger have in mind, in advocating the sublation of art and everyday life, or an unprecedented active role for the recipient of a work. "The recipient's attention no longer turns to a meaning of the work," says Bürger, "but to the principle of construction," or production (1984:81). The sensory impact of the subverted fragments in montage, or simply the expression of contumacy, leads not only to greater critical acumen, but the possibility of self-expression, on the model of the work in question. For Raphael, as for Benjamin and Bürger, the work of art is a form of expression that "connects a *sensual* appropriation of the world to an ideational or *cognitive* mode of apprehension"—or form to content, affect to intellect. Through a "reconstitutive description, . . . experienced by any viewer, . . . the energy in the work is released. [A]rt leads from the work to the process of creation" (Barrett 1987:87–88; italics added).

34. Graeme Turner concentrates on the historical evolution in analysis of the relation between texts and contexts, or audiences (1990:87–130, 162–66).

35. Like many postmodern theorists of desire, Chambers tends to construe the body as a text, through aestheticized, "transcedent modes of reading," as Colin Mercer puts it, as opposed to a concern with the actual techniques through which people employ various cultural forms, and their specific affective results (1991:71).

36. In touting the virtues of cultural studies, Giroux et al. find that in "North American Universities the study of culture is so fragmented that concerted cultural critique is almost impossible." Intellectual specialists are so alienated from the rest of society that they seem, finally, its most genuinely "uncultured" members (Giroux et al. 1984:472–73).

37. Jim Collins argues that British cultural studies contrasts production with the heterogeneity of everyday life as if nothing good can come of the production process, a conventional pessimism about the homogeneity of capitalist culture that denies the possibility of "conflictive textual production in tension-filled environments" (1989:22–24). But any tendency to associate all commercial production with a monolithic dominant culture is specifically refuted by Richard Johnson, at least, who disavows the excesses of "economism," concerned with the means of capitalist cultural production, and "productivism," the inference of "the character of a cultural product and its social use from the conditions of its production." The conditions of production include the circulation of "a stock of already existing cultural elements drawn from the reservoirs of lived culture or from the already public fields of discourse," an injection of significant conflicts over language and discourse (1986/87:55–56).

38. Todd Gitlin likewise argues that the presumably anesthetizing "global shopping center" includes "pluralist exuberance and critical intelligence" (1989:58). See Frith and Horne (1987:3–25), an analysis of negative conceptions of postmodernism that argues for the positive possibilities of contemporary cultural practices.

39. If truly "anti-authoritarian and iconoclastic," Harvey says in a similar

vein, ideas associated with postmodern art (more than theory)—the democratization of taste and celebration of difference, for example—"could be deployed to radical ends" (1989:353).

40. This celebration of play in and of itself is often a species of formalism: Fiske describes the grotesque bodily excesses of professional wrestling as Bakhtinian carnival (1989:81–90), but omits reference to wrestling's content, which is heavily authoritarian, racist, and sexist. The contradictory iconography Madonna presented a few years ago, as simultaneous virgin and whore, has received the same formalist interpretation, as a "postfeminist" freeplay of signifiers (see Fiske 1987; Kaplan 1987)—as if teenage females, during a period of mass-media backlash against women, could have gained any strength merely through devotion to images. Frith appears to satirize this view in asserting that the teenage singer Tiffany "really does matter" (1988a:79).

Lisa Lewis, in contrast, takes a more concrete, historical view of the "style imitation" sparked by Madonna and other female performers who struggled to open up MTV, finding in it a virtual feminism, rather than a belated postmodern variety. She also chides the women's movement for not recognizing the significance of adolescent experience and even assigning it negative connotations (1990:163–71, 223–24), possibly implicit in the "post" (literally "after") feminist terms.

41. British cultural studies has been criticized for neglecting black experience as well, by Paul Gilroy. One exception to his criticism is Hebdige's *Subculture,* which documents the role of punk in revealing the unacknowledged relationships between black and white youth subcultures (see Gilroy 1991:122).

42. On the relation of an aggressive, rebellious feminism to the avant-garde, see Suleiman (1990), though her overly broad definition of avant-gardism includes questionable versions of postmodernism.

The terms of aggressiveness here might be contrasted with Radway's *Reading the Romance,* an ethnographic study of women who read romance fiction. Radway champions those readers' creative forms of resistance, but in terms of a "limited, . . . minimal but nonetheless legitimate . . . protest"—not the sort of protest suggested by Morris's terms. Radway would have "we who are commited to social change" (an invocation of a vanguard that has received some criticism) encourage the development of something stronger [1984:222]).

43. See Garber and McRobbie (1976); McRobbie (1980). For overviews of feminism in cultural studies, see Brantlinger (1990) and Long (1989).

44. McRobbie notes a particular blindness to the use of literary texts in youth culture, which the second half of this book should correct.

45. On feminism and anarchism, see H. Ehrlich et al. (1979:233–79).

Chapter 2

1. This chapter focuses on mass communication for the sake of brevity, but does offer some discussion of another institution central to youthful experience, education.

2. To post-Marxists, for example, the perpetual, ongoing social struggle to "produce" texts through their "articulation," or interpretation and use, leaves no completed moments by which to judge either the text's initial meaning (inscribed in production) or its reception (Grossberg 1988:168–70).

3. The postmodern abandonment of judgment is founded on the Frankfurters' pessimism, in many cases, as the previous chapter indicates concerning Fredric Jameson.

4. Strummer/Jones, "White Riot" and "Complete Control," *The Clash,* CBS/Epic Records JE 36060, 1979.

5. Scholarly specialists have usually preferred the abstraction characteristic of formalist analysis, but the material, realist question of control inevitably confronts any actual oppositional practice (as opposed to detached academic theory), when it collides with the monologue of power. The formalist position has been contradicted, for instance, in the recent experience of Asian and Eastern European dissidents. If the technology (or "form") of a medium like television facilitates the dispersal of totalitarian propaganda, those dissidents have credited the variety and pervasiveness of other electronic communications forms with providing alternative sources of information at the same time, essential to maintaining civil society outside the state. It was *access* to those forms that was critical, in other words. In the West as well, it is not something intrinsic to mass communications that poses the severest obstacle to dissident politics, but their control by corporate conglomerates (rather than the state, as in the East). Even advertising, which most clearly reduces discourse to pure form (i.e., images), works primarily through repetition and saturation, which suggests that monopolizing communication facilitates its effects. This is precisely why cultural studies has focused on subcultural groups that have turned the media against their owners, however briefly, counteracting this dominance of expression.

6. See R. Johnson for a critical reponse to Murdock's "economism," or the emphasis on "more brutally-obvious 'determinations'—especially mechanisms like competition, monopolistic control, and imperial expansion, . . . typically the work of capitalist business" (1986/87:55). Graeme Turner presents a more sympathetic account of Murdock's work on political economy, noting Johnson's objection to it (1990:190–92).

7. Rosier assessments of postmodernism, questioning monolithic constructions of a dominant culture, argue that the mass media have multiplied to the extent that "power is elusive, and there is no longer any telling where the 'plan' comes from" (Eco, qtd. in Collins 1989:17). But the *range* of messages and voices widely available in public discourse is inarguably limited; dominant news sources like *Time* magazine and *The MacNeil-Lehrer Report* have asserted that "there's no left in the United States," on the evidence of their own closure. There may be a plethora of communications forms, but what are most people seeing and hearing? If the plurality of communications is uncontrollable, why aren't more people? In repudiating negative absolutism about the mass media, postmodernist theory at the opposite pole seems just as detached, denying "any coordinated system to assign . . . specific discourses for specific audiences, [since] ownership does not guarantee unity of effect" (Collins 1989:12, 41).

8. A decade of corporate mergers and acquisitions, with tangible assets broken up and workers released in order to absorb the resulting debt, actually exacerbated the decline of the economic infrastructure. Taxpayer money was used to *socialize* the *losses* of corporations (through bailouts and tax exemptions) and wealthy individual rentiers (most outrageously in the savings-and-loan debacle and its aftermath, the greatest theft in history organized by the state). At the same time, massive tax cuts *privatized* the *profits* of both. With the resulting grotesque concentration of wealth, increasingly maldistributed between affluent professionals and poorly paid service workers, a resurgence of conspicuous consumption hardly reflected prosperity.

9. On the complicity of the mass media in defaming striking miners, see Cockburn (1989b). On the history of American labor relations, see Davis (1986:102–53).

10. The frequent description of advanced capitalism as a quasi–avant-garde force, however, requires the qualification that its profess ideology may affirm tradition even as it is swept away, by the encouragement of ever-greater consumption and so on. (And reflexive abandonment of tradition characterizes modernism—or "modernization," in the terms of capital—not the avant-garde, which sought to recover moments of antagonism from the past.) The recent "folklore of capitalism" in the United States, paradoxically, works through "a constantly *changing* repertoire of perceptions and maxims of value—American values—that are presented as *unchanging*, . . . even as capitalism's voracious need for change and innovation insists . . . on continually changing the rules, and replacing the scenery" (A. Ross 1989a:9).

11. On recent rhetoric in the mass media that blames the victims, specifically impoverished blacks, see Cockburn (1989a).

12. Concern for the powerless, on the part of leftists or liberals, typically entails a call for a public program to remedy social injustice; the right successfully equated such programs with an increase in state power and an erosion of individual autonomy, further articulating individualism with unfettered free enterprise (Fiske 1989:164).

13. "Right-wing statists like Reagan now get elected by posing as libertarian, populist opponents of big government that their constituents believe is socialistic, although in fact it is plutocratic"—socialism for the rich—"and becoming more so with the election of every antigovernment conservative" (Lazere 1987:85).

14. This mistake also had something to do with the formal conservatism of Springsteen's music (see Frith 1988b:94–101).

15. Marton/Escamilla, *Strange Attraction,* Black Hole, 1989.

16. See "The Wembley Concert" (1990).

17. The mass media, however, play a stronger, more consolidated role in political legitimation in times of economic crisis, even taking over this task from traditional state organs like public schools. Now superfluous to the one function they served, they have thus been left to rot, under Reagan's regime broken up into a class-segregated mixture of private and public schooling.

18. Leisure time, however, actually declined after the pivotal year of 1973;

consumerism has instead been fueled by increasing rates of work, according to the economist Juliet Schor (1991).

19. On reification, see Lukács (1971:83–110); Debord (1983:#1–53); Jameson (1979:130–41). Ball's definition, like Lukács's, derives from Marx's concept of commodity fetishism: the products of *human* activities and relations take on a life of their own, in an apparent relation between *things* (see Marx 1977:163–66).

20. In general, says Jameson, reification "renders society opaque: it is the lived source of the mystifications on which ideology is based and by which domination and exploitation are legitimized" (1977:212). This is too static a conception of ideology, however; if reification in labor and leisure renders the domination of some humans by others seemingly inevitable and natural, ideology involves the work done to combat as well as to reinforce that mystification.

21. The specialist conservators of art, in abstracting aesthetic expression out of its social bases, might now be understood as purveyors of this effect. Lukács's work on reification includes a critique of specialization: the "more intricate a modern science becomes and the better it understands itself methodologically, the more resolutely it will turn its back on the ontological problems of its own sphere of influence and eliminate them from the realm where it has achieved some insight" (1971:104).

22. Herbert Schiller, however, considers claims for the "active audience" only a contemporary updating of the old "limited-effects" paradigm in media studies, which likewise underestimates the influence of the mass media (1989a:136–56).

23. See "The Call-Up" (1987); Frith (1987a); Selbin (1988).

24. For a more theoretical discussion of media criticism based in readings of "political economy," see Gurevitch et al. (1982).

25. The history of the "October surprise" story, concerning the Reagan campaign's possibly treasonous arrangements with Iran during the 1980 presidential election, is a good case in point; when the story did finally break thanks to Gary Sick's investigation, mainstream periodicals such as *The New Republic* and *Newsweek* rushed to discredit him.

26. The orchestrated horror at such uncivilized conduct later required particularly schizophrenic contortions, in denying any comparison when the United States destroyed an Iranian passenger jet. Possible U.S. complicity in the Korean airliner tragedy, documented by Seymour Hersh among others, remains censored by the dominant media.

27. Political turmoil in less spasmodic forms also appears as "good-against-evil conflict," especially in television news, though evil is evoked more vaguely, "in 'faceless enemies' and 'bizarre cults' " outside the mainstream. Reproducing the evocation of paranoia by political authority, whether about the Soviets or the urban poor, the news media in the United States persistently presented a nation under siege through much of the 1980s (Hallin 1986:39).

28. On the news media's propagandistic coverage of the Persian Gulf War, and the Pentagon's manipulation of it, see Fairness and Accuracy in Reporting (1991); Kemper and Baldwin (1991); E. Larsen (1991); Ray (1991); Volpe and

Ridgeway (1991).

29. See "The Missing Bodies" (1991).

30. It should be emphasized that the idea of a human nature is not inherently reactionary, but has often been "a revolutionary rallying cry" (Eagleton 1990:409).

31. Williams has suggested that mass culture's frequent depiction of domestic and international police actions embodies, in debased form, earlier modernist assumptions of habitual competitive violence. The representative of order is distinguishable from the outlaw only by a nominal identification with authority, confirming the seemingly inevitable destructiveness of every level of society (1989:130–31).

32. This is not to say that dilemma in understanding the elemental forces that shape the world occurs for no better reason than the success of neoconservative twaddle. In this century, the possibilities of technological progress have consistently borne the contradictory but apparently concomitant horrors of total war, nuclear terror, environmental disaster, and so forth. The increasing relief of the human individual's struggle with nature for survival has seemed to require a corresponding expansion of social organization and—consequently and para-doxically—repression. The further technology and society advance, apparently, the more destructive, repressive, and terrifying they become. This paradox was theorized by the Frankfurt School as the "dialectic of enlightenment" (see Horkheimer and Adorno 1987), referring to the period when philosophy, as well as society, enthroned "instrumental reason," with the industrial revolution. This view, developed primarily out of Freud, Marx, and Weber, is extremely nostalgic, hearkening to some primeval relation with nature, under the influence of Friedrich von Schelling's counterevolutionism (Anderson 1979:81–83, 91).

The Frankfurt argument may be pitched in excessively absolutist terms, but its general features are indisputable. Instrumentality or rationalization, the quantification and division of labor into mechanical tasks, represses what natural impulses might be expressed in human activity. This same technological standardization, in culture, impedes communication. This is no inadvertent effect of industrialization; cultural, economic, and political authorities must suppress public discourse on the systemic contradictions of modernization, which would throw their direction of society open to question. (The solution to reification, in Lukács's terms, would be to grasp the social totality, and the fact that it is not natural or inevitable, but quite unnaturally favorable to its elite.) As a result, people can only internalize the chaos they find, and often "surrender themselves to artificially constructed mass egos that promise to restore their links with the past and futures," à la authoritarian populism, Nazism, and so on (Rosenberg, qtd. in Marcus 1989:43).

Chapter 3

1. A dense poststructuralist version of a similar, deleterious transition from voice to writing can be found in Deleuze and Guattari's *The Anti-Oedipus*.

2. Benjamin stands distinctions like Kant's on their head in "The Work of

Art in the Age of Mechanical Reproduction," in which *contemplation* appears as an asocial, passive absorption in art, while *distraction,* the term conventionally used to deride the mass audience, ironically designates a critical habit in reception.

3. Christgau cites McClary (1991) as a singular exception.

4. See also Foucault (1979:3–31, 195–228), and the criticisms of such theory in Dews (1984); Hebdige (1988:66–70); Said (1983:220–25).

5. For an overview in one text of relevant work in both fields, see Habermas (1979:1–94). Habermas, not unlike Bakhtin, associates the development of antiauthoritarian impulses with the maturation of youth into control of the material force of language (1975:14, 90–92).

6. The question remains, however, whether Lacan's account of the subject actually buttresses a theory of collective agency. His description of the linguistic formation of the subject consists largely of visual metaphors (the "mirror phase," the "gaze," and so forth) that have only stoked postmodern theorists' preoccupation with the power of the image and the abstraction of experience. On this basis, Robert Stam draws a stark contrast between Lacan and Bakhtin: the former "makes subjectivity dependent upon the recognition of an irreducible distance separating self from other, and in so doing, turns psychic life into a series of irremediable losses and misrecognitions." Human beings, driven continually by "lack," are perpetually susceptible to unsatisfied desire, in Lacanian theory. Bakhtin, in contrast, "foregrounds the human capacity to mutually 'author' one another, the ability to dialogically intersect on the frontiers between selves. One becomes 'oneself' ... *with another's help"* (1989:5–6). This point is crucial, later, in describing the relationship between individual and collective agency.

7. Leslie Roman, on the basis of her ethnographic study of women in punk, similarly disavows accounts that uncritically romanticize the degree of consciousness and intention in subcultures. She prefers the concept of "asymmetric subjectivity," designating the different degrees of verbal and nonverbal, conscious and unconscious discourse any person as well as group embodies (1988:143, 145). Individuals and groups do not necessarily inhabit consistent subject positions, either, across the range of their cultural experience.

8. Though Foucault, and Deleuze and Guattari in *The Anti-Oedipus,* advocate an anarchism of sorts—"difference over uniformity, flows over unities, mobile arrangements over systems"—the new subject groups or collectivities that they envision are predicated on deindividualization, or "schizoanalysis," since the "individual is the product of power." Deleuze and Guattari may hold, like other critics of traditional aesthetics, that the "greatest force of language was only discovered once a *work* was viewed as a machine, producing certain effects, amenable to a certain use," but the utility they have in mind serves only the unconscious desires of individuals, who are reconceived as "desiring-machines." *The Anti-Oedipus* shares the poststructuralist assumption that language "represents nothing" and that power, inscribed in and through writing and other media controlled by power, has given the lie to appeals to the authenticity of the voice. Meaning is not discovered and confirmed in the social use of a text, but is nothing other than the schizophrenic desiring-machine's use of it (Foucault

1983:xiii–xiv; Deleuze and Guattari 1983:109, 205). Society, in one characterization of such theory, is merely an assemblage of agents "with no sense that their self-realization might flourish within bonds of mutuality" (Eagleton 1990:393).

9. True dialogue, according to the Situationists, involves a common project "sustained only by the self-discipline of individuals proving themselves in the coherence of the theories and acts through which each member strives to merit his [or her] joint responsibility with all the others" (Knabb 1981:177).

10. Bringing art alone into play will not do, however, unless linkage with cognitive and moral discourses (also in specialist hands) occurs as well (Habermas 1983:11–12).

11. For similar views in anarchism, see Bakunin (1980:237); Kropotkin (1971:202–6). Eagleton adds that much postmodernist theory, in emphasizing "difference" and plurality alone, has disastrously abandoned this position.

12. Writing on Bakhtin, Linda Hutcheon reiterates that parody can be not only progressive—"a threatening, even anarchic force"—but also regressive, an "authorized transgression" ventilating hostility toward authority through regulated mockery. She undercuts this dialectical view in the Bakhtin essay, however: one line, that the "presupposition of both a law and its transgression bifurcates the impulse of parody," resembles hackneyed postmodernist denunciations of anarchism for supposedly affirming the law it transgresses; and she takes the questionably sober view that Bakhtin's concept of carnival is limited to the paradox of authorized transgression. Hutcheon never entirely excludes the possibility of parody and/or Bakhtinian carnival renovating and renewing discourse, though (1989a:99–103). In their original moments, the strongest youth subcultures have hardly been authorized, and if at some point they become commercially incorporated, they continue for some time, nonetheless, to provoke visceral responses, whether enthusiasm or condemnation.

13. If Williams's early use of the concept *structure of feeling* emphasizes material experience at the expense of a more abstract, structural frame, in subsequent work he is much more cognizant of the mediation of ideology through material social processes. Eagleton once caustically observed, on the other hand, that Williams was talking about ideology (like everyone else) all along, but the material emphasis in describing the structure of feeling, in *Marxism and Literature,* seems distinctive from the abstraction in nearly all analyses of ideology. On problems with Williams's concept, see Turner (1990:57–58).

14. Lefebvre worked briefly with the Situationists and taught, at Nanterre, many of the students involved in the May Revolution in 1968.

15. Lefebvre's understanding of the moment also presents a sharp contrast with the modernist's ethereal significant moments, such as the epiphany, and their "eternal contemporaneity" (Williams 1989:76), which excluded historical change.

16. Fiske's refutation of much previous critical inquiry and its elitism, however, is in fact hardly populist at all. At the heart of his work is a thesis derived from de Certeau, similarly indebted to poststructuralism, and also reminiscent of Bourdieu's work on "the practical sense," which appears in de Certeau. The academic construction of discourses about everyday life diminishes it, Fiske ar-

gues, because those engaged in everyday practices do not themselves engage in larger (theoretical) generalizations about their experience, or refuse to do so (see the following note, on the elitism of this argument). It would be wrong, therefore, to expect popular culture to be radical, in the sense of combining practice with theory. Bourdieu, in his "theory of practice," likewise finds no "strategic intention" in everyday practices, though professing to valorize them: "it is because subjects do not know, strictly speaking, what they are doing, that what they do has more meaning than they realize" (qtd. in de Certeau 1984:56). (De Certeau disapproves of the terms of unconsciousness, though he attributes purposiveness only to an amorphous mass.)

Fiske, in his conclusion, chastises the left for privileging direct political action, as Hall and others have, but seems to regret himself the limitation he finds in the politics of popular culture, a progressive "micropolitics" at a good distance from the truly radical "macropolitics" of political organization (1989:159, 188, 192–93).

17. Colin Mercer also makes the extreme judgment that cultural theorists "don't know what people actually do with culture," as if academic discourse emerges out of *total* isolation. Cultural analysis, in his view, should concentrate more on "techniques" in using culture—"what people actually do"—rather than seeing lived experience as "a repository of meanings to be deciphered" through overly general, intellectualized aesthetic codes (1991:63, 71–72). Although this redirection of inquiry resembles Fiske's argument, in the work discussed here Fiske merely infers the uses of texts from the texts themselves.

First-hand studies of the actual use of culture (like ethnography), however, may themselves be guilty of condescension and reductiveness, if ordinary people's experience is considered alien to aesthetic interpretation, as Mercer seems to argue, which implies that everyday pastimes are transparent in meaning, relatively easy to understand. Richard Johnson's encouragement of recourse to the scholar's own personal experience (1986/87:69, 79), in interpreting lived cultures, seems more balanced than Mercer's dichotomy between first-hand experience and second-hand critical reading, since any recounting of the former is inevitably just as subjective. The latter, furthermore, virtually always includes an analogical component, or a connection drawn at some level (usually unspoken) between the critic's own life, his or her own feelings and thoughts, and those perceived in the subjects in question, at whatever chronological or geographical distance. The lack of effort at such analogy, as in contemptuous dismissals of popular musics and youth subcultures, is the actual liability of much aesthetic interpretation.

18. Peter Wicke points out, however, that if videos standardize the perception of songs, it would be more accurate to find that they continue and extend the marketing process already extant in rock, rather than creating some new sensorium. The most celebrated "postmodern" videos, furthermore, actively dissolve meaning rather than fixing it, though this tends only to confirm the experience of televisual flow (1990:158–73). Dick Hebdige also disagrees with the view that rock videos necessarily "concentrate yet more attention on the (incidental/suspect) visual dimension and distract attention away from . . . the speak-

ing, singing, living human voice" (1988:236–37). He lauds the possibilities opened up by the Talking Heads' "Road to Nowhere" video, which undermines narrative coherence through both the song lyrics (including David Byrne's vocal performance) and a pastiche of indirectly referential images, creating an ultimately affirmative statement on coping with postmodern uncertainty.

Scholars of mass culture have paid a great deal of attention to MTV on somewhat the same postmodernist basis (see Frith and Horne 1987:166–69), but often in less qualified "postmodernist celebrations of fragmentation and disruption." Considering the frequent, quite coherent appeal to white male adolescent fantasies, however, rock videos certainly still "nail down meaning" (Bhat 1989:15), with the "postmodern" elements the exception to the rule, occurring largely in brief graphic interludes. Wicke ultimately agrees that the majority of rock videos are superficial and thoughtless, that the important thing "is simply to be present," as in all advertising, from which they derive their techniques. Even most of the celebrated postmodern videos, despite their flexible meanings, only reinforce "standard ways of looking at the world," or the experience of fragmentation characteristic of advertising; the diffuse sights and sounds come to seem rather similar in light of their economic function. He does also offer a realist (rather than formalist) defense of music videos: less narrowly controlled for marketing purposes, more open-ended ones (like "Road to Nowhere") could have the potential to deepen and enhance the viewer's imaginative experience of both music and television (1990:168, 170–71).

Lisa Lewis finds that a more straightforward struggle for meaning is also possible, via MTV, in new forms of "female address" in the 1980s that "satisfied three groups: female musicians, who had been searching for a more complex and subjective mode of self-representation; female audiences, who wanted a system of textual discourse comparable to the prominent male-adolescent discourse; and even MTV, whose primary prerequisite was the delivery of a youth audience to advertisers" (1990:222). For this last reason, MTV was also happy to see black rap performers become prominent in the nineties, though their original access came through a token presence grudgingly granted by the network. Rap videos, often locked into static narratives, have displayed the same mixed results as rock ones, which is not surprising since they share the same commercial imperatives and, in particular, many of the same attitudes towards women.

19. See Bakunin on the role of antiauthoritarian youth, in particular, as "fraternal instructors of the people" (1980:233).

20. Noam Chomsky, for example, commends Bakunin's "sharp critique of the technical intelligentsia—the Marxists in particular," who seek managerial roles and "just plain privilege," like their capitalist counterparts. Anarchism, in contrast, "offers no position of privilege or power to the intelligentsia. In fact, it undermines that position. As a result, it's not particularly attractive to many of them and in in fact, the number of anarchist intellectuals, though there are some, has been quite limited as compared to those who associated themselves with one or another variety of so-called Marxism" (1987:20–21).

21. As Bakunin says in *God and the State*, "Does it follow that I reject all authority? Perish the thought." The specialist knowledge of "the savant" in any

field should be respected, but while "reserving always [the] incontestable right of criticism and censure. I do not content myself with consulting a single authority in any special branch; I consult several and compare their opinions, [recognizing] no *infallible* authority" (1980:229).

22. Boon, *3-Way Tie (For Last)*, SST 058, 1985.

23. With respect to the issue of attaching excessive importance to the motives and organization of producers, another difficulty in the aftermath of punk has been the privileging of independent music, distributed on a smaller scale than corporate rock, with less massive promotional plugging. The network of petit-bourgeois bohemian-entrepreneurs behind punk rock was not inconsiderable in its impact by any means, to be sure, and such developments, haphazard and organic, still cannot be reproduced by the music industry: "this gives the grass-roots element in rock the power, at certain key moments, to disrupt seriously the music industry and, at least temporarily, to alter its balance of power" (Harron 1988:184). The postpunk mythos of the "indie" company had already declined considerably by 1991, however, when Rough Trade records, a bellwether begun in the punk era, went bankrupt. The head of a leading indie subsequently declared that the "whole notion of alternative is a ghetto for backwards-looking people right now" (Poneman, qtd. in McDonnell and Mapp 1991:57). Independence in the music industry appeared to be reduced to a question of market shares, not a full-scale alternative production process. The decline of the indies indicates the inevitable confrontation, in cultural studies, with the realities of political economy, here simply the significance of profit and loss for both major and independent companies.

In considering the possible uses of mass-reproduced music, Frith's fairly recent dissociation from cultural studies poses another qualification of subcultural theory, though it also marks an unusual form of postmodernist cynicism. Returning pessimistically to an older "productivist" emphasis, he finds that any authenticity heard in rock music is actually "already determined by the technological and economic conditions of its production." He rejects, on this basis, the assumption that rock music might be a model for collective subcultural expression, whether by directly representing particular audiences, or even simply by encouraging radical consumption. His dismissal of the subcultural model reflects an absolute concentration on the corporate marketing of rock music, a theory that the only dynamic in popular music lies in the "multinationals 'fishing' for material, pulling ideas, sounds, styles, performers from the talent pool and dressing them up for worldwide consumption" (1988c:130). Whereas most critics of postmodernist culture construct highly abstract theoretical models of a monolithic cultural repression, Frith reaches somewhat the same end *empirically,* by asserting the primacy of production: "what is possible for us as consumers . . . is a result of decisions made . . . by musicians, entrepreneurs and corporate bureaucrats, made according to governments' and lawyers' rulings, in response to technological opportunities" that determine the final product (1988b:6, 12).

This emphasis on the economics of distributing music, however, may overcompensate for the tendency of cultural studies to concentrate on the seeming variety of voices in rock music, and on the range of their uses by consumers.

Andrew Ross asserts, in contrast, that "moments of change and reinvestment of cultural energy, especially those ushered in by new cultural technologies," are always moments "when opportunities exist to contest, reconstruct, and redefine existing terms and relations of power" (1989a:213). Frith does argue elsewhere for the commercially unexpected consequences of changes in popular music making, which his formulations above would appear to rule out. Such changes may occur in technology (or production), in audience tastes in stars and styles (or consumption), or in some combination thereof. Even in this observation, though, he leans towards technologism, arguing that the "major disruptive forces in music in this century have been new devices, technological breakthroughs" that increase (usually inadvertently) consumer control of music (1988c:129; 1980:57).

24. The reference to "adaptations" suggests the commonality of avant-garde montage and subcultural style.

25. Levi-Strauss's work has also been compared with that of Bakhtin, in their common concern with ritualistic and/or carnivalistic inversions of cultural hierarchies like high and low, youth and age (see Stallybrass and White 1986:16–17).

26. This revision in Chambers's own work, unfortunately, has tended to devolve into postmodernist insistence on the fragmentation of experience, and a concomitant conception of style as a noncoherent assemblage. Something more than *eclecticism,* in Chambers's terms (reminiscent of Jameson's use of *pastiche*), might still be the result of oppositional expropriations.

27. Hebdige has gone a long way, then, toward taking into account Gary Clarke's criticism (1990) of the original work on subcultures in the 1970s. Clarke challenges excessively homogeneous descriptions of subcultures, especially in relation to social class, and insists on more heterogeneous accounts, out of concern with a perceived elitist tendency in cultural studies, a concentration on stylistic innovators. He exaggerates the problem in Hebdige's original work on punk, however, in which the moment of style is not as narrowly conceived, both chronologically and demographically, as Clarke suggests, but in fact is just the opposite, in the lack of identification of the actual persons involved. And his argument for considering "the individual life trajectories" of youths in subcultures, rather than stylistic ensembles, can lead to a paralysis in which nothing can be said to have been accomplished until the exact roles of many of the agents involved have been documented.

It is certainly fair to criticize renderings of subcultures as "static and rigid anthropological entities" in which all members of a subculture operate in the same class location, and presumably solve the same problems with the same degree of commitment. But even if "subcultures are diffuse, diluted, and mongrelized in form," beyond the original members whom cultural studies presumably privileges, it seems excessive to assert that style is such a vague concept that it cannot be countenanced as an objective category. The assemblages of texts and commodities are verifiable enough, as is their impact, if the question of who was responsible is less clear-cut. A suggestive model for further creative practices might be found in fiction as well as in fact, anyway; the ultimate use value of that model in everyday life is the test that matters. If, finally, cultural studies overemphasizes innovators and the original moment of creative assemblage, as opposed to the moment when the style becomes widely available, the terms of Clarke's own concern with "mass selling"—the "firm stake" of many stylistic innovators in the commodity market—begin to suggest an elitism as well, in conjuring up the inexorability and degradation of commercial incorporation (1990:82–84, 89–92). From any reasonable view, the incorporation of deviant expression hardly begins to approach any degree of completion.

Chapter 4

1. Even when most successful, certainly, the resulting ideology continues to accomodate to some extent the interests and values of subordinate groups; common sense is always negotiated, always spontaneous and volatile to some degree. The dominant bloc extends its mastery of the economy into culture by transforming conceptualization and mores in a direction which does not always pay direct, "immediate profits to the narrow interests of any particular class," if it does favor "the development and expansion of the dominant social and productive system" (Hall 1982:85). Contrary to rosier uses of Gramsci (see Turner 1990:210–15), however, this does not mean that the extent of struggle remains profound at every point in time. When dominant ideas encompass a wide enough range in reference and explanation, the contradictions in common sense are less "subject to tests of internal coherence and logical consistency," causing injustices of an immediate, material sort "to appear as mere exceptions . . . within this larger structure" (Hall et al. 1978:155). To fracture that structure on a wide scale requires that the practical knowledge in common sense must connect with "philosophy," or a larger historical self-consciousness. (These terms resemble Hegel's observation that conformist common sense suppresses contradictions, and philosophical thought recognizes and refuses to accept them.) Everyday good sense and realism, it should be emphasized, if less extensive in outlook than philosophy, do also serve an essential purpose in mitigating the distance of theory from popular life (see R. Johnson 1991). (A similar recovery of cognitive and moral discourse from specialists, in Jürgen Habermas's theory, would facilitate communicative reason.)

The expansion of practical knowledge is no easy achievement, given the narrow control of mass communications; in relation to earlier discussion of authoritarianism in entertainment and information, the general omission of strongly oppositional ideas and views, in a culture concentrated in corporate hands, might be understood as a significant component of the postwar hegemony of affluence, in the United States as well as England. At the very least, though, the prevailing common sense does always erode under the weight of its contradictions, with the ruling bloc continually shoring it up. When enough people decide to knock it down entirely, that is a truly historic moment.

2. Given the nettled literary ambivalence about claims for affluence, their hostility towards television derives in part from its centrality to those claims, as much as the inheritance of traditional elitism. Their predecessor in this regard

was George Orwell, though the 1941 essay "England Your England" made the same points with regard to books and radio; Stuart Laing (1986) documents the manipulations through which earlier theses of cultural embourgeoisment, like Orwell's, were adjusted to fit the 1950s and television.

3. Peter Hitchcock's description of the Angry Young Men as a "cultural event" usefully details the way in which *Declaration* exploited the Angry label at the same time it purported to rebuke it, as the Movement had in its own case. In general, right up to the present, in criticisms of the label *Angry* it is actually unclear who did the labeling, except for uncouth journalists denounced in the abstract. As a new sensation seemingly with a life of its own, in any case, Angry and/or working-class writers "who previously might have found it extremely difficult to [overcome] the elitist pretensions of the culturati now found themselves swept into the center of the [high] cultural arena," with the effect of containment (1989:29–33, 58). Haut bourgeois culture, however, under threat with the changes signaled by mass culture, hardly had to extend itself to incorporate the Angries. They complained about this defusing, but were in fact readily assimilable; their nonconformity was limited to upsetting prevailing literary taste. Though some class feeling between different strata of the middle class was involved, "professional blockage rather than political outlook was the issue" (Sinfield 1989:233).

Thus the writers identified with the Movement and the Angry Young Men may express a common disillusionment with both culture and society, but that discontent remains confined to a relatively narrow rebellion against the literary establishment or "Mandarins." The disinterest in any larger politics reflects in part the disappointment that had set in by 1950 with Labour's misbegotten experiment with socialism, undermined by continuing austerity, the reluctance of upper–middle-class politicians to eradicate entirely the class structure in education and public institutions, and adherence to America's position in the cold war. This "lack of achievement [was] matched ... over the same period in the world of literature and the arts," says Robert Hewison, who cites J. B. Priestley's lament in 1949 that "we are revolutionaries who have not swept away anything."

A vogue for logical positivism set in, disparaging universalizing ethical and moral arguments such as those characteristic of socialism, in favor of a practical, empirical politics; hence Wain's disparagement of the working class and a society organized by the quasi-socialist Labour party. Orwell's principled aversion to both political dogma and centralized state power became widely influential, converted into more of an anti-Communist quietism than he ever intended, perhaps, with virtually all leftist politics associated with Stalinism. (Some of this quietism was no accident, given the covert CIA funding of the literary magazine *Encounter,* edited by Irving Kristol and Stephen Spender.) Other writers from the thirties, the so-called Auden group, became objects of derision for having been drawn out by political conflicts. By the late 1940s, merely "the wish to believe" was considered the appropriate material for literature. In this atmosphere, the concern of younger writers was narrow and self-serving, an assault on the upper–middle-class Mandarin caste epitomized by the older generation of Bloomsbury, as well as Auden, Cyril Connolly, John Lehmann, Spender, and Waugh, which dominated the literary world. If fundamentally conservative, in their vehemence against their elders, members of the Movement and the Angries could appear a major rebellion in English culture nonetheless (Hewison 1981:3–5, 27–28, 43–44, 60, 64, 86–87, 118–26, 141; see also Sinfield 1989:44–50, 233–35).

4. At the same time, Whiteley notes, the political implications of the ownership and control of communications technologies "were largely ignored by the IG" (1987:50).

5. Malcolm Bradbury, in *Eating People Is Wrong* (1959), has a young novelist sum up the cultural and social confusion of contemporary writers: "Here's the boys with the big fannies slapping everyone on the back and saying 'You've never had it so good.' What can the poor old novelist do? . . . He just sits on his arse, too, like everyone else, but it's a thin angry arse and he doesn't sit so comfortably."

6. Osborne's misogyny reflects a somewhat convoluted relation to modernism, specifically Bloomsbury figures such as E. M. Forster. Bloomsbury made a positive association between the feminine (or personal) and literary practice, opposed to the masculine public world (Sinfield 1989:62–63, 81), and thus was identified with effeminacy in the Movement's repudiation of the earlier literary establishment. The opposition drawn between feminine and masculine culture is appropriated by Osborne, but recast in more conventional form, in depicting a negative, disabling continuity between feminized (private) leisure and (public) mass culture.

7. In the midst of this negative montage, high culture—"too intellectual"— falls into music-hall burlesque, symptomatic of the ravages of cultural leveling. One notable routine is "T. S. Eliot and Pam," with Eliot standing in for Punch: "'she said she was called a little Gidding [as in Eliot's *Four Quartets*], but she was more like a gelding iron!' Thank you." Typically, the reference to "gelding" associates cultural decline with the loss of virility.

8. Sinfield corrects the association of jazz and race in Kenneth Tynan's contemporaneous review of the play, accordingly (1989:261).

9. M. Wilde/Youngstar, *Roots of British Rock,* Sire SASH-3711-2, 1975.

10. Lest there be any confusion, regarding the critique of modernism in chapter 1: this is not a matter either of "making it new" for art's sake, like Ezra Pound, or consolidating an elite tradition, like T. S. Eliot, but of remaking popular music with a keen eye to both the musical past and the immediacy of present social experience.

11. The teds' desire to escape, to some extent, social class reflects their clash with the parent working-class culture. Discretionary income and new leisure pastimes on which to spend it were more a luxury of youth, in-between school and domesticity, and an oft-remarked source of antagonism for working-class adults (see Hall et al. 1978:158). The teds, and subsequent working-class youth subcultures to different degrees, have typically functioned at the intersection between the parent and dominant cultures, mediating between their own experience and that of working-class tradition. That tradition, threatened with obsoles-

cence in the fifties, was in some ways defended as well by the teds. Their sense of territoriality, for example, traditional in delinquent "street corner" gangs, either resisted or at least contradicted the perception (and the reality) of the breakup of working-class families and neighborhoods by new tower-block housing and the like. One sociologist, at some distance from the fifties, even asserts that the teds were fundamentally aware "of belonging to the working class and want[ed] to emphasize that fact" (Cashmore 1984:27). If older "entrenched, immobile" working-class consciousness was a distinct liability, as some in the New Left thought (Anderson, qtd. in Sinfield 1989:256), the combination of nontraditional and traditional attitudes among the teds would seem a virtue.

12. The "colour problem" was addressed by moving to reduce the numbers of Commonwealth, that is, nonwhite immigrants (Hill 1986:30).

13. MacInnes, as a Beat, had a triumvirate of interests that appear in each of his "London novels," *City of Spades* (1957), *Absolute Beginners,* and *Mr. Love and Justice* (1960): black immigrants, teenagers, and ponces (pimps). If he was uniquely in touch with the fifties, this was due to his ability "to empathize to an almost uncanny degree with the younger generation" because of his psychological makeup. If MacInnes sought only the marginally criminal—the African waterfront boy, the teenager, the ponce, and the drug user—he did find criminality, in more innocent forms of corruption, to be a "creative and daring alternative to a life of mindless drudgery." He remembered his adolescence in Australia as the most vital moment in his life, in both its pain and exhiliration. Once ensconced in England, in late adolescence, with his grandparents, the Mackails—his grandfather held the Oxford Chair in poetry—while his mother, novelist Angela Thirkell, went to work in earnest, MacInnes "became critical of his artistic heritage" (which included Kipling). He especially rejected pre-Raphaelites like his great-grandfather Burne-Jones, who "had turned their backs on a happy animal side of life for which I hankered" (Gould 1983:xiii, 34, 45, 51, 114).

Thus he always sought the outsider, within the limits of the mildly criminal, romanticizing—and patronizing—blacks in particular. Jazz musician Kenny Graham says that MacInnes, despite the genuineness of his enthusiasm, "had a don's mentality, was all calculated." In jazz, he sought "all the things he wasn't, taking all the time," and was rebuffed by black musicians as a result. What MacInnes sought most of all in his Beat/White Negro avocation, and his homosexuality, was "a kind of literary matricide," in the attempt to break through to his cold-blooded mother by means of documented outrageous behavior—"Mothers are supposed to love their sons," the narrator complains in *Absolute Beginners.* After Angela Thirkell's death, says Gould, without her "to shock with his familiarity with the underworld and his rejection of the values she espoused, the urge to write waned" (1983:86, 140, 158).

14. Osborne, among others, called him the J. D. Salinger of Britain, and the style of *Absolute Beginners* does suggest nothing so much as *Catcher in the Rye.* The actual argot is minimal, a few generic terms like "tax-payer" or "absolute beginner," and mostly suggests Beat, rather than teenage, speech: "That's crazy! It nearly shook me rigid!" The frequent expression of sentiment, the most salient

quality of the narration, comes straight from Holden Caulfield. The narrator says that his father's melancholia "makes me demented, because really he's got a lot of character," the same overcompensation for alienation characteristic of Caulfield, expressed in the same gushing cadence. One line is taken almost directly from the last line of *Catcher in the Rye:* "That's what always happens if you try to tell the truth, they always [get] angry with you when they hear it, and dislike you for it." (Holden concludes that if you tell the truth, you wind up missing everybody, something of a zen koan.) When the narrator carries on about books—"somebody else's mind opened up for me to look into"—he provides the same straightforward humanist declaration at the center of *Catcher.*

Chapter 5

1. A general shift in focus occurred in Sillitoe's work, as a result, with a less vocal condemnation of social injustice and "an increasing emphasis on the suffering experienced by particular," more intellectual individuals. *The Death of William Posters* not only removes his radical interests onto the international level, but also onto the solipsistic ground of a quest for a "new man," reminiscent of modernists such as Lawrence and Nietzsche, while dismissing, of course, the English worker's beguilement by television. (On the continuing intellectual reaction against television, in the sixties, see Hewison 1987:10–14.) Since the early sixties at least, "Sillitoe has sought to weave a mystique about the creative processes of the novelist," who, in his words, represents "the life spirit of society," using "senses that those who live on the surface don't always imagine existing" in the mindless age of mass communications (Atherton 1979:23, 45–46, 52).

Storey, in *Flight into Camden* (1961), portrays a "dead" working-class family, torn apart by the traditional puritanism of the parents and the educational opportunities afforded their children, suggesting that older working-class attitudes are destructive anachronisms. In *Jubb* (1963), Keith Waterhouse is no longer concerned with a fairly broad social milieu—like the Americanization execrated in *Billy Liar*—apart from brief, passing treatments of the housing situation and organized racism; instead, he presents a deceptive, ultimately harrowing portrayal of the grimmest sort of psychopath. *Jubb* was published in the same year as John Fowles's study of another working-class maniac with a minimally developed class resentment, *The Collector.* The two novels indicate the terrain on which literature, even in works with class themes, was operating: not only the psychological field, but also the space opened up by an increasing tolerance of sexual frankness, as in the explicit homosexuality of Storey's *Radcliffe* (1963). (The end of Victorian standards is usually dated with the test case involving D. H. Lawrence's *Lady Chatterly's Lover*, in 1959, which resulted in the acquittal of Penguin Books on obscenity charges.)

It is tempting to conclude that playwright Joe Orton, among the literary, understood the sixties best, in eschewing reference to his working-class background. He neither tricked up working-class life with conventional literary aspirations emphasizing introspection and bourgeois individualism, nor accepted the supposed sexual liberation in the sixties as a sign of genuine liberality. (As a gay person, he was understandably less credulous; the liberalized Sexual Offences Act was not passed until the year he died, 1967.) Instead, he launched a persistent critique of repressive desublimation—the release of libidinal energy into certain "specialized" or narrowly contained areas like leisure entertainment, at the expense of oppositional political energies. Orton's plays, especially *What the Butler Saw,* present one large portrait of sexually hyperactive people, apparently "liberated" in the sexually frank consumer society, but in reality utterly at the mercy of political and bureaucratic authority.

2. Burgess may have picked up the whole Augustinian/Pelagian historical schema from early literary criticism on Greene by Walter Allen.

3. One wonders why Alan Sinfield, writing on the frantic chase for satisfaction through consumption in the sixties, countenances the demands of labor for "as much money as possible to pay for the life wasted, the time lost," an acceptance of those very conditions, and then dismisses youth cultures as "incoherent" (1989:279–80)—apparently out of conventional leftist preference for direct political forms like labor organizations. In exploring leisure instead, the mods— with no faith in the rewards of labor, as Tom Wolfe indicates—would seem much more lucid and resistant than their elders, and far less resigned to the alienation of the workplace.

4. On class differences in Swinging London, even among some associated with the mods, see Wolfe (1969:82); Platt (1985:139– 40).

5. See, for example, "The Campus Entrepreneurs" (1967).

6. Hebdige also attributes a considerable influence on punk to pop art's "facetious quotation" of high and popular culture, and its parody of cultural commerce conducted at both levels (1988:142–43).

Chapter 6

1. See Jameson (1977:207–8; 1979:133–40); Löwy (1985:54–55); Lunn (1982:151–60); and Wolin (1982:183–97). Even Peter Bürger reverts to a conventional execration of Benjamin's essay on art and mechanical reproduction. It is simply not true, however, that Benjamin "tends to ascribe emancipatory quality to the new technical means (film) as such." As Bürger recognizes at another point, Benjamin's essay on mechanically reproduced art presents "a hypothesis for the *possible* diffusion of a mode of reception [generated by the shock effect] that the dadaists were the first to have intended" (1984:27–33; italics added).

2. On the Situationist role in May 1968, see Caute (1988:227–28); Marcus (1989:31–33, 353–57, 424–31); Plant (1992:94–107); Sussman (1991).

3. Ball cites Hedbidge's *Subculture* on the aberrant uses of commodities in subcultural styles, but observes that commercial culture also engages in the fragmentation and reassembly of its images and products. Ball thus comes to a fashionably postmodernist conclusion, that mass culture itself is now one long skein of detournements, a "cult of the displaced object [in which] detournement has become axiomatic to profit-making" (1987:36)—the same abuse of the con-

cept of detournement, treated as a mere register of postmodern fragmentation, elaborated by Sadie Plant (1992:112). Mass culture may thrive on pastiches of images and narratives, but it only practices a very literal form of montage, in its flow of images. Ball does not recognize any distinction between pastiche and a more vibrant critique, as McRobbie (1986) puts it, in cross-references across high and popular culture. Ball fails, moreover, to cite Hebdige's connection of subcultural style and the avant-garde tradition, trivializing the former by ignoring both its analogies and very real basis in the latter, especially in the reemergence of the Situationist International itself in the punk subculture.

4. The Situationists believed, in fact, that one of the primary difficulties of the Paris Commune—reconciling its members' desire for autonomy with some sort of organizational coordination—reflected an *insufficient* development in the technology of communication.

5. The pessimism of his more recent *Comments on the Society of the Spectacle,* published in France in 1988, still retains a purposeful, radical political edge missing in epigones such as Jean Baudrillard (see Debord 1991; Plant 1992:168).

6. Much like the SI's practice of detournement, Bakhtin's conception of carnival stresses the replacement of the hierarchies of official culture with a collective cultural community in everyday life. Through *mésalliances* mixing up and down the sacred and the profane, carnival would also expose usually concealed forces, particularly the resentment offical culture works to pacify or suppress outright (Lachemann 1988/89:141–42).

7. The Situationists' role as intermediary between the original avant-garde and punk appears fairly conspicuously in their use of the term *ensemble* to describe this milieu, the language of subcultural sociology as well.

8. An appendix in a new edition of the book (Omnibus Press, 1987) provides Fred Vermorel's perspective on the Situationist International.

9. The Pistols even lived out the most harrowing scene in the novel, a graphic razor attack on Pinkie. In June of 1977, when the group had just released the partially antimonarchy song "God Save the Queen," at the height of jubilee festivities, Rotten and drummer Paul Cook were slashed in razor and knife attacks by patriotic monarchists. The Vermorels bring out the scarifying violence that pervades *Brighton Rock,* in juxtaposing newspaper reports of the incident with Greene: "every man had his razor out, the long cut-throat razors which the sun caught slanting low down. [T]he man immediately facing him leant across and slashed his knuckles. Pain happened to him, and he was filled with horror and astonishment." The further violence done to the Pistols, highlighted by the Vermorels, lay in the incredulity of the news media; having created much fiction about punk violence, they requested the display of scars as proof that right-thinking Englishmen could do such violence.

10. These descriptions strongly suggest Thomas Hardy's character "Father Time" in *Jude the Obscure,* who represents a new, hopeless generation, prematurely aged by hardship and indifference. Greene may also have had in mind Joseph Conrad's Stevie in *The Secret Agent,* a novel Greene explicitly invoked four years earlier in *It's a Battlefield.* Stevie, however, only serves ironic purposes

in Conrad's novel: in a mockery of radical cant, Stevie performs the only actual anarchist act while everyone else talks; his form of "vacancy" lies in the chaotic, half-witted mind assigned him, as the true anarchist.

11. Jones/Matlock/Cook/Rotten, *Never mind the bollocks here's the Sex Pistols,* Virgin Records V2086, 1977.

12. A native avant-garde sprang up in England, in fact, not so much in the Auden generation, with which Greene is identified, but in younger critics like Alick West. His concerns in *Crisis and Criticism* (1937) bear a good deal of similarity to those on the continent, especially to Benjamin and Bakhtin's materialist linguistics.

13. Auden, who argued at the same time for a living popular cultural tradition, released the wide-ranging anthology *The Poet's Tongue* in 1935, "with the intention of erasing the social distinction between highbrow and lowbrow" (Hynes 1977:166). As well as songs for plays like *The Dog Beneath the Skin* and *The Ascent of F6,* he composed a number of lyrics meant to be performed as cabaret, including the "Twelve Songs" found in *Collected Shorter Poems.* MacNiece was a more ardent proponent and user of popular music (see "Eclogue for Iceland"), championing cultural "vulgarity" in his "self-proclaimed role of common man": "I am all against the rarefying effects of good taste, and have no sympathy with the idea that artists are people who should not soil their fingers with life.... In the case of music, I have a vulgar preference for something with a tune" (qtd. in Hynes 1977:295).

14. McRobbie, interestingly, emphasizes the importance of Walter Benjamin's youth in his work, as well: "Benjamin was himself politicized [in part] by the constraints and hypocrisies of bourgeois society as they imposed themselves on the life of the young adult. The Youth movement which Benjamin belonged to was greatly concerned [with] rigid authoritarianism" in a variety of social spheres (1992:153). It is tempting to conclude that the most genuinely radical artists and critics are those who remain forever young, in their outrage at injustice.

15. "'Minhas lealdades sao fluidas,' diz Greene: O autor inglês, morto em 3 de abril, revela suas afinidades com o anarquismo," *Folha de Sao Paulo* 18 May 1991; trans. Arthur Efron.

16. Bergonzi's conclusion that "Greene was never an explicitly political writer" is clearly true only in the narrow sense of his lack of political theory. Otherwise, Greene's mania for personal revenge increasingly turned to social targets during the thirties. His paradigm, as Bergonzi puts it, is hardly an idiosyncratic Catholicism distinct from the Marxist model of others in the Auden generation (1978:64). He found religion inextricably involved in contemporary life in the midthirties, specifically in the Spanish Civil War and in the extirpation of Catholicism in the Mexican state of Tabasco (documented in *The Lawless Roads*). This political dimension led him to incorporate his Catholicism into his work for the first time, in *Brighton Rock,* published twelve years after his conversion. Some later novels focus on Catholic themes to an obsessive extent, as in *The Heart of the Matter* (1948), which prompted George Orwell to dismiss Greene for merely rehashing the convention of the "sanctified sinner," who strikes grace-

ful poses on the brink of hell. But the initial introduction of somewhat the same theme, in *Brighton Rock*, remains balanced by the novel's continuity with the politics of the preceding secular works. This balance accounts in large part for the superiority of this early achievement, in relation to the subsequent works for which he is best known (and sometimes discounted, à la Orwell).

17. Why Greene, in 1938, would focus on Wordsworth might be explained by the apparent debt of *Brighton Rock* to Thomas Hardy's *Jude the Obscure* (1896): besides the strong resemblance between descriptions of Father Time and Pinkie, Hardy mocks the same line from the Immortality Ode. The novels appear to share a common whipping-boy, Matthew Arnold, whose heedless extolment of Oxford as "the home of lost causes" reappears in Pinkie's pursuer, Ida Arnold, whose "remorseless optimism" and absence of "pity for something she didn't understand" suggest the Arnoldian sanctimoniousness Hardy excoriates.

18. Sherry (1989) points out that Greene first transmogrified this line in a 1937 review of a film about the schooling of the poor, written at the same time as *Brighton Rock*.

19. Richard Wolin has related Benjamin's rediscovery of the significance of allegory, a highly arbitrary practice, to the extreme subjectivism of his modernist contemporaries. In isolating the quality of subjectivism, however, he omits Benjamin's political concerns, culpably misaligning him with Symbolism, with Joyce, Proust, and their belief in "the validity of fragmentary or problematical art as the form of expression appropriate to ages of decline" (1982:76). But Benjamin hardly accepted the inevitability of decline, and he certainly never validated the deliberate obliqueness of Symbolism. He may have been fascinated by both modernism (particularly Baudelaire) and the avant-garde, but he "never assumed that Kafka and Surrealism were engaged in the same project" (Pinkney 1988:127). As Bürger points out, the fragments drawn together by the allegorist—or avant-gardist—compose the opposite of the organic symbol, directly attacking the impression of autonomous wholeness intended by the modernist text (1984:69, 72, 82).

20. See Lukács (1971:101–9), the text Benjamin has in mind on reification and law.

21. Young gang members in England have long held to an oppositional morality, in a codified commission of crimes against property laws. Greene, because of his familiarity with the resentment of the adolescent gangster, not any special sociological knowledge, gives body to it in fiction. Greene's conceit, the result of his purely intuitive knowledge, lies in making his own Catholicism the young hoodlum's oppositional moral code. By Pinkie's lights, "nobody could say he hadn't done right to get away from [Nelson Place], to commit any crime," precisely the point illuminated by Benjamin, concerning the origin of allegorical evil in social oppression. Crime offered "working-class youths momentary reprieve from their inferior social identity, [an] opportunity to conquer feelings of hunger, failure and insignificance, and to assert a proud and rebellious identity through which its members could feel masters of their own destiny." Such crime might even be understood as a "discriminating response" proving the political import of "anger, resentment, and hostility" (Humphries 1981:175, 179, 182,

239). Crimes with this basis can thus "be classified as 'social' in the sense that they [express] a conscious, almost political challenge" to the social order and its values (Hobsbawm, qtd. in Hall et al. 1978:187; see also 186–89, 358–64). In the English youth riots of 1981, for example, "'Politics' and 'pleasure,' crime and resistance [were] meshed and confounded" (Hebdige 1988:34). Pinkie's pride in his crimes likewise derives from a code based in social identity, as much as his Catholic certainty that they will earn him damnation. Because of Greene's emotional kinship with this existence, he captures it fully.

22. Jones/Matlock/Cook/Rotten, *Never mind the bollocks here's the Sex Pistols*. Burchill and Parsons claim that "Anarchy in the U.K." was written by Jamie Reid (1978:33). On this question of authorship, McLaren has described Rotten as a "marvelous poet, with me inspiring him here and there" (Isler 1983:24). McLaren and Reid undoubtedly supplied Rotten with some ideas.

23. In winning such a reaction, the Pistols in particular resembled the Dutch Provos of the sixties, a group loosely associated with the Situationists. The Provos had given "a new twist to the old idea of propaganda by deed through deliberately goading governments into showing their most brutal faces" (Woodcock 1986:9). But the Situationists ultimately condemned the Provos for failing to develop "a coherent revolutionary critique" (Plant 1992:91).

24. McLaren's personal history included sit-ins at Croydon and Goldsmith Colleges of Art, and occupations of the London School of Economics and the University of London Union, but he never actually made it to France in 1968.

25. A *Vanity Fair* reporter named Craig Bromberg has written an egregious, inexplicable, grotesquely establishmentarian biography that treats McLaren's career solely in terms of his business dealings, condemning his failure to observe the standard operating practices of economic and legal "reality"; the author's obliviousness to cultural issues is typified by his inane notion of what detournement means (1989:103, 203–4). The book that accompanied the 1988 retrospective show at The New Museum of Contemporary Art, *Impresario* (Taylor 1988), is quite worthwhile, however.

26. The Pistols, by some accounts, were asked by McLaren "to mould themselves into a certain kind of image"; Rotten "was fabulous when he allowed us to play our hunches," says McLaren, who describes himself as having "utilized" the group (Vermorel 1978:171; Watts 1979:36). He aimed to be both "blatantly commercial (and thus resist the traditional labels of art and Bohemia) and deliberately troublesome (so that the usually smooth, hidden gears of commerce were always on noisy display)" (Frith and Horne 1987:132). Reid, who had been involved in the Suburban Press, a Situationist collective, since helping McLaren organize a student sit-in at the Croydon art school in 1968, says that McLaren originally wanted simply to promote his shop, Sex, and apparently was unhappy with the band's working-class, confrontationist attitudes. He reverted to Situationist ideas, which he and Reid had helped percolate in England since 1968 (assisting with Christopher Gray's book, for example), only "as things started to snowball, [and] everybody got more ambitious" (Reid and Savage 1987:55). His ironic play with the mass media was only made possible by the genuine, unmistakable anger of Rotten, which supplied an authentic sense of

threat. McLaren's one talent, a not inconsiderable one, was that of "an appropriator, a juxtaposer (and sometimes just a poser)," who could use people, could "spot the one potential anti-star among all one's customers" (Carr 1988:40).

Though McLaren has long been denigrated as a cynical manipulator, and his subsequent projects (the group Bow Wow Wow, the albums *Duck Rock, Fans,* and *Waltz Darling*) have been uneven, his commitment to confrontation in 1977 thus seems a genuinely alacritous seizure of the moment. At one point in the semidocumentary film *The Great Rock and Roll Swindle,* McLaren, in a news conference, is clearly shaken by the fact that the Sex Pistols were not only effectively banned from performance, but also unable to venture safely out-of-doors—hardly the picture of gleeful exploitation.

27. Reid's work appears, for example, on the cover of the single "Holidays in the Sun," which features two instances of detournement: one an advertisement supplied with banal captions ("nice young lady") that previously appeared in Christopher Grey's English anthology *Leaving the 20th Century;* the other an insertion of the song's lyrics, clichés from from European economic and political discourse, into the balloons of a saccharine cartoon advertisement for a Belgian travel agency. See also Marcus (1989:28–35, 438).

28. Besides exposing the hegemonic function of the media, over the long term the punk parody of depravity has had the salutary effect of drawing out elitist scholarly judgments on mass culture, confirming their persistence. The academic severance of the avant-garde and mass culture has emerged in regrettably hostile responses on the left to Greil Marcus's *Lipstick Traces,* for example. The impunity with which Marcus was dismissed by some also reflects long-standing antipathy on the left towards any semblance of anarchism (as opposed to more conventional political dogmas), and towards politics focused on everyday culture (as if authoritarian attitudes inculcated through leisure consumption posed no stumbling block at all to social change). But Johnny Rotten, Marcus points out, "had never learned the language of protest, in which one seeks a redress of grievances, and speaks to power in the supplicative voice, legitimating that power by the act of speaking: that was not what it was about. . . . He denies the claims of his society with a laugh, then pulls the string on the history of his society with a shift of vowels so violent that it creates pure pleasure" (1989:7, 13).

Eagleton, otherwise a champion of the Benjamin-Brecht position in undiluted form, draws the line at punk, and its presumably "supremely pointless spectacle": "From [Dada] to spitting punks is a sharper declension than Mr. Marcus seems to think. [H]is enthrallment with punk leads to a drastic underplaying of its less savoury aspects: the infantile self-indulgence, the violence and machismo, the postpolitical nihilism, the inexorably squalid conclusion for the likes of Sid Vicious, who killed his girlfriend and later died of an overdose." Particularly in mistaking punk for nihilism, Eagleton's stereotypical litany of violence and vomit blithely offers up a hazy recollection of something like the *Sunday Mirror* version of punk, a cavalier attitude he would never take to an art form more suited to his tastes. He is also wrong to dissociate "the politically orthodox avant-garde, . . . sober, technological and socially minded," from "carnivalesque subculture," an "anarchistic parody of it" (1989:12). His description of the former would appear to have in mind Benjamin and Brecht, but a subculture like punk, in its anarchist subversion of spectacle, is hardly a parody of the avant-garde, but a direct, meritorious descendent of it.

While Andrew Ross fairly criticizes Marcus's mystification of the history of the avant-garde, he travesties punk itself in some regards, such as the strange assertion that it demolished interchange between producers and audiences out of contempt for the latter, when just the opposite is the case. He also believes that the Situationist International were unmitigated elitists, and hence lacked the "analytic power" to include "popular desires" in their work, presumably exactly like the Frankfurt School (1989b:109–11). The SI, of course, especially Raoul Vaneigem, wrote about desire and everyday life almost obsessively. See also the uncomprehending review of Marcus by Santoro (1989).

29. Ernst Fischer offers a robust description of the dialectic between form and content, derived from Hegel: "content changes incessantly, at times imperceptibly, at other times in violent action; it enters into conflict with the form, explodes the form, and creates new forms in which the changed content becomes, for a while, stabilized once more." Hanns Eisler's *Cantata on the Thirteenth Anniversary of Lenin's Death* provides a concrete example of what this dialectic entails. Despite the abstract formal character of the music, it does possess "concrete, socially determined elements," based not simply in Brecht's text (the given content), but in the emotive task of appropriately mourning Lenin, that is, without traditional pathos. Eisler thus had to find a new style, based in "simplicity, precision, economy, austerity of musical gesture pointing far into the future—not into a mysterious beyond but into a brighter material world" ostensibly brought about by Lenin's work. This was not form for form's sake, "but form determined by a new content" (1986:124–25, 185–86).

30. See, for example, Pattison's misbegotten *The Triumph of Vulgarity* (1987), and Frith's review of Pattison (1987b). See Marcus (1986:78–79), on Lawrence Grossberg's (1986) bisection of song lyrics from music in writing on punk. Dave Marsh (1987), in reviewing the Clash's "This Is England," finds that indecipherable lyrics in no way obscure the song's essential rage, conveyed in Joe Strummer's tone of voice.

31. Jim Collins similarly defends objective discussion of "style" (against the argument of reader-response critics that physical descriptions are entirely arbitrary interpretations by readers) by pointing out that communication never occurs in a purely "tension-less environment," but in a dialogical relation fraught with the sender's designs (for better or worse) upon the receiver (1989:85).

32. The success of Greene's novel, though, ultimately results not just from sheer vitriol, but from a collision of very different cultural languages both high and low, both conformist and dissident. Bakhtin describes such "dialogization," an artistic "system" of languages, as defining the novel as a genre. The "social diversity of speech types," notably including "tendentious languages" set against the "languages of authorities," is "the basic distinguishing feature of the stylistics of the novel" (1981:263, 416).

33. Wohlfarth (1988) suggests Benjamin's reversal of Nietzsche, but seems reluctant to emphasize it.

Bakhtin's concept of the "dialogical imagination," in its antiauthoritarianism, can also be connected with Nietzsche's concept of *ressentiment*, Michael André Bernstein (1989) has argued. He considers the point, however, an *objection* to Bakhtin, even invoking fascism and madness—rather than just the opposite—as the logical outcome of *ressentiment*. To Bernstein, the multiple voices in Bakhtin's "dialogue" are as dark and threatening as they are life-enhancing.

34. In the same year, Norman Denzin was one of the first academics to argue that sound mattered more than lyrical content in popular music (Frith 1988b:119).

Fischer, writing ten years earlier on form and content in music, represents an estimable, unacknowledged predecessor to this material understanding, and those that follow. Music, including rock and roll, is "a means of stunning or exciting the senses," provoking automatic associations and collective emotions with the possibility of "direct participation," as in dance, in which the music "acquires a *content* through the . . . excitement of the dancers." That content is a social element finding "expression in the musical form alone" (1986:187, 189), in mood and emotion—the same sense in which Bakhtin and Benjamin understand form and content melting down.

35. The bluntness of the accompanying music, characterized by frenetically strummed, simple chord forms played on highly distorted electric guitars, was more a technologically based populist assault on commercial rock music, particularly expensively produced, virtuoso art rock.

Laing recognizes to some extent that the responses of the punk audience mattered equally as much as the music. In this matter he follows Marcel Proust's concepts of the *mémoire involontaire* and *volontaire*, used by Benjamin (in writing on Baudelaire) to characterize integrated and traumatic responses, respectively, to urban life and culture. Laing suggests that the shock effect, for the punk listener, may "include a pleasure in the awareness of how the other, 'traumatized' listener will be discomforted," particularly the mainstream pop audience (1983:81). This point helps explain how a distinctive subculture may form around a particular musical form, but it hardly begins to suggest the further creative activity in the punk subculture. Due to his Marxist desire to find directly class-conscious cultural activity, the imaginary, prepolitical symbolic forms of resistance described by cultural studies seem not only inadequate but delusory to Laing, and even altogether unengaged with the production apparatus of leisure culture. Most of the left, says Frith, similarly "rejected any suggestion that punk reality was constructed. Punk for them was simply a transparent image of a real youth condition" (1980:56). Johnny Rotten himself denounced hard-line leftists for "just using" a music that they otherwise despised (not that this is the case with Laing).

36. Barthes, however, who seemed sympathetic to youth music in essays like "Musica Practica," would, in *The Pleasure of the Text*, denounce all mass culture as repetition, simple *plaisir*, and attribute *jouissance*, a higher pleasure, to a

necessary retreat from mass culture into higher forms. *Jouissance* has all the earmarks of the old "romantic ideal of the [unique] individual who experiences such pleasure, and who does so beyond the appeal of ideology" (Turner 1990:220; see also Huyssen 1986:211–12).

37. Fischer, in a similar though briefer history of music, makes the same argument for distinguishing music intended to produce a uniform effect from music that serves a collective social need.

38. For a detailed comparison and contrast of the New York and London punk scenes, see Savage (1991).

39. Of all these elements (besides black leather attire), the fanzine has proven the most enduring in youth culture, continuing to proliferate to this day. As the place where "the particular social vocabularies and ideological formulations that constitute [the group] may be socially constructed, argued, and clarified" their authorship "distributed throughout the subculture at large" (James 1988:178). In this form of direct expression, one finds clearly documented evidence of the empowerment of individual agents by such phenomena as a common love for a particular music (or other cultural forms).

40. Chambers likewise finds a paradoxical combination of chaos and sense: the symbolic labour alerted the eye to "a 'shocking' reworking of 'culture' and 'class.' Proud of its 'dumbness,' punk was yet the most articulate of subcultures: anti-art in its intention, it adopted a politics of ruptural aesthetics," subverting mainstream political discourse (1985:181).

41. Lester Bangs (1987) documents the racism of many on the New York punk scene, but the handling of race in English punk presents some genuinely positive moments, if a mixed picture nonetheless.

42. See Worpole (1985), however, for criticism of Harrison's failure, in *V.*, to realize the intended embodiment of the forces at work in the miners' strike.

43. Lydon/Laswell, *album,* Elektra 9 60438-1, 1986.

44. This is not to say rap is indebted to punk, since they emerged at roughly the same time (in the late seventies), and rap's exploitation of the resources at hand has distinctive roots in African-American culture (see Toop 1984). The recording of "World Destruction" by Afrika Bambaataa, the South Bronx DJ whose Zulu Nation helped bring rap to prominence in 1979, and John Lydon (née Johnny Rotten) would seem to acknowledge some sort of common ground, though, as the Cold Crush Brothers' "Punk Rock Rap" most certainly does.

References

Adler, Jerry, et al. 1990. "The Rap Attitude." *Newsweek,* 19 March, 56–63.

Adorno, Theodor W. 1941. "On Popular Music." *Studies in Philosophy and Social Science* 9:17–48.

———. 1981. "Perennial Fashion—Jazz." *Prisms.* Trans. Samuel and Sherry Weber. Cambridge: MIT Press.

Ahlberg, Brian. 1988. "Anarchy in the USA (And Canada)." *Utne Reader,* Nov./ Dec., 14–17.

"All the King's Men." 1981. In *Situationist International Anthology. See* Knabb 1981.

Allain, Marie-François. 1984. *The Other Man: Conversations with Graham Greene.* Trans. Guido Waldman. New York: Penguin.

Allsop, Kenneth. 1964. *The Angry Decade.* Port Washington, N.Y.: Kennikat.

Anderson, Perry. 1979. *Considerations on Western Marxism.* London: Verso.

———. 1983. *In the Tracks of Historical Materialism.* London: Verso.

———. 1988. "Modernity and Revolution." In *Marxism and the Interpretation of Culture,* ed. Lawrence Grossberg and Cary Nelson. Urbana: University of Illinois Press.

Atherton, Stanley. 1979. *Alan Sillitoe: A Critical Assessment.* London: W. H. Allen.

Attali, Jacques. 1985. *Noise.* Trans. Brian Massumi. Minneapolis: University of Minnesota Press.

Avrich, Paul. 1988. *Anarchist Portraits.* Princeton: Princeton University Press.

Bagdikian, Ben H. 1983. *The Media Monopoly.* Boston: Beacon.

———. 1987. Introduction. *The Media Monopoly.* 2d ed. Boston: Beacon.

———. 1989a. "The Lords of the Global Village." *Nation,* 12 June, 805–20.

———. 1989b. "Missing from the News." *The Progressive,* August, 32–34.

Bakhtin, Mikhail. 1981. "Discourse in the Novel." *The Dialogic Imagination: Four Essays,* ed. and trans. Caryl Emerson and Michael Holquist. Austin: University of Texas Press.

————. 1984. *Rabelais and His World*. Trans. Hélène Iswolsky. Bloomington: Indiana University Press.

Bakunin, Michael. 1971. "God and the State." In *The Essential Works of Anarchism,* ed. Marshall S. Shatz. New York: Bantam.

————. 1980. *Bakunin on Anarchism*. Ed. and trans. Sam Dolgoff. New York: Black Rose.

Ball, Edward. 1987. "The Great Sideshow of the Situationist International." *Yale French Studies* 73:21–37.

Bangs, Lester. 1973. "1973 Nervous Breakdown." *Creem*, Dec., 35–37, 72–76.

————. 1987. *Psychotic Reactions and Carburetor Dung*. Ed. Greil Marcus. New York: Knopf.

Barnes, Richard. 1979. *Mods!* London: Eel Pie.

Barrett, Michèle. 1987. "Max Raphael and the Question of Aesthetics." *New Left Review* 161:78–97.

Batsleer, Janet, et al. 1985. *Rewriting English: Cultural Politics of Gender and Class*. New York: Methuen.

Benjamin, Walter. 1969. "The Work of Art in the Age of Mechanical Reproduction." *Illuminations*. Trans. Harry Zohn. New York: Schocken.

————. 1973. "The Author as Producer." *Understanding Brecht*. Trans. Anna Bostock. London: New Left Books.

————. 1977. *The Origin of German Tragic Drama*. Trans. John Osborne. London: New Left Books.

————. 1978. "Surrealism." *Reflections*. Trans. Edmund Jephcott. New York: Harcourt Brace Jovanovich.

————. 1985a. "Construction Site." *One-Way Street and Other Writings*. Trans. Edmund Jephcott and Kingsley Shorter. London: Verso.

————. 1985b. "Eduard Fuchs, Collector and Historian." *One-Way Street*. See Benjamin 1985a.

Benn, Linda. 1990. "White Noise: The Long, Sad Story of TV Criticism." *Voice Literary Supplement*, Dec., 14–16.

Bennett, Tony. 1980. "Popular Culture: A 'Teaching Object.'" *Screen Education* 34:17–29.

————. 1982. "Popular Culture and Hegemony in Post-war Britain." In *Politics, Ideology and Popular Culture (1)*. Milton Keynes: Open University Press.

————. 1986. "Introduction: Popular Culture and 'the Turn to Gramsci.'" In *Popular Culture and Social Relations,* ed. Tony Bennett et al. Philadelphia: Open University Press.

Bennison, Steve, and Andrew Spicer. 1991. "Cultural Studies at A Level?" *Magazine of Cultural Studies* 3:18–22.

Berger, John. 1972. *Ways of Seeing*. New York: Penguin.

————. 1985. *The Sense of Sight*. New York: Pantheon.

Bergonzi, Bernard. 1978. *Reading the Thirties: Texts and Contexts*. London: Macmillan.

Bernstein, Michael André. 1989. "The Poetics of *Ressentiment*." In *Rethinking Bakhtin: Extensions and Challenges,* ed. Gary Saul Morson and Caryl Emerson. Evanston: Northwestern University Press.

Bérubé, Michael. 1991. "Just the Fax, Ma'am: Or, Postmodernism's Journey to Decenter." *Voice Literary Supplement,* Oct., 13–17.

Bhat, Gouri. 1989. "Year of the Women? Liking Guns N' Roses and Living with Myself." *buckethead* 3:14–17.

Bicat, Anthony. 1970. "Fifties Children: Sixties People." In *The Age of Affluence. See* Bogdanor and Skildelsky 1970.

Bishop, Kathy. 1988. "Pop Provocateur: Malcolm McLaren Tackles Broadway." *Elle,* Oct., 140–42.

Bogdanor, Vernon, and Robert Skildelsky, eds. 1970. *The Age of Affluence, 1951–64.* London: Macmillan.

Bold, Alan. 1976. *Thom Gunn and Ted Hughes.* New York: Barnes & Noble.

Bond, Edward. 1977. *Plays.* Vol. 1. London: Methuen.

Bourdieu, Pierre. 1984. *Distinction: A Social Critique of the Judgment of Taste.* Trans. Richard Nice. Cambridge: Harvard University Press.

———. 1991. *Language and Symbolic Power.* Trans. Gino Raymond and Matthew Adamson. Cambridge: Harvard University Press.

Brake, Mike. 1980. *The Sociology of Youth Culture and Subcultures: Sex and Drugs and Rock and Roll?* London: Routledge & Kegan Paul.

Brantlinger, Patrick. 1983. *Bread & Circuses: Theories of Mass Culture as Social Decay.* Ithaca: Cornell University Press.

———. 1990. *Crusoe's Footprints: Cultural Studies in Britain and America.* New York: Routledge.

Brecht, Bertolt. 1964. *Brecht on Theatre: The Development of an Aesthetic.* Ed. and trans. John Willett. New York: Hill and Wang.

Breton, André. 1969. "Political Position of Today's Art." *Manifestoes of Surrealism.* Trans. Helen R. Lane and Richard Seaver. Ann Arbor: University of Michigan Press.

———. 1978. "Manifesto for an Independent Revolutionary Art." In *What Is Surrealism?: Selected Writings,* ed. Franklin Rosemont. New York: Monad.

Bromberg, Craig. 1989. *The Wicked Ways of Malcolm McLaren.* New York: Harper & Row.

Browne, Nick. 1987. "The Political Economy of the Television (Super) Text." In *Television: The Critical View,* ed. Horace Newcomb. New York: Oxford University Press.

Budd, Mike, et al. 1990. "The Affirmative Character of U.S. Cultural Studies." *Critical Studies in Mass Communication* 7:169–84.

Buhle, Paul. 1990. "America: Post-Modernity?" *New Left Review* 180:163–75.

Burchill, Julie, and Tony Parsons. 1978. *The Boy Looked at Johnny.* London: Pluto Press.

Bürger, Peter. 1984. *Theory of the Avant-Garde.* Trans. Michael Shaw. Minneapolis: University of Minnesota Press.

Burgess, Anthony. 1986. "Introduction: A Clockwork Orange Resucked." *A Clockwork Orange.* New York: W. W. Norton.

———. 1978. *1985.* Boston: Little, Brown.

———. 1970. *The Novel Now.* New York: Pegasus.

Burke, Kenneth. 1966. *Language as Symbolic Action*. Berkeley and Los Angeles: University of California Press.

Buttigieg, Joseph A. 1987. *A Portrait of the Artist in Different Perspective*. Athens: Ohio University Press.

Calinescu, Matei. 1987. *Five Faces of Modernity*. Durham: Duke University Press.

Callinicos, Alex. 1989. *Against Postmodernism: A Marxist Critique*. Oxford: Polity.

"The Call-Up." 1987. *Rock & Roll Confidential* 49:1–2.

"The Campus Entrepreneurs." 1967. *Newsweek*, 25 Sept., 88–90.

Carr, C. 1988. "Never Mind the Bollocks, Here's the Impresario." *Village Voice*, 27 Sept., 40.

———. 1990a. "The Situationist Situation: What We Talk About When We Talk About the Avant-Garde." *Voice Literary Supplement*, April, 18–19.

———. 1990b. "The War on Art." *Village Voice*, 5 June, 25–30.

Carson, Tom. 1988. "What We Do Is Secret: Your Guide to the Post-Whatever." *Village Voice Rock & Roll Quarterly*, Fall, 21–26.

———. 1990. "Rocket to Russia." In *On Record: Rock, Pop, and the Written Word*, ed. Simon Frith and Andrew Goodwin. New York: Pantheon.

Carter, Sandy. 1991. "Rock and War." *Zeta Magazine*, May, 89–92.

Cashmore, E. Ellis. 1984. *No Future: Youth and Society*. London: Heinemann.

Caute, David. 1988. *The Year of the Barricades: A Journey Through 1968*. New York: Harper & Row.

Chambers, Iain. 1985. *Urban Rhythms: Pop Music and Popular Culture*. New York: St. Martin's.

———. 1986. *Popular Culture: The Metropolitan Experience*. New York: Methuen.

———. 1987. "British Pop: Some Tracks from the Other Side of the Record." In *Popular Music and Communication*, ed. James Lull. Newbury Park, Cal.: Sage.

———. 1988. "Contamination, Coincidence, and Collusion: Pop Music, Urban Culture, and the Avant-Garde." In *Marxism and the Interpretation of Culture*. *See* Anderson 1988.

Chomsky, Noam. 1987. *The Chomsky Reader*. Ed. James Peck. New York: Pantheon.

———. 1989. "The Tasks Ahead III: Problems of Population Control." *Zeta Magazine*, Nov., 11–18.

Christgau, Robert. 1991a. "Curse of the Mekons." *Village Voice*, 21 May, 75, 78.

———. 1991b. "Madonnathinking Madonnabout Madonnamusic." *Village Voice*, 28 May, 31, 33.

Chua, Lawrence. 1988. "Malcolm McLaren: Master of Manipulation." *W*, 5–12 Sept., 20.

Clark, T.J. 1982. *The Absolute Bourgeois: Artists and Politics in France 1848–1851*. Princeton: Princeton University Press.

———. 1984. *The Painting of Modern Life: Paris in the Art of Manet and His Followers.* Princeton: Princeton University Press.

Clarke, Gary. 1990. "Defending Ski-Jumpers: A Critique of Theories of Youth Subcultures." In *On Record. See* Carson 1990.

Clarke, John. 1976. "Working Class Youth Cultures." In *Working Class Youth Culture,* ed. Geoff Mungham and Geoff Pearson. London: Routledge & Kegan Paul.

Cockburn, Alexander. 1986. "Beat the Devil." *Nation,* 29 March, 446–47.

———. 1987. *Corruptions of Empire: Life Studies and the Reagan Era.* New York: Verso.

———. 1989a. "Beat the Devil." *Nation,* 24/31 July, 113–14.

———. 1989b. "Beat the Devil." *Nation,* 21/28 August, 194–95.

Cohen, Phil. 1980. "Subcultural Conflict and Working Class Community." In *Culture, Media, Language. See* Hall 1980.

Cohen, Stanley. 1972. *Folk Devils and Moral Panics: The Creation of the Mods and Rockers.* London: MacGibbon and Kee.

Cohen, Stanley, and Paul Rock. 1970. "The Teddy Boy." In *The Age of Affluence. See* Bogdanor and Skildelsky 1970.

Cohn, Nik. 1970. *Rock from the Beginning.* New York: Pocket Books.

———. 1975. *The Rolling Stones.* New York: Circus.

———. 1988. "Delinquent in Derry." *Granta* 25:169–78.

Collins, Jim. 1989. *Uncommon Cultures: Popular Culture and Post-Modernism.* New York: Routledge.

Consolo, Dominick P. 1962. "Music as Motif: The Unity of *Brighton Rock.*" *Renascence* 15:12–20.

Coon, Caroline. 1978. *1988: The New Wave Punk Rock Explosion.* New York: Hawthorn.

Cooper, D. E. 1970. "Looking Back on Anger." In *The Age of Affluence. See* Bogdanor and Skildelsky 1970.

Cunningham, Valentine. 1988. *British Writers of the Thirties.* New York: Oxford University Press.

Davis, Mike. 1986. *Prisoners of the American Dream.* London: Verso.

Debord, Guy. 1981a. "Detournement as Negation and Prelude." In *Situationist International Anthology. See* Knabb 1981.

———. 1981b. "Methods of Detournement." In *Situationist International Anthology. See* Knabb 1981.

———. 1981c. "Preliminaries Toward Defining a Unitary Revolutionary Program." In *Situationist International Anthology. See* Knabb 1981.

———. 1981d. "Report on the Construction of Situations and on the International Situationist Tendency's Conditions of Organization and Action." In *Situationist International Anthology. See* Knabb 1981.

———. 1983. *Society of the Spectacle.* Detroit: Black & Red.

———. 1991. *Comments on the* Society of the Spectacle. Trans. Malcolm Imrie. New York: Verso.

Debord, Guy, et al. 1981. "Theses on the Paris Commune." In *Situationist International Anthology. See* Knabb 1981.

de Certeau, Michel. 1984. *The Practice of Everyday Life*. Trans. Steven Rendall. Berkeley and Los Angeles: University of California Press.

Deitcher, David. 1990. "A Fine Disregard: 'High and Low' Keeps the Faith at the Modern." *Village Voice*, 16 Oct., 99–100.

de Lauretis, Teresa. 1987. *Technologies of Gender*. Bloomington: Indiana University Press.

Deleuze, Gilles, and Félix Guattari. 1983. *The Anti-Oedipus*. Trans. Robert Hurley, Mark Seem, and Helen R. Lane. Minneapolis: University of Minnesota Press.

DeMott, Benjamin. 1990. *The Imperial Middle: Why Americans Can't Think Straight About Class*. New York: Morrow.

Dews, Peter. 1984. "Power and Subjectivity in Foucault." *New Left Review* 144:72–95.

Doctorow, E. L. 1986. "The State of Mind of the Union." *Nation*, 22 March, 327–32.

Eagleton, Terry. 1976. *Criticism & Ideology*. London: New Left Books.

———. 1981. *Walter Benjamin or Towards a Revolutionary Literary Criticism*. London: New Left Books.

———. 1983. *Literary Theory: An Introduction*. Minneapolis: University of Minnesota Press.

———. 1986. "Capitalism, Modernism and Postmodernism." *Against the Grain*. London: Verso.

———. 1988. Foreword. In *The Emergence of Social Space*. See K. Ross 1988.

———. 1989. "Rotten, Vicious and Surrealist." *New York Times Book Review*, 9 April, 12.

———. 1990. *The Ideology of the Aesthetic*. Cambridge, Mass.: Basil Blackwell.

Eastman, Max. 1955. *Reflections on the Failure of Socialism*. New York: Devin-Adair.

Ehrlich, Cindy, ed. 1975. *The Rolling Stones*. New York: Straight Arrow.

Ehrlich, Howard, et al., eds. 1979. *Reinventing Anarchy*. London: Routledge & Kegan Paul.

Ewen, Stuart. 1976. *Captains of Consciousness: Advertising and the Social Roots of the Consumer Culture*. New York: McGraw-Hill.

———. 1988. *All Consuming Images*. New York: Basic Books.

Ewen, Stuart and Elizabeth Ewen. 1982. *Channels of Desire: Mass Images and the Shaping of American Consciousness*. New York: McGraw-Hill.

Eysteinsson, Astradur. 1990. *The Concept of Modernism*. Ithaca: Cornell University Press.

Fairness and Accuracy in Reporting. 1991. *Extra! The Gulf War Special Issue*. May.

Felski, Rita. 1989. *Beyond Feminist Aesthetics: Feminist Literature and Social Change*. Cambridge: Harvard University Press.

Fischer, Ernst. 1986. *The Necessity of Art*. Trans. Anna Bostock. New York: Penguin.

Fiske, John. 1987. "British Cultural Studies and Television." In *Channels of*

Discourse, ed. Robert C. Allen. Chapel Hill: University of North Carolina Press.

———. 1989. *Understanding Popular Culture.* Boston: Unwin Hyman.

———. 1992. "Cultural Studies and the Culture of Everyday Life." In *Cultural Studies,* ed. Lawrence Grossberg, Cary Nelson, and Paula A. Treichler. New York: Routledge.

Fletcher, Angus. 1964. *Allegory: The Theory of a Symbolic Mode.* Ithaca: Cornell University Press.

Foucault, Michel. 1979. *Discipline and Punish: The Birth of the Prison.* Trans. Alan Sheridan. New York: Vintage Books.

———. 1983. Preface. In *The Anti-Oedipus. See* Deleuze and Guattari 1983.

France, Kim. 1992. "Angry Young Women." *Utne Reader,* September/October, 24–26.

Freire, Paulo and Henry A. Giroux. 1989. "Pedagogy, Popular Culture, and Public Life: An Introduction." In *Popular Culture: Schooling and Everyday Life. See* Giroux and Simon 1989.

Frith, Simon. 1978. "The Punk Bohemians." *New Society,* 9 March, 535–36.

———. 1980. "Music for Pleasure." *Screen Education* 34:51–61.

———. 1981. *Sound Effects: Youth, Leisure, and the Politics of Rock'n'Roll.* New York: Pantheon.

———. 1987a. "The Industrialization of Popular Music." In *Popular Music and Communication. See* Chambers 1987.

———. 1987b. "Roll Over Beethoven." *Nation,* 28 March, 405–7.

———. 1987c. "We Win Again." *Village Voice,* 29 Dec., 83.

———. 1988a. "The Adman's Loop." *Village Voice,* 17 May, 79.

———. 1988b. *Music for Pleasure.* New York: Routledge.

———. 1988c. "Video Pop: Picking Up the Pieces." In *Facing the Music,* ed. Simon Frith. New York: Pantheon.

Frith, Simon, and Howard Horne. 1987. *Art into Pop.* New York: Methuen.

Frith, Simon, and Angela McRobbie. 1990. "Rock and Sexuality." In *On Record. See* Carson 1990.

Fussell, Paul. 1975. *The Great War and Modern Memory.* New York: Oxford University Press.

Garber, Jenny, and Angela McRobbie. 1976. "Girls and Subcultures." In *Resistance through Rituals. See* Hall and Jefferson 1976.

Garlitz, Barbara. 1966. "The Immortality Ode: Its Cultural Progeny." *Studies in English Literature* 6:639–49.

Garofalo, Reebee, ed. 1992. *Rockin' the Boat: Mass Music and Mass Movements.* Boston: South End.

Gendron, Bernard. 1986. "Theodor Adorno Meets the Cadillacs." In *Studies in Entertainment: Critical Approaches to Mass Culture,* ed. Tania Modleski. Bloomington: Indiana University Press.

Geras, Norman. 1987. "Post-Marxism?" *New Left Review* 163:40–82.

Giardina, Denise. 1989. "Solidarity in Appalachia." *Nation,* 3 July, 12–14.

Gilroy, Paul. 1991. *'There Ain't No Black in the Union Jack': The Cultural Politics of Race and Nation.* Chicago: University of Chicago Press.

Gindin, James J. 1962. *Postwar British Fiction*. Berkeley and Los Angeles: University of California Press.

Giroux, Henry A. 1988. *Schooling and the Struggle for Public Life: Critical Pedagogy in the Modern Age*. Minneapolis: University of Minnesota Press.

Giroux, Henry, et al. 1984. "The Need for Cultural Studies: Resisting Intellectuals and Oppositional Public Spheres." *Dalhousie Review* 64:472–86.

Giroux, Henry A., and Roger I. Simon. 1989. "Popular Culture as a Pedagogy of Pleasure and Meaning." In *Popular Culture: Schooling and Everyday Life,* ed. Henry A. Giroux and Roger I. Simon. Granby, Mass.: Bergin and Garvey.

Gitlin, Todd. 1982. "Prime Time Ideology." In *Television: The Critical View,* ed. Horace Newcomb. New York: Oxford University Press.

———. 1989. "Postmodernism Defined, At Last!" *Utne Reader,* July/August, 52–61.

Gosling, Ray. 1980. *Personal Copy: A Memoir of the Sixties*. London: Faber and Faber.

Gould, Tony. 1983. *Inside Outsider: The Life and Times of Colin MacInnes*. London: Verso.

Gramsci, Antonio. 1971. *Selections from the Prison Notebooks*. Ed. and trans. Quintin Hoare and Geoffrey Nowell Smith. New York: International.

———. 1988. *An Antonio Gramsci Reader: Selected Writings, 1916–1935*. Ed. David Forgacs. New York: Schocken.

Graña, César. 1964. *Bohemian Versus Bourgeois: French Society and the French Man of Letters in the Nineteenth Century*. New York: Basic Books.

Gray, Christopher. 1974. "The Construction of Situations: An Introduction." In *Leaving the 20th Century: The Incomplete Work of the Situationist International,* ed. and trans. Christopher Gray. London: Free Fall.

Greene, Graham. 1971. *A Sort of Life*. New York: Simon and Schuster.

———. 1980. *Ways of Escape*. New York: Simon and Schuster.

Gresham, Jewell Handy. 1989. "The Politics of Family in America." *Nation,* 24/31 July, 116–22.

Gripsrud, Jostein. 1989. "'High Culture' Revisited." *Cultural Studies* 3:194–207.

Grossberg, Lawrence. 1983. "Cultural Studies Revisited and Revised." In *Communications in Transition: Issues and Debates in Current Research,* ed. Mary S. Mander. New York: Praeger.

———. 1986. "Is There Rock after Punk?" and "Reply to the Critics." *Critical Studies in Mass Communication* 3:50–74, 86–95.

———. 1988. "Putting the Pop Back in Postmodernism." In *Universal Abandon? See* A. Ross 1988.

———. 1989a. "The Circulation of Cultural Studies." *Critical Studies in Mass Communication* 6:413–21.

———. 1989b. "Pedagogy in the Present: Politics, Postmodernity, and the Popular." In *Popular Culture: Schooling and Everyday Life. See* Giroux and Simon 1989.

Guérin. Daniel. 1970. *Anarchism: From Theory to Practice.* Trans. Mary Klopper. New York: Monthly Review.

Gurevitch, Michael, et al. 1982. *Culture, Society and the Media.* New York: Methuen.

Habermas, Jürgen. 1975. *Legitimation Crisis.* Trans. Thomas McCarthy. Boston: Beacon.

———. 1979. *Communication and the Evolution of Society.* Trans. Thomas McCarthy. Boston: Beacon.

———. 1983. "Modernity—An Incomplete Project." In *The Anti-Aesthetic: Essays on Postmodern Culture,* ed. Hal Foster. Port Townsend, Wash.: Bay.

Hall, Stuart. 1980. Introduction. *Culture, Media, Language: Working Papers in Cultural Studies, 1972–79.* Ed. Stuart Hall et al. London: Hutchinson.

———. 1981. "Cultural studies: Two Paradigms." In *Culture, Ideology, and Social Process,* ed. Tony Bennett et al. London: Open University Press.

———. 1982. "The Rediscovery of 'Ideology': Return of the Repressed in Media Studies." See Gurevitch et al. 1992.

———. 1986a. "On Postmodernism and Articulation: An Interview with Stuart Hall." *Journal of Communication Inquiry* 10:45–60.

———. 1986b. "The Problem of Ideology—Marxism without Guarantees." *Journal of Communication Inquiry* 10:28–44.

———. 1988. *The Hard Road to Renewal: Thatcherism and the Crisis of the Left.* New York: Verso.

———. 1990. "The Emergence of Cultural Studies and the Crisis of the Humanities." *October* 53:11–23.

———. 1992. "Cultural Studies and Its Theoretical Legacies." In *Cultural Studies. See* Fiske 1992.

Hall, Stuart, and Martin Jacques, eds. 1983. *The Politics of Thatcherism.* London: Lawrence and Wishart.

Hall, Stuart, and Tony Jefferson, eds. 1976. *Resistance through Rituals: Youth Subcultures in Post-war Britain.* London: Hutchinson.

Hall, Stuart, and Paddy Whannel. 1965. *The Popular Arts.* New York: Pantheon.

Hall, Stuart, et al. 1978. *Policing the Crisis: Mugging, the State, and Law and Order.* New York: Macmillan.

Hallin, Daniel C. 1986. "We Keep America on Top of the World." In *Watching Television,* ed. Todd Gitlin. New York: Pantheon.

Haraway, Donna. 1989. "A Manifesto for Cyborgs: Science, Technology, and Socialist Feminism in the 1980s." In *Coming to Terms: Feminism, Theory, Politics,* ed. Elizabeth Weed. New York: Routledge.

Harris, Daniel. 1992. "Make My Rainy Day." *Nation,* 8 June, 790–93.

Harron, Mary. 1988. "Pop as a Commodity." In *Facing the Music. See* Frith 1988c.

Harvey, David. 1989. *The Condition of Postmodernity: An Enquiry into the Origins of Cultural Change.* Cambridge, Mass.: Basil Blackwell.

Hebdige, Dick. 1976. "The Meaning of Mod." In *Resistance through Rituals. See* Hall and Jefferson 1976.

———. 1979. *Subculture: The Meaning of Style*. London: Methuen.

———. 1987. "The Impossible Object: Towards a Sociology of the Sublime." *New Formations* 1:47–76.

———. 1988. *Hiding in the Light: On Images and Things*. New York: Routledge.

Heller, Scott. 1990. "Cultural Studies: Eclectic and Controversial Mix of Research Sparks a Growing Movement." *Chronicle of Higher Education*, 31 Jan., A4+.

Herman, Edward S., and Noam Chomsky. 1988. *Manufacturing Consent: The Political Economy of the Mass Media*. New York: Pantheon.

Hewison, Robert. 1981. *In Anger: British Culture in the Cold War 1945–60*. New York: Oxford University Press.

———. 1987. *Too Much: Art and Society in the Sixties 1960–75*. New York: Oxford University Press.

Hill, John. 1986. *Sex, Class and Realism: British Cinema 1956–1963*. London: BFI.

Hitchcock, Peter. 1989. *Working-Class Fiction in Theory and Practice: A Reading of Alan Sillitoe*. Ann Arbor: UMI.

Hitchens, Christopher. 1989. "Minority Report." *Nation*, 25 Sept., 302.

———. 1990. "Minority Report." *Nation*, 24 Dec., 794.

Hoare, Philip. 1991. "Anarchy in the U.K.? Forget It." *The Independent*, 28 May, 14.

Hoffman, Abbie. 1987. "Closing Argument in Trial of CIA Protestors." *Nation*, 2 May, 562–63.

Hoggart, Richard. 1961. *The Uses of Literacy: Changing Patterns in English Mass Culture*. Boston: Beacon.

Horkheimer, Max, and Theodor Adorno. 1987. "The Culture Industry: Enlightenment as Mass Deception." In *Dialectic of Enlightenment*. 1944. Trans. John Cumming. New York: Continuum.

Huelsenbeck, Richard. 1989. "En Avant Dada: A History of Dadaism." In *The Dada Painters and Poets: An Anthology*, ed. Richard Motherwell. Cambridge: Harvard University Press.

Humphries, Stephen. 1981. *Hooligans or Rebels?: An Oral History of Working-Class Childhood and Youth 1889–1939*. London: Blackwell.

Hunter, Ian. 1988. "Setting Limits to Culture." *New Formations* 4:103–23.

———. 1992. "Aesthetics and Cultural Studies." In *Cultural Studies. See* Fiske 1992.

Hutcheon, Linda. 1989a. "Modern Parody and Bakhtin." In *Rethinking Bakhtin. See* Bernstein 1989.

———. 1989b. *The Politics of Postmodernism*. New York: Routledge.

Huyssen, Andreas. 1986. *After the Great Divide*. Bloomington: Indiana University Press.

Hynes, Samuel. 1977. *The Auden Generation: Literature and Politics in England in the 1930s*. New York: Viking.

Indiana, Gary. 1991. "Victory Lite: Notes on the Postwar Culture of Resentment." *Village Voice*, 11 June, 28–35.

Ireland, Doug. 1989. "Press Clips." *Village Voice,* 15 August, 8.

Irving, Katrina. 1988. "Rock Music and the State: Dissonance or Counterpoint?" *Cultural Critique* 10:151–70.

Isler, Scott. 1983. "Malcolm McLaren: From the Eye of the Storm." *Trouser Press,* May, 20–25, 55.

Jaggar, Alison M. 1989. "Love and Knowledge: Emotion in Feminist Epistemology." In *Gender/Body/Knowledge: Feminist Reconstructions of Being and Knowing,* ed. Alison M. Jaggar and Susan R. Bordo. New Brunswick, N.J.: Rutgers University Press.

James, David E. 1988. "Poetry/Punk/Production: Some Recent Writing in L.A." In *Postmodernism and Its Discontents. See* Kaplan 1988.

Jameson, Fredric. 1977. "Reflections in Conclusion." In *Aesthetics and Politics,* ed. Ronald Taylor. London: New Left Books.

———. 1979. "Reification and Utopia in Mass Culture." *Social Text* 1:130–48.

———. 1984. "Postmodernism, or The Cultural Logic of Late Capitalism." *New Left Review* 146:53–92.

———. 1987. "Reading without Interpretation: Postmodernism and the Videotext." In *The Linguistics of Writing: Arguments between Language and Literature,* ed. Nigel Fabb et al. Manchester: Manchester University Press.

Jauss, Hans Robert. 1988/89. "The Literary Process of Modernism From Rousseau to Adorno." *Cultural Critique* 11:27–61.

Jay, Martin. 1973. *The Dialectical Imagination: A History of the Frankfurt School and the Institute of Social Research 1923–1950.* Boston: Little, Brown.

Jefferson, Tony. 1976. "Cultural Responses of the Teds: The Defence of Space." In *Resistance through Rituals. See* Hall and Jefferson 1976.

Jessop, Bob, et al. 1985. "Thatcherism and the Politics of Hegemony: A Reply to Stuart Hall." *New Left Review* 153:87–101.

Johnson, Pauline. 1987. "From Virginia Woolf to the Post-Moderns: Developments in a Feminist Aesthetic." *Radical Philosophy* 45:23–30.

Johnson, Richard. 1986/87. "What Is Cultural Studies Anyway?" *Social Text* 16:38–80.

———. 1991. "Frameworks of Culture and Power: Complexity and Politics in Cultural Studies." *Critical Studies* 3:17–61.

Kaplan, E. Ann. 1987. "Feminist Criticism and Television." In *Channels of Discourse. See* Fiske 1987.

———, ed. 1988. *Postmodernism and Its Discontents: Theories, Practices.* New York: Verso.

Kellner, Douglas. 1982. "TV, Ideology, and Emancipatory Popular Culture." In *Television: The Critical View. See* Gitlin 1982.

Kemper, Vicki and Deborah Baldwin. 1991. "War Stories." *Common Cause Magazine,* March/April, 18–23.

Khayati, Mustapha. 1981. "Captive Words: Preface to a Situationist Dictionary." In *Situationist International Anthology. See* Knabb 1981.

Kipnis, Laura. 1986. "'Refunctioning' Reconsidered: Towards a Left Popular Culture." In *High Theory/Low Culture. See* MacCabe 1986.

———. 1988. "Feminism: The Political Conscience of Postmodernism?" In *Universal Abandon? See* A. Ross 1988.

Knabb, Ken, ed. and trans. 1981. *Situationist International Anthology*. Berkeley: Bureau of Public Secrets.

Kovel, Joel. 1988. "The Victims of Anticommunism," *Zeta Magazine*, Jan., 84–89.

Kozol, Jonathan. 1975. *The Night Is Dark and I Am Far From Home*. New York: Continuum.

Kropotkin, Peter. 1971. "The Conquest of Bread." In *The Essential Works of Anarchism. See* Bakunin 1971.

Lachemann, Renate. 1988/89. "Bakhtin and Carnival: Culture as Counter-Culture." *Cultural Critique* 11:115–52.

Laclau, Ernesto. 1977. *Politics and Ideology in Marxist Theory*. London: New Left Books.

Laing, Dave. 1978. "Interpreting Punk Rock." *Marxism Today*, April, 123–28.

———. 1983. *One Chord Wonders*. London: Open University Press.

Laing, Stuart. 1986. *Representations of Working-Class Life 1957–64*. London: Macmillan.

Lang, Curtis J. 1990. "The Hole in America's Stocking." *Village Voice*, 25 Dec., 38–48, 179.

Larsen, Elizabeth. 1991. "Watching between the Lines." *Utne Reader*, May/June, 26–28.

Larsen, Neil. 1990. *Modernism and Hegemony: A Materialist Critique of Aesthetic Agencies*. Minneapolis: University of Minnesota Press.

Lazere, Donald. 1987. "Conservative Media Criticism: Heads I Win, Tails You Lose." In *American Media and Mass Culture: Left Perspectives*, ed. Donald Lazere. Berkeley and Los Angeles: University of California Press.

Leavis, F. R. 1933. "Mass Civilization and Minority Culture." *For Continuity*. Cambridge: The Minority Press.

Lee, Martin A., and Norman Solomon. 1990. *Unreliable Sources: A Guide to Detecting Bias in News Media*. New York: Lyle Stuart.

Leighten, Patricia. 1989. *Re-Ordering the Universe: Picasso and Anarchism 1897–1914*. Princeton: Princeton University Press.

Leland, John. 1991. "Welcome to the Jungle." *Newsweek*, 23 Sept., 53–54.

LeMoyne, James. 1981. "Oi—Music to Riot By." *Newsweek*, 31 Aug., 35.

Lesage, Julia. 1988. "Women's Rage." In *Marxism and the Interpretation of Culture. See* Anderson 1988.

Lessing, Doris. 1958. "The Small Personal Voice." In *Declaration. See* Maschler 1958.

Levy, Ellen. 1986. "The Packaging of America." *Dissent*, Fall, 441–46.

Lewis, Lisa. 1990. *Gender Politics and MTV: Voicing the Difference*. Philadelphia: Temple University Press.

Lipsitz, George. 1990. *Time Passages: Collective Memory and American Popular Culture*. Minneapolis: University of Minnesota Press.

Little, Hilary, and Gina Rumsey. 1989. "Women and Pop: A Series of Lost Encounters." In *Zoot Suits and Second-Hand Dresses. See* McRobbie 1989.

Lloyd, David. 1990. "Analogies of the Aesthetic: The Politics of Culture and the Limits of Materialist Aesthetics." *New Formations* 10:109–26.

Loeb, Paul. 1990. "Most Students Today Are Individualists, Not Activists." *Utne Reader,* May/June, 56–62.

Long, Elizabeth. 1989. "Feminism and Cultural Studies." *Critical Studies in Mass Communication* 6:427–35.

Lovell, Terry. 1980. *Pictures of Reality: Aesthetics, Politics and Pleasure.* London: BFI.

Löwy, Michael. 1985. "Revolution Against 'Progress': Walter Benjamin's Romantic Anarchism." *New Left Review* 152:42–59.

Lukács, Georg. 1964. "The Ideology of Modernism." *Realism in Our Time.* Trans. John and Necke Mander. New York: Harper & Row.

———. 1971. "Reification and the Consciousness of the Proletariat." *History and Class Consciousness.* Trans. Rodney Livingstone. Cambridge: MIT Press.

Lunn, Eugene. 1982. *Marxism and Modernism: An Historical Study of Lukács, Brecht, Benjamin, and Adorno.* Berkeley and Los Angeles: University of California Press.

Maayan, Myriam D. 1989. "From Aesthetic to Political Vanguard." *Arts Magazine,* Jan., 49–53.

MacArthur, John R. 1991. "Last Word from Graham Greene." *Progressive,* June, 25–28.

MacCabe, Colin. 1978. *James Joyce and the Revolution of the Word.* London: Macmillan.

———. 1986. "Defining Popular Culture." In *High Theory/Low Culture: Analysing Popular Television and Film,* ed. Colin MacCabe. New York: St. Martin's.

———. 1987. "Opening Statement: Theory and Practice." In *The Linguistics of Writing.* See Jameson 1987.

McCarthy, Thomas. 1978. *The Critical Theory of Jürgen Habermas.* Cambridge: MIT Press.

McClary, Susan. 1985. "Afterword: The Politics of Silence and Sound." In *Noise. See* Attali 1985.

———. 1991. *Feminine Endings: Music, Gender, and Sexuality.* Minneapolis: University of Minnesota Press.

McDonnell, Evelyn, and Ben Mapp. 1991. "Rockbeat." *Village Voice,* 4 June, 57.

McGrath, F. C. 1986. *The Sensitive Spirit: Walter Pater and the Modernist Paradigm.* Tampa: University of South Florida Press.

MacInnes, Colin. 1961. *England, Half English.* New York: Random House.

McRobbie, Angela. 1980. "Settling Accounts with Subcultures: A Feminist Critique." *Screen Education* 34:37–49.

———. 1986. "Postmodernism and Popular Culture." *Journal of Communication Inquiry* 10:108–116.

———, ed. 1989. *Zoot-Suits and Second-Hand Dresses: An Anthology of Fashion and Music.* Boston: Unwin Hyman.

———. 1991a. "Moving Cultural Studies On: Post-Marxism and Beyond." *Magazine of Cultural Studies* 4:18–21.

———. 1991b. "New Times in Cultural Studies." *New Formations* 13:1–17.

———. 1992. "The *Passagenwerk* and the Place of Walter Benjamin in Cultural Studies: Benjamin, Cultural Studies, Marxist Theories of Art." *Cultural Studies* 6:147–69.

McRobbie, Angela, and Jenny Garber. 1976. "Girls and Subcultures: An Exploration." In *Resistance through Rituals. See* Hall and Jefferson 1976.

Malcomson, Scott L. 1989. "Aux armes, historiens!" *Village Voice,* 18 July, 58–60.

Marcus, Greil, ed. 1969. *Rock and Roll Will Stand.* Boston: Beacon.

———. 1982. "The Long Walk of the Situationist International." *Voice Literary Supplement,* May, 13–19.

———. 1986. "Critical Response." *Critical Studies in Mass Communication* 3:77–81.

———. 1989. *Lipstick Traces: A Secret History of the Twentieth Century.* Cambridge: Harvard University Press.

———. 1990. "Corrupting the Absolute." In *On Record: Rock, Pop, and the Written Word. See* Frith and McRobbie 1990.

Marcuse, Herbert. 1964. *One-Dimensional Man: Studies in the Ideology of Advanced Industrial Society.* Boston: Beacon.

Marsh, Dave. 1987. [untitled]. *Nation,* 27 December/3 January, 747.

Marsh, Dave and Phyllis Pollack. 1989. "Wanted for Attitude: The Right-Wing Attack on Rock." *Village Voice,* 10 Oct., 33–37.

Marx, Karl. 1964. *The Economic & Philosophic Manuscripts of 1844.* Trans. Martin Milligan. New York: International.

———. 1977. *Capital.* Vol. 1. Trans. Ben Fowkes. New York: Vintage.

Maschler, Tom, ed. 1958. *Declaration.* New York: E. P. Dutton.

Meisel, Perry. 1980. *The Absent Father: Virginia Woolf and Walter Pater.* New Haven: Yale University Press.

———. 1987. *The Myth of the Modern: A Study in British Literature and Criticism after 1850.* New Haven: Yale University Press.

Melly, George. 1970. *Revolt into Style.* London: Penguin.

Melman, Seymour. 1991. "Military State Capitalism." *Nation,* 20 May, 649, 664–68.

Mercer, Colin. 1986. "Complicit Pleasures." In *Popular Culture and Social Relations. See* Bennett 1986.

———. 1991. "Neverending Stories: The Problem of Reading in Cultural Studies." *New Formations* 13:63–74.

Middleton, Peter. 1990. "Vanishing Affects: The Disappearance of Emotion from Postmodernist Theory and Practice." *New Formations* 12:125–42

Middleton, Richard. 1981. "'Reading' Popular Music." In *Popular Culture: Form and Meaning (2).* Milton Keynes: Open University Press.

———. 1986. "In the Groove, or Blowing Your Mind? The Pleasures of Musical Repetition." In *Popular Culture and Social Relations. See* Bennett 1986.

Miliband, Ralph. 1984. *Class Power and State Power.* New York: Schocken.

Miller, Mark Crispin. 1986. "Prime Time: Deride and Conquer." In *Watching Television*. *See* Hallin 1986.

———. 1990. "Hollywood: The Ad." *Atlantic Monthly*, April, 41–68.

"The Missing Bodies." 1991. *Lies of Our Times*, June, 17.

Modleski, Tania. 1986. "Femininity as Mas(s)querade: A Feminist Approach to Mass Culture." In *High Theory/Low Culture*. *See* MacCabe 1986.

Moi, Toril. 1985. *Sexual/Textual Politics: Feminist Literary Theory*. New York: Methuen.

Moretti, Franco. 1983. *Signs Taken for Wonders: Essays in the Sociology of Literary Forms*. London: New Left Books.

Morris, Meaghan. 1988. "Banality in Cultural Studies." *Discourse: Journal for Theoretical Studies in Media and Culture* 10:3–29.

Morris, William. 1984. "Popular Art." *News from Nowhere and Selected Writings and Designs*. Ed. Asa Briggs. New York: Penguin.

Morrison, Blake. 1980. *The Movement: English Poetry and Fiction of the 1950s*. New York: Methuen.

Mowitt, John. 1987. "Music in the Era of Electronic Reproducibility." In *Music and Society*, ed. Richard Leppert and Susan McClary. New York: Cambridge University Press.

Muncie, John. 1982. "Pop Culture, Pop Music and Post-war Youth: Subcultures." In *Popular Culture: Politics, Ideology and Popular Culture (1)*. Milton Keynes: Open University Press.

Murdock, Graham. 1989. "Cultural Studies: Missing Links." *Critical Studies in Mass Communication* 6:436–40.

Murdock, Graham, and Robin McCron. 1976. "Youth and Class: The Career of a Confusion." In *Working Class Youth Culture*. *See* Clarke 1976.

Nadeau, Maurice. 1965. *The History of Surrealism*. Trans. Richard Howard. New York: Macmillan.

Nathan, Debbie. 1990. "The Ritual Sex Abuse Hoax: What McMartin Started." *Village Voice*, 12 June, 36–44.

Nelson, Cary. 1989. *Repression and Recovery: Modern American Poetry and the Politics of Cultural Memory*. Madison: University of Wisconsin Press.

Newman, Michael. 1989. "Revising Modernism, Representing Postmodernism: Critical Discourses of the Visual Arts." In *Postmodernism: ICA Documents*, ed. Lisa Appignanesi. London: Free Association.

Nixon, Rob. 1989. "Culture Heroes: Williams and Hall for the Opposition." *Voice Literary Supplement*, Oct., 15–17.

O'Flinn, Paul. 1975. *Them and Us in Literature*. London: Pluto.

Oldham, Andrew Loog. 1965. Liner Notes. *The Rolling Stones Now!* London PS 420.

Osborne, John. 1958. "They Call It Cricket." In *Declaration*. *See* Maschler 1958.

Pareles, Jon. 1991. "Now Is the Summer of Discontent." *New York Times*, 25 Aug., 20–22.

Parenti, Michael. 1986. *Inventing Reality*. New York: St. Martin's.

Pattison, Robert. 1987. *The Triumph of Vulgarity: Rock Music in the Mirror of Romanticism*. New York: Oxford University Press.

Pearson, Geoffrey. 1984. *Hooligan: A History of Respectable Fears.* New York: Schocken.

Pindell, Howardena. 1990. "Colonial Culture." *Lies of Our Times,* Dec., 4–5.

Pinkney, Tony. 1988. "Understanding Modernism: A Response to Franco Moretti." *New Left Review* 167:124–27.

———. 1989. "Editor's Introduction: Modernism and Cultural Theory." In *The Politics of Modernism. See* Williams 1989.

Plant, Sadie. 1992. *The Most Radical Gesture: The Situationist International in a Postmodern Age.* New York: Routledge.

Platt, John. 1985. *London's Rock Routes.* London: Fourth Estate.

Polan, Dana. 1986. "Brief Encounters: Mass Culture and the Evacuation of Sense." In *Studies in Entertainment. See* Gendron 1986.

———. 1987. "Bertolt Brecht and Daffy Duck: Toward a Politics of Self-Reflexive Cinema?" In *American Media and Mass Culture: Left Perspectives. See* Lazere 1987.

———. 1988. "Postmodernism and Cultural Analysis Today." In *Postmodernism and its Discontents. See* Kaplan 1988.

Poole, Mike, and John Wyver. 1984. *Powerplays: Trevor Griffiths in Television.* London: BFI.

Priestley, J. B. 1934. *English Journey.* London: Heinemann.

———. 1957. *Thoughts in the Wilderness.* London: Heinemann.

Radway, Janice. 1984. *Reading the Romance: Women, Patriarchy, and Popular Literature.* Chapel Hill: University of North Carolina Press.

Rapping, Elayne. 1990. "TV Guides." *Voice Literary Supplement,* Dec., 17.

Ray, Ellen. 1991. "The Killing Deserts." *Lies of Our Times,* April, 3–4.

Read, Herbert. 1953. *The Philosophy of Modern Art.* New York: Horizon.

———. 1967. *Art and Alienation: The Role of the Artist in Society.* New York: Horizon.

———. 1971. *Anarchy and Order: Essays in Politics.* Boston: Beacon.

Reed, Lou. 1991. "The Velvet Underground Meets the Velvet Revolution." *Utne Reader,* Jan./Feb., 104–6.

Reid, Jamie, and Jon Savage. 1987. *Up They Rise: The Incomplete Works of Jamie Reed.* London: Faber & Faber.

Reszler, André. 1973. "Bakunin, Marx and the Aesthetic Heritage of Socialism." *Yearbook of Comparative and General Literature* 22:42–50.

Reynolds, Simon. 1991. "Boredom + Claustrophobia + Sex = Punk Nirvana." *New York Times,* 24 Nov., 25.

Ridgeway, James. 1991a. "Stormy Weather: The Government Is Witholding Information—But We Didn't Tell You That." *Village Voice,* 11 June, 21–22.

———. 1991b. "This Time, We Won." *Village Voice,* 19 Feb., 21–22.

Roberts, Julian. 1982. *Walter Benjamin.* London: Macmillan.

Rohan, Marc. 1988. *Paris '68: Graffiti, Posters, Newspapers and Poems of the Events of May 1968.* London: Impact.

Rolleston, James L. 1989. "The Politics of Quotation: Walter Benjamin's Arcades Project." *PMLA* 104:13–27.

Roman, Leslie G. 1988. "Intimacy, Labor, and Class: Ideologies of Feminine Sexuality in the Punk Slam Dance." In *Becoming Feminine: The Politics of Popular Culture,* ed. Leslie G. Roman and Linda Christian-Smith. New York: Falmer.

Ross, Andrew. 1988. Introduction. In *Universal Abandon?: The Politics of Postmodernism,* ed. Andrew Ross. Minneapolis: University of Minnesota Press.

———. 1989a. *No Respect: Intellectuals & Popular Culture.* New York: Routledge.

———. 1989b. "The Rock'n'Roll Ghost." *October* 50:108–17.

Ross, Kristin. 1988. *The Emergence of Social Space: Rimbaud and the Paris Commune.* Minneapolis: University of Minnesota Press.

Rubin, Joan Shelley. 1992. *The Making of Middlebrow Culture.* Chapel Hill: University of North Carolina Press.

Russell, Charles. 1985. *Poets, Prophets, & Revolutionaries: The Literary Avant-Garde from Rimbaud through Postmodernism.* New York: Oxford University Press.

Said, Edward. 1983. *The World, the Text, and the Critic.* Cambridge: Harvard University Press.

Santoro, Gene. 1989. "This Magic Moment." *Nation,* 29 May, 744–47.

Savage, Jon. 1991. *England's Dreaming: Anarchy, Sex Pistols, Punk Rock, and Beyond.* New York: St. Martin's.

Schiller, Herbert I. 1987. "Information: Important Issue for '88." *Nation,* 4/11 July, 1, 5–6.

———. 1989a. *Culture, Inc.: The Corporate Takeover of Public Expression.* New York: Oxford University Press.

———. 1989b. "Pitchers at an Exhibition." *Nation,* 10 July, 37, 55–57.

Scholes, Robert. 1985. *Textual Power: Literary Theory and the Teaching of English.* New Haven: Yale University Press.

Schor, Juliet. 1991. *The Overworked American: The Unexpected Decline of Leisure.* New York: Basic Books.

Schulps, Dave. 1978. "Andrew Loog Oldham." *Trouser Press,* June, 18–20.

Schulte-Sasse, Jochen. 1984. "Foreword: Theory of Modernism versus Theory of the Avant-Garde." In *Theory of the Avant-Garde. See* Bürger 1984.

Schwartz, Jim. 1989. "Struggle for the Soul of the Union." *Nation,* 3 July, 7–10.

Scialabba, George. 1988. "A Thousand Points of Blight: What Ronald Reagan Left Behind." *Village Voice,* 8 Nov., 26–29.

Selbin, Eric. 1988. "Are Records Soon to Be Extinct?" *Utne Reader,* July/August, 18.

Shames, Laurence. 1989. "What a Long, Strange (Shopping) Trip It's Been: Looking Back at the 1980s." *Utne Reader,* Sept./Oct., 66–71.

Shattuck, Roger. 1968. *The Banquet Years: The Origins of the Avant Garde in France, 1885 to World War I.* New York: Vintage.

Shaw, Greg. 1975. Liner Notes. *Roots of British Rock.* Sire SASH-3711-2.

Shepherd, John. 1987. "Music and Male Hegemony." In *Music and Society. See* Mowitt 1987.

Sherry, Norman. 1989. *The Life of Graham Greene, Volume I: 1904–39*. New York: Viking.

Shor, Ira. 1986. *Culture Wars*. New York: Routledge & Kegan Paul.

Sinfield, Alan, ed. 1983. *Society and Literature 1945–1970*. New York: Holmes & Meier.

———. 1989. *Literature, Politics, and Culture in Postwar Britain*. Berkeley and Los Angeles: University of California Press.

Smith, Barbara Herrnstein. 1988. *Contingencies of Value: Alternative Perspectives for Critical Theory*. Cambridge: Harvard University Press.

Smith, Paul. 1988. *Discerning the Subject*. Minneapolis: University of Minnesota Press.

———. 1989. "Pedagogy and the Popular-Cultural-Commodity-Text." In *Popular Culture: Schooling and Everyday Life*. See Giroux and Simon 1989.

Smoler, Fredric Paul. 1991. "The Head of the Class." *Nation*, 21 Jan., 67–68.

Solomon, Maynard, ed. 1979. *Marxism and Art: Essays Classic and Contemporary*. Detroit: Wayne State University Press.

Sonn, Richard D. 1989. *Anarchism and Cultural Politics in Fin de Siècle France*. Lincoln: University of Nebraska Press.

"The Sound and the Fury." 1981. In *Situationist International Anthology*. See Knabb 1981.

Stallybrass, Peter, and Allon White. 1986. *The Politics and Poetics of Transgression*. London: Methuen.

Stam, Robert. 1988. "Bakhtin and Left Cultural Critique." In *Postmodernism and Its Discontents*. See Kaplan 1988.

———. 1989. *Subversive Pleasures: Bakhtin, Cultural Criticism, and Film*. Baltimore: Johns Hopkins University Press.

Steinhorn, Leonard. 1990. "Spin Control." *In These Times*, 4–10 April, 24.

Stevenson, Ray, ed. 1978. *Sex Pistols File*. London: Omnibus.

Stewart, Kathleen. 1988. "Nostalgia—A Polemic." *Cultural Anthropology* 3:227–39.

Strauss, Steve. 1969. "A Romance on Either Side of Dada." In *Rock and Roll Will Stand*. See Marcus 1969.

Street, John. 1986. *Rebel Rock: The Politics of Popular Music*. New York: Basil Blackwell.

Stubbs, David. 1989. "Fear of the Future." In *Zoot-Suits and Second-Hand Dresses*. See McRobbie 1989.

Sulieman, Susan Rubin. 1990. *Subversive Intent: Gender, Politics, and the Avant-Garde*. Cambridge: Harvard University Press.

Sussman, Elisabeth, ed. 1991. *On the Passage of a Few People through a Rather Brief Moment in Time: The Situationist International 1957–1972*. Cambridge: MIT Press.

Taylor, Paul, ed. 1988. *Impresario: Malcolm McLaren and the British New Wave*. Cambridge: MIT Press.

Tesich, Steve. 1991. "Breaking Away from Ourselves." *Nation*, 18 March, 334–36.

Toop, David. 1984. *The Rap Attack: New York Jive to New York Hip Hop.* Boston: South End.

Traube, Elizabeth G. 1992. *Dreaming Identities: Class, Gender, and Generation in 1980s Hollywood Movies.* Boulder: Westview.

Trilling, Lionel. 1967. "On the Modern Element in Modern Literature." In *The Idea of the Modern in Literature and the Arts,* ed. Irving Howe. New York: Horizon.

Turner, Graeme. 1990. *British Cultural Studies: An Introduction.* Boston: Unwin Hyman.

Tzara, Tristan. 1989. "Lecture on Dada." In *The Dada Painters and Poets. See* Huelsenbeck 1989.

Ulmer, Gregory L. 1983. "The Object of Post-Criticism." In *The Anti-Aesthetic. See* Habermas 1983.

Vaneigem, Raoul. 1974a. "Self-Realisation, Communication, and Participation." In *Leaving the 20th Century. See* Gray 1974.

———. 1974b. "The Totality for Kids." In *Leaving the 20th Century. See* Gray 1974.

———. 1983. *The Revolution of Everyday Life.* Trans. Donald Nicholson-Smith. London: Left Bank.

Vermorel, Fred, and Judy Vermorel. 1978. *The Sex Pistols: The Inside Story.* London: Universal.

Volosinov, V. N. 1986. *Marxism and the Philosophy of Language.* Trans. Ladislav Matekja and I. R. Titunik. Cambridge: Harvard University Press.

Volpe, Nicole, and James Ridgeway. 1991. "How to Win: 32 Examples of the Press on a Leash." *Village Voice,* 26 March, 17–18.

Wain, John. 1958. "Along the Tightrope." In *Declaration. See* Maschler 1958.

Ward, Tom. 1985. "The Situationists Reconsidered." In *Cultures in Contention,* ed. Douglas Kahn and Diane Neumaier. Seattle: Real Comet.

Warren, Ellen. 1988. "Bush Attacks on Economic Issues." *Austin American-Statesman,* 26 Oct., A3.

Watts, Michael. 1979. "Malcolm McLaren." *Melody Maker,* 16 June, 35–40, 50–51.

"The Wembley Concert: Untouched by U.S. Eyes." 1990. *Lies of Our Times,* May, 20.

Whiteley, Nigel. 1987. *Pop Design: Modernism to Mod.* London: Design Council.

Wicke, Peter. 1990. *Rock Music: Culture, Aesthetics and Sociology.* New York: Cambridge University Press.

Wieck, David. 1979a. "The Habit of Direct Action." In *Reinventing Anarchy. See* Ehrlich 1979.

———. 1979b. "The Negativity of Anarchism." In *Reinventing Anarchy. See* Ehrlich 1979.

Williams, Raymond. 1977. *Marxism and Literature.* New York: Oxford University Press.

———. 1980. *Problems in Materialism and Culture.* London: New Left Books.

————. 1983. *Culture and Society 1780–1950.* New York: Columbia University Press.

————. 1989. *The Politics of Modernism: Against the New Conformists.* New York: Verso.

Willis, Paul. 1978. *Profane Culture.* London: Routledge and Kegan Paul.

————. 1981. *Learning to Labor: How Working Class Kids Get Working Class Jobs.* New York: Columbia University Press.

Wilson, Edmund. 1984. *Axel's Castle: A Study in the Imaginative Literature of 1870–1930.* New York: Norton.

Wohlfarth, Irving. 1988. "Resentment Begins at Home: Nietzsche, Benjamin, and the University." In *On Walter Benjamin: Critical Essays and Recollections,* ed. Gary Smith. Cambridge: MIT Press.

Wolfe, Tom. 1969. *The Pump House Gang.* New York: Bantam.

Wolin, Richard. 1982. *Walter Benjamin: An Aesthetic of Redemption.* New York: Columbia University Press.

Wollen, Peter. 1989. "The Situationist International." *New Left Review* 174:67–95.

Wood, Ellen Meiksins. 1986. *The Retreat from Class.* London: Verso.

Woodcock, George. 1986. *Anarchism.* 2d ed. New York: Penguin.

Woodmansee, Martha. 1988/89. "Toward a Geneology of the Aesthetic: The German Reading Debate of the 1790s." *Cultural Critique* 11:203–21.

Woodworth, Fred. 1979. "Anarchism." In *Reinventing Anarchy. See* Ehrlich 1979.

Worpole, Ken. 1983. *Dockers and Detectives.* London: Verso.

————. 1985. "Scholarship Boy: The Poetry of Tony Harrison." *New Left Review* 153:63–74.

Young, Charles M. 1977. "Rock Is Sick and Living in London: A Report on the Sex Pistols." *Rolling Stone,* 20 Oct., 69–78.

Young, Michael, and Peter Willmott. 1957. *Family and Kinship in East London.* New York: Pelican.

Zinn, Howard. 1980. *A People's History of the United States.* New York: Harper & Row.

Index